# Who Cleans
the Park?

# Who Cleans the Park?

*Public Work and Urban Governance in New York City*

JOHN KRINSKY AND
MAUD SIMONET

*The University of Chicago Press   Chicago and London*

The University of Chicago Press, Chicago 60637
The University of Chicago Press, Ltd., London
© 2017 by The University of Chicago
All rights reserved. No part of this book may be used or reproduced in any manner whatsoever without written permission, except in the case of brief quotations in critical articles and reviews. For more information, contact the University of Chicago Press,
1427 E. 60th St., Chicago, IL 60637.
Published 2017
Printed in the United States of America

26 25 24 23 22 21 20 19 18 17    1 2 3 4 5

ISBN-13: 978-0-226-43544-2 (cloth)
ISBN-13: 978-0-226-43558-9 (paper)
ISBN-13: 978-0-226-43561-9 (e-book)
DOI: 10.7208/chicago/9780226435619.001.0001

Library of Congress Cataloging-in-Publication Data

Names: Krinsky, John, author. | Simonet, Maud, author.
Title: Who cleans the park? : public work and urban governance in New York City / John Krinsky and Maud Simonet.
Description: Chicago ; London : The University of Chicago Press, 2017. | Includes bibliographical references and index.
Identifiers: LCCN 2016034613 | ISBN 9780226435442 (cloth : alk. paper) | ISBN 9780226435589 (pbk. : alk. paper) | ISBN 9780226435619 (e-book)
Subjects: LCSH: Parks—New York (State)—New York—Employees. | Parks—Maintenance—New York (State)—New York.
Classification: LCC SB482.N72 K75 2016 | DDC 333.78/309747— dc23 LC record available at https://lccn.loc.gov/2016034613

♾ This paper meets the requirements of ANSI/NISO Z39.48–1992 (Permanence of Paper).

# Contents

*List of Abbreviations vii*

1. Introduction 1
2. The Workers 26
3. The Work 67
4. The Workplace 99
5. Public-Private Partnerships 131
6. Institutional Boundaries, Accountability, and the Integral State 167
7. The Politics of Free Labor: Visibility and Invisibility 192
8. Valuing Maintenance, Valuing Workers 217

*Afterword 250   Acknowledgments 259*

*Notes 261   References 277   Index 287*

# Abbreviations

| | |
|---|---|
| APSW | Associate Park Service Worker |
| APRM | Associate Parks and Recreation Manager |
| CPW | City Park Worker |
| CSA | City Seasonal Aide |
| DPR | Department of Parks and Recreation |
| JTP | Job Training Participant |
| PEP | Parks Enforcement Officer |
| P4P | Partnerships for Parks |
| PIP | Parks Inspection Program |
| POP | Parks Opportunity Program |
| PPS | Principal Park Supervisor |
| PS1 | Park Supervisor, Level 1 |
| PS2 | Park Supervisor, Level 2 |
| SYEP | Summer Youth Employment Program |
| WEP | Work Experience Program |

ONE

# Introduction

Central Park, Manhattan. Summer 2009, 9:45 a.m.: A sixty-something-year-old white woman works on her knees, pulling weeds from the edges of a flagstone pathway. She wears a blue t-shirt with the Central Park Conservancy logo on the front and VOLUNTEER emblazoned on the back. She works next to an African American man in his late thirties or early forties, who also wears a Central Park Conservancy shirt, but with STAFF on the back. They work for the next forty minutes before taking a break, pulling weeds together.

Upper Manhattan. Fall 2008, 8:30 a.m.: Ray[1], a second-generation Latino man in his mid-thirties, a City Park Worker, takes five Job Training Program participants in a van to clean playgrounds in the district. All the JTPs are African American and Latina women from their 20s to their 50s, and each wears a royal blue t-shirt with the Parks Department logo on the front and STAFF written on the back. George, about fifty, also Latino, is also a City Park Worker and wears a dark blue shirt with a Parks Department patch and his name embroidered on the pocket. He takes five additional Job Training Program workers in another van to make the rounds of other playgrounds. Ray will get out of the van and clean alongside them; George will not. Ray, as a low-level permanent parks employee, should not be driving the van and supervising Job Training Program participants. George, who has an official "crew chief" designation, can do so, and gets paid several thousand dollars more per year than Ray for his supervisory role.

## Who Cleans Your Park?

For New Yorkers, if they bother to think about it, the answer to the question "Who cleans your park?" would be complex: It might be welfare-to-work trainees, volunteers, unionized city workers (working within or outside their official job descriptions), summer youth workers, workers for private, nonprofit parks "conservancies," staff of companies working under contract, and people sentenced to community service. Immediately, this answer suggests something important about a larger set of social relationships, namely, that public services are no longer necessarily provided primarily by public workers. Moreover, in spite of the sound and fury about bloated public-sector unions and their distended pay and benefit packages, a greater amount of public service work is being done either for free or at lower cost due to the reorganization of the public workplace.

This book is an investigation of the conditions under which New York City's parks are maintained, of changing labor relations and contracts of the parks' cleaners, and of their relations at the workplace with each other. It argues that we cannot understand these unless we also try to understand the ways in which the city's institutions have changed—with the Parks Department sometimes at the avant-garde. We must also, in turn, comprehend how and why even more encompassing changes in urban political economy shape these institutional changes. Thus, this book is based on a bet, namely, that by looking at who cleans the parks in New York City, we can enter, even provoke, a larger conversation about life in contemporary cities, and New York City in particular.

The Department of Parks and Recreation is a microcosm of New York City's governance as a whole and a case in which current trends in urban governing are thrown into bold relief. The study seeks answers to several empirical questions, all of which flow from the confluence of several literatures in the sociology of work and urban political economy, public administration, nonprofit organizations, civic service, and volunteering. What does this reorganization mean and entail for workers who maintain the parks and who have different statuses and different places in the hierarchies of the workplace? And what does it mean for the public who enjoys the park, the city government in charge of delivering this public service, and private actors who involve themselves in the governance of parks and may also derive private benefits from it?

Many of these questions can be asked of other workplaces and other agencies or firms, of course. Most of us by now have seen significant changes occur in our places of work, or are aware of "how things used to be." For professors in the United States, for example, the shift to adjunct labor—often graduate students, but also others, who teach courses as do regular faculty but with little job protection and at about a quarter of the cost per course—has been a regular feature of higher education over the past twenty years, along with apparently more momentous policy changes, such as ending tenure, desired by many college administrators and boards of directors.[2] The parceling off of apparently skilled from less-skilled aspects of a job and the redistribution of this work within workplaces is as common in universities as it is in factories or in public agencies. The trick, however, is that the process is often incomplete, so that, as with adjunct faculty, it is also common that people with very different statuses in the workplace with respect to pay, benefits, legal protections, and so forth are doing the same exact work.

A further aspect of the changes in contemporary labor markets and workplaces is the growing reliance on unpaid or low-paid labor, justified by claims that the workers performing this labor are trainees or are mainly contributing their labor on a volunteer basis, for civic purposes or for "the love of it." Scholars of "digital labor," moreover, argue that the profit-generating activity of Internet use is a type of unremunerated labor that is no less labor because it may be play or a host of other things besides.[3] Additionally, the vast proliferation of internships, which has just recently begun to become controversial in the United States, provides companies and public-sector offices (politicians and public managers, for example) with millions of hours of free labor[4] as well as opportunities to screen potential applicants for real employment. As with graduate students who teach course loads commensurate with those of their own professors, however, interns run the risk of displacing the need for the very jobs they hope to gain in the future.

As important is the reorganization of work and workplaces through complex networks of subcontracting. Across a wide range of jobs, from day labor to garment work, to temporary office work, these often drive down pay and stymie efforts by workers and their allies to hold anyone accountable for poor and even sometimes dangerous working conditions, arbitrary work schedules, and other characteristics of "degraded" and "precarious" work.[5] In the public sector, some of this reorganization takes the form of privatizing work once done by public workers and public-private partnerships of various sorts that leverage private funds for public purposes.

## Why Parks? Why New York?

Parks crystallize several important aspects of contemporary urban life and policy, each double-sided: they are quintessential public places

CHAPTER ONE

whose good upkeep tends to benefit private property owners in their vicinities; they exist for leisure—both for residents and visitors—and are yet also workplaces; and their maintenance is a "normal" public service, like libraries and street cleaning, rather than a critical service like firefighting, ambulance services, or policing, but they attract intense interest and community involvement. Parks maintenance also spans the spectrum of skilled to unskilled work, and parks workers have historically been public employees, though the proportion of public employees maintaining parks has shrunken. Accordingly, tracing the history of employment and conditions of parks workers reveals the ways in which politics and policy have intersected with attempts to regulate labor markets, make peace with or fight unions, and privatize the administration of public services.

New York City is at once exceptional with respect to other US cities and also both a testing ground for policy and a keen adapter of others' policy innovations to a larger and more directly globally connected context. New York's size and complexity—and that of its parks system—usually means that its governance involves a greater variety of organizations, and thus the labor force involved in public service involves more different types of workers than do those of other cities. This means, therefore, that in New York City, other cities see experiments, such as the public-private parks-management partnerships, as potential models, while at the same time analysts can see multiple types of arrangements simultaneously, which they might see one at a time in other places.

Furthermore, New York City is emblematic, in many respects, of the changes in urban governance that have unfolded for the last forty years and is thus a "critical case"[6] in which one can study larger trends in urban public management and politics writ large. These trends have often been described as being "neoliberal," reflecting, at least in part, a set of policy preferences that, in the name of freedom and efficiency, favor private enterprise and minimal state action to ensure social equality. Neoliberal urban policy, based on public austerity, privatization, hostility to unions, and orientation to private-market policy solutions, found its first major laboratory in New York City beginning with the fiscal crisis of 1975–1977. The "roll back" of what historian Joshua Freeman has called New York's "social democracy"—an extensive public hospital and clinic system, a top-flight and free public university system, extensive public and subsidized housing programs, widespread public day care centers—was a model for urban policy under Ronald Reagan and was expressly geared toward generating private investment in cities to replace public investment.[7]

If we go much farther back, however, we can see in parks the contours of a much more clientelistic form of public administration: parks laborers—like many unskilled and semi-skilled workers—were drawn primarily from the ranks of ethnically segregated wards and rewarded with jobs for political loyalty by machine politicians. By the early 1950s, little had changed, except that union agitation beginning in the 1930s—and the vast expansion of public resources during the New Deal—had weakened the hold of political patrons and party bosses on public employment.

By the mid-1950s, the city's parks laborers paved the way to public-sector collective bargaining in the early 1960s, well ahead of most public-sector workers around the country. Taking on the powerful parks commissioner Robert Moses, public parks workers forced him to abide by Mayor Robert F. Wagner Jr.'s order to collectively bargain with unions representing the majority of workers in a given civil service title. In a series of demonstrations in 1955, they charged Moses with being an "absentee owner" of a zoo containing a species of worker that "Resembles Normal American Worker BUT Has No Collective Bargaining; Has No Grievance Machinery; Has No Dignity on the Job"[8]

In forcing Moses to bargain, they dealt the master city builder—who used parks as a way to tie together his housing and highway-development plans—one of his first major political defeats.[9] In 1961, parks laborers signed the first officially bargained contract with the City. By 1967, parks workers and other municipal workers had gained statutory collective bargaining rights, grievance procedures, security, and the modest comforts of working-class life.

These modest comforts would quickly begin to unravel, however. During the city's fiscal crisis in the 1970s, the City pioneered the use of welfare recipients and volunteers to undercut lower-skilled unionized civil service jobs, and it began to forge partnerships with nonprofit organizations to farm out responsibility for managing public amenities to the private sector. This was also the period in which the Central Park Conservancy and the Prospect Park Alliance were formed. The Central Park Conservancy began as an alliance of three separate, smaller volunteer groups, mainly comprised of people living close to the park. Led by Elizabeth Barlow Rogers, an urban planner and park historian who had written a book on Frederick Law Olmsted and Central Park, the Central Park Conservancy began to take greater and greater responsibility for the park—not just doing volunteer work and raising money for capital repairs and improvements but becoming in charge of daily management as well. The Conservancy and the Prospect Park Alli-

CHAPTER ONE

ance—led by Tupper Thomas, an idealistic transplant from the Midwest who followed Mayor John Lindsay's call to public service in the mid-1960s—were supported from the beginning by the City. Under Parks Commissioner Gordon Davis, the city's two most prominent parks were assigned administrators who would also be responsible to their own, private nonprofit organizations, and therefore were put under pioneering public-private partnerships. Bryant Park, a much smaller park behind the public library's main branch on 42nd Street (the one with the iconic lions in front), was given over to the Bryant Park Restoration Corporation (BPRC), a business improvement district, or BID, with the authority to levy a supplementary tax on local business owners. The park, which had fallen into a state of disrepair, became completely privately administered, and its redevelopment was the centerpiece of a larger revitalization of the area around Times Square. The broader importance of these conservancies is that they were early forays in New York City's experimentation with public-private partnerships and betokened a shift in the way urban public services were and could be delivered. The deepening, *direct* involvement of private interests in administering parks signaled a shift toward what urban political scientists call "regimes," that is, an approach to governing, combining and institutionalizing private and public power, which, while open to some popular influence, has elites at its core.[10] The founding of the three conservancies show that no single model of public-private partnership need be dominant and that a regime can sustain a good deal of internal variety in spite of common elements such as nonprofit status, nonunionized workforces, and lower labor standards. Further, these conservancies underscore the centrality of real estate value to the postcrisis regime in New York City and the shifting balance of power to real estate interests in the city at a time when the local state took a leading role in setting up public-private partnerships but fused its agenda for them with those of the new elites. The result has been that public investment in parks and their maintenance has been extremely uneven across the city and that the work to maintain these investments has fallen most on the shoulders of those who benefit least.

## Why Now?

Recent attacks on public-sector workers and their benefits, heard across statehouses and city halls, in newspaper editorials and among both major parties, tend to ignore the real changes undergone by the public-sector workforce over the past thirty years. New York's public sector is an important case, in part because it has been on the leading edge of efforts to diversify and weaken the rights of its labor force, and because it is widely seen as privileged, as it is highly unionized and has politically connected unions. The public parks maintenance and operations workforce also represents a low- and moderately skilled workforce whose jobs are most easily redistributed among workers with less power. As increasing numbers of parks maintenance jobs are privatized to well-funded nonprofit organizations, and as increasing numbers of jobs are reallocated to temporary welfare-to-work trainees, the ability for such workers to make a career in the public service decreases. Today, on any given day, the majority of the people actually cleaning parks in New York are participants in the city's Parks Opportunities Program (POP), which provides six to nine months of full-time work and associate (not full) union membership, with one day per week for training in a range of possible activities, for former welfare recipients. POP is administered on a contract with the city's welfare department (the Human Resources Administration), and workers are defined by a special job title, Job Training Participant (JTP).

Overall, today's parks workers are divided between those who retain collective bargaining and grievance procedures and those who do not. The first group includes public workers and, to a different extent, welfare-to-work trainees. The second contains newer categories of workers, including privately contracted employees of parks conservancy groups, volunteers, workfare workers, and people sentenced to community service by the courts. These are further divided into those who are visible and recognized *as workers* and those who are not; those who are paid a wage and those who are not; and those who are at the park worksites voluntarily and those who are not. Like their counterparts in the 1950s, who demonstrated against Robert Moses, they are not "regular" workers, but they are, in many ways, the new normal.

The financial crisis that began in 2008 has cast a new light on many things, including the parks maintenance model that has developed since the late 1970s and early 1980s. The private sources of funding that sustain several large conservancy organizations, including Central Park, are no longer as secure as they once were. The possibility of cutting budgets and relying increasingly on private funds, on volunteers, or on welfare-to-work workers may have passed its peak effectiveness. In recent lean years, the Department of Parks and Recreation has struggled to meet the high standards of cleanliness and good repair that it set for itself (in most parks) in the fat years. Frequent shortages of

CHAPTER ONE

staff or equipment have begun to compromise the complex edifice of parks maintenance and operations management. Further, as the crisis —and the brief Occupy movement—have thrust inequality once more into the foreground, parks workers and users alike have begun to question the fairness of privately administered parks and the partnerships they entail getting what seems to be preferential attention from the public sector. They also question the fairness of labor contracts that purport to "transition" workers into permanent employment but often confront a lack of available jobs beyond the ones they are providing at barely sustainable levels of income.

The questions we face now, therefore, are ones about how the whole system works and how people working in it adjust to it, understand it, and understand their roles in it. On one level, we are engaging questions typical of the sociology of work, which ask about how workers perceive their workplaces, interact within them, create and resist power hierarchies, and generally get motivated to work. On another level, by treating the category of "workers" more broadly, we raise the question of where the boundaries of "work" lie and how they can shift. Here, we have recourse to feminist studies of work that insist that what is "visible" institutionally *as work* excludes a wide array of activities that may not be *employment* but are certainly work.[11] Further, following the more recent institutional focus of studies of work, we extend the study of work to parks workplaces as sites of "governance"—government and its extensions out to nongovernmental organizations. In so doing, we extend questions about work to areas more frequently understood to belong to studies of urban politics and policy, welfare and workforce development policy, volunteering and civic service, and street-level bureaucracy.

### Researching Parks Maintenance

#### *A Tree Falls in Brooklyn*

When we began this project, we had hoped, above all, to observe parks maintenance worksites up close. Our first thought was to volunteer with the Central Park Conservancy. It has a program whereby volunteers can work with Zone Gardeners—those charged with the horticultural and maintenance upkeep of specific areas of the park—for three hours a day, several days a week. Because our research protocol, approved by the board at City College that vets the ethics of research with human subjects, did not allow us to use deception in our research, we quickly realized that we could not proceed as planned. In order to become a volunteer Zone Assistant, you have to sign several pages of nondisclosure agreements; writing about your experiences is not allowed. After some unsuccessful negotiations with the Conservancy, we decided instead, that in order at least to get a *feel* for parks work—to use the tools of the trade—we should find an alternative place to volunteer.

We found the Monday group of volunteers in Prospect Park with a phone call. Showing up at the Vale of Cashmere, a somewhat careworn area on the park's northern end, we met a volunteer coordinator who furnished us with rakes and bags, and advice to pace ourselves: "Remember, it's just another day in the park!" There were no confidentiality agreements to sign, though there was a sign-in sheet. After stepping over a large dead rat, we set to work, raking a thick carpet of leaves from a long, sloping stair, as the coordinator suggested we do.

About two hours into our work—in which blisters began to form between our thumbs and forefingers where we were holding the rakes—a tree suddenly collapsed and shattered where we had been standing not twenty minutes earlier. We alerted the coordinator, who took it in stride and worked with us to clear the debris. We, on the other hand, were a little taken aback by what we felt was a close brush with injury or worse. We wondered whether we might be covered by the City's workers' compensation insurance had anything more serious transpired.

The following Thursday, we returned to the park, this time with a larger group, with different coordinators, and set to work weeding an area not far from a parking lot and ice-skating rink. After some brief instruction from the coordinators about which weeds we were meant to pull, we donned the cotton work gloves provided by the coordinators and started to pull burdock. If you've ever pulled burdock, you know that it has a deep root (which is edible and also used for medicinal purposes) and thousands of burrs that stick to anything as if it were Velcro. Between the burdock burrs and what was likely poison ivy, we both emerged from that day with aching backs and itching in places we did not even know existed.

After some time, John decided to take a break and pick up a garbage bag and grabber. These were provided for volunteers who did not want to weed. He found an area, nearby, that was clearly used for sexual liaisons, as the ground was littered with condom wrappers, condoms, and—in a strange juxtaposition—candy wrappers and lollipops. Picking up trash with a grabber ends up being mind-numbing work, and it is difficult to do quickly. You need just enough dexterity and attention to pick up small pieces of trash with the tool (which you squeeze in order to bring the two "fingers" at the tip together), but it is difficult to maintain your focus on the task, no matter how intriguing the detritus.

Parks work, we found, can be both dirty and uncomfortable, even when it's a nice day in the park. But we also found that among the volunteers, there was a good deal of camaraderie. Many volunteers appeared to be regulars and to know each other, and during breaks, one volunteer brought cookies for everyone (apparently, he did this often). Bagels, brought by the coordinators, are the center of a break time, when people socialize for twenty minutes or half an hour before getting back to work. And yet, unlike in Central Park's Zone Assistant program, volunteers did not seem to be working alongside many of the "regular" workers. Prospect Park volunteers were put to maintenance tasks that were set aside for them. Moreover, in both Central Park, in a weekend volunteer program, and in Prospect Park, we found that volunteers could be somewhat insular, making little conversation with new volunteers, short of establishing their own expertise as workers, dispensing advice—or criticism—about how best to do the job.

*Gaining Entry*

We were still left outside of the Parks Department proper and no amount of work with the Prospect Park crews—segregated as they were from the main maintenance workforce—would get us closer.

We decided to take the bull by the horns and just begin. We chose another park with a conservancy, but one in which there were few volunteers and no clearly structured volunteer program. Madison Square Park, in the lower reaches of midtown Manhattan, takes over several city blocks, having been set aside by the 1811 Commissioner's Plan of New York City as a military parade ground. Now, densely shaded by trees, the park is bustling during the day as area office workers and others lounge on its chairs, appreciate its frequent public art installations, and queue up for burgers and shakes at the Shake Shack—a takeout restaurant run by one of the park's largest benefactors, the restaurateur Danny Meyer. One day, we simply walked into the park and approached the first person we saw wearing a Parks Department staff t-shirt. We told her that we were researching a book about people who worked in the parks, and she told us in no uncertain terms that she was not allowed to speak with us. She referred us to her supervisor, and he to his. This was not going to work from the bottom up.

After calling around to various people John knew in community-

**Table 1.1** Interviewees by position or role in parks

| Position | Number | Position | Number |
| --- | --- | --- | --- |
| Volunteer | 11 | CPW | 17 |
| Volunteer coordinator | 4 | APSW | 2 |
| P4P | 1 | Gardener | 1 |
| Park advocate | 3 | PS1/PS2/PPS | 17 |
| Grounds crew (conservancy) | 11 | PEP | 3 |
| Foreman (conservancy) | 2 | Associate Park Service Manager | 4 |
| Zone Gardener (conservancy) | 1 | Administrator & upper management | 13 |
| Management (conservancy) | 5 | Chief/deputy chief of operations | 8 |
| WEP | 1 | Comm/ass't comm | 4 |
| JTP | 18 | Union | 7 |
| CSA | 4 | Conservancy board members | 2 |

level government in New York, we finally got the name of someone who was described as "helpful." An upper-level manager in one borough, this contact, whom we will call Peter, responded to a request for a meeting. There, we asked about the whole organizational set-up of the Parks Department and its partnerships; discussed the parks workforce, its functional divisions, and its composition; and, crucially, secured permission to speak with and interview district-level Managers and Supervisors, as well as whatever other staff they decided to recommend or make available to us.

After having pursued a wide range of interviews in four parks districts (districts are roughly consistent with the city's fifty-nine community districts, which function as local planning and administrative bodies) in the first borough, we pursued the same strategy in three others; speaking with Peter's equivalents in the other boroughs, we gained similar access—until we were finally shut out. In addition, we contacted "Friends of" parks groups, conservancies, and volunteer groups directly, as they were not bound by the City's policies of clearing all encounters with the public with upper Parks Department management. In the end, we conducted more than 120 interviews in eleven districts with people actively involved in cleaning and maintaining New York City's parks (see table 1.1) and with parks managers, advocates, and union officials.

*Insider and Outsider*

We approached our interviews from different vantage points: John is from New York—born and raised—and has studied the welfare politics and labor politics of New York for more than fifteen years. Maud, from Paris, has had several sojourns in the United States for her comparative research on French and American civic engagement. Nevertheless, in spite of her familiarity with New York, she did not enter the research with the granular level of historical and collective memory of New York's politics that John did. Where John frequently approached interviews by trying to establish some point of connection with the interviewee, Maud often specifically positioned herself as an "outsider," more naive about New York City than our collaboration would make possible. The dual insider-outsider roles we took on allowed us to selectively probe more deeply into some issues in interviews and, in others, be certain that the interviewees' viewpoints were more carefully and slowly explained. In both cases, we found that most of our interviewees spoke long and freely.

There were other ways in which insider and outsider roles helped us to negotiate our field research. After the Central Park Conservancy turned down our plan to become Zone Assistants, we sought other ways to speak with workers for the Conservancy. At the time we were beginning our research—and quite likely related to the Conservancy's reticence—District Council 37 of the American Federation of State, County and Municipal Employees (DC 37 AFSCME), the city's largest public-sector union, was attempting to organize and unionize Conservancy workers. Through his previous research on workfare, John had done some work with a poor people's organization in East Harlem, Community Voices Heard (CVH). CVH had long been an opponent of workfare programs and had been one of the groups that was instrumental in pressuring the City to create POP and transitional jobs. Thus, it also worked with DC 37 to monitor the program. Through those and other points of collaboration, CVH's director was asked to chair a community support network for the DC 37 organizing drive in Central Park. Through John's contacts, we were able to work through DC 37 to speak with some of the workers involved in the Central Park Conservancy unionization drive. In introducing us to the organizing committee, DC 37's organizing director cited John's workfare book: "He wrote a book that helped us a lot; I have his book in my office."

Shortly afterward, and wanting to get a broader sampling of voices from the Conservancy, John figured out another possible way "in," via a friend of his parents who had a longstanding relationship to the Conservancy. The friend facilitated access to top staff members of the Conservancy, and these staff members then chose workers for John's interviews.

As we then had access to the Central Park Conservancy from "above" *and* "below," so to speak, we decided that it would be best to divide the labor and to keep it scrupulously divided. Maud stuck with interviewing union activists and even went out into the field with organizers on their rounds to see how people reacted to the union and spoke about their work outside of the supervisory orbit of the Conservancy itself. By the time she was finished with her interviews—and had to return to France—she had earned the moniker of "sister" from those in the union. John, by contrast, worked from "above." We quickly realized that entering from these two doors—the workers supporting the union, the management resisting the drive—not only shed light on an ideologically conflicted organization but also on a racially divided workforce. While Maud's interviewees from the Conservancy were almost exclusively African American and Latino, of John's interviewees, selected by management, there was just one African American and one Latina in seven. We decided not to go to the park together until both of us had concluded our interviews and were extremely careful not to let information from one "field" seep into the other lest we break trust with our interviewees on either end.

Even so, John *had* to ask about the union drive during his interviews, even with handpicked workers (all of whom either told him they opposed the union, were indifferent, or felt as if it were unnecessary), and as part of a much larger interview schedule about their work and their workplace he asked about the lines of communication when things go wrong. At last, a top administrator called John into his office and told him that he was making "[his] workers nervous" by talking about the union. John reassured him that this was a small part of the interview but that as a researcher, he would be remiss if he ignored it. John did not believe that the administrator was at all reassured and subsequently interviewed several Parks Department employees who were not under the direct supervision of the Conservancy.

For her part, Maud began to get a sense of both the idealism and the frustrations of a union drive. Though a nonprofit, the Conservancy fought the union drive as many employers do, with meetings with workers to discourage unionization and by doing their best to find out who supported the union and who did not. The Conservancy had faced down two previous unionization drives and knew how to navigate the difficult legal terrain of the fight, as well. And when the Conservancy faced financial difficulties linked to the financial crisis and fired thirty-one workers, pro-union workers were disproportionately among those let go. For its part, the union—without a recent history of organizing new workers—did not commit commensurate, or even sufficient, resources to a campaign in which it faced an adversary with enormous resources and a stellar public reputation. It devoted few organizers to the campaign, in spite of the lead organizer's insistence that Central Park was a litmus test for the union's ability to "follow the work" and maintain its strength in the face of the privatization of public services. Though the union organized a solidarity committee of sympathetic community groups and religious leaders, the committee did not have clear or frequent marching orders and it could not sustain a larger campaign to shame the widely beloved conservancy in the eyes of the public—or even more specifically, in the eyes of its supporters and volunteers.

Being an outsider to this—but being let *inside*—let us get a fuller picture of the reasons that some of the changes we document in this book have not met stiffer resistance from organized labor.[12]

At other points, however, the insider-outsider roles were reversed—or at least mixed—largely according to expertise. John had never studied volunteers, while this was Maud's specialty. Accordingly, Maud was the point of contact with all of the volunteers and used *both* the insider knowledge of volunteering culture and the outsider status and exoticism of being a "French researcher" to make quick contact with volunteer groups in Brooklyn, Queens, and the Bronx, as well as with the Partnerships for Parks, the Parks Department's public-private partnership with the private-but-publicly-created City Parks Foundation that fosters volunteer activity in parks around the city. Further, Maud's expertise in civic service and volunteering was the basis of our attempts to understand the strong role of the state in organizing and supporting volunteer efforts, an aspect of volunteering that is often hidden from view.[13]

Two other aspects of insider and outsider roles were important. First, our team of research assistants—two who helped to conduct interviews and two others who primarily helped code the interviews—was diverse. Marcela Gonzalez, a sociology graduate student from Argentina, and Kenn Vance, a political science graduate student from California, were the main assistants for the interviewing phase, and both were given districts to cover after accompanying Maud and John on several interviews first.[14] As students at the City University Graduate Center, both Marcela and Kenn had adjunct teaching jobs in addition to their research assistantships and studies. They immediately understood the stakes of studying contingent work, though neither had experience in parks. Yet, even as outsiders, they had been in New York for years and could draw on neighborhood ties and the familiarity of daily interaction in their interviews. By giving them districts to cover that were near to their homes, we were able to ensure that they began to get a clear sense of local work dynamics in their districts.

Second, the research assistants who helped with the coding of interviews, Samantha Halsey and Andrew Miller (and Kenn Vance also contributed), were outsiders in the sense that they were involved in few interviews but needed a strong orientation to the research in order to understand what they were coding. This forced us, as a research team, to be clear about all the roles of every worker and organization in the parks.

## *Hearing It and Bearing It*

Net of the insider and outsider roles we played as the core of the research team, we also found that working together made it easier to deal with some of what we would come to find out in the course of the research. New York City is a city of vast inequality. However much it prides itself on being a tolerant and almost dizzyingly multicultural city, it is also a place that, within just a few miles, contains some of the wealthiest and poorest census tracts in the country. This inequality is not just a matter of income; it is encoded in relations of race, ethnicity, and gender as well. And it is found in frequent reports of sexual harassment of Job Training Participants or reports that JTPs—who are overwhelmingly African American and Latina women—sometimes trade sexual favors with supervisors in exchange for easier work. In either case, the confluence of poverty, race and ethnicity, and gender inequality can break over an interview like a wave of acid.

Sometimes, the traces are subtler but can be encountered in the same day, such as the time that John and Maud did a morning interview with a City Park Worker and John did an afternoon interview with a Conservancy supporter. The former interview was done in a park house—a squat building in a playground with a small office sandwiched between two bathrooms—and the latter in a beautiful park-side apartment. The recordings of the interviews register the differences starkly: the morning interview contended with the frequent sound of toilets flushing through the pipes that ran over the top of the office, while the afternoon interview was punctuated by the tinkle of silver on china, as John sipped tea with his interviewee. In the morning we heard about favoritism, sexual harassment, and the economic hardships of low-level city workers; in the afternoon, the conversation turned to philanthropy and to how "thuggy guys" from the union were intimidating the workers.

Talking through these contrasts was a crucial part of our work, both because they are analytically telling and important to the story that unfolds in the following chapters and because the research posed real emotional ups and downs—outrage, despair, cynicism, and a great deal of humor—that are important to process in order to be able to continually expose yourself to difficult-to-hear stories.

### *Watching and Being Watched*

Throughout our research, we were keenly aware that we were not only observing people cleaning and maintaining New York City's parks. As ethnographers everywhere know, we were also being watched. Having been shut out of volunteering in Central Park, we instead took to watching volunteers and Zone Gardeners work together. From our early field notes:

CENTRAL PARK—WEDNESDAY, SEPTEMBER 24, 2008
We are sitting on a bench, near the Harlem Meer, since 9 o'clock in the morning. We're watching a volunteer and an employee from the Central Park Conservancy working together, taking the weeds out of the cobblestones around the walk. Yesterday, at the same time, we were doing the same thing in another part of the park, near Belvedere Castle and the Turtle Pond. A volunteer and a gardener were also working together in that zone, weeding on both sides of a fence. Like the "duo" we are watching today, they were part of the Zone Assistant program of the park: volunteers who sign up for one or two mornings a week to join the Zone Gardener's staff for various nonmechanical tasks. At 11h45, as we are watching and taking notes on our bench, another employee of the Conservancy stopped his golf-cart near us, looked and smiled at us, and said, "You guys gotta find yourself a real job!"

If we never, therefore, felt completely secure in our access to the parks —and, especially, each time we approached an upper-level borough manager for "access"—this insecurity was confirmed in February 2010 when the top hierarchy of the Parks Department, not the park commissioner but someone close to him in the Arsenal, sent an e-mail to every park district in the five boroughs preventing anyone from talking to us or our research assistants.

Here are the notes Kenn Vance, who was on site conducting an interview when that e-mail was sent, took from that morning:

I went to do a prescheduled interview with an APSW I had met several times prior at the Park House. . . . Since I was waiting for the APSW I went for a cup of coffee and ran across Sophie Tyler, the Park Administrator, who commented that I was becoming like another staff member I was around so much. I responded that I was "just trying to wrap things up" and she laughed.

When the APSW returned I said hello and he went inside. Sophie poked her head out the door and asked, "What is your last name?" I said who I was and she asked who John Krinsky was, the name sounded familiar. I reminded her that he had talked to her last summer and was one of two principal researchers and that the other was Maud Simonet who had been around the other day as well. She said something to the effect of "It's a funny world" and went back to her office.

I started the interview with the APSW and was following up on the fact he was a provisional APSW when Sophie knocked (on the wrong door) to the locker room, "Is everybody decent? Can I come in?" I said yeah and told her she was at the wrong door and opened the correct one and let her in. She told me that she had just gotten a call from her chief that said basically all these interviews were to be discontinued. This was surprising to her since last summer she had checked it out and done interviews with us. But she had to ask me to stop the interview for the time being.

I told her I didn't know about this whole thing and she said she had just gotten the e-mail and then checked it out. I told her the news had not gotten to me yet. I also tried to strongly imply that the whole thing was a mix up and interviews proceed again.

Her demeanor seemed to put the APSW at ease—she even said to him, "You didn't do anything wrong, we—I and all the Supervisors—did interviews last summer." He told me, without my asking, that he would still do an interview—he had no problem with it—once everything was okayed again.

I asked who Sophie was hearing this from and she said . . . the main offices for all city parks (the Battery? or the Armory? someplace or building that sounded vaguely militaristic to me[15]). I apologized and she apologized and said hopefully I would be back after we get this thing sorted out and she said sure. Then I got on the phone as soon as I was away and called Maud.

We never got back. After two years in the field, and interviews conducted with over one hundred people, the research process, at least inside the Parks Department, was suddenly interrupted. Any interview with park employees became strictly forbidden. A Park Manager—the title of those in charge of one or a few districts—with whom we had very good relations even told us that the borough commissioner had called him and asked for the list of all the persons to whom we talked in his districts. Our research ethics protocol prevented us from disclosing the names we knew, and because our research protocol anticipated risks to those who did not remain anonymous, we did not even keep records of the names. But the anxiety in his voice when he called us, his request that we not call him on his professional cell phone anymore but only at home, and even his little joke ("I don't know what you guys have done but considering the amount of stress around here I would not be surprised to find your picture on the first page of the *Daily News* tomorrow!") set the tone.

We did manage to meet with top management at the Parks Department after having been shut out of the districts, and they provided us with some important data on POP afterwards. Further, we acknowledge that we were actually lucky to be able to conduct that many interviews and visit that many parks and parks houses around the city during these three years. Under Mayor Giuliani's administration we would probably not have been able to conduct any research project of this kind in any city agency. Nevertheless, it is important to note that a significant culture of secrecy surrounds the operations of public agencies in New York today and has at least since the 1990s. When asking questions about work and working conditions in the parks, it is not difficult to see why, even though the vast majority of workers with whom we spoke had mostly good things to say about their jobs.

### Looking at Parks through Different Lenses

Looking at parks through the lenses of the sociology of work and the politics of public administration entails a shift in the prevalent ways of seeing: any visit to a local bookstore will reward you with beautiful picture books of parks, sometimes with photographs taken when the park is not in use—creating pastoral landscapes divorced from the city—or showing parks users within the landscapes. But none show parks maintenance workers, even though in the course of a visit to a park, and particularly to a park that is routinely photographed, like Manhattan's Central Park, it is impossible to avoid them. Nevertheless, the emphasis of these books is on the design and development of parks.

There are, of course, exceptions. Roy Rosenzweig and Elizabeth Blackmar's masterful *The Park and the People*, a social history of Central Park,[16] is close to unique in its multifaceted treatment of the park, and other works such as Oliver Cooke's *Rethinking Municipal Privatization*[17] focus on the Central Park Conservancy. Both address workers but focus specifically on a single park, even while raising important issues—which we take up as well—about the meaning of public and private space. By and large, however, the workers who maintain parks are left out of focus.

Our approach to parks is first and foremost one rooted in seeing the parks as workplaces. There is no doubt that they are much, much more than that. Nevertheless, studying parks in this way enables us to see them as a kind of multilayered system that is otherwise difficult to take in all at once. Accordingly, in the chapters that follow, we move through this larger picture in stages: First, in chapter 2, we take a close-to-the ground look at the different kinds of workers who clean parks, at their work in chapter 3, and in chapter 4 at their workplace relations. Second, in chapter 5, we introduce the new webs of organization involved in parks maintenance and governance, and present the varied types of groups—public, nonprofit, and partnerships—that now maintain parks. In chapter 6, we discuss how these organizations blur the boundaries between public and private and how the changes operated in the governance of public parks could be understood in terms of Antonio Gramsci's conception of the "integral state," in which political and civil society are mutually constituted and mutually reinforcing. Third, we consider, in chapter 7, the ideological production of this integral state through the process of using and legitimizing different types of unpaid labor. Chapter 8 summarizes our findings and concludes by bringing the distinct parts of our argument together. It considers both the ways in which value is extracted from the process of parks maintenance via labor displacement and increased real estate values, and the ways in which contemporary park maintenance fits in with broader neoliberal modes of governance.

In taking this view of parks maintenance work, we are moving stepwise up levels of analysis, from an analysis of labor contracts and workplaces through organizations and up to larger public policies and to an understanding of the state that, in its diverse composition, is producing them. We are convinced that by doing this, we are able to see dynamics that studies confined to one or the other level might miss. Our approach is a bit like using Google Earth. We begin by zooming into the street-level view, where you can literally see the gum stuck to the sidewalk (at least in New York City), and then up to the neighborhood view, where the picture is a bit more schematic but represents a different—but no less true—picture of our object. We conclude by zooming out further, taking in larger issues and broader context. At each stage, a different language is necessary to describe what we see. But taken as a whole, the interesting problem is to relate one view to the other.[18]

*Analysis of the Workplace*

At the level of studying workplace relations, our study joins many others in finding that job quality—in terms of security of employment, levels of compensation and benefits, quality of rights and representation at work, and autonomy over work—has decreased relative to what it had been before the mid-1970s and the onset of market-oriented, "neoliberal" public policy.[19] Typically, however, these observations have been made for private, for-profit workplaces, in large part because a clear link exists between efforts to reduce job quality and impose new, more "flexible" arrangements on a firm's workforce and the ability of that firm to move capital to areas with ever-cheaper labor costs and to realize profits amid a suddenly expanded, global set of competitors, suppliers, and customers. Further, studies of the service economy have shown significant segmentation of labor markets: the "good jobs" with higher pay, benefits, security, and career paths are segmented from "bad jobs" that lack these things.[20] In what follows, we certainly see the segmentation of the workforce in parks, but we see it increasingly in the public sector and the private, nonprofit organizations that manage some parks, both of which are, in theory, insulated from the profit motive. Taken together as a system combining public and private—and within private, for- and nonprofit elements—New York's parks system allows a comparison and consideration of the complementary aspects of public and private, good and bad jobs.

An important aspect of work life that is set against the more general properties of a job is how workers respond to their workplaces, their supervisors and managers, and to each other. These are important issues largely because they affect the degree to which workers can form common experiences upon which to act collectively in the service of common interests. Thus, understanding what *actually* happens at the workplace, among workers with different statuses, helps to understand the power that different workers—and their supervisors, and their supervisors' supervisors—have both to determine what happens at work and also how it is interpreted, is presented to outside audiences, and forms the basis of mobilizing workers to do the work asked of them.

There are few studies of blue-collar work in public workplaces and fewer still that look at the effects of organizational change on the experience of public work.[21] Nevertheless, if we do not understand what difference it makes—to workers themselves, to labor markets, to careers, and to the ability of relatively unskilled workers to develop and to earn a steady living in the public service—whether this work is being done by volunteers, nonprofit employees, civil service workers, welfare-to-work program participants, workfare workers, people sentenced to community service, or youth employed for the summer, we fail to understand one basic public policy that shapes inequality in the city. The creation of certain groups of workers that are almost powerless in the workplace leaves the door open both to the more intimate violations of a workplace sexual economy and harassment and the more generalized practices of making it increasingly difficult for people to earn a living.

## *Analysis of Organizations*

Studying parks maintenance and operations in New York entails studying many organizations at once. One has to be open to the fact that contemporary public services are organizationally complex and that this complexity affects the workplace and the workers in fundamental ways. Even here, we have reduced some of the complexity of our field by excluding from our study those spaces that are often regulated by the Parks Department but that are "privately owned public spaces," or POPS, such as public atriums or vest-pocket parks in midtown Manhattan, often created as a result of zoning regulations and negotiations between real estate developers and the City. We have also excluded state parks that are in the city. Even so, by looking at the operations of a single agency—the Department of Parks and Recreation—we have to understand how other city agencies, such as the Human Resources Administration, and nonprofit agencies, such as the Partnerships for Parks, Central Park Conservancy, Prospect Park Alliance, Madison Square Park Conservancy, and many others, intersect with the work and staffing of the public agency.

We find, for example, instances where public employees are *also* private employees, even while doing the same job, an arrangement that seems less problematic in terms of conflicts of interest and accountability because of the nonprofit status and civic missions of the private partners. The terms of some of the public-private partnerships to manage parks are such that top managers collect half their pay from the Department of Parks and Recreation and half from the nonprofit agency they lead. We also find instances of subcontracting for maintenance, where the Broadway Mall Association contracts with social-service organizations that provide maintenance crews from among their clients.

For more than twenty years, literature on public administration has spoken of "governance" rather than "government."[22] This is the idea that organizations beyond the official channels of government are critical to actually getting anything done in the public realm. This change in terminology both reflects and analyzes a shift away from more centralized government programs and the appearance of new questions about how democratically elected governments can—or should—hold private organizations, for- and nonprofit, with self-appointed leadership, accountable for the provision of public goods.

Other disciplines, such as sociology, political science, and geography, have also noted the shift to "governance" but have most often addressed this shift through more "macro" studies of the changing relations of states, capital, and civil society. As noted earlier, "regime theory" in urban political science deals directly with the intertwining of public and private interests in governance and tries to distinguish among regime types based on the configuration of, and predominance of, the organized interests involved. Urban geographers, from both Marxist and feminist traditions, also have sought to understand governance in similar ways to regime theorists but have focused not just on the traditional locus of politics and public administration but on the governance of workplaces, neighborhoods, and households, as well.[23] Some have noted that the boundaries among these categories of actors have now blurred to a significant degree. The state looks increasingly like the "integral state" described by Antonio Gramsci: a combination of institutions that span a range between more purely coercive functions and those engaged in gaining the active consent of the citizenry.[24] Whether a given institution is explicitly "public" or "private" is less important; the meanings of each become increasingly less clear as their functions intertwine and their civic missions resonate with each other.

Although the reordering of public and private seems to us to be clearly true, there is little work that ties it back to the workplace and very little of anything concrete that is known about the consequences for workers in an increasingly complex web of relationships among public and private actors. Though *governance* may blur public and private organizations and sectors, it is nevertheless true that from the standpoint of the *labor regulation*, the sectors continue to differ, and to do so significantly. Public-sector workers are covered under extensive civil service laws, with definite job titles and responsibilities, regular performance reviews, and appeals procedures. They are required to wear official uniforms and to segregate their private activities from their public ones. This is far less straightforwardly the case for private workers. Further, there are significant differences between civil-service-regulated labor and policies that purport to be public solutions to private problems, such as workfare, welfare-to-work, youth unemployment, and community-service sentences. Perhaps the starkest contrast is that between civil-service-regulated public employment and volunteer work, in which, at least in principle, there is no regulation and no coercion or compulsion, only private initiative, freely applied.

Another contrast between public and private sectors that remains in the face of governance lies in the issue of unionization. In contrast to workers in private-sector firms, in which workers have seen their unions shrink and almost disappear from the scene, workers in the public sector have seen their unions expand or stabilize. The shift from government to governance, of course, has something to do with this: faced with new collective bargaining procedures and increased economic demands from unionized public workers, public employers in the 1970s often sought to reduce the power of these unions by shrinking the public sector and privatizing some of its functions.[25] This is certainly the case in New York City, and perhaps especially true with respect to parks maintenance. As Henry Stern, who was parks commissioner under Mayors Ed Koch and Rudolph Giuliani and a parks official during the 1960s, told us with respect to unionized civil-service employment: "All of the safeguards make it very difficult to use resources effectively." Therefore, ways to skirt the rules become imperative for effective management of the parks. This suggests, further, that contemporary conservative ideas about the power of public-sector unions—which see them as being able to choose their bosses through the electoral system, and therefore being capable of cynically manipulating public commitments and budgets through their influence—greatly exaggerate the actual power that public workers have.[26] Only by looking at the organizational changes wrought by governance and at the workplace relations that they produce can we begin to take a measure of the ways in which workers and their unions wield power or not. As the profiles that opened this chapter suggest, there are a great number of practices at parks workplaces that fall outside of strict enforcement and regulation of civil service codes and union rules, even if the presence of these regulations still exerts some influence on workplace and political relations.

CHAPTER ONE

## *Analysis of Contemporary Urban Politics*

Analysts of contemporary cities often view the proliferation of institutions of governance as a key aspect of neoliberalism. In contrast to the austerity programs that characterized the onset of neoliberal governance starting in the mid-1970s (significantly including the enormous rounds of public retrenchment during New York City's fiscal crisis), the current form of neoliberal governance does not cut services back: it attempts to enhance services even while cutting public employment by redistributing public work away from public workers. The "rollout" of neoliberal programs is, as sociologist Bob Jessop explains, often accompanied by elements of governance that do not accord to a pure "market" logic or appear to be oriented toward profit-making activities.[27] Instead, they draw on mixed strategies of what he calls neostatism, neocorporatism, and neocommunitarianism. Neostatism, for example, contributes public-private partnerships under state direction; neocorporatism involves the broadening of public, private, and civic stakeholders in governance; and neocommunitarianism contributes an expansion of the "role of the third sector," or civic and community-based organizations, in governance and service provision.

Attention to the neoliberal reordering of urban service provision and public work also draws us to consider the *indirect* role that parks maintenance has in supporting new, dominant conceptions of good city governance and of its purpose. With the expansion of the financialization of the global economy and, in particular, the growing global importance of investments based on real estate value, cities, including New York, attempted to reinvent themselves so as to maximize real estate value and to market themselves globally as "places" to be and to own property.[28] The refurbishment of the city's parks infrastructure that began at the tail end of the fiscal crisis with the formation of Central Park Conservancy, Prospect Park Alliance, and the Bryant Park Restoration Corporation has continued and has brought significant development and commercial activity back to the Times Square area, Madison Square, Union Square, West Chelsea and the West Village (where the High Line runs), and, in different ways, many other parks, especially in Manhattan and Brooklyn. The maintenance of this infrastructure is critical for the success of the real estate value-boosting initiatives to which these efforts are tied, and so parks maintenance work participates in a dynamic of indirect capital accumulation. To be sure, there are public benefits tied to parks maintenance—many people, and not just those who own adjacent property, benefit from well-maintained public amenities. Nevertheless, when considering the private value that is derived from parks maintenance, it becomes clear that the push to cut public budgets and average worker pay continually involves a distinctive form of exploitation combining both public and private organizational decisions.

Significantly, too, this exploitation maps onto existing categories of inequality and, very often, deepens them. The sociologist Loïc Wacquant[29] has argued persuasively that the current practices of welfare reform and mass incarceration are contemporary ways of reinforcing racial and gender hierarchies: welfare reform allows the state to hassle and control a population significantly composed of poor women of color, while mass incarceration allows the same for men. Moreover, just as prison labor has become a lucrative industry, so workfare and welfare-to-work programs have helped to staff otherwise-decimated public services. All of this, moreover, began at a crucial point of transition: ethnic succession in public services—and particularly in lower-skilled public services—began to shift significantly toward African American and Latino workers after the 1970s fiscal crisis (the process had begun earlier but last-hired, first-fired rules ensured that the full effects were delayed).[30] Thus, the conversion of regular civil-service jobs in which one could make a career to high-turnover jobs, seasonal and part-time employment, and "program" slots further undermined the economic prospects of those hoping to benefit from public employment's apparent advantages. To be sure, many still do, and public employment is still an important ladder into more stable economic circumstances. But for many more, this opportunity has been foreclosed.

TWO
---

# The Workers

> Some people come from the jail working for parks. Some community service. Some park assistants. We are so many different . . . **JOB TRAINING PROGRAM PARTICIPANT, BROOKLYN**

When Alvin left the active military to join the reserves, he went to the Veterans' Administration for a job referral. Initially sent to Manhattan's garment district to pull coat racks from workshop to workshop, and from workshop to showroom, Alvin was turned off by the company there:

This was 1986. And all the guys that were there, they were all smoking weed, and they were bums and winos, and I did it for a couple of weeks, and I went back and said, "Listen, I'm going to college, I'm a veteran, you gotta be able to do better than that. I know how to read and write, you know. This is like people who . . ." So the guy said, "You know what? You happen to be lucky, there's a massive hiring for the Parks Department. And go there on such and such date, dress business attire." And I like the Parks Department . . . well, maybe I never focused on it, didn't pay too much attention. And I went down there like in August and in November I got hired as a Park Service Worker.

Like hundreds of others hired in the Parks Department in the mid-1980s, Alvin benefited from the recovery of New York City from the fiscal crisis that defined its politics in the 1970s and early 1980s and the relative stability and availability of advancement opportunities of a public-sector job. We sit in an office in a "park house"—a squat building with an equipment storage area and public bathrooms, one of hundreds around the city built by Robert Moses in playgrounds and parks—as Alvin describes his first job with the Parks Department:

> We would do really good jobs. I happen to take a lot of pride in the work that I do, because we used to take parks that were completely neglected, full of weeds, we would change benches, we would do a lot of painting of graffiti, and I did that for a few years . . . And you know, I was very happy because it was a good job, city job, good benefits, but it was very menial tasks. It was raking and painting and stuff like that . . .

Alvin, a tall and muscular man in his late forties who retains his military bearing, then got promoted and worked his way up to Parks Supervisor, passing through the ranks of Associate Park Service Workers, who operate heavy equipment and drive the "heavy packer," a garbage truck with a sixteen-cubic-yard capacity.

Like Alvin, Harlan is a second-level Supervisor, having worked his way up through the Maintenance and Operations hierarchy through civil service exams. Unlike Alvin, he was able to take the test for Principal Park Supervisor (PPS), which gives him responsibility over multiple districts. Alvin also has this responsibility, but his title, Parks Supervisor 2, is an "in-house" title, which means that it is an appointment by the Parks Department separate from the civil service system. Harlan began as a City Park Worker, a civil service title that consolidated, or "broadbanded," several other separate titles, including the Park Service Worker. Like Alvin, Harlan is a military veteran who benefited from the expansion of the parks workforce in the 1980s and from the promotional opportunities it provided. But already in the 1990s, Harlan began to see troubling changes, particularly in the appointment of managers. "There's a lot of us who came up through the ranks together, and [when confronting a problem], it's like: 'What would Mr. Marcos do? What would Mickey do?'" But now, "These [managers], they come in off the street, they haven't come up through the ranks. They don't know how to clean a bathroom because they never have cleaned a bathroom."

The Supervisors are not the ones who normally clean the bathrooms, of course. This job falls primarily to the Job Training Program workers who make up between a third and over a half of the department's maintenance and operations workforce. These workers, who in fiscal year 2010 were 92.6 percent black and Latino and 74.1 percent female,[1] work in the department for six to nine months a year as part

CHAPTER TWO

of a welfare-to-work program called the Parks Opportunity Program (POP). Job Training Program workers, universally known as "JTPs," do much of the dirty work in the parks and the most menial tasks. As temporary, seasonal workers, they are paid less than City Park Workers (CPWs), otherwise the lowest civil service rank in the Maintenance and Operations wing of the department. In 2010, JTPs made $9.21 an hour as against between $14.02 and $16.12 for CPWs. They do not receive pension credits and do not have full union-member status. JTPs are often on "mobile crews" that clean multiple parks, playgrounds, and traffic medians over the course of their 7 a.m. to 3:30 p.m. shifts. They are shepherded from one place to the other in vans or in pickup trucks driven either by CPWs or by "crew chiefs," who are either CPWs or Associate Park Service Workers (APSWs), who get a "step-up" promotion worth more than $3,000 a year in order to take on the responsibility of supervising JTPs' work.

Alvin and Harlan, like many other parks workers we interviewed, have made their careers in the Parks Department amid the changes in its workforce. They will have seen and been part of shifts in the organization of work and categorization of workers that can be described with reference to two main processes, in which there are finer variations, namely, *broadbanding* and *segmentation*. Broadbanding refers to the consolidation of many categories of work into fewer. Segmentation refers to the expansion of the number of categories of worker, and especially to the creation of distinctions among them in terms of pay, workplace rights, and supervisory discretion and the erection of barriers to mobility among them. At first glance, it seems as if these dynamics work in opposite directions; the one seems to contradict the other. Yet, as this chapter will make clear, these dynamics together create a complex and variegated workforce but do not undermine each other, in part because the specific policy changes that contribute to these dynamics did not all occur at once. Neither, however, did they occur in clear phases, so that their overlap both results in—and reinforces—a workforce whose internal divisions are difficult to bridge. We take up these two dynamics in the first two parts of the chapter, leading with broadbanding and following with segmentation. We treat each broadly: we extend past the technical aspects of combining categories of work in our discussion of broadbanding; we treat segmentation as both a practice of proliferating new kinds of labor contracts and an analytic device that shows how these labor contracts—both formal and informal, within the Parks Department and outside of it—restructure the workplace and make the passage from one contract to another rare. The overall picture that emerges is akin to what David Weil has called a "fissured workplace," in which systems of contracting and restructuring enable the degradation of previously decent jobs into more insecure and contingent ones.[2]

## Broadbanding

Broadbanding has a circumscribed and precise meaning: it is the combination of several job categories or "titles" under a single civil service title. Broadbanding often takes away promotional steps within a title, and it gives more freedom to managers to put workers to tasks that before broadbanding might have triggered supplementary payments for "out-of-title" work.

Here, we begin our discussion with broadbanding and follow its several implications through the labor policies of the Parks Department, including the switch from fixed-post to mobile crews, and the recently interrupted, long-term practice of avoiding civil-service testing. The core of the story is that the reorganization of work through broadbanding is one method to increase administrative and managerial power over key aspects of the workplace, from hiring to labor allocation and from evaluation to promotion.

Since the fiscal crisis in the late 1970s, broadbanding has been one of several strategies employed by municipal managers in their attempt to make service delivery more efficient. Because different job titles entail different sorts of work, upper-level parks managers and "good government" groups such as the City Budget Commission fear that workers who may have substantially similar tasks may nevertheless be able to refuse to do specific tasks if they fall under a neighboring job title. To the frustration of agency managers, then, it may be impossible to get an employee to perform a given task, given the personnel on hand. More likely, the manager will get a worker to do the task, but if it is normally in a different title, the worker can file a grievance and get compensated at the level at which the relevant civil service title demands. By including more tasks within a given civil service title, broadbanding does away with this problem. It also increases managerial control by giving managers the flexibility to demote workers within a title from one "assignment" or "in-house" position to another without the due process that demotion across titles would trigger. In combining titles, promotional opportunities also shrink because there are fewer steps in an agency's career ladder.

The Park Service Worker title, which became the CPW title in 1986, was the result of a large-scale broadbanding in 1977. As the fiscal crisis dragged on, the City tried to make its civil service more efficient. Accordingly, after negotiation with District Council 37, the main union representing city workers, over the match of the new titles with representation by the council's locals and pension classification, it folded sixteen titles into four. The Park Service Worker title was created out of Custodial Assistants, Attendants, Watchmen, and Ticket Agents. Associate Park Service Workers combined Water Plant Operators and Motor Vehicle Operators and also inherited some of the tasks of Gardeners and Climbers and Pruners. Several other titles were combined to create two levels of parks Supervisors, the Parks Supervisor and the Principal Park Supervisor.[3]

Combining job titles can have contradictory effects. On one hand, in their normal course of work, workers are exposed to more tasks, and can theoretically advance more quickly through the ranks by learning more aspects of parks operations. On the other hand, because the titles are broader, there may be less opportunity to advance because with fewer rungs, the likelihood that a higher rung will have vacancies is lower.

The consequences of broadbanding for advancing through the ranks, then, are that the jump from CPW to APSW depends on the worker getting a different kind of driver's license and passing the promotional test. The Parks Department's Parks Opportunity Program offers driver's education classes for JTPs. But simple, diligent work over a long period of time cannot earn one a promotion to a new position unless these conditions are met. Accordingly, as Harlan noted, even Debris Collectors would compete with each other under the older system: "It was like, 'I've got seven-and-a-half tons, you picked up five-and-a-half.' Now, there's no incentive. People always were looking to get promoted, so they'd shine. Now, they're not hiring people through the ranks, so you don't have that."

Management power also increases through the generation of "in-house" titles such as crew chief and Parks Supervisor 2 (PS2), which are not civil service ranks. By agreement with District Council 37, CPW "crew chiefs" earn the APSW pay for supervising workfare (WEP), Job-Training, and community-service workers. The only thing that distinguishes a crew chief is that he or she drives JTPs, WEP workers, or community-service workers in a twelve-passenger van from one worksite to another. If one takes a crew of three JTPs in a pickup truck, one is not doing a crew chief's work. If, however, the same three JTPs who showed up to work that morning are taken in the van, it should be a designated crew chief who takes them out. Therefore, depending on the actual staffing levels in a given district, crew chief designation can be arbitrarily made by a manager. And as with any set of more or less arbitrary decisions, this opens up room for favoritism. As one CPW who had actually been taking crews out in the van on and off for two years said:

> I'm doing the work anyways. I just want to get paid for it . . . two years of doing crew chief work and I'm not getting paid for it. . . . It's basically about who you know in this agency. Like if you pretty much are a quiet person and don't know anybody, then you might just stay the way you are. Like see I like to bug [my Supervisor] and tell him, "Listen, I know you could get me the step-up, please, man." It's more money, you know?

Though the CPW could bring a grievance with his union since the step-up to crew chief was collectively bargained, he said that doing so, in spite of voluminous trip records, could result in his getting "blackballed" and transferred to a more difficult district even if he won. This is common throughout the civil service, in spite of the alleged power that unions have over the workplace. It is worse in a context in which layoffs are being discussed or implemented. When, in 1991, the Parks Department laid off all of its 124 Laborers and reallocated their work to CPWs and APSWs, union leaders complained. The president of the CPWs' union argued that "They use the threat of layoffs to force mainly minority employees into out-of-title work in jobs that others were paid much more to do. It's slave labor and it's discrimination." The president of the unionized parks Supervisors claimed: "We don't like to give out-of-title assignments, but higher management intimidates the staff. Everyone is afraid that more layoffs will mean their job."[4] Even where grievance machinery is available, many workers do not use it out of fear for their jobs or for their current assignments.

Thus, the management—that is, those above the union-represented Supervisors in the hierarchy—could more easily decide who among existing Supervisors they would promote to the jobs with the most operational responsibility for maintenance and operations.

### *From Fixed-Post to Mobile*

The broadbanding of many parks titles made possible the most basic, visible change in the organization of maintenance and operations work in the Parks Department, namely, the switch from assigning parks maintenance workers to specific parks in "fixed posts" to assigning them to "mobile units" that attend to multiple parks and playgrounds. Charles Brecher and Raymond Horton, longtime budget watchdogs in New York, describe this shift as directly stemming from budgetary concerns following the fiscal crisis of the 1970s. They note, as well, that the shift has had some adverse consequences, even though it is also an example of improved efficiency in deployment of personnel (the primary concern of their organization, the Citizens' Budget Commission, a business-led "good government" group founded amid the city's fiscal crisis in the 1930s). Specifically, they note that not having parks employees stationed in parks on a permanent basis increases the likelihood of vandalism, since there is nobody around to deter vandals. This, in turn, makes considerably more work for the mobile crews, as vandalism—taking the form of graffiti, broken fences and benches, or even the impromptu moving of play equipment and lawn borders to create skate-park obstacles (reported by one of our interviewees who worked in a park in Queens)—occupies a disproportionate amount of time and resources to undo.

When Robert Moses developed 758 playgrounds in his tenure as parks commissioner,[5] he did so with the idea that in these playgrounds, the department would provide supervised play. The very movement that argued for the importance of playgrounds and became important in their design—tied with progressive good-government movements in the late nineteenth and early twentieth century—also assumed that play would be supervised by adults. The "recreation" part of the name "Department of Parks and Recreation" speaks to that legacy, and there are still summer youth workers who run activities in playgrounds in the summer months, as well as a regular staff of recreation employees in a range of positions, most often in the larger recreation and sports centers in neighborhoods around the city that house after-school programs, weight rooms, gyms, and pools. Nevertheless, the vast majority of parks and playgrounds have not had assigned recreation workers since shortly after they were developed during the New Deal. Cuts in New Deal programs and the onset of World War Two ended that. But even during the 1990s, the number of recreation workers went into free fall. From 371 recreation workers citywide in 1991, the total declined to eighty ten years later.[6] Given that most of these were deployed in the recreation centers, the only permanent public presence in playgrounds across the city would be either parks maintenance staff or Parks Enforcement Officers (PEPs).

The move from fixed-post to mobile crews changed this considerably. There are still workers assigned to fixed posts, but they are a tiny minority. Moreover, even where parks supervisors prefer to have fixed-post workers in principle, they understand that their ability to get all the parks in their districts cleaned on a daily basis means that having a single worker assigned to a single site—and particularly one authorized to drive a vehicle with other workers—can compromise the cleanliness of other sites. They also sometimes remark that the assignment of fixed-post workers to specific parks is a result of inequalities in political power. For example, a parks supervisor in Brooklyn looked forward to the retirement of one of her CPWs because that would give her the opportunity to move staff around. If the playground in the middle of a gentrified portion of her district lost its fixed-post parkie, the parents would "raise holy hell at the Community Board . . . I could never do it." She continued, "In a perfect world, would I want everyone fixed-post? Would I prefer a fixed-post? Absolutely. But now, I need him to drive a vehicle." Then, indicating a poorer area in the district she had just shown us on a tour of the area, she asked, "Why should they get less?"

Even apart from the deterrent effect on vandalism that fixed-post workers can have, other supervisors indicate the lack of "deep cleaning" and a decline in understanding of parks by maintenance workers that follows the move to mobile crews. One supervisor in Harlem suggested that simply removing litter, glass, and graffiti—key areas on the department's Parks Inspection Program evaluation sheet—while important, still missed other facets of maintenance. It would be less likely, for example, for members of a mobile crew to clean benches, or notice that a piece of play equipment had a screw loose or that a piece of soft matting around a play structure had torn slightly. Without actually spending time in the park, he said, you cannot tell what needs to be done. He mentioned that he can listen to a game of basketball and tell if the hoop needs tightening. A mobile crew going through the same playground at seven in the morning will never get that basic maintenance information.

And what about PEP officers? Of course PEP officers are not typically understood as integral to the maintenance and operations of parks. They are instead understood as providing security. Nevertheless, by 2010, PEP was at the center of controversy that was closely akin to the question of which parks get fixed-post workers. According to the chairwoman of the City Council Committee on Parks, there were ninety-two full-time PEP officers available for parks citywide, "with an additional eighty-three officers that are contracted by conservancies and other private entities to work in specific parks. There are often just a few at-large officers on duty at any given time for the entire borough of the Bronx, whereas in a single park in communities of greater means, there might be a dozen." PEP officers are unarmed but have the right to make arrests and to issue tickets for infringement of Parks Department rules. They also often enforce "quality of life" measures, which in many cases means rousting homeless people from sleeping on benches or preventing homeless people from storing their belongings in secluded sections of parkland.

At McCombs Dam Park in the Bronx, a volunteer lamented the absence of PEP officers and fixed-post park maintenance workers. On a tour of the park, he showed how a break-in occurred in the supplies closet for a sports program there. McCombs Dam Park is opposite the new Yankee Stadium (built with tens of millions of taxpayer subsidies) and has recently undergone a $23 million expansion and renovation. It has a beautiful running track and well-used soccer fields and baseball diamonds with the same grass that is used across the street at the stadium. The volunteer pointed to broken fences around a handball court where drug dealers hang out and said that the city stands to lose its investment in the park in a few years if it does not commit the resources for fixed-post supervision of the park.

The more "mainstream" of New York City's parks advocacy organizations, New Yorkers for Parks (NY4P), joined the Citizens' Budget Commission (CBC) to release a report in 2007 in which they argued that the Parks Department still does not allocate enough resources to maintenance and relies too much on the capital budget for replacement of parks features that are subject to wear and tear. NY4P and CBC claim that there is too little preventive maintenance and that this is driven by the demand to produce low year-to-year operating budgets, even as capital budgets for parks expand. While NY4P and CBC do not connect this problem with staffing—they call, in fact, for measures that might exacerbate some of the problems that mobile crews produce—they indicate another way in which the department tries to manage its operational challenges as the depths of maintenance, operations, and security suffer in response to the shift from fixed-post to mobile crews and the systematic inequalities in allocating PEP officers.

*Civil Service and Promotion*

As job descriptions in the Parks Department have changed, so too has the department's reliance on civil service examinations as a means for promoting its workers. For a good part of the 1980s and 1990s—and even into the 2000s—the department relied on "provisional" appointments of Supervisors and Managers, while the City did not offer promotional exams to allow existing civil service workers to rise through the ranks. This changed in the later 2000s as lawsuits forced greater compliance with civil service law. One lawsuit, occurring on Long Island, resulted in a ruling that provisional employees could not be given tenure rights under a union contract, and this meant that New York State agencies had to begin to give civil service exams more often. The second lawsuit, which the City settled for $21 million, was a class-action suit charging that the department's provisional hiring practices were systematically skewed against black and Latino employees and showed a pattern of discriminatory promotion.[7] The lawsuit, *Wright v. Stern*—settled by the department and the class of black and Latino plaintiffs in 2008—alleged that the City skirted promotional tests, did not post jobs, did not do regular evaluations, and generated jobs for which the department preferentially tapped outside hiring pools. If job openings are not posted, and performance evaluations not always done, workers cannot apply for promotional positions, and provisional promotions are made solely on the basis of supervisors' discretion. Moreover, Commissioner Henry Stern developed a program in the 1990s called the "Class Of" program, to recruit graduates of top universities to work in administrative positions in Parks. There was a large disproportion of whites in the "Class Of" program, and they were given access to higher-level training, even while Stern discontinued a different program that had been "successful in grooming managers for the agency."[8]

We will return to some of the implications of this at the worksite in later chapters. For the moment, however, it is important to understand several points about broadbanding: First, the collapsing of distinctions across job categories implied in broadbanding has both direct and immediate—though sometimes contradictory—effects for workers in the broadbanded titles with respect to promotion, incentives, and out-of-title pay. Second, broadbanding gives managers increased discretion with respect to the allocation of workers across the necessary maintenance tasks, but also with respect to promotion and hiring. This wider discretion enabled the switch from fixed-post to mobile crews by consolidating the tasks of those most likely to be assigned to mobile crews, at least at first. At the same time, this widened discretion also has the contradictory effect of generating more internal distinctions through the creation of "in-house" titles and unofficial promotional tracks. More importantly, broadbanding ushered in a much more general dynamic of segmentation: the same impetus of budget- and staff cuts that made broadbanding appear to be an important efficiency tool also led to the proliferation of new kinds of (mostly) non-civil-service titles and work contracts in parks maintenance work.

## Segmentation

Labor economists and sociologists have long understood that labor markets are not continuous gradients of insecure to secure jobs, lower pay to higher pay, or unskilled to skilled. Instead, they are "segmented" to different degrees depending upon the ways in which they are regulated.[9] This means that internal "job ladders" or "labor markets" in a firm or organization are discontinuous, with some jobs filled by a large pool of people with high turnover, low job security, and low pay, and others filled by a smaller pool of people, often with more skills, who have significant job security, higher pay, and reliable benefits. This is no less true—at least now—in the public sector than in the private sector. It is especially striking in the Parks Department in part because it has become increasingly segmented since the 1970s and particularly so since the 1990s.

### *Segmentation as a Category of Analysis*

Scholars of labor and employment talk about "labor market segmentation" not only as a *practice* but also as a category of analysis. Segmentation speaks to the division of labor markets into "primary" and "secondary" segments: primary markets are characterized by relatively stable employment, autonomy at work, and expectation of payment. Secondary labor markets are characterized by high turnover and insecurity, high levels of supervision, and less expectation of continuous employment. Whether one or another job fits into the primary or secondary designation is generally a matter of judgment: the categories are marked by gradients along a number of axes, rather than firmly bounded from each other. And yet labor market scholars argue that within a given labor market or sometimes within a firm (an "internal labor market"), primary and secondary jobs are fairly well bounded *from each other*, with few passages between them via promotion.

In their sociology of work, *Work Under Capitalism*, Chris and Charles Tilly compared various sorts of "labor contracts" or arrangements between workers and their employers with respect to the potential for

# THE WORKERS

"short-term monetization" of their labor and the "extent of time discipline." For Tilly and Tilly, "short-term monetization" refers to the effort workers put in based on their expectation of getting paid (nondeferred compensation). "Extent of time discipline" refers to the control one has over one's time at work; it increases the less control you have.[10] This is the skeleton of figure 2.1. The shaded area represents labor-market work and the unshaded area represents noncommodified work. The diagonal line through the labor market suggests the boundary between "primary" and "secondary" labor markets.

Primary labor markets are those in which high levels of control over work time and high potential for payment predominate (though not necessarily high wages or salaries when compared to those outside a given firm or organization). They are, therefore, marked by greater stability and low turnover and the presence of within-segment promotion opportunities. Secondary labor markets, by contrast, are large, low-wage turnover pools. With little control over one's work, and little potential to earn money within the organization, secondary-market workers have little incentive to stay and are easily replaced by employers, and they will often turn over quickly. Accordingly, management incentives differ according to segments, too. In primary markets, efforts to secure loyalty, appeals to professional pride, and contests for coveted management jobs predominate. In secondary markets, "em-

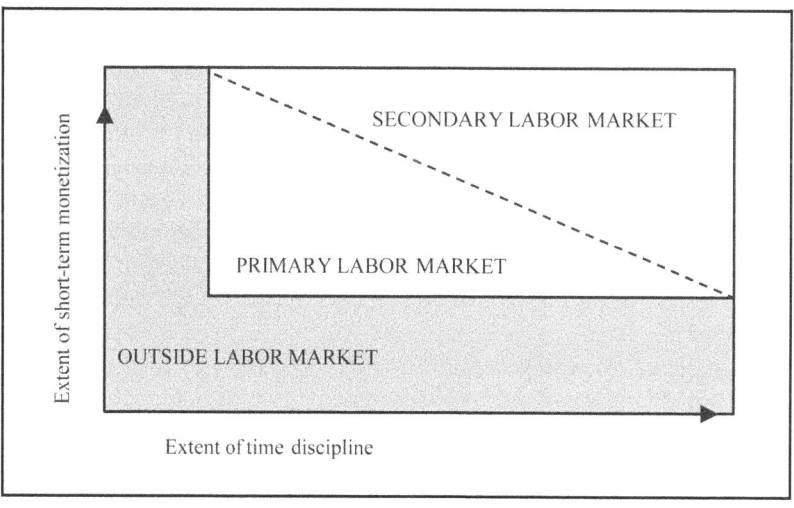

2.1  Labor-market segments (Tilly and Tilly, 1998)

ployers see workers as more interchangeable and expendable"[11] and are likely either to manage by means of tangible results by punishing workers for failing to meet a standard (as in piecework, but also other systems of assessment) or simply by driving them through the threat of job loss.

One important aspect of figure 2.1 is especially important to highlight: There is space in the figure for *nonmarket work*. One can imagine an independent craftsperson or artist in the upper left, with a high expectation of short-term financial reward but nearly no time discipline. Volunteers may be closer to the bottom left: they can withdraw their labor at will. Prisoners, slaves, and workfare workers will be closer to the bottom right, again outside of the labor market. Housework, unpaid digital labor, and other forms of work that are not as often understood in comparison to other kinds of labor relations are also outside of the market and somewhere along the lower strip of low short-term monetization.

As a depiction of segmentation, however, the figure is limited: First, it is static. Students of contemporary labor markets such as Marc Doussard and David Weil speak of "degraded work" and "fissured workplaces" to indicate, respectively, the ways in which employers in certain sectors have aggressively pushed workers into secondary-market jobs and decimated primary labor markets in their fields, and the ways in which subcontracting distributes workers across the segments in a common workplace with multiple employers. Second, though we might think of workfare workers—who get no pay but their welfare benefits and are required to work as a condition of receiving them—as being part of the coerced, "nonmarket" segment, it is equally the case that they work in expectation of receiving these benefits and so could be considered as being in the secondary labor market. Similarly, volunteers might also be trying to make contacts for a parks-related business or be required to participate as a condition of their employment at a corporation. Moreover, trainees on the job for several months may, in fact, supervise summer youth workers, for example. How do we think of these?

In practice, then, segmentation itself—and not just in combination with broadbanding—can appear paradoxical: particular jobs or labor contracts may proliferate; they may become more unequal and cut off from each other in terms of promotional ladders; and yet, even within this broad framework, each is marked by a peculiar mix of autonomy, pay levels, security, duration, and responsibility that do not neatly sort out into primary, secondary, and non-labor-market work.

THE WORKERS

## *Segmenting the Parks Workforce: Creating a Subtier of the Workforce*

Beginning in the early 1970s, the City developed workfare programs and other welfare-to-work programs and used some of these workers for general parks maintenance. Since then, their numbers have fluctuated and, with them, the City's dependence on them to do the bulk of the basic work of parks maintenance. The widespread move to mobile crews after the fiscal crisis corresponded with the expansion of the city's workfare program, which was then called the Public Works Program, under Mayor Edward I. Koch. By 1984, the Parks Department was using 1,775 workers in the program, while also assigning Park Service Workers and Laborers to mobile crews. As the Public Works Program waned in the last five years of the Koch administration, and as more workers were hired into the Parks Department and other agencies, mobile crews were composed mainly of regular parks workers. But as the city began to sink again into fiscal crisis in the 1990s, Mayor Dinkins began to expand workfare again, focused primarily in the Parks Department (along with the continued use of workfare in the Human Resources Administration). Between April 1990—four months after Dinkins took office—and April 1994, at the same point in Rudolph Giuliani's first term, the number of City Park Workers declined by 22 percent, from 1,553 to 1,200.[12] It would decline again by another third to 803 over the following five years. In November 2006, there were 514. The expansion of workfare was critical, therefore, to maintaining the mobile crews.

An aide to Mayor Giuliani, Richard Schwartz—who originally had been hired in the 1980s by Henry Stern and returned during Stern's second run at Parks—developed plans for an expansive workfare program, the Work Experience Program (WEP). Under WEP, welfare recipients would receive their welfare checks and food stamps, but no further compensation. In WEP, which was mandatory for most welfare recipients, workers were defined as compensating the city for the aid they received, rather than as being paid for the work they did. By 1997, two years after WEP began a historic expansion, there were more than 38,000 welfare recipients working in city agencies and contracted nonprofit organizations at any one time.[13] They worked between twenty and thirty-five hours per week and were concentrated in four agencies: the welfare agency (the Human Resources Administration, or HRA), the Department of Citywide Administrative Services (DCAS), Sanitation, and Parks. In the Parks Department alone, there was an average of over six thousand WEP workers, with more than three thousand in the field at any one time. WEPs did work that more than six hundred full-time workers did before they were laid off in the early 1990s.

Several community organizations and unions had opposed WEP's expansion. For three years, they tried to get the city council to pass legislation creating "transitional jobs" that would, unlike WEP, enable workers to have "employee" status and, thus, workplace rights and a wage. Because of the division of powers in New York City, activists and their lawyers thought that if the city council could create a "program" with time-limited jobs, it would not preempt the mayor's power to staff the executive agencies as he saw fit (a state court later disagreed). Amid a good deal of political wrangling, the city council passed legislation to create 7,500 transitional jobs in 1999 and overrode a mayoral veto. Nevertheless, taking his cue from the bill, Mayor Giuliani shortly thereafter announced the creation of the Parks Opportunity Program (POP), a transitional jobs program in the Parks Department.[14]

Beginning in late 2000, POP enrolled 2,500 welfare recipients who were nearing the end of their federally covered five years in the welfare program. POP enrollees were given a four-day work week in the field and had one day a week for training coordinated through the Parks Department. The training was done in house and by contract. It included GED classes, "job-readiness" classes and job search, driving classes for both regular and commercial driver's licenses, horticulture, and security services. The positions were to last for eleven months and to be defined as "seasonal" work, meaning that POP workers were ineligible for regular municipal workers' health and pension benefits. But as City Seasonal Aides, POP workers did have the right to representation by DC 37, were treated as "employees" under the law, and were compensated at wages commensurate to those earned by regular employees who performed the same tasks (usually City Park Workers).

By the end of 2001, however, as the first cohort of POP workers neared the end of their contract, the Giuliani administration attempted to transfer the POP workers to a contract under TempForce, a private temporary jobs agency. The terms of that deal were to be that the average POP worker would see her pay reduced by more than three dollars per hour (from about $11) so that TempForce could be paid to manage them without significantly adding to the cost of the program. Though the contract was nullified when the Bloomberg administration took the reins of city government in early 2002, the attempt indicated a central problem at the heart of POP, namely, that it closed the gap between the costs of regular employment at the kind of "free labor" represented by WEP and its predecessors. As New York City's finances suffered with the "dot-com" bust and the effects of the attacks of September 11, 2001, these crises focused significant attention of both mayors—Giuliani and Bloomberg—on slashing budgets.

In 2003, Mayor Bloomberg proposed to DC 37 that POP workers' pay be cut by fifty cents per hour. DC 37 balked, while the local representing City Seasonal Aides was set to accept the deal, which was less draconian than earlier administration proposals. The local, Local 983-Motor Vehicles Operators, was the base of one of the leaders of an internal reform movement in DC 37. It clashed regularly with the general district council leadership. For its part, that leadership argued that it was unfair to bargain concessions for workers at the bottom rung of public service. In response, the Bloomberg administration cut the program entirely, only to reinstate it with a new job title, Job Training Participant, at a far lower wage ($7.50 per hour) than the original POP program and for a six-, rather than eleven-, month tenure. Two years later, DC 37 regained the right to represent JTPs in the POP/JTP program. Because JTP turned into a six-month job assignment, JTP workers were not eligible for full union rights and were folded into the union as "associate members" with reduced dues and no self-governance structure.

In the interviews we conducted with "regular"—that is, civil service—workers, we found that perceptions of JTP and WEP varied a great deal. Some conflated the programs. Even an upper-level manager did so, suggesting that whatever the merits of POP and JTP relative to WEP, perceptions of the program were often influenced by the continuity of the demographics of the WEP-POP-JTP workers, by their subordination, and by the governing structures at the workplace associated with the program.

And yet, other workers—and particularly supervisors—strongly distinguished the programs, and almost all in favor of JTP, though they had significant criticisms of the program, having to do with their inability to hire JTPs permanently and the concomitant waste of training resources. WEP, however, posed the greatest operational difficulties.

Specifically, because WEP is a program by which welfare recipients "work off" their welfare checks, their schedules are set by dividing the value of their benefits by the minimum wage. This means that WEP workers at a given worksite may have quite different numbers of required hours: some may have hours set by food-stamp budgets alone, others by budgets for different family sizes, and still others' budgets may be affected by small amounts of other income, including earned income. For district managers dealing with mobile crews, this is a potential scheduling nightmare. It means that CPWs and crew chiefs

CHAPTER TWO

have to keep track of who needs to be picked up from which worksite at what time.

During most of our research, there were few WEPs in the parks. By 2008, when we began our research, they had mostly been supplanted by JTPs in maintenance and operations roles. Nevertheless, in one district in Brooklyn, WEP was reintroduced as a pilot for a potential expansion, and by the summer of 2009, the district had equal numbers of WEP and JTP workers, about fifty to sixty of each. One Supervisor expressed reservations about the arrangement, and particularly about the unfairness the workers were likely to perceive of working in the same sorts of tasks, side by side, under quite different conditions of employment. Moreover, it would be a challenge to have newer WEP workers working alongside JTPs without the JTP workers supervising the WEP workers' work, which was not allowed. The entire experiment came to a rapid halt, however, when one of the Supervisors apparently submitted time-sheet paperwork to the welfare agency, the Human Resources Administration (HRA), several hours after the deadline. The computer tracking system at HRA recorded all of the WEP workers in the district as not having been at work over the previous two weeks, and all were sent failure to comply (FTC) notices, which can result in the loss of their benefits. Once the mistake was discovered, every effort was made to rectify the situation, but WEPs were once again—temporarily—withdrawn from the parks.

Still, by 2011 a greater number of WEP workers were assigned to parks across several districts, while the number of JTPs began to decline. With the transfer of federal money to state and local governments from the 2009–2010 "stimulus" running out, the resulting budget squeeze put pressure on parks as well as on every city agency. The result is that in spite of the stated preference of the top parks managers for JTP, WEP had been expanding. Though compared to the levels of the late 1990s, the number of WEPs became quite small (DPR reported in February 2012 that it averaged 225 WEP workers per week, working on average fewer than twenty hours per week, but that it had already started 602 WEP workers in their parks assignments), it represents a significant increase, even as the department planned a reduction of 800 JTPs for fiscal year 2013.

In the midst of this, DPR strove to put a good face on WEP. An employee of the month in the fall of 2011 was someone tasked with implementing the reintroduction of WEP. And in February 2012, the "Commissioner's Corner" newsletter profiled one former WEP worker who was then assigned to JTP:

In the spring of 2011, Mark was assigned to Morningside Park as a Work Experience Trainee, under the supervision of Horticulture Trainer PS Joseph "Joe" Spano. Mark quickly learned the operations of the park and absorbed knowledge from his supervisors. Ten months later, he is now able to perform most duties like a seasoned horticulturist, including the designing and planting of flower beds, and performing plant and tree care and maintenance. According to PS Spano, "Mark was a true asset to us at Morningside Park . . . He is a self-motivated individual . . . and always puts 100% effort into every job he takes on."

After working as a Work Experience trainee with Parks for 10 months, Mark Lilly was hired as a JTP in Queens in February, 2012. Congratulations, Mark! What a great example of how hard work and dedication pays off.

Sincerely,
Adrian Benepe

Though Mark is able to work as a "seasoned horticulturalist," DPR celebrates moving him from nonmarket work into contingent work, where but for the timing of staffing policy, he might have made the move from JTP to CPW, that is, from contingent to secure employment.

The civil-service ranks—the CPWs, APSWs, PS1s, and PS2s—are in the primary labor market, where promotional opportunities exist and where increasing responsibility, and therefore control over one's own time, tends to go along with increasing pay. Job Training Program workers and City Seasonal Aides are in the secondary labor market: theirs is regular employment, but seasonal and interchangeable; there is no expectation of loyalty on either the workers' or employers' part. In the case of JTPs, their employment is statutorily limited to six- or nine-month positions. Based on pay records, the median JTP worker from the years 2008 and 2009 remained in the program for just over ten weeks before either being fired, finding other employment (including promotion), or leaving the program for other reasons. Of 13,536 people who entered the JTP program over those two years, 4,682 completed all six of the minimum program months. CSAs, on the other hand, can be called back season after season. This is a good arrangement both for workers with a tenuous hold on labor-market work and for managers seeking experienced but cheap workers. Further, managers can sometimes secure renewable and better-paid CSA positions for JTPs, or can sometimes secure hourly paid CPW jobs. In the years 2008 and 2009, for example, of 13,536 JTPs to pass through the agency, about 163 were promoted to CSA positions and eighty-two to CPW positions (including both hourly and annual CPW positions). Thus, though it is possible to cross into the primary labor market, such transitions are exceedingly rare.

CHAPTER TWO

Parks workers understand and often lament this segmentation. Michael, a CPW in Manhattan, told us: "We get a lot of JTPs that come through here and they're fabulous workers, they really work—and you get some that really don't care, they don't care if they get fired—but the ones that really work, we always ask for extensions, see if we can get them permanent, and it never happens. I mean, it hasn't happened in like a while, like maybe a year or two." Harlan, a Supervisor, echoed this: "I feel bad, 'cause we're not hiring. You can't even hire the good ones."

Even within-segment hiring, though more common, is rare. In a group interview, several workers talked about one's promotion to CSA from JTP:

Joseph: I have 16 years with the CSA. She started, she's a JTP, and she started as a JTP. If your performance, your job, work performance, your attendance, lateness, all the things that bosses want from the employee, are very good, you can, they'll make you CSA. But it's, the turnover is very high. . . . She wanted the job. And a lot of the JTPs don't. A lot of them come from single-parent homes, and they're just basically looking to get paid. And the turnover, I mean, how many became CSA when you made it? Just you, right?
Maricel: Yeah. Just me, out of . . .
Joseph: How many? Sixty? Seventy?
Maricel: Yeah.

Another worker at the same site—a beach—said that he had been working as seasonal for about twenty-five years and wanted to become permanent but could not, since he did not have his driver's license. Unlike permanent workers in DPR, he could not take advantage of the Parks Academy, which provides in-house training programs. Accordingly, seasonal workers tend to rely both on unemployment benefits and on odd jobs to take them through the months between October and April, until they get called back—if they do—to Parks:

So I do those on Saturdays. I do state teacher's exams, as a proctor. I participate in that as a proctor. I do high school SATs. But I do just enough so I can still get unemployment. . . . Like I got one on the twenty-fifth, next Saturday. So as long as you keep your balance, you can actually make it. Because I've been working, I've been a CSA long enough, you know, I get a nice piece of money from the unemployment also. And if you work that out right, it runs right until the next season. . . . I mean, you couldn't have a wife and four kids and do it that way. I'm single, so it's easy for me to work through it like that. Not that I don't want to be a full-time employee. That's my goal still.

Workers have also noted that within-segment distinctions are important from the point of view of dignity. Specifically, many workers—and several supervisors—made a strong distinction between WEP and JTP, though the tasks done in each are nearly identical, though WEP workers and JTP workers are vulnerable to many of the same types of harassment, and though the profile of people in each program is the same, that is, mainly black and Latina women who have little hope of advancing across the barrier separating primary and secondary labor markets. The fact that JTP is employment at a wage competitive with work demanding low skill levels in the private sector makes it far more appealing, despite its temporary nature, than WEP, which many view as akin to slavery. Despite the fact that several supervisors we interviewed slipped and spoke about JTP and WEP interchangeably, there is some consciousness on the part of most of the administration that WEP is profoundly unpopular: as one top administrator said, "We prefer to pay people a wage."

From a longer, historical viewpoint, the Parks Department's workforce segmentation appears not exactly as a *reversion* to a time prior to unionization and collective bargaining, when employees served at the pleasure of the commissioner and had virtually no rights at the workplace, but still as an *undoing* of a good number of the protections that unions won since the 1950s. Though there were civil service titles in the 1950s, even prior to Mayor Robert F. Wagner Jr.'s decision to open up collective bargaining to public workers and to introduce a "Career and Salary Plan" in 1954 to formalize job ladders, pay scales, and raises, union efforts were directed toward institutionalizing a primary labor market through the mechanism of civil service *and* bargaining.[15] Work in this primary market—regardless of worker skill level—would be secure, have opportunities for merit-based promotion, and enable public workers to gain a foothold in the middle class. Since the fiscal crisis in the 1970s, however, there has been an increasing—though incremental—move from market to nonmarket work, and hence to work outside of the primary labor market and even outside of the secondary labor market (as in the cases of WEP and volunteers, however differently their work is valued). This shift, in turn, reverberates throughout the agency as work is reorganized and titles are redefined accordingly.

In addition to WEPs and, later, JTPs, non-labor-market workers supplemented the shrinking Parks workforce. Volunteers, both from corporations and individuals organized by Parks Department–sponsored nonprofit groups, as well as summer youth workers and referrals from the court system, also appeared with greater frequency at worksites. And seasonally hired staff who do the work mainly of CPWs and JTPs —called City Seasonal Aides, or CSAs—also work in parks and playgrounds at levels determined by annual funding availability.

Segmentation in the Parks Department was not limited to the reallocation of work from permanent to temporary, and from unionized workers to trainees and workfare workers. One of the more significant changes was the growth in the number of workers for parks conservancies, private nonprofit groups that in some cases won contracts from the City to manage specific parks or even groups of parks during the 1990s and the first decade of the twenty-first century. These organizations, often organized with the help of the Parks Department and its nonprofit arm, Partnerships for Parks, hire their own workers to take care of maintenance either as a fully private workforce or alongside Parks Department employees. These workforces are not subject to civil service rules and have not yet been successfully unionized; they are "at-will" employees.

### *Nonprofit Parks Organization Staff*

Segmentation takes place both within the Parks Department's workforce and in the parks maintenance workforce as a whole, extended through the department's contracts. "Friends of" organizations and the Partnerships for Parks that fosters and supports them are extensions of a set of private experiments that began in the wake of New York City's fiscal crisis of the 1970s. These experiments—comprising first Central Park and Prospect Park in Brooklyn, and then, quickly, Bryant Park, next to the main branch of the New York Public Library on 42nd Street—brought private management to parks. These experiments set up nonprofit organizations with different names and slightly different missions: the Central Park Conservancy, the Prospect Park Alliance, and the Bryant Park Restoration Corporation. More will be said about their contrasts in subsequent chapters, but for the time being, what is important is that they began to supplement—and supplant—regular city workers with their own, privately hired and managed, nonunionized staff. Further, these groups—and particularly Central Park Conservancy and Prospect Park Alliance—relied on significant numbers of volunteers and have devoted a great deal of energy to developing extensive and intensive volunteer programs that significantly affect the maintenance of the parks under their care.

From the beginning, the Central Park Conservancy sought to compensate for what they considered to be the management failures stemming from the outsized power of the parks workers' unions and the general lack of discipline in the city workforce. One response to the apparent inefficacy of the management of maintenance staff in Central Park was a complete redefinition of tasks, put into effect with the Conservancy's own workers. The Conservancy's "zone management" system divides the park into forty-nine zones and puts a single "Zone Gardener" in charge of each one. The Zone Gardener is in charge of coordinating all the planting and maintenance work within the zone and supervises a crew of assistants, volunteers, and "Grounds Technicians". All, to a great extent, share work and tasks; Zone Gardeners and Grounds Technicians both deal with trash, weeding, repairing and putting up wire fencing, and planting, as well as raking leaves, shoveling snow, and other seasonal tasks. Grounds Technicians do more basic maintenance work, while others do more horticultural work, but the larger idea is that everyone in the park should be aware of—and able to perform—each other's tasks as a maximally flexible workforce. The Zone Gardeners, however, are accorded a significant amount of responsibility and autonomy and have to have more horticultural training and experience.

Zone Gardeners are, however, in the lower end of a larger management hierarchy, and a separate line of authority—not including Zone Gardeners—governs park-wide crews, such as turf crews, tree crews, and night maintenance crews. These latter are overseen by a Foreperson and Coordinators, in ascending order. Zone Gardeners answer to them as well, and zones are grouped into sections that are assigned Forepersons and Coordinators. Personnel decisions begin to be made at the Coordinator level, and the upper levels of the hierarchy coordinate work with the Chief of Operations, who plans out maintenance strategy for the entire park.

The difference between the Conservancy hierarchy and that of the civil service is pronounced. Not only are the physical tasks of the work not fairly strictly delimited, but there is much more room for personal favoritism in hiring, firing, and promotion decisions. Richard Gilder, a cofounder of the Central Park Conservancy and a prominent board member, criticized the "bureaucratic, seniority-based system" under

CHAPTER TWO

which union workers were managed and compared it unfavorably to Central Park's system, in which

> The Conservancy's great advantage comes in staffing. It hires and pays its horticulturists, groundskeepers, and cleanup crews as any private employer would. If they do well, they advance. If they do poorly, they're fired. Conservancy staffers are flexible enough to do more than one task, so they can be assigned to whatever job needs doing most urgently. And most crucial perhaps, the Conservancy is able to instill a real sense of pride in those who work for it; they come to think of Central Park as *their* park.[16]

The Zone Gardener system has a kind of implicit promotional ladder, as well. People can be hired as seasonal workers and then be asked to join the permanent crew. Unlike the Parks Department, however, Central Park Conservancy does not generally hire the same people as seasonal workers from one season to the next, since the management of the Conservancy does not want to create the expectation for eventual permanent employment for people they cannot hire permanently at once. Once on the permanent crew, many workers begin as Ground Technicians, sometimes hoping to be promoted to Zone Gardener. Some areas of the park—those without significant horticultural needs, such as the perimeter areas—do not require a Zone Gardener at all; they are overseen by Grounds Technicians and their Forepersons and Coordinators. If a Grounds Technician becomes a Zone Gardener, therefore, he or she will be assigned a zone requiring significant horticulture work. For Eve, a Foreperson we interviewed with nearly five years' experience as a Zone Gardener, the zone system "gives you a really great sense of ownership and recognition of what's going on in your site that someone who's just passing by might not recognize." In other words, the zone system ensures that all areas of the park have fixed-post personnel.

Even among workers who had recently been fired by the Conservancy following the 2007 fiscal collapse (which hurt many foundations, and thus their grantees as well), we found evidence for pride in the park, but also complaints about the lack of transparency in staffing decisions and the inadequacy of the "open-door policy" of the upper management as a grievance mechanism. Among them, we encountered criticisms of the management structure, which is unsurprising (though it was, perhaps, surprising how measured the criticisms were). Raymond, fired suddenly after nearly twenty years with the Conservancy—a tenure that should have indicated his "doing well"—told us that

The park has improved a lot. A lot of repairs have been done. We took all different sections . . . that has been repaired, redone, a lot of pathways have been redone where the band shell is, Bethesda Fountain has been redone . . . and around the fountain itself, the Great Lawn, the North Meadow ball fields, Hecksher ball fields, Hecksher playground, these places have been repaired where donations have been given to have these repairs and to pay for the maintenance and operation that goes on each and every day in all of these areas. The Harlem Meer . . . the first couple of years after the lake was first done it had irrigation in it to keep oxygen into the water. Eventually that went out. They built an island inside the Harlem Meer for wildlife, such as swans, some swans have been born there. . . . Baby ducklings are born in the area.

At the same time, like City Park Workers, Raymond complained that supervisors did not necessarily understand the work that those under them did and suggested that the ideology of management favored those without on-the-ground knowledge:

You have some people that have gone to school and got their degrees in certain business aspects, and you have some people that went to training school to run these skills, vocational schools or what have you. . . . They hire the ones with the degrees first, but the ones that have on-the-job training or vocational training, they'll get rid of them first before they get rid of the ones that have the degrees. With soft hands. Never done anything out in the field. They know how to read a blueprint but cannot get out and do the work that is needed to be done when it comes [to] hands-on work, to be able to stand out with their worker and work with them, stand by them and sweat with them, assist them. You have some supervisors that do and some supervisors that don't. . . . The supervisors that don't do no work will still be there, riding around, getting fat, and calling on the phones from the next. . . . "Oh, this person is just sitting there, they're not doing anything." And it's like that throughout the whole park. . . . There's certain supervisors that have their little pets. I've seen that. I've seen a lot of good, and I've seen a lot of bad.

Both Raymond and other former Conservancy workers complained that personnel procedures were opaque and subject to manipulation. While it is true that they had all been fired, and all had supported a unionization drive, each had specific stories in which they gave examples of unfair situations in which other workers were fired for having had poor evaluations, or were denied raises because of poor evaluations, even when they had recently been promoted, either from seasonal positions to permanent ones or from one permanent one to another. The larger idea to which this speaks is that workers within the

CHAPTER TWO

Central Park hierarchy have less recourse to rules and procedures than do civil service workers, and between the Zone Gardener and other positions up the hierarchy, the path to promotion is far less clear than it is under the civil service. Even if, as we have said, the City tries to skirt the civil service procedures, these procedures still impart some measure of transparency on the jobs and promotion pathways within the department.

Zone Gardeners also supervise volunteers. Central Park has several types of volunteers, including more than seventy in its Zone Assistant program. Zone Assistants typically come one or two mornings a week and join the Zone Gardener's staff, working closely with the Zone Gardener or Grounds Technicians on tasks that do not require the use of power tools such as mowers or weed-whackers (which volunteers are not allowed to handle for liability reasons). There are also weekend crews of volunteers who engage in a group maintenance or horticulture activity every Saturday. Eve, the Foreperson, also explained that they would "never leave a volunteer all alone" and that it's nicer for the volunteer if they work side by side with a Zone Gardener.

Central Park Conservancy workers also work with regular municipal parks workers, since there are still about two dozen of the latter in Central Park, almost all with more than fifteen years' experience in the park. The Conservancy's workforce grew steadily since its founding in 1980. First, it supplemented the more than 300 municipal workers in the park, mainly with horticulturists and gardeners and then, increasingly, with general maintenance workers. The City began to stop replacing workers who transferred to other parks districts or who quit or retired from their jobs, so by the time that the Central Park Conservancy won a "master contract" to maintain the park in 1998, more than half of the almost 250 workers in the park were its own employees. Since then, the number has grown, and the number of municipal employees has shrunken to about 10 percent of the workers in the park. The city workers are assigned two areas in the park (much like Zone Gardeners) and also run large packers to pick up the garbage.

Private parks staff in other parks have different sorts of positions, and the arrangement of the workforce differs from that in Central Park mainly because of the relatively smaller size of the other conservancies' workforces or because of the smaller size of the parks. For example, Bryant Park, the first park for which management was privatized in the early 1980s, is quite small and completely maintained by its own staff, with only district Managers and Supervisors from the City who pass through the park to inspect it. Prospect Park, on the other hand, which is managed by the Prospect Park Alliance, a nonprofit that formed shortly after the Central Park Conservancy, works much more closely with city workers and blends them into combined work teams with its own employees. Of 106 full-time employees listed in its 2011 annual report, eighty-seven are paid for by the Alliance. Most of the city employees are concentrated in the volunteer, landscape management, and maintenance departments. There are extensive volunteer opportunities in Prospect Park, as well; some areas of the park are mainly maintained by volunteer crews, and regular teams of volunteers (supplemented by community service sentencees) engage in large clean-up, weeding, and leaf-removal projects twice a week. In maintenance, they are mainly supervisory personnel who, in turn, supervise the JTPs who do the bulk of the cleaning; JTPs also work indoors in several of the park's attractions, such as the skating rink. Tupper Thomas, the former, long-time president of the Prospect Park Alliance and Administrator of Prospect Park, suggested that this relationship with the Parks Department is the result of long-standing underfunding of regular Parks staff:

Thomas: We have close to 100 employees, and that's a milestone. The Parks Department has a very small number. It's probably . . . twenty working for the Parks Department.

John: Including supervisors?

Thomas: Yes. But the welfare-to-work is huge. So we can have as many as forty people at a given time.

John: Through JTP.

Thomas: Through JTP. So the JTP program is how we clean this park.

John: I see.

Thomas: That's the people who are out there doing it every day. So the Parks Department is the supervision of most of that, and then the ones who clean the bathrooms, playgrounds, and landscape are mostly JTP. So that program has been saving the Parks Department, because of the number of regular employees that we've lost.

Nonprofit private park management organizations, therefore, engage a wide range of practices with respect to the use of their own staffs, city workers, and combinations of the two. Madison Square Park's conservancy, for example, hires its own staff to maintain the park and also draws upon the services of a CPW crew chief and a fluctuating number of JTPs. Their tasks overlap considerably, but they tend to divide up even that small park, with respect to areas to clean and tasks to complete. For example, JTPs in Madison Square Park will generally not do horticultural work, but both JTPs and Madison Square Park Conservancy workers will spend a good deal of the fall removing leaves, a good deal of the spring and summer removing garbage, and a significant amount of time removing snow when there are cold winters.

*Volunteers*

If WEP workers represent one pole of the City's attempt to rely on nonmarket work for basic parks maintenance and operations tasks, volunteers represent the other. The one is nonmarket labor done under the compulsion of welfare rules; the other is nonmarket labor based on freely given time.

Two main types of volunteer are used in park maintenance: the occasional corporate volunteer and the more regular volunteer with one of the hundreds of parks support organizations ("Friends of . . . Park") or private parks conservancies. The Partnerships for Parks, an organization jointly run by DPR and the private City Parks Foundation (itself a creature of DPR), organizes and supports "Friends of" groups to care for neighborhood parks and estimates that 56,000 volunteers gave their time to parks in 2011, and in 2007 estimated that a total of 1.7 million hours were given. This is the equivalent of roughly 850 full-time workers' work, on a base of 3,000 or so city workers. Volunteers are not only involved in maintenance and operations work. They also run weekend programs and special events and volunteer in recreation centers.

According to DPR administrators, "in most cases the 'Friends of' or volunteers are not doing daily maintenance. Most of the 'Friends of' groups, most of the parks people, come out episodically, or maybe there's one person who comes out every day and does a little bit of pruning or weeding or something. But the vast majority of our volunteers volunteer episodically." And yet this does not mean that the volunteers are not critical to the maintenance of the parks, or of specific parks. As one park manager recently remarked after the parks advocacy group New Yorkers for Parks and the accounting firm Ernst and Young teamed up for a volunteer day painting walls around a basketball court and picking up litter, "Volunteerism plays such a vital role in helping us reach our goals—especially now with staff cuts in the Parks Department." Though basic maintenance is rarely the sole thing done by the corporate or "Friends of" volunteers, tasks like painting, and sometimes gardening, which might otherwise be deferred are seen by managers as a good fit for volunteers. Said one Manager in Queens:

It's icing. I would count it as icing. . . . For the district level, for them to plan, they may say that with the fall project, we'll have the volunteers come and paint all the fencing around this playground, and that's something that they're not going to get around to normally. So that's a nice bit of icing. Something that, you know, is a problem but I just don't have the resources to give to it. So when the volunteers come, if they can take care . . . you put thirty people painting a fence, that's a lot quicker than one person painting it every afternoon.

Sometimes, however, the character of parks is defined by volunteers. For example, a regular corps of volunteers maintained the plantings in a small neighborhood park in Manhattan because there were no gardeners or assistant gardeners assigned to the district. For smaller neighborhood parks, "Friends of" groups can be important coordinators both of volunteer workdays—often involving horticultural work, painting, and litter removal—and the people who draw attention to maintenance problems at meetings with parks managers.

Moreover, in certain parks, volunteers adopt whole areas of the park as their own, caring for it with support from, and often tools provided by, the district. For example, one Brooklyn Supervisor summed up his park's volunteering activities:

For the dog run, we have people who take care of the dog runs, and they do touch base with me. When they need wood chips [or] they set up a project, they send me an email, "Get me two loads of wood chips, get me tools, wheelbarrows, rakes, whatever, bags," and I basically, I inspect [that park], I'm responsible for working with them. You also have the moms, who take care of an area inside the playground over there.

It is not that JTPs or other mobile or fixed post workers will not, therefore, go in these areas; it is rather that the maintenance needs of these areas are partially met by volunteers, decreasing the need for more frequent visits or for the diversion of regular staffing resources into special projects. Because volunteers are often seen by parks supervisors as "icing" rather than the "cake" itself, figuring out how to integrate them into the work of a district can be a challenge. And yet, as this exchange makes clear, their contributions can sometimes be fundamental to the overall condition of parks when they get a "deep cleaning."

Maud: So there's some challenge with the volunteers, right?
Supervisor: It's a challenge, but once you understand it, it could be a tool, a useful tool. . . . I'll give you an example. We had volunteers Saturday in one of our parks. They generated seventy-nine bags of garbage. So that's a help. That's a

big help. Because they did things we usually don't do. We do basic cleaning. They went there, got the leaves out, got the weeds out, cleaned up the garden area. Bottom line is they got seventy-nine bags, which is great.

Not all volunteers are self-managing, though. As the same Supervisor told us,

It's important that I send somebody that's going to know our intentions. What they want done with that. Certain things we might not want. Volunteers say, "We want to paint everything!" Mm . . . certain colors, really, not certain colors. Certain colors might not be what we want. We don't want yellow park houses or purple . . . no. We got basic colors. Green or brick red. Sometimes that will be nice. Gotta steer them in that direction. "If you want to paint them, it's gotta be this way. Not rainbows . . ."

A further development in the department's use of volunteers is the innovation of positions of volunteer coordinators, not just for privately run parks conservancies (about which, more below) but also at the borough level and, occasionally, at the level of some midsized parks with their own administrators. In one midsized park in Brooklyn, for example, an administrator has built up a significant relationship with corporations and local community residents, after having built up the volunteer program in a larger park. She mainly uses volunteers for horticultural projects rather than maintenance projects and integrates community volunteers (sometimes recruited through appeals on Internet volunteer websites) and larger groups from corporations in her work plans, which she tailors at once to the project needing attention, the volunteers, and the day in the week:

Administrator: Yeah, and the other thing about our park is that we don't have that much to paint. . . . Anyway, I wouldn't paint benches on a weekend, because that's when people come sit on the benches. I wouldn't paint the picnic tables on the weekend, because that's when they get used. So that would be something we'd do with corporate volunteers or staff.
Maud: The corporate volunteers, they can come during the week, right?
Administrator: Almost all of them come during [the week]. It's called work release time, which sounds like you're getting released from jail, right? A good corporation would give their employees a day that they can come out during the work week, so instead of coming to the office, you came to the park and volunteered. Some companies have like a team-building project on the weekend. Those are generally not as well attended.

Across the city, even away from parks with well-established volunteer programs, Partnerships for Parks cultivates "Friends of" groups and encourages them to take on increasing responsibility for their parks. Though few, if any, of these groups eventually take over operations of their parks, to the extent that they can act as conduits of volunteers, "Friends of" organizations can make the difference between parks that look polished and those that look run-down.

The kernel of the Partnerships for Parks' efforts in many neighborhoods is often the presence of one or two people who are committed individual volunteers. These are people who—often out of professional or serious amateur interest—get involved with gardening tasks, usually with permission from the City (sometimes retroactive!) and with some, though often minimal, support from local parks districts. Others get involved in volunteering because they hope to reserve parts of their local parks for dog runs and are then drawn into design and planning processes, fundraising, and, ultimately, maintenance efforts for dog runs. Gardeners and "dog people" are crucial to recruiting others in their neighborhoods. The gardeners or other environmental professionals (e.g., an elementary-school science teacher who has organized parks walks and clean-up projects with her students) also frequently get as involved in the organizational activities of volunteering as with the work itself: we found, for example, Mary, a landscape gardener, who no longer lives in the neighborhood in which she founded a "Friends of" group but who both continues to work with the group and has been appointed to the board of directors of a local land trust whose mission is to acquire land for parks and environmental preservation. Similarly, Jennifer, head of another "Friends of" group in Manhattan, told us that she could imagine a career in the Parks Department with all that she had learned as a volunteer. Of course, there are other individual volunteers who spurn larger organizational entanglements. Richard, a professional gardener, has befriended the chief horticulturalist in a prestigious park in Manhattan and continues to volunteer there, gardening as he has for thirty-five years, and well before the installation of a conservancy in the park. In all these cases, the connections between civic engagement and professional commitment are difficult to disentangle. The symbolic rewards for volunteering are clearly there, but so are the rewards of forging new professional paths and social ties. Beyond this, as well, the Partnerships for Parks also holds classes in conjunction with the Parks Department's training academy, to certify "citizen pruners" in order to try to ensure some level of regular, volunteer care for the Million Trees campaign undertaken by Mayor Bloomberg, in which the City has committed to planting one million trees.

## *Community Service Sentencees*

Another category of unpaid worker doing routine maintenance in parks is people sentenced to community service by the courts for violations or misdemeanors. Like WEP workers, they are not doing labor-market work, since they are not being paid for their work; arraying them in terms of effort expended in expectation of pay ("short-term monetization" in Tilly and Tilly's schema) would not be possible. Over the course of the late 2000s, as WEP workers were not yet being assigned to cleaning duties in large numbers again and as JTP numbers began to decline, we found increasing numbers of workers assigned to community service by the courts in alternative sentencing programs in the field, doing the same tasks that JTPs, WEPs, and CPWs otherwise did. Most of the alternative sentencing program participants—known colloquially as "community service"—we encountered were adults, though interviewees among regular parks workers indicated that a mix of adult and juvenile offenders are sent to clean parks.

People doing court-ordered community service nearly always staff mobile crews and, depending on who shows up to a given district on a given day, may be put on crews alongside JTPs or WEP workers, but they may also be put on their own detail with their own crew chief (or a non-crew-chief CPW who officially "helps" rather than "manages" the crew). Most community service workers come on weekends, in large part because many are working during the week. But there are districts that get them every day. Usually, management staff in a district will get a week's notice from the courts about how many workers—and who—are going to show up. Not all do. Nevertheless, they are a part of the workforce for which supervisors need to plan, especially since the compulsory nature of the position means that workers sometimes try to get out of their punishments and leave the parks before their service is complete. One district Supervisor in Queens also cited safety concerns with respect to her placement of community service workers on mobile crews:

But we don't put them in stationary spots. They're mobile. So they gotta go mobile crew. We don't put them in a park house for the day. Because a lot of times they don't tell us why they're doing community service. It could be not such a bad thing, it could be bad things. We're not supposed to get nothing violent. This is not the place. Especially when there's children around. Can't have that. But sometimes people get mixed in there and they don't really tell us why. It's one of those, "not my business" kind of things. Or it is my business if they're given to me.

Said one district Supervisor in Brooklyn:

So it's something that we have to account for. We have to make room for them. They cannot be left alone. They cannot be unattended. They cannot be left to do things, and there's not [an] honor [system] with that. They need to be immediately, directly supervised. They gotta be watched.

A district Supervisor in Harlem told us the procedures of signing community service sentencees in and out of work. Separate parks workers had to sign workers in and out, partly in response to incidents in 2008 in which the Department of Investigation caught lower-level parks workers taking bribes from community service sentencees (or investigators posing as them) to fraudulently sign them in and out.

Because community service work is strictly a punishment without even the pretense of mobility or reward for hard work, it can be difficult to manage. Managers and front-line parks workers reported occasional conflicts that escalate, but most of the reported problems occurred with youth. One Supervisor at a beach district reported:

You get a few knuckleheads, you know, fifteen-, sixteen-year-old kids that . . . you know, want to be Johnny Tough Guy, and you have to explain to them, "It's either do the work that we need you to do or go back to court! I'm not going back to court! You're the one going back to court. It's up to you." And when Mommy and Daddy find out that I sent them home and they come by and talk to me and I say, "Well, if Johnny Knucklehead would just pick up the bag and the grabber like I asked him to instead of telling me to go jump and how high and whatever," and that's when he gets a little smack in the head and parents tell me, "Whatever you want my son or daughter to do, they will do."

The same Supervisor described other challenges, too, amid the imperative of getting the work that needs to done accomplished:

But then you'll get the kids who live here . . . who don't get along with one another, and they're all in the same boat where they all have to do community service together, so now we're playing provider of somebody that we need the services of and at the same time playing kindergarten cops, so . . . it goes with the territory. I can laugh about it, but the ultimate goal is to get them to do their hours and provide us with cleaning the beach, painting a bench, doing whatever is needed for that day.

In spite of its evident expansion, however, alternative sentencing program use in the parks appears to have proceeded fairly smoothly, perhaps in part because it is just another step on the already-existing continuum of compulsory labor used for mobile crews. Along with mixing JTPs, WEPs, and community service sentencees on mobile crews, the CPWs who work with them sometimes understand them as being comparable.

> CPW: Yeah, they know they not getting paid, so they work like a person that ain't getting paid. You can tell sometimes the difference. Somebody got a little more pep in their step than others. They got the attitude, "I'm not getting paid." But they getting done, I can't tell bad about anybody, they doing what they gotta do. Some of these people are sentenced to long times, so I start feeling sorry for them, like, "What, you still here?" [chuckles] They telling me, one dude has six months, and he just left! They say he was here for a while. He did, like, one person JTP term!
> John: Was he coming in four days a week or just on weekends or something?
> CPW: No, he was coming every day.

### *Summers: Seasonals, Youth Workers, and Step-Ups*

One interesting wrinkle in the picture of segmentation is that parks maintenance work changes according to the season. So does staffing. Of course, as we have already seen with seasonal workers, the whole picture of who cleans your park will change according to the time of year. The Parks Department focuses its hiring seasonally, concentrating its JTP workforce in the months from March through November. Conservancies such as Madison Square Park Conservancy hire seasonal workers for the summer months, while less-intensive conservancy groups, such as the Friends of Fort Greene Park in Brooklyn, will avail themselves of increased numbers of JTPs or WEP workers and will also have summer youth program workers of various sorts provided by the Parks Department. Programs for youth such as "Green Teens" and "Green Applied Projects for Parks" combine education and training activities with general maintenance and horticulture work (e.g., weeding and planting). The Green Applied Projects for Parks (GAPP) program, for example, was designed for roughly 200 18–24 year-olds who were out of work. Administered through the POP program, GAPP participants, like JTPs, had one day a week for education and training and four days a week for parks work, generally done in teams, under the supervision of crew chiefs or Supervisors. GAPP was a five-week program (May-June) and paid $8.10 per hour (or more than a dollar less than JTP). A *chance* at a seasonal job with Central Park Conservancy or another such organization was held out as one incentive for good performance on the job.

These programs tend to patch holes in parks during the summer, since a large number of JTPs, CPWs, APSWs, and Supervisors are drawn out of the districts and larger parks to the beaches and pools. Here, many full-time municipal employees get a chance to "step up," or be promoted to a new civil service position on a seasonal basis. Step-up promotions are provisional and based on Supervisors' and Managers' recommendation, rather than on a competitive exam. They can result in significantly more money for the worker, as well as know-how and experience in a higher-ranked position, should the worker ever try for promotion through the civil service exam. It is common for districts to promote several CPWs to be seasonal APSWs or Supervisors (or to promote APSWs to Supervisors) during a summer season; this can make staffing difficult, particularly in finding sufficient numbers of drivers for mobile crews. Accordingly, CPWs can be borrowed from district to district and given crew chief step-ups, or JTPs can be put on fixed-post duties. In cases, such as Central Park's, that purposely avoid using many public workers, budgetary problems such as those that resulted in layoffs in early 2009 and the expanded use of the park during the summer months (both in terms of intensity and in the number of hours the park is used) meant shuffling workers' schedules and rotating crews onto evening shifts that had not been asked to work evenings before.

Finally, summers bring significant numbers of special events to parks, and these present logistical challenges to parks maintenance, on one hand, and a frequent chance for overtime pay for all grades of nonmanagerial workers, from JTPs through PS2s. Again, overtime is determined on a personal basis and at the discretion of the supervisor. Significantly, too, contractors brought in to run special events also come with their own clean-up crews and must pay significant deposits to ensure that the cleanup for which they are contractually responsible actually occurs. Finally, private parks managers, such as the Prospect Park Alliance, have hired municipal parks workers on a per-diem basis (on non-City hours) to staff special events, as well.

CHAPTER TWO

# The Growing Diversity of Labor Contracts in Parks: A Fissured Workforce

The Parks Department has increasingly relied on workers it does not employ to clean the parks. What David Weil calls "fissuring" happens when large corporations stop directly employing the people who make their products or provide their services and rely instead on contractors who, in an effort to compete with each other, drive wages and working conditions down. This is perhaps best known in the garment industry, where short production runs and stiff competition have resulted in infamous working conditions, often slave-like conditions of labor, and horrific industrial tragedies. But even in local-serving industries, such as construction, as Doussard points out, systems of subcontracting have often led to the degradation of working conditions, including even the ability of workers to get regular work and the resultant displacement of competition and work discipline onto the workers themselves.[17]

Fissuring in the Parks Department is not driven by the same direct profit motive, nor does it look the same as among large firms. Nevertheless, the Parks Department *has*, in effect, taken a large organization and begun to distribute the work it used to do to more independent entities, including courts and district attorneys' offices, conservancy and "Friends of" organizations, and even individual volunteers. Though we see more of the internalized competition among WEPs and JTPs—at least among those who hold out hope for being hired into the department and for crossing from non- and secondary-labor market segments into the primary labor market—we also can see some of this in the more formal partnerships the Parks Department has formed.

## *How it Works*

In order to get a synthetic sense of how a fissured workplace looks in parks, it is helpful to look at a single park, with the knowledge that the segmentation and fissuring of the workforce in the Parks Department and its partners differs from place to place and across time.[18] McGolrick Park in the Greenpoint neighborhood of Brooklyn is a shady oasis with tall, mature trees and a neoclassical, colonnaded pavilion that distinguishes it from most of the utilitarian Robert Moses–era park houses. This serves as the headquarters of Brooklyn's Parks District 1. On a late summer's weekday afternoon, the park is a hive of activity, even though there are few people using the park aside from a

THE WORKERS

cluster of people on benches that line the paths and a few mothers and caretakers with strollers. Under one especially thick stand of tall trees, about twenty kids in the city's Summer Youth Employment Program are putting leaves in large piles in large black plastic bags. They have been given rakes and shovels and charged with clearing a blanket of leaves that has fallen on the lawn beneath the trees, both recently and, evidently, as far back as the previous fall. They are overseen directly by a tall man in a blue t-shirt with "STAFF" emblazoned on the back. He is in the Job Training Program, and though he has no supervisory capacity, he is clearly supervising the summer youth workers. He has taken on a considerable amount of responsibility and is in and out of the main office in the park shelter, getting equipment and checking in with his own supervisor about what needs to be done and when.

This JTP—unlike many others—was "fixed-post" in McGolrick. He reported directly to one of the district's Parks Supervisors Level 1 (PS1). Others, however, would arrive at the park after their shifts in a van. These JTPs, mostly women, were on mobile crews, and sometimes worked alongside WEP workers, who had recently come back into the district in maintenance and operations work. Sometimes, as well, mobile crews would go out in the district—and from other districts in the city—composed of JTPs and community service sentencees referred from the district attorney's office. They were driven by CPW "crew chiefs," while other CPWs were assigned to McGolrick and to nearby McCarren Park, the largest park in the district. The Associate Park Service Workers (APSWs) in the district would make the rounds of the district in a heavy packer, collecting the trash and detritus that the fixed-post CPWs, JTPs, WEPs, summer youth, and community service workers would pick up and put into heavy black garbage bags.

For their part, the PS1s report to a PS2 who does less direct supervision of staff and more coordination of staffing throughout the large district, along with inspections of playgrounds and trouble-shooting maintenance problems. PS1s and PS2s also coordinate with district-assigned repair workers (nearly always one per district, at most) and with borough-wide crews assigned to do more technical repairs, such as plumbing or tree pruning or removal. They also supervise the Assistant Gardeners in the district, who, with crews of WEP workers selected (at the time) by the Gardeners themselves from the larger pool of WEPs in the district, attended to all of the plantings in the district and paid special attention to decorative areas of McCarren Park. The PS2 reports to the Parks and Recreation Manager (PRM or Associate PRM), who is not only in charge of the maintenance and operations of the parks in the district but also responsible for the recreation workers, such as those who work at the pools in the summertime. McCarren Park, a five-minute walk from McGolrick, has one of the largest pools in the city, though it was in disrepair and disuse for decades, save as a venue for summer rock concerts. Its reopening in 2012 involved a greater number of recreation staff.

In the case of District 1, there exists another layer of management. District 1 is the only parks district that has been put under a private administrator. Unlike other public-private partnerships that have been formed to manage parks, District 1's is district-wide and goes beyond a single park to all of the district's more than 100 DPR-managed properties. The private organization with joint management responsibility for the district is the Open Space Alliance for North Brooklyn (OSA). OSA, for its part, has been a primary force in getting the City to invest in parks in North Brooklyn, in the rapidly gentrifying areas of North Williamsburg and Greenpoint, and has raised private funds and has induced thousands to volunteer to improve open space, especially along the waterfront. OSA's executive director serves as the Administrator for North Brooklyn Parks. And though OSA now has a small paid staff, including a volunteer coordinator, not all of the positions are actually funded through the organization itself; some are paid for by the Parks Department.

Particularly striking is the fact that at least six categories of workers have significantly overlapping jobs but vastly different statuses. Summer youth, community service sentencees, Job Training Program workers, WEP workers, and City Park Workers have substantially overlapping jobs, though they are differentiated, as we discuss in the next chapter, by a range of regular and allowable tasks that characterize each type of work (such as cleaning bathrooms for WEP workers and JTPs, using power equipment for JTPs and CPWs, and driving light vehicles for CPWs). Volunteers in District 1, as elsewhere in the city, do a range of tasks from cleaning parks and painting benches (as do all the others) to planting bulbs and horticulture (as WEP workers did, and as JTPs have done on special crews elsewhere in the city).

*Looking Backward*

Now, imagine that we could locate all of the types of workers, working side by side in McGolrick Park, or elsewhere in the city, in the space defined by Tilly and Tilly's diagram in figure 2.1. Even here, we would have problems in getting analytic leverage on the segmentation in the department because the segmentation—and fissuring through contracting—has unfolded over a period of more than thirty years.

If you were to have joined the Department of Parks and Recreation in the late 1970s or early 1980s, you would have likely been hired into a civil service job with union representation. The pay would not have been great; the unskilled and semi-skilled work of parks maintenance would have meant that you would struggle a bit financially. But you would have steady work. You would have grievance procedures, health benefits, and therefore some buffer against the increasingly contingent and unstable employment affecting a lot of other unskilled and semi-skilled laborers.

In truth, of course, you probably would not have been hired at all until the mid-1980s, when the city's finances stabilized and it began to hire workers again. Nevertheless, you would have encountered some controversy with respect to the broadbanding of multiple Parks civil service titles and the concomitant reduction in the number of people assigned to particular tasks. You would, in other words, have been hired into the department at a point at which District Council 37 began to lose some measure of power over the workplace but in which union rules were often enforced and civil service rules mainly respected.

The condition of the parks was another thing. Fewer than 60 percent of parks properties citywide got "acceptable" ratings by the City's own reckoning. Management was a shambles, and capital improvements were nearly nonexistent. Maintaining the parks was an exercise in trying to keep up with litter, graffiti, and vandalism and in staying safe. Many parks were simply given over to drug dealers and users at least at certain times of the day, and even the big, landmark parks like Central Park bore the scars of several decades of underinvestment in everything from underground plumbing to turf replacement.

As the 1980s progressed, however, you would begin to see new sorts of workers showing up at the same worksites in which you were working. If you were in Central Park, the Central Park Conservancy would have a growing staff; in Bryant Park, the Bryant Park Restoration Corporation would close the park and reopen it with its own staff. You would begin to see community service sentencees come into parks districts on weekends to work off their court-mandated sentences. You would see a first wave of workfare workers, during the mid-1980s, doing work once done by the lower-level civil servants. And you would see—even as early as the mid-1970s—a small but growing corps of volun-

CHAPTER TWO

teers, mostly maintaining plantings, but increasingly getting involved in general parks maintenance. The union would periodically raise objections, but an expansion of hiring in the parks under Mayor Koch in the mid-1980s softened some of the blow of the encroachment of new sorts of workers on civil service workers' turf.

Figure 2.2 summarizes some of the shifts that took place in the parks maintenance workforce. It does not, perhaps, adequately represent the rupture of the early 1990s, when Mayor Dinkins came into office faced with a depressed city economy and demands from bond raters to shrink the municipal budget. Parks maintenance was hit hard, and the contemporaneous flare-up of the crack epidemic meant that the outdoor drug trade and the violence associated with it spilled into the parks, as did the decades-long simmering housing crisis that blossomed into mass homelessness in the 1980s and continued to grow through the decade.

As the parks maintenance workforce was nearly cut in half, the parks suffered significantly. During the last days of the mayoral administration of David Dinkins, and with far greater speed under Mayor Rudolph Giuliani, the alternative workforce began to become far more important. Workfare workers were sent to parks and new crew chief positions were created to supervise the massive shift from fixed-post to mobile crews (a shift that had been underway for a decade already, but which also took on greater importance in the second fiscal crisis).

| Inside DPR | Broadbanding and new titles created | Workfare expands (PWP) DPR hiring | Layoffs | Workfare expands (WEP), crew chief title begun privatization experiments | POP/JTP begun, WEP shrinks | POP/JTP wage and program time cut | JTP shrinks WEP temporarily expands | New hiring |
|---|---|---|---|---|---|---|---|---|
| Non-DPR | | Conservancies founded | Community service sentencing begins | Bryant Park reopens under BPC | Partnerships for Parks Founded Central Park master contract | Conservancies multiply "Friends of" groups multiply Volunteering expands | | |
| Year | 1975 | 1980 | 1985 | 1990 | 1995 | 2000 | 2005 | 2010 | 2015 |
| Economic Crises | Collapse of NYC manufacturing, oil crisis, real-estate glut | | Stock market crash | | | Dot-com bubble burst | post-9/11 recession | Subprime bubble burst, financial crisis | |
| Political Crises | NYC fiscal crisis | | | Second fiscal crisis | | 9/11 | | Occupy Wall Street | |
| Mayor | Beame Koch Dinkins Giuliani Bloomberg de Blasio | Multiple Commissioners | Davis | Stern | Gotbaum | Stern | | Benepe | White Silver |

2.2 Changes in maintenance work and organization in context

As a regular city parks worker—say a CPW—you would have encountered a significantly changed workplace in the 1990s. Chapter 3 discusses the results of these changes. For now, consider that, had you survived the layoffs of the early 1990s, you would have begun to see several important shifts take place around you. Workfare, and later JTP, become the dominant workforce of people doing the tasks you once did and to a certain degree still do. You would have to deal with more volunteers and particularly volunteers associated with "Friends of" groups that began to spring up around the city thanks to the Partnerships for Parks. Often, you would "appreciate the help" that these volunteers provided—you might never get the benches painted in the park otherwise. But you also would see that your own numbers were dwindling and that your own work and knowledge of the parks was considered to be less important. The fact that the City was offering fewer and fewer promotional exams and instead hiring Supervisors on a "provisional" basis meant that apart from summer step-ups, you might not have the opportunity to advance that you might have had in previous years.

Now consider the landscape you would encounter if, instead of a CPW, you were a WEP worker or a JTP, coming into the parks in the late 1990s or 2000s. If you were a WEP, you might bounce from park to park, mostly on mobile crews and for an indeterminate period of time. You would have no or few rights connected to your work since you would not be considered an "employee." Though court cases begun in the 1990s and lasting through the 2000s established more rights for workfare workers, the City did its best to restructure WEP so as to become less like a regular job and, therefore, to again escape regulation. If you were a JTP, you might well have been a WEP worker before. You might therefore experience JTP as a step-up, a "real job," even if it lasted only six months. No matter how hard you worked, how assiduously you arrived at your worksite on time—even travelling halfway across the city to do so—the best you could really hope for would be a three-month extension. You might very occasionally see your coworkers promoted beyond this, but only in exceptional cases and when hiring was possible in the department. And, during most of the 1990s and 2000s, if you were in either WEP or JTP, chances were that you were a young woman of color. And by virtue of the fact that both programs are linked to the welfare system, you were certainly poor; you would enter the workplace with a set of well-worn stigmas associated with welfare receipt and welfare mothers. You entered into a workplace in which you had little choice *but* to be there, though WEP was more coercive than JTP, at least in a formal sense.

In the next chapter, we turn to the work you would do—what actually goes into parks maintenance—and we look more carefully at who does what and how the distinctions between and among workers are maintained according to the division of labor.

THREE

# The Work

This isn't rocket science; we pick up dog shit. PARK SUPERVISOR II, MANHATTAN

So it's just housekeeping, all kinds of housekeeping. Park-keeping! ALICE, VOLUNTEER, PROSPECT PARK

Harlan, the seasoned Parks Supervisor quoted above, shakes his head and points to the gravelly erosion on the concrete surrounding a flagpole in a Manhattan playground. The concrete, which is carved with animal figures, has been worn away and chipped. "You see this?" Harlan asks. "This is from the snowplow and too much salt in the winter." He then explains that oversalting in order to prevent ice buildup after a snowfall corrodes the concrete. The divot in the concrete, he says, is from a heavy snow plow driven into the playground attached to a pickup truck in order to clear paths in the snow. Neither, he tells us, would be necessary if there were enough people to manually shovel snow in the winter. But that is rarely the case, as the "season" for Job Training Program participants—when more are assigned to parks—runs from May through November. And neither would be necessary if the department would allow the district to close the playground—which is adjacent to a school—instead of insisting that paths through the snow are cut within hours.

Another day, Harlan tells us about what might be called "playground sense"—though he does not use the term. It involves testing the equipment oneself—getting on the swings, sliding down slides, and being sure to inspect

CHAPTER THREE

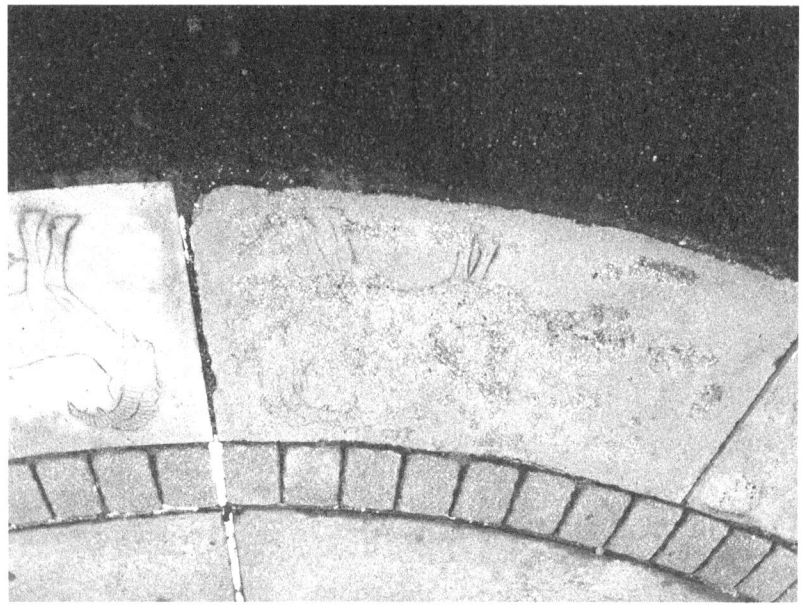

3.1   Ruined ornamentation from excessive salt and mechanical scraping

parks not just when they are empty, at seven in the morning, but also when they are full and being used by hundreds of kids. Testing swings can alert you to erosion in the hooks and joints that attach them to the swing-set bar in ways that visual inspection cannot as easily. Sliding down a slide can alert you to a rattle that indicates a loose screw beneath the structure. Any of these, Harlan says, can result in injuries to children if left undetected. And inspecting playgrounds when they are being used can reveal loose basketball rims that could not be detected without hearing the way they vibrate when a basketball hits them.

Harlan's tour of a playground reveals a distinction between practical and technical knowledge that translates poorly into discussions of work that distinguish between skilled and unskilled labor. Accordingly, while Harlan observes that Park Managers who have not risen through the ranks "don't know how to clean a bathroom," bristles at some superiors' suggestion that Supervisors and Managers should be college graduates, and indicates the importance of a significant range of practical knowledge, he is also realistic about what most of the job of cleaning the parks entails: "This isn't rocket science," he says. "We pick up dog shit."

Human waste, too. Alex, a retired CPW, told us of working in an outer-borough park in the mid-1980s and regularly having to hose down and scour an area that served as a latrine for an encampment of homeless people. This activity resulted once in his slipping, tearing ligaments in his knee, and lying in the sudsy slick of excrement. He still limps.

"Cleaning" is not just any kind of work activity.[1] It is associated with waste and pollution on one side, as Harlan and Alex explicitly refer to it, and with domestic work on the other side, as Alice, the volunteer quoted above, but also other women we interviewed, expressed. Most of the time, these two symbolic associations are plainly related or even resonate together, as when cleaning the park means cleaning the park house's or the beach's bathrooms. But "park-keeping" for Alice does not mean cleaning Prospect Parks' bathrooms, as it actually does for some JTPs we will quote in this chapter. It means taking care of the park gardens, "beautifying" the park, even if this may sometimes involve a good amount of physical work and contact with waste and polluted material or species.

In this chapter, we look more closely at what work is involved in "cleaning parks" (from picking up trash to gardening, from shoveling snow to cleaning bathrooms) and how this work is divided across the different types of park, types of park-management agencies (i.e., public or private), the different seasons, and also, and most importantly, across the different types of workers. If any of the workers we have interviewed may be found at one point of the day with a broom cleaning up the stairs or with a grabber pick up small pieces of trash, only a few would use machines like a blower, plant new bulbs, or clean bathrooms. This division of labor among workers has different layers: on the most formal and visible layer it has to do with status segmentation (civil services rules or volunteer safety rules) that allows for one category of worker to do a specific number and variety of tasks and no more. On a deeper layer, division of labor in the Parks Department—as elsewhere—has to do with broader social hierarchies. Assigning specific tasks—the ones symbolically closer to domestic and polluted work, for instance—to specific categories of workers who happen to be mostly poor black and Latina women is both a product of class and race and gender relations and the structural device through which these hierarchies are reasserted in specific places and institutions.

The association with "dirty work,"[2] with domestic work, and the assumption that no real skills are needed to do most park-cleaning and maintenance work helps to justify the general trend we have noted toward the casualization of this work and the segmenting of the labor

CHAPTER THREE

force between those with technical knowledge or sufficient practical knowledge to take on a supervisory role and those without. Importantly, however, the segmentation of the labor force means that many of the workers do not—and *will not*—get the chance to develop their practical knowledge of the work. As we saw in the last chapter, a mainly male, fixed-post workforce used to characterize the Parks Department staff. As such, these "parkies" would do a wide variety of tasks. The result was that they could get a sense of the whole set of tasks that were required for maintenance, a sense that was crucial to climbing the civil service career ladder. Moreover, though their tasks necessarily involved *some* "dirty work," they were not largely defined by it. In contrast, with the paradoxical specialization of parks maintenance through the combination of broadbanding and segmentation we discussed in the last chapter, a hierarchy of tasks matches roughly to existing social hierarchies of race and gender.

In what follows, we begin with a description of the variety of tasks involved in cleaning parks and in composing the jobs people do. We then focus on the logics driving the division of tasks within the park worksites and the park workforce.

### Garbage

There is a lot of garbage in New York City's parks.

One way of thinking about this is that 100 gallons equals about half a cubic yard. A heavy packer—large garbage truck—holds sixteen cubic yards of garbage. Most of the fifty-nine parks districts in New York City send a heavy packer's worth or more (Central Park, for example, sends many) of garbage to the dump. At roughly 3,200 gallons per truck, that's 188,800 gallons of garbage *every day*, and that does not count the garbage from small packers (six cubic yards each) or the much larger volumes of trash generated in the summer and with special events.

Much of this garbage is quite small. It includes cigarette butts, paper coffee cups, plastic lunch containers, and the like. Some of it, however, is quite large: some parks, particularly in fairly remote areas of the city, like parts of Staten Island, have a problem of illegal dumping, where car tires—and even junked cars—and construction debris join the refuse stream. By and large, however, the garbage in the parks is small and removed mainly by JTPs and community service workers, often working alongside crew chiefs, but also often on their own.

Grabbers and broom-and-dustpan sets are the most common tools applied to the task, which means that collecting garbage is one of the most labor-intensive jobs done in the Parks Department. In addition to this, clearing garbage means pulling full garbage bags out of large public garbage cans several times a day and getting them to the designated pick-up point, where APSWs and their (usually) JTP helpers will pick them up and load them into the back of a packer (or the CPW will do it if the district has a light packer). To get a sense of the work, we quote a JTP at a small Manhattan park, speaking about his day:

When I first get in, like Thompson, nine times out of ten, he get here early. He be here around like seven. So most of the time when I come here he be already started pulling the trash out of the cans already. But being that he wasn't here, I kind of picked up where he left off, so I kind of pull the cans, or I do, I think that's more important, because they be like, when the bosses or supervisors come around, they do a quick scan of the perimeter, so I try to do the main garbages in the front so we looking good, and then I grab the grabber and a plastic bag and get all the debris around the park, work my way inside. That's about it.

In a roughly six-acre park, this can take a four-person work crew all morning. Many smaller parks or playgrounds are left with one or two JTPs "on mobile" who get dropped off for much of the day at a single site and almost exclusively deal with the garbage, clearing litter and emptying garbage cans as the park is being used. For many other playgrounds, a crew of JTPs and a crew chief comes through at some point during the day—starting in the morning around seven o'clock—to clean up.

As with many of the maintenance tasks, garbage removal is not a foreign activity to workers in the parks, whether they are JTPs or higher-ranked workers. On the other, the scale and diversity of parks in New York City make the work both vastly different than it is at the level of a single home, and yet never free of "contamination by its domestic origins."[3] The contrast is similar to that between cooking a meal for two and cooking in a high-volume restaurant and similar, too, in the sense that the relationship between the domestic and unpaid work and the public paid work is also a relationship that has usually been divided by gender. And the workers understand the difference, too. Nora, a JTP who worked in a Brooklyn park, had the following exchange with Maud:

Maud: Is it the first time you've done maintenance work?
Nora: Yeah, first time. Well, I can't really say first time. First time I'm getting paid for it. Because I do it at home. I clean at home . . . I have that down pat. But first time I'm getting paid for it, and first time I'm doing it in a vast area.

CHAPTER THREE

The Central Park Conservancy employs both daytime crews and evening crews, reflecting the nearly constant use of the park from dawn until 1 a.m. every day. Though, as with the regular DPR crews, Central Park Conservancy employs some seasonal workers (or has in some years and not others), its core daytime staff work under a Zone Gardener, and therefore have a range of tasks, not necessarily chiefly focused every day on trash removal, though the job of Grounds Technician is the closest equivalent of the JTP in terms of the work given to the title. A smaller crew of Grounds Technicians, under night crew supervisors, work in the evenings, after the final runs of DPR APSWs who still do the trash-bag pickups and dump runs in heavy packers.

**Leaves**

Clearing leaves probably runs a close second to garbage removal for the attention of the regular maintenance workforce. New York City's parks have hundreds of thousands of trees; Central Park, alone, has 24,000. By far, most of these trees are deciduous, and the fall brings an enormous task of leaf removal. If left unattended, leaves decompose into acidic compounds that ruin lawns and stain concrete, both of which would produce far costlier conditions for parks than removing them does. Although playgrounds tend to have fewer leaves than do regular parks, most playgrounds in the city also have a significant number of trees that line their perimeters. As soon as leaves start to fall—usually in October—and at least until the first snowfall, leaf removal is a preoccupation of park-maintenance efforts. Leon, a Park Manager in Brooklyn, explained:

Once summer's over, fall gets here. Look how many trees we got. All these leaves need to be collected. Sometimes we don't end until like the end of December collecting leaves, or January. We gotta do leaf blowing, you know. And it's not an easy task to rake and use the blowers and collect all those leaves, and if you don't have enough people, it takes time to do it.

If the leaves have not been cleared by the winter, they may accumulate, but they still must be cleared later on. The work is done by JTPs, WEP workers, and volunteers.

There are multiple ways of clearing leaves, but most involve rakes or leaf blowers. Some parks, such as Central Park, do not use leaf blowers because doing so both uses gasoline and because the blowers make

3.2 Leaves whose acid imprinted them in stone steps after not being raked in a timely way

enough noise to disturb residents in the high-end apartment buildings that surround the park on three sides. Other conservancies, such as that in Madison Square Park, with fewer staff and few volunteers use blowers, but only after eight o'clock—again, to cut down on the noise. Some DPR-managed park districts have some leaf blowers, but typically not enough to handle all of their needs; others have none at all. All, therefore, typically depend on simple raking—which is more labor intensive—for most of their leaf-removal needs. Susan, the administrator for a midsized park, complained about her leaf situation, casting it as a matter of resources and bureaucracy:

Susan: We do it all by hand. When it comes to leaf raking, we don't have a leaf blower. We rake it by hand.
Maud: How come?
Susan: Mostly because of money. Because oh, you know, "We give you a truck, we don't have a truck to give to another park . . ."

The centrality of leaf removal is hard to overstate. And raking is heavy work. When we volunteered for a day in a park in Brooklyn, the volunteer coordinator, sensing two—perhaps overeager—novices, told us to pace ourselves, take it easy, and to take breaks. Faced with a stair that was covered ankle-deep in old leaves, we ignored his advice. Three hours later, the stair was clear, but our muscles hurt for days afterward, and our blisters from the rakes took a week to heal.

JTPs who may otherwise be picking up garbage understand the difference between garbage and leaves: "Like there's always gonna be leaves for now. Take time out doing the leaves. That's the most manual labor. Gotta bend down, put it in the top, take it over there." JTPs who start in leaf season may do little else for their six-month stints other than pick up leaves and garbage. Another JTP told us: "Yeah, that's all they've been talking about lately. They told me . . . the time that I start . . . said I'm gonna be leaf man. So we focus on leaves."

### Weeds and Invasive Species

Both clearing leaves and weeding are familiar to anyone who has ever had to deal with lawn care or has ever tended a garden. The technology is essentially the same: weeding is done with one's hands and a trowel, and with a weed-whacker. But as with leaf removal, technological fixes are few, and weed-whackers take training to use.

The principal distinction of weeding in parks is its diversity and volume. Weeding also involves removing *any* invasive plant species, and therefore must be done with supervision and care. Weeding can entail pulling up chest-high bushes of burdock, with its prickly burrs, from an area half the size of a city block, or pulling up small saplings where they have taken root. It can also entail getting on one's knees with a trowel and "edging" the weeds and grass, clearing them from spilling over from lawn areas into pathways. As Alice, the Prospect Park volunteer quoted above, told us:

> We edge, which sounds like a fuddy-duddy thing, but these things are important, because you have grass growth there, it's going to compromise both the roadway and the pathway, and gradually it encroaches, there's no pathway left. Not so much on the drive, but also on some of the paved pathways.

It should be acknowledged, however, that weeding is a kind of deep cleaning that is done in parks with conservancies, in special areas given over to plantings, by volunteers, or simply rarely, when resources allow. One does not see edging and weeding very often in the hundreds of playgrounds run by DPR, and it's not a typical task done by

JTPs on mobile crews. As Alvin, the Parks Supervisor we met in the last chapter, told us:

Well, for example, there's paths in [one park] that we'll never hit. It's a slope. And to take care of it you would need a town. And that's what we did. We had fifty kids with rakes just rake the entire path, and the slope, and then we had tons and tons of debris, branches, and weeds, something like that, it pays, because you have manpower. But edging? Having them pull out weeds from the cracks with scrapers and ice choppers, you know what an ice chopper is? Remove the weeds. If you have a lot of people that do that, I don't have the luxury to do that on a daily basis, because my people are just overwhelmed with all the work.

Though some JTPs get basic training in plant identification (typically those who do a special POP horticulture training program), conservancy workers often get trained in this, so that they weed, if not independently from a supervisor, at least on a predictable basis. As for lawn care: parks with large lawns usually either have conservancy crews that mow and keep up the lawns, or they get the lawns mowed periodically by borough crews with tractor-driven mowers. Few districts have their own mowers for large lawns.

3.3   Stone steps cracked from neglect and failure to "edge"

CHAPTER THREE

## Snow

Snow is unpredictable in New York City. Many snowfalls are light and do not accumulate. But several times in an average winter, snow accumulates, clogging traffic, covering cars parked on the street, freezing over, and then melting into lakes of gray slush. Snow often means that many playgrounds will be locked, though others will be open, with paths shoveled through them and ice broken up as soon as possible. Parks will be open. This means that paths must be shoveled through snow, both on the pathways and on the stairs. Moreover, tree branches that break off with the weight of the snow must be cleared and hazardous areas marked off.

Again, equipment to do this is limited, which, in turn, results in a great deal of labor-intensive work and in subpar results. As Robert, a Supervisor in Brooklyn, told us:

Robert: Yeah, we get the people who get the grass, like the borough crews, and when the snow and the ice is really bad sometimes the borough crew comes by and does our perimeter. But our staff does all the paths, and we have to have all your paths free of snow and ice in the winter. Like, even if it's a little tiny playground that nobody goes in, that has gates you can actually lock up, we're not allowed to keep it open. This park I understand, a lot of people use it as a cut through to get to the subways. But that being said, we don't have a single piece of mechanized equipment, and we don't have a truck. We do a lot of hand . . . they give us blowers, snow blowers, but a snow blower can only be used if there's a certain height of snow. If you get less than an inch and a half or two inches of snow, the snow blower's useless. You have to do it by hand. The old-fashioned way.

John: And you need a lot of people . . .

Robert: I'm out there. I'm out there helping them out. Because if you don't get it within the first twenty-four hours, and you have a real cold night, then the next day you're going to be breaking ice, and you're going to be applying salt. And what happens with the salt, you apply it, and then when it melts you gotta sweep it, and it's . . .

John: So you try to get away without salt.

Robert: I like to not salt if at all possible. It also is detrimental to any horticulture. Grass or gardens, it kills them. It kills trees. If it's a relatively new sidewalk it cracks the sidewalk . . . So we don't use sodium chloride like we should use. We just use rock salt. Sodium chloride is less damaging to plants and to concrete.

Maud: You don't get it?

Robert: We get the cheapest. Which is rock salt. You know what I mean? And sometimes the JTPs, they don't know.

In one district in Manhattan, we interviewed workers after nearly the entire district's staff was spending the morning breaking ice in a string of playgrounds. It was late February and the number of JTPs in the district had dwindled to zero. A significant snowfall had blanketed the city a week before and low temperatures meant that a sheet of ice froze on the playgrounds several inches thick. Only when the temperature climbed above freezing were the workers—including the Supervisors—able to break the ice.

Getting caught short of equipment in the snow was a common theme among supervisors. Susan, an Administrator of a medium-sized park, told us:

And in fact we don't have a snow blower. We're in a thirty-acre park with significant pathways. You should see these guys working! It's heartbreaking to see how hard they have to work outside. It's insane. And then because we're on a hill, you clear all the paths, and then every path is clear, and then it starts to melt, and then at night it freezes, and then you have to cut through ice again. And then you're schlepping the salt from here to this end of the park, that end of the park, it's . . . salt is heavy! So it's a ridiculously stupid . . . we don't have a single salt spreader. You know, the little machine that ch ch ch . . . we don't own one of those in this park. It's *stupid*.

It is particularly in matters like this that having a conservancy helps. Conservancies' ability to raise even modest amounts of money helps to defray the cost of equipment such as snow blowers, salt spreaders, and leaf blowers. Susan, whose park has a conservancy, mentioned that she is likely to ask the conservancy to pay for equipment that the Parks Department cannot or will not allocate to her park.

## Bathrooms

If you talk to longtime New Yorkers about parks, they might recall a time in the not-too-distant past when it was difficult to find a working bathroom in a park. Many bathrooms in park houses were locked or the toilets clogged, the sinks overflowing, and the floor littered, wet, and smelly. This simply is rarely the case anymore.

There are hundreds of bathrooms in New York City's parks, in playgrounds, in larger parks, and on the beaches. They are cleaned daily—

CHAPTER THREE

and in the summer, often many times a day—and replenished with toilet paper, paper towels, and soap.

Who does it? Cleaning bathrooms is clearly associated with bodily functions, fluids, and waste. It is therefore quintessential "dirty work," though certainly garbage removal—and even the incidental garbage removal that must be done when weeding—can be just as associated with bodily excreta in its various forms. As with most dirty work, the task falls to those lowest in local status hierarchies. In the case of the Parks Department, it falls almost exclusively to JTPs and WEPs.

Recall that almost 75 percent of JTPs are women and almost 93 percent are African American or Latina. While it is clear that JTPs make up the bulk of cleaning crews in the parks and therefore do most of the tasks associated with cleaning more than anyone else does, cleaning bathrooms tends to be a job that *nobody* but JTPs and WEPs do. Volunteers are not asked to do it, and CPWs, crew chiefs, and Supervisors only do it in a pinch.

Male JTPs clean bathrooms, too. So, too, do the men hired by the Doe Fund, Inc., a nonprofit organization for homeless recovering addicts that provides maintenance staff for many business improvement districts in the city and for parks like the jointly state-city-administered Hudson River Park. Nevertheless, cleaning bathrooms is still largely understood as women's work. The manager of a smallish park, run by a private conservancy, summed up his view of parks maintenance work thus: "I don't want to be sexist, but it's a job for men, except, we need bathroom attendants, who are females, for the bathrooms." Even in parks where there were men and women who were JTPs, women were more likely to clean the bathrooms. In one, which has both JTPs and conservancy workers, Maurice, a JTP, after summing up his morning, added, "The girls probably take care of the bathrooms already, and once everybody else did their jobs and everybody working together, you hit the whole place, like probably the leaves or whatever."

At the same time, he denied that there is a *strictly* gendered division of labor, and even suggested that some of the dirty work actually has skill or technique attached to it:

Kenn: You think it's pretty happy with the division of labor, guys go out, do the perimeter of the park, while the girls do the bathrooms in the morning? Is that sort of the way that it . . .

Maurice: It's not the way, it's just that the girls already overpopulated with the women before the men, anyway, so just do it . . . it's funny you said that, because I just told Dani today, said, "You know what? Before you leave, you gotta show me how to clean the bathroom," and she laughed. I said, "Not that I don't know how to clean a bathroom, I clean my bathroom all the time, but how you clean it without touching things? You gotta teach me the technique! Teach me how to clean it . . ." You know, I'm not a crazy neat freak, but I'm finicky about touching certain things, too. I be on my hand sanitizer pretty hard.

Nevertheless, the only place we encountered men who regularly cleaned the bathrooms was at the beaches, where bathrooms were in constant use and in constant need of maintenance and where seasonal workers also attended to their care. Here, especially, men and women were concerned about being in the bathrooms of the opposite gender, both for the dangers and for the possibility of accusation of untoward activity. In fact, this appeared to create a certain amount of anxiety for the workers. At a group interview at a large beach, two seasonal workers and a PS1 explained how they handle the situation:

Martin (PS1): That's the good thing about having male attendants at male bathrooms and female at the female, is you interact, when female attendants have to go inside, there's not a male attendant to clean up, the male public to female . . . that's where . . .
Yariza (Seasonal): Yeah, I have that all the time. So that's an issue where I become . . .
Alston (JTP): A girl once showed up at my place, where I had to . . .
Martin: Either a Supervisor will come down . . . Like if they have to clean the female side, I'll stand in front of the door for the fifteen, twenty minutes, whatever it takes, five minutes . . .
John: So you want to have two people there . . .
Yariza: Yeah, you gotta have a man for the male side . . .
Alston: That's right.
Yariza: Like if a male comes in, and they get all offended because . . . , they come in and they look at me like, "This is the males' bathroom . . . ?"
Alston: And if they say something . . .
Yariza: Yes, a little disrespectful or outrageous to where you feel uncomfortable, or you're not that safe in that bathroom by yourself with a bunch of males. I had that problem all the time.
John: So then, do you then actually, if you have to end up cleaning the male bathroom . . . ?
Yariza: I usually, when I end up cleaning the male bathroom, I usually have a PEP officer, male PEP officer, come, if he is around, or I'm next to a lifeguard station . . . I ask him to please keep an eye on me while I'm in the bathroom. I will call Joe

or any of my other Supervisors, just to say that I'm going to be in the males' bathroom, and just if I could have someone over here to help me out, to keep an outside view.

Cleaning bathrooms in parks takes both practical knowledge of social situations and practical knowledge of tasks whose optimal performance may not be obvious. Alston, the seasonal worker at a large beach—he has been a seasonal for over a decade—explained another aspect of practical knowledge relevant to cleaning bathrooms.

Alston: Like, keeping your tools clean. Like, your mop is dirty. You have to clean your mop. Otherwise, you're going to be washing the floor, you know what I mean? Don't put it back on the floor. It's little things like that that people don't know . . . Keeping your tools clean, especially in bathrooms, with floors, mops are very clean. I clean my mop. . . . And I didn't know that when I first started. I heard that from somebody. I would never think about washing the mop! But everything is different. People don't know that. You'd be surprised. People don't do that.
Maud: So who's teaching the newcomers? People on the site, from the job . . . ?
Alston: Yeah, I walk in, the bathroom stinks, this guy, I take him on the side and pull him in and say, "Look, you gotta clean the mop."

Alston, a seasonal worker, has outlasted almost all the permanent staff in his beachside district, and so, during the summer months, he is able to pass his practical knowledge on to newcomers. Similarly, Maurice sought help in learning how to clean the bathroom properly without having to drown in his hand sanitizer. Think for a moment about how Harlan, the Supervisor with nearly thirty years' experience in parks, bemoaned the fact that most managers had "never cleaned a bathroom" and so did not know how. We begin to see, then, in the mundane dirty work of bathroom maintenance, the ways in which the segmentation of the labor force, by relegating to a temporary workforce tasks that require a certain practical knowledge to do effectively, systematically risks losing that knowledge. This makes the work less likely to get done well, more unpleasant to perform, and harder to supervise effectively.

## Painting

Describing the use of Summer Youth Employment Program (SYEP) workers in his district, Ronny, a district Supervisor at a beach, told us:

Usually we give them projects to do, like they'll go into a certain area and paint all the benches, do some weeding, and move on to another section. It's not really . . . I mean I'm sure on Mondays they're being used for the daily maintenance, but then they try to get them to do the things that need to be done, but you don't really have the resources to do normally.

This captures both the use of SYEP workers in maintenance and operations work (which we only mentioned in passing in the last chapter) and also the reality of painting in the Parks Department. Except for failure to paint over graffiti, which is often done by a CPW or supervised by a crew chief—to be sure it gets done quickly—painting is not considered to be basic maintenance. It is rather an enhancement that is done as regularly as possible but that sometimes falls to the wayside in an understaffed department. Because this is the case, "easier" districts—ones that are cleaner overall—will often get paint jobs and other enhancements more readily than more difficult ones. Comparing two districts he had worked in Manhattan, one CPW discussed his current district in favorable terms: "Yeah. Definitely. It's easy. Cleaner. You don't have to clean as much. There's mostly like, painting and things like that, and that nature, but over there it's like, gotta deal with dog poop and rude people . . ."

Because painting is an enhancement that can be done periodically rather than every day, it is also a job that is often reserved for special crews, whether they are SYEPs or, as they often are, volunteers. In our interviews, we found that volunteers and painting were frequently paired subjects, as suggested in the last chapter. One parks administrator explained some of the logic for assigning the task to corporate volunteers: because they come in during the weekdays, one is not in the position of getting weekend volunteers to paint benches or fences when the park is used the most. Nevertheless, this all depends on a park's having a reliable source of volunteer labor. As one borough-wide administrator told us, painting is part of the "deep cleaning" that depends on scarce labor resources:

It's changed when you don't have . . . like when somebody's there, they can almost do like a deep cleaning. They can run out, get all the glass and litter first. They can get into maybe washing things down, and some painting . . . and it's not happening as much. It'll happen when we have events or different things going on, where you . . . bring the resources in to do it. But for somebody to be there every day and do it, it's just not there.

Overall, in talking to workers about the work they did, we got the sense that a park staffed by conservancy workers, such as Central Park or Madison Square Park; with significant volunteer programs, such as Prospect Park; or with the regular use of special teams of youth workers or workers in the GAPP program—a new program begun in 2012 for eighteen- to-twenty-four- year-olds under a contract with the Human Resources Administration—could be sure more regularly that fences and benches were painted and in good shape than could smaller neighborhood parks or playgrounds in busy districts cleaned by mobile crews of JTPs.

In addition to the problem that painting is an important but not everyday activity, its allocation to volunteers and special crews is a function of its being relatively more pleasant to do than many other tasks and carrying with it a measure of instant gratification: one can see the results of a newly painted iron fence or line of benches much more readily than one can see painstaking weeding or routine garbage collection. Moreover, painting requires planning and materials, from paint to rollers and pans. Corporate volunteers and "Friends of" groups often provide these materials; Park Supervisors often provide them for smaller-scale volunteer activities. Alvin, the Parks Supervisor, summed up how he coordinates volunteer activities like painting with the Partnerships for Parks, highlighting the way in which painting—and horticulture—are more attractive to volunteers:

> I want to get a group that's going to paint. So that means you can't use children. You gotta use adults. Children are . . . they want to paint, but more of it ends up on the floor, they're not careful. Or you can say, "Listen, I want people that know a little bit about horticulture. I want to do a little planting, I want to do some grass edging, I want to paint the wrought iron fence." Usually we don't give them the nasty jobs like picking up garbage and cleaning up bathrooms, because if you do that you might not want to volunteer next time . . . No, really, that's the truth. My employees do the ugly work. The bathrooms, picking up dog feces . . . dead animals.

### Fences

Though folklorists and students of proverbs will confirm that the saying "Good fences make good neighbors" is ambiguous and filled with historical nuance, in parks its meaning is very tangible. Fences abound in parks and are critical to park maintenance. Three types of fencing are most typical in parks. Heavy wrought-iron fencing often surrounds playgrounds and other facilities, such as staging areas for Parks Department staff and vehicles. This is the type of fencing that requires periodic painting, both to keep from looking shabby and to provide protection from the elements and rust. Chain-link fences are also extremely common and also appear around playgrounds, staging areas, and ballfields. These are built higher—often to heights of fifteen to twenty feet—and play an important role in actually keeping people out of restricted areas. Finally, light, portable, chicken-wire fencing—about four feet high—is used in parks to restrict access to planted areas and lawns. The ubiquity of this light-wire fencing in many parks has been criticized by some park-user groups, but administrators and managers insist that it is critical to keeping the parks in good repair and presentable to the public.

Fencing is both a work saver and a source of work. For example, a fenced-off field that has recently been reseeded with grass will result in a green lawn from the spring through the fall. If it is not fenced off, the seeds will be disturbed and the young grass trampled, and the field will remain a brown patch of dirt. Similarly, after heavy rains, sports fields with natural grass will be unusable for a day, or they will turn into mud pits and be ruined as grassy areas to play for the rest of the season or require expensive new sodding. Even rotating the use of lawns in good weather can allow them to recover from overuse. For this reason, one can find fenced-off lawns and fields in Central Park and other parks during high season. Further, the chicken-wire fencing can be used to create impromptu areas in parks that facilitate other tasks. For example, chicken-wire pens can be constructed quickly for piles of leaves that keep them from blowing back all over the park if there will be a time lag between raking and removal.

But if good fences make good parks users, parks users also sometimes disturb the fences, either by accident or on purpose. When they do, it often takes more than a JTP crew supervised by a crew chief or a CPW to fix fences. While light-wire fencing can be replaced easily—it is simply rolled onto stanchions and affixed with plastic ties—chain-link fencing requires the work of a district "handyman" or skilled maintenance worker. Broken fences can be a safety hazard and are thus important to fix quickly.

The range of tasks regularly done by maintenance crews in Central Park and in other conservancies is somewhat larger than is true for the JTP and other mobile crews that predominate in publicly managed

CHAPTER THREE

parks. One Grounds Technician we interviewed from Central Park discussed the benefit of having multiskilled Zone Gardeners, alluding to fencing as one of a range of tasks to which they attend:

So that's why they have it. Zone Gardeners, because he'll stay in maybe one specific area, say for instance, Central Park, Columbus Circle, he's a Zone Gardener for Columbus Circle, so he takes care, keeping that area pruned, grass cut, fences and a little bit of everything done . . . So what will happen is, now that the seasonals coming in, he may get one to two seasonals to work with him, so that they'll take the, more or less, the perimeter, clean up, and he'll concentrate on his planting, weeding, stuff like that, or sometimes they'll help him. Sometimes they have to put up fencing or take out some bushes and plant new bushes, you know, change of season every year you have different flowers, so at certain times of the year you have to change.

**Playground Equipment and Benches**

The skilled maintenance workers assigned to every district—or every several districts—do not just install and maintain fences. They are the point people for most of the features of parks and playgrounds on which parks users sit or play. Broken benches, for example, are usually fixed by the maintenance workers, who can replace bolts and wooden or plastic composite bench slats. Loose screws or other repair problems with playground equipment, too, are usually fixed by the maintenance workers, though CPWs also can do this kind of work. Maintenance workers will also attend to broken or damaged sections of boardwalks at the beaches (though some of these are being replaced by lower-maintenance concrete, instead of wooden planks). These features must be inspected regularly by Supervisors, as they are directly related to the safety of park users. If Supervisors do not find problems with benches, playground equipment, or boardwalks, park users will. As Alston, the seasonal at the beach, told us about feedback from the public:

Yeah. They want to talk to you. Straighten things out, like the boardwalk. I just want to report these things happening around me. Just tell the Supervisor. Need to be fixed. I can't fix it, because I'm not a maintenance man. I do ordinary little fixing things, but I don't fix the whole nine yards. I don't get that pay, what they get [laughs]. I would do it if I got the moolah!

Similarly, CPWs and maintenance workers maintain basic plumbing, fixing park-house bathrooms and water fountains and sprinklers. One CPW told us that if there is a problem, "I will do it, electrical work, plumbing work, all that I can do. Not all. If there's something that needs to be done professionally or by the book, we call the professional from the Parks Department, the plumbing department." Maintenance workers are more skilled than CPWs, by and large, but even they call in the "shops"—the skilled plumbers, electricians, arborists, etc.—when they confront more difficult issues.

The problem is that there *aren't* maintenance workers for every district, and there is more than enough work for the maintenance workers who are in the department. Geoffrey Croft, who is the president and founder of the New York City Parks Advocates, related a story in an interview that captures part of the problem that results from short-staffing maintenance workers:

One of the things I was explaining not that long ago, I was out at a park in the South Bronx, and I came across this bench, and this bench was, I photographed it years earlier, and this JTP was there, and it was an older man, and you could tell these people have pride in their work and pride in their community and want to do the right thing. So he's saying that he got in trouble because he tried to fix that bench. He tried to put in a work order, the bench has been broken for years, but he was saying that, you know, he went out of title and tried to fix this bench because he kept calling the maintenance and there was no maintenance, he said, you know, kids and grandmothers play on this bench.

The shortages are borne out, too, in the audits performed by the city comptroller's office. Though the comptroller found that the vast majority of work orders required by the Parks Inspection Programs inspectors and by Parks Supervisors (in their independent inspections) were performed within thirty days, and found as well that so-called "immediate attention" work orders were also finished within the required thirty-day period, a small but significant minority of those immediate attention work orders were not, leaving hazardous conditions in place. Table 3.1 gives a sample of the longest completion times for Immediate Attention orders across all the boroughs, and also illustrates the kinds of work that maintenance workers and craftspeople from the "shops" do.

Supervisors are tasked with making sure that these work orders are put into the maintenance management system—now automated on handheld devices—and actually performed. But with shortages of

CHAPTER THREE

**Table 3.1** Selected immediate attention orders, 2011–2012

| Hazard | Playground | Date Reported | Date Repaired | Days Elapsed |
|---|---|---|---|---|
| Weld loose railing on play equipment. 5-foot fall hazard | Benson Playground | 5/26/2011 | 2/15/2012 | 266 |
| Exposed bolt on bottom railing of play equipment | Ethan Allen Playground | 4/19/2011 | 1/11/2012 | 267 |
| Trip hazard—missing cobble stones on East 68th Street opposite fire hydrant | Hickman Playground | 5/9/2011 | 3/31/2012 | 327 |
| Worn out s-hook at bottom of climbing chains | McCaffrey Playground | 4/20/2011 | 2/16/2012 | 302 |
| Uplifted concrete trip hazard on sidewalk outside playground | Gutenberg Playground | 4/16/2011 | 2/16/2012 | 306 |
| Dead limbs hanging over play equipment | Matthews-Palmer Playground | 6/5/2011 | 5/24/2012 | 354 |
| Uncovered manhole | P.S. 42/Almeda Playground | 7/30/2011 | 2/12/2012 | 198 |
| Hole in handball court surface, trip hazards at curb, by comfort station, and work-out play equipment | Captain Rivera Playground | 11/12/2011 | 8/9/2012 | 271 |
| Check all shackles on top of swings, at least four are worn | Lopez Playground | 9/11/2011 | 5/24/2012 | 257 |

Source: "Audit of the Repair and Maintenance of Playgrounds by the Department of Parks and Recreation" (Brooklyn: Office of the New York City Comptroller, 2012), appendix 2.

skilled workers to do the work, there is a queuing process that prioritizes those work orders that the Parks Inspection Program (about which more in the next two chapters) inspectors put into the system. This does not necessarily sit well with the Supervisors who have to manage the completion of the orders. As Henry told us:

We're the ones who are going to monitor and repair. But if it's a priority if *they* turn it in. If *I* turn it in they'll say it's not a priority. Which to me is not right. We all work together. Why should I jump because *he* gave it to me? What's wrong with *my* work order? Why is it taking three fucking months, sometimes longer?

The comptroller's audit does not mention staff shortages, but it is precisely the queuing of the work in response to severely limited resources that means that new conditions found by the centralized inspections may take priority over other outstanding work that Supervisors already know is necessary to ensure park users' safety. As if in recognition of this fact, the Parks Department, in early 2013, announced that it would hire forty-five additional maintenance workers (which works out to just under one per district) along with an additional 170 CPWs.

**Plowshares and Pruning Hooks**

Our research here focuses mainly on the question of cleaning and clearing debris in the parks, not on horticulture and tree care. Nevertheless, the overall experience of parks maintenance—for workers and users alike—is obviously tied up with both. The repair and maintenance of fencing, for example, is often related to efforts to preserve planting, and stumps from trees that have been removed, missing or eroded paving stones from tree pits, and overhanging branches all affect the maintenance and safety of playgrounds and parks. Furthermore, both elements of parks maintenance figure importantly on any evaluation of the overall condition of parks, whether from outside evaluators, such as the advocacy organization New Yorkers For Parks, or from internal inspections carried out by supervisors and by inspectors from the Parks Inspection Program.

*Horticulture*

While there is no doubt that cleaning bathrooms is "dirty work"—unpleasant because of its associations and the realities of what dirty bathrooms can look like—horticulture can also be dirty and difficult. Quite literally, horticulture focuses on putting things in and taking them out of dirt, and it can be by turns painstaking, backbreaking, and prickly. Nevertheless, the results of horticulture—including the weeding we described above—can be magnificent and involve much more aesthetic rewards than do painting, leaf removal, weeding, and cleaning toilets. Moreover, gardening is a common enough leisure activity, and rather like the difference between a marathon and a backbreaking day of manual labor, similar levels of effort and sweat are commonly valued differently by participants based on the cultural valences of the activity itself, the kinds of feedback given to those doing the activity, and the degree of choice one has in carrying it out.

Visitors to Central Park in the springtime cannot help but be impressed by the riot of color that the thousands of tulips, daffodils, mums, azaleas, rhododendrons, and other flowering bushes and trees present. Springtime in Madison Square Park brings more flowering bushes and extensive beds of tulips. Gardens blossom in all the parks districts, too; daffodils, especially, are a harbinger of spring around the city.

But daffodils need to be planted. So do tulips, mums, and dozens of other kinds of flowers found throughout the city's parks. This, of course, involves digging into dirt with a trowel, burying bulbs in late fall, and waiting until they bloom in the spring, or planting the flowers in the springtime itself.

The Parks Department employs Gardeners and Assistant Gardeners. In 2010, in the middle of our research, there were fifty-three Gardeners and ninety-eight Assistant Gardeners on payroll. While some are employed in the department's extensive nursery on Staten Island, others are deployed in the districts and larger "flagship" parks. Other horticulture work—on many Greenstreets, for example—is carried out by private gardening firms under contract with the Parks Department.

Many districts do not have Gardeners or Assistant Gardeners assigned to them, while others, like District 9 in Manhattan, with both Morningside and St. Nicholas Parks, which are midsized, landscaped parks, have two. Conservancies have their own gardeners who design and oversee plantings in their parks. For districts without Gardeners, however, enterprising Supervisors and volunteers have often done beautification projects, getting flowers and other plants from the Parks Department nurseries, from the Partnerships for Parks, or from conservancies whose gardeners have extra plants, bulbs, and flowers to donate. Conservancies will sometimes raise money specifically for plants, as does the Central Park Conservancy Women's Committee, which encourages minimum thirty-five-dollar donations for daffodils, tulips, and mums.

Much of the actual horticultural labor—beyond the fairly complex tasks of designing planted areas, choosing environmentally appropriate plants, and choosing plants appropriate to the level of maintenance that can be expected to occur—is done by volunteers. Semi-annual "It's My Park" days, coordinated by the Partnerships for Parks, bring thousands of volunteers to parks in the spring and fall to engage in a range of maintenance projects, with planting a significant activity among these. Supervision of these plantings falls to a range of parks workers, from CPWs to Supervisors, and to volunteer coordinators from the Partnerships or to local leaders of "Friends of" park groups that trigger the Partnerships' involvement. Coordination of plantings is a more regular occurrence in parks with gardeners, whether these are conservancy-run or not. The importance of supervision of horticultural activities was underscored by Meg, a Supervisor in Brooklyn:

In that particular case I had a Gardener there, given that they were doing horticulture, and he can say, "Well this is a weed, but this isn't a weed. It might look like a weed now, but it's going to flower soon. This is intentionally put here. This was unintentionally growing." So someone would have to oversee the volunteer group to make sure it goes well.

For more regularly planted parks, watering, pruning, weeding, and switching out plantings may fall to groups of workers other than volunteers, as well. A Parks Opportunity Program course available to POP-JTPs assembles a special horticulture crew that does special projects around the city, and which is trained by a longtime Parks Department Gardener-turned-Supervisor. Further, Summer Youth Employment Program workers, workers in the Green Applied Projects for Parks corps, and even WEP workers have been put to horticultural projects, again, typically supervised by Gardeners or Assistant Gardeners. In conservancy-run parks, conservancy workers, either working under a Gardener or, in the case of Central Park, a Zone Gardener, will often do planting, weeding, and light pruning, as well as removing invasive tree species (when the trees or bushes are young enough to do so without power tools).

*Trees*

The close call we had with a collapsing tree in Prospect Park, which we mentioned in chapter 1, made us sensitive to the importance of tree care in parks. Two other things alerted us to the work of tree-care. First, it turns out that during the course of our research, our close call was far from the only—or most serious—incident. The parks advocate Geoffrey Croft has listed six cases of serious injury or death in the period between 2009 and 2012 from falling tree limbs. And he has documented several more recent cases. He notes that at the time, the parks commissioner, Adrian Benepe, blamed one death in Central Park from a falling elm limb on the weight of the wet snow that had fallen earlier in the day but failed to cite a work order from the Central Park Conservancy that had recommended the removal of the tree two months earlier. Similar delays were implicated in the grave injury of a young father and software engineer, Sasha Blair-Goldensohn, whose case was widely publicized at the time of his injury in July 2009. And as the comptroller's report shows, hanging tree limbs are a fairly common danger. In its audit of Brooklyn's parks, for example, it found that of sixty-three possible "immediate attention" orders, eight involved hanging limbs.

CHAPTER THREE

The second thing that alerted us to the importance of tree care was that Mayor Michael Bloomberg, as part of his large-scale PlaNYC—an effort to redesign parts of the city to make it greener and more sustainable—initiated the "Million Trees" project. The Million Trees campaign is exactly what it sounds like: an effort to plant one million trees in New York City. As people who almost had one tree come down on our heads, and who were aware of dangerous backlogs in tree care, we were interested in who would look after one million new trees even as the existing ones might be in need of attention.

The work of tree care is, it turns out, quite complex from an organizational point of view, and therefore several types of workers do this work. To begin with, the Parks Department is charged with maintaining 650,000 street trees in the city. Nevertheless, responsibility for some—for example on some "Greenstreets" or traffic medians—lies with the Department of Transportation, and the responsibility for many others lies with property owners. Nevertheless, in leafy boroughs like Queens, Brooklyn, and Staten Island, the borough-wide tree crews are in charge of inspecting and maintaining hundreds of thousands of street trees, even while the borough crews across the city are tasked with maintaining the nearly two million trees already in New York City's parks.

Within the Parks Department itself, there has been—until a round of hiring in 2013—a steady reduction in the number of tree Pruners and Climbers, as overall staffing levels have declined in Maintenance and Operations. In 1979, for example, there were 330 full time workers in Forestry and Horticulture. Cuts in 1980 reduced that number to 284, and the numbers continued to drop, so that in 1990 there were 192 full-time employees in Forestry and Horticulture. Many of these cuts were to Gardeners, to be sure. Nevertheless, the number of Climbers and Pruners has also declined. In 2007 there were 112 Climbers and Pruners; in 2012, there were ninety-two Climbers and Pruners and forty foresters (forestry specialists), only fifteen of whom were assigned to tree care.[4] The budget for forestry declined by almost 75 percent even as the number of trees to be inspected and maintained increased. The result has been that—before the recent increase in Climbers and Pruners—trees were put on a twenty-year inspection and pruning cycle, rather than the seven-year cycle that Partnerships for Parks called ideal. Moreover, as reported in the 2012 Mayor's Management Report the number of trees pruned in the "established cycle" fell to under 10 percent from around 15 percent in fiscal years 2009 through 2012.[5] Other city data, however, show that the department responds to pruning requests well within the week-to-month windows required by specific types of conditions. Accordingly, a picture emerges of tree care by regular department staff and tree crews that, while emphasizing safety, suggests that Holly Leicht, the former executive director of New Yorkers for Parks, is correct when she says that "They're so under-resourced that it becomes more about putting out fires and responding to complaints than about a long-term maintenance strategy."[6] Or, as one Bronx Supervisor said in testimony at a trial involving a bicyclist injured by a falling limb: "We are a complaint-generated organization. So we only inspect any complaints that come in."[7]

As in other areas, such as gardening, the Parks Department increasingly has relied on volunteers for tree care, both for trees in parks and—perhaps most importantly—for street-tree care. Jay, a volunteer in Queens, explained:

That's why they really push, though, getting certified citizen tree pruners. Because if you're planting a million trees, and there are already so many, you need a tremendous volunteer base to work on this, because otherwise it's not going to happen. I mean, I can't say the property owners and managers are not going to do it, but I don't know that many realize the extent of their responsibility for that.

Another volunteer coordinator told us:

I think the Partnership [for Parks] is offering more classes more regularly. They're offering them either free or with sort of a refunded fee. That's how we got so many people is . . . we said . . . "If you even have a smidgeon of interest in this please sign up, and if you complete the class we'll refund the expense." And we set everyone up with tools, we had food during the meetings to try to encourage it. But since then I think they've made the classes more accessible. They also have a whole tree academy program that they're doing. I think last year was possibly the first or second year, and then they're doing it again this year. . . . But it's a huge commitment. So it's impressive that they get a fair number of people, like ten or fifteen people to go through it, depending. But I think that there's no way that they're going to have this many street trees—and they need them, though—without a pretty substantial volunteer force behind it.

The New York City Street Tree Consortium—now simply called Trees New York—"was founded in 1976 as a volunteer response to New York City's devastating cutbacks in forestry and tree-related community services"[8] and provides training and certification for "citizen pruners" who are authorized to prune trees as they identify the need to do so and who also provide a wide range of tree-care services such as watering and repair of tree beds. Trees New York claims to have trained 11,500 adults and 6,000 young people in tree care. Because of the decentralized nature of a citizen-pruner program, and because districts do not use citizen pruners in a systematic way, it is difficult to quantify the work that citizen pruners do, though one volunteer leader in Queens tries to get crews of citizen pruners to email him to let them know what they have done.

There are clear limits, however, to the kinds of work these volunteers may do. Citizen pruners must keep their feet on the ground; in other words, they are not authorized to climb ladders or—in contrast to the department's Climbers and Pruners—climb trees or get into cherry pickers to reach tree limbs. They may only prune what they can reach. Accordingly, they are unable to deal with the most hazardous conditions.

It should also be noted that Supervisors, who are the ones tasked with inspecting trees in the parks—they are the ones who submit work orders to forestry crews—receive almost no formal training to recognize tree hazards. Neither do CPWs, who are also charged with reporting hazardous conditions to their Supervisors. While the Parks Department training academy does offer a course on trees, it is not mandatory for any regular, front-line maintenance workers.[9]

The parks managed by private conservancies have a range of arrangements for dealing with tree maintenance. The richer conservancies, like Central and Bryant Parks', have their own staffs, sometimes supplemented by outside contractors. Central Park has its own tree crew with trained arborists; they inspect all of the park's more than 24,000 trees and respond, as well, to Zone Gardeners' reports of problems. Nevertheless—and statistically, it would also have to do with the enormous traffic Central Park enjoys—the park has been the site of many serious and even fatal injuries. Indeed, except for injuries caused by street trees, extremely few of the serious injuries from *parks'* trees have occurred in ones centrally managed by the Parks Department.

One final, important aspect of tree care is tree and stump removal. The department's forestry crews cut down more than 16,000 trees in fiscal year 2012, in response to complaints and to monitoring of conditions. Yet, as New Yorkers for Parks has indicated, amid the annual budget cuts from 2008 through 2012, there was no allocation for removing tree stumps, so these have tended to linger, preventing new trees from being planted in the old ones' place or preventing reuse of the particular tree bed.[10]

## Unusual Maintenance

Three times during the course of our research, significant disasters struck New York and its parks. The first time was in August 2009, when a freak windstorm blew down hundreds of trees in Riverside and Central Parks in Manhattan. The area of Central Park called the Great Hill suffered extensive damage. Five years later, the wood chips generated by the recycling of the downed trees formed a mountain in a nearby area of the park. The second, Hurricane Irene, destroyed more than 150 trees in Prospect Park. And in 2012, Hurricane Sandy flooded the city and destroyed miles of beachfront boardwalk in the Rockaways, in Queens, damaged waterfront parks around the city, and blew over or destroyed thousands of trees, including several that killed people beneath them.

In all of these cases, the response was an all-hands-on-deck affair that put regular public workers—and especially forestry division workers—on the frontline of recovery, saw Park Supervisors coordinating massive efforts to reclaim and rehabilitate their parks, involved private landscaping and construction firms in off-budget (i.e., unbudgeted for the Parks Department) repair and restoration work, and, at the same

3.4   The aftermath of Hurricane Sandy, Juniper Valley Park, Queens (photo credit: Mike Gannon, Queens Chronicle)

time, detracted little—if at all—from the overall effort to maintain parks citywide.

## Divisions of Labor

The work we have described in this chapter—and its brief excursions into questions of staffing levels and funding, which will be taken up again in subsequent chapters—is the basic set of tasks that keep parks operating in a way that is generally aesthetically appealing and usually safe for the public. These tasks are carried out unevenly, however. This is true both from the point of view of the absolute levels at which they are performed across districts and parks because of historical shifts in staffing levels, and from the point of view of the division of labor across worker categories.

In the previous chapter, we described the segmentation of park maintenance workers' labor contracts. Here, we take a different look at the division of labor in parks by focusing on the tasks different types of worker do. Naturally, supervisory responsibility will most likely mean that workers who must oversee others will not do the exact same work. And it is unsurprising to have some hierarchy in a workplace, based on qualifications such as civil service exams or on experience and seniority. Nevertheless, there are other logics driving the composition of the parks workforce and the division of tasks within it.

### Scarcity and Cost Saving on Labor

The first logic driving the composition of the parks workforce is simply one of cost savings on labor. Though this is related to questions of skill and expertise, it is also part of the long-term movement we described in the last chapter from fixed-post to mobile and from permanent to temporary labor contracts. As we have described here, there are various types of "deep cleaning," for example, that simply cannot be accomplished by mobile crews of JTPs, community service sentencees, or WEP workers. These workers, of course, cost the department far less than do regular employees, like CPWs. The divisions of labor in conservancies vary considerably according to the proportion of the staff the private organization hires in the park in question. In Central Park, for example, Grounds Technicians fulfill the role that JTPs fulfill in regular parks, but with a broader variety of regular tasks. The Zone Gardeners, by contrast, fulfill the CPW role, but also take on the role of Assistant Gardeners. In parks with less extensive conservancy staff, such as Prospect Park, existing crews of CPWs and JTPs clean the park, while Prospect Park Alliance's staff performs a wide variety of less-routine work, such as volunteer coordination and landscaping projects. Conservancies, with their ability to draw on private donations, have fewer scarcity-driven problems that shape the division of tasks among their workforces in that—as opposed to run-of-the-mill Parks Department–administered parks—they can arrange their management contracts to both respond to the department's scarce resources *and* to maximize their own, while keeping Parks Department staff on whatever essential functions the conservancy does not care to take on or cannot do efficiently (such as trucking garbage to the dump). Even here, however, changes in the work tasks, division of labor, and schedules could be driven by scarcity. In January 2009, for example, the Central Park Conservancy faced a budget crisis as several of its donors reduced their financial commitments to the organization due to losses from the financial crisis or to the collapse of Bernard Madoff's Ponzi scheme. It laid off thirty-one workers and decided against hiring summer seasonal workers that year. Instead, it reshuffled the schedules of its workers so that daytime workers had to do some stretches of evening duty, which involved less specialized planting work and more simple refuse removal. As one highly ranked official in the Conservancy told us, the plan was a disaster for morale: "Nobody liked it."

Scarcity also has driven the changes in the work of the skilled workers in the shops. Tree care and all sorts of other work orders have been subject to delays—and tree pruning schedules have been scaled back from a seven-year cycle to a twenty-year cycle—due to chronic staff shortages. Accordingly, too, much of the response to longer-term maintenance tasks has taken the form of emergency repairs and responses to complaints, rather than to planned, long-term maintenance. We will discuss some of the consequences of this—both operational and political—in later chapters.

Finally, the reintroduction of WEP workers to the parks where JTPs once worked—a sort of reversal of the initial advocacy victories that forced the introduction of JTP in the early 2000s[11]—was clearly driven by the hopes of reducing costs to the city for the labor it deploys. As the Independent Budget Office—a city agency charged with analyzing budgets and the costs of city programs—describes it:

One initiative is replacing Job Training Program (JTP) participants at the parks department with federally funded Work Experience Program (WEP) workers, for a

CHAPTER THREE

city savings of $6.8 million this year and $13.9 million next year. According to the Mayor's budget office, 330 full-time equivalents were cut in 2012 and additional cuts will be made to bring the total reduction in fulltime equivalents to 700 for 2013 (about half the program). Individuals who would have been assigned to the parks department via JTP are now assigned as WEP workers; while WEP workers perform similar duties with no city-funded costs, they can only work roughly half as many hours as JTPs.[12]

When considered *only* from the point of view of the work performed by WEPs or JTPs, the initiative seems to have no real impact: JTPs have longer hours, but they do the same work as WEPs. But if considered from the point of view of *supervision*, the impact of the initiative would be significant. Recall that WEP workers' schedules are not as regular as those of JTPs, since the number of work hours required of them is linked to the value of their welfare benefits. Accordingly, even though new hiring expanded the ranks of CPWs significantly—largely making up for recent attrition—had the WEP expansion continued the new workers likely would have spent more time ferrying WEP workers from place to place than they would have with a workforce of JTPs.

*Daily vs. Occasional Tasks*

The difference between daily maintenance tasks and occasional ones also shapes the division of labor in parks maintenance but, again, does not do so in a straightforward way. While it is true that much of the daily maintenance work is carried out by workers under a variety of labor contracts—City Park Workers, City Seasonal Aides, WEPs, JTPs, community service sentencees, and APSWs—it is also the case that much of this work varies on a seasonal basis. The movement within the department in the summer season—where permanent workers often "step up" to higher positions at beaches and pools, or fill in for other stepped-up employees in the districts—means that even CPWs and APSWs may spend a quarter to a third of their work years doing work that they ordinarily do not.

The division between daily tasks and occasional tasks distinguishes much of the work dividing those attending to that which needs to be "cleared" and those attending to that which needs to be fixed or put in place. In other words, clearing garbage, snow, and leaves is an activity that goes on every day, while fixing benches, fences, swing sets, water fountains, and boardwalk slats (jobs typically done by maintenance workers), and painting, weeding, and planting (jobs often allocated to volunteers), are activities that are more occasional.

Some of the distinction between these two sets of jobs, however, also breaks down in the setting of private conservancies. Central Park Conservancy, for example—and to a different extent, several other conservancies with their own staffs—divides tasks less than is typical in the Parks Department, in part to reinforce that overall care for the park is the responsibility of everyone on staff, rather than something that is subordinate to strict job descriptions. This, after all, is part of the Central Park Conservancy's founding narrative for why it hired its own, nonunion workers. As Richard Gilder, a philanthropist and conservative activist who is a significant donor to, and founding board member of, the Central Park Conservancy, argued in 1997:

Conservancy staffers are flexible enough to do more than one task, so they can be assigned to whatever job needs doing most urgently. And most crucial perhaps, the Conservancy is able to instill a real sense of pride in those who work for it; they come to think of Central Park as *their* park.

Though the Parks Department has many fine people in Central Park, they work under a bureaucratic, seniority-based union system. Rigid union job descriptions can create a ready excuse for leaving work undone. When scores of fish died of a mysterious ailment in the Rowboat Lake a few years back, Parks Department workers maintained—rightly, no doubt—that retrieving them wasn't in their contract. Some of the Conservancy's gardeners took care of the problem while the city workers looked on.[13]

## *Symbolic Division of Tasks*

It is difficult to believe that Central Park's gardeners were enthusiastic about cleaning up loads of dead fish. Indeed, it was their nonunion status and their ability to *be assigned* to urgent tasks as much as their "sense of pride" in the park that led them to step in where city workers would not. But the way that this story works is, at least in part, by reversing the symbolic order that should otherwise obtain, in which lower level public employees whose job it somehow "ought" to be to do the most unpleasant of tasks are shown to be both operationally and morally stunted by more "flexible" workers who exhibit more "pride" in their jobs and in the park.

The normal—or normative—symbolic order is that lower-level workers do the most unpleasant tasks, or the "dirty work." As Alvin suggested, above, volunteers are not asked to clean bathrooms, pick up dog feces, or dispose of dead animals. But it is not as if sweeping up a dead bird or shoveling excrement—or picking up dozens of used condoms—is impossible to encounter while doing weeding or preparing a site for planting. And it is not as if any of these tasks are any *less* pleasant, in the end, than being covered in itchy burrs from removing burdock or getting poison ivy while weeding. Instead, there are some tasks that are more readily defined as symbolically dirty—typically those dealing with waste—and others that are just as dirty but are symbolically cleaner. Parks administrators are reluctant to *ask* volunteers to do this dirty work. Moreover, most of the *regular* parks workers *also* do not do this dirty work. Rather, it is those people whose social status is lower—people who are on welfare or still in the orbit of the Human Resources Administration (WEPs and JTPs) or who are subject to the correctional system, or even those who are poor enough to work seasonally and rely on unemployment benefits and informal-sector work for the rest of the year—who are most often put to these tasks. They are far more likely to be black and Latino than other workers in the parks and more likely to be women, too. They, too, are a "flexible" workforce, and they, too, may take pride in their work, and often do. But they enjoy a different status in the workplace, a status shaped by relations beyond the workplace. Yet because the translation of inequality from one setting to the next is neither always straightforward nor automatic, we turn in the next chapter to the relations of workers with each other in the workplace.

FOUR

# The Workplace

A maintenance technician for several years at the Central Park Conservancy before he was fired in 2008, Jackson was still quite upset when we interviewed him several weeks after his dismissal.

So again, as we're going along, the rules are changing, and they're changing them to their benefit, not yours, so again I was getting disillusioned. I like the job because I'm outside, and I'm meeting people, and the day is going by. You got the kids. It is a nice job. But what makes it so hard and so stressful is the little nitpicking that they do. The way they make you feel very uncomfortable if you make suggestions on how to make your job easier. "No. That's how we do it here. Well, if you don't feel satisfied, you know . . . here's the door." And they give you that look like, "It's up to you. If you don't like it leave." That was the attitude. . . . They pick and choose their people who they feel they can work with, who's gonna do what they say without questioning.

Disgruntled as he clearly was, Jackson's observations squared with other stories we heard about the work environment in the Conservancy. But as important are several themes that recur in parks workplaces, whether in private conservancies or in the Parks Department itself. These include the plasticity of rules and the seeming arbitrariness of supervision, at least from the point of view of many of the workers; the frequent lack of any regard for any bottom-up input into how best to do a given job; and a pervasive sense that favoritism is really the principle by which parks workplaces operate.

CHAPTER FOUR

We have already discussed the division of labor in parks and the ways in which city policy has brought different kinds of workers into competition with each other by assigning them similar work—for example, JTPs and WEPs with CPWs, or conservancy workers with public workers—but here, while we touch on this again, from time to time, we will focus on the ways in which the entire system of staffing shortages, of privatization, and of the growth of nonstandard labor in parks also creates competition among workers with the *same* work status.

Taken together, the apparent arbitrariness of supervision, the lack of positive bottom-up feedback mechanisms, the pervasive sense of favoritism, and the encouragement of competition among workers ends up producing workplaces that are governed by a kind of dual system, corresponding loosely to the segmented labor markets discussed in chapter 2. For "regular" civil service workers, workplaces are still largely governed by civil service codes and union contracts. To be sure, there is some deviation from solid rules, as there is in any bureaucratic system. But for WEPs and JTPs, and, to a large degree, for conservancy workers, governance based on the personal proclivities of supervisors prevails, often with troubling results and sometimes—as is the case with systems relying on personal power—with ones that workers appreciate a great deal. As the French sociologist Nicolas Jounin writes, "The subtle equilibrium of paternalist relations at work relies on assuring certain protections without guaranteeing them; they are always favors to win and never rights to protect."[1] And for volunteers and community service workers, who are outside of career paths in the parks, but participate in them, these divisions may not be clearly visible at all.

We begin here, however, by revisiting some of the ways in which workers are divided from each other and made to compete with each other. But we also show the ways in which the nature of competition among workers changes depending both upon overall management strategies and priorities and upon the kinds of workers that are put into competition. Further, we show that not all competition occurs with respect to the performance of the work itself; in a paternalist system, competition also occurs for favors. In the parks, this is widely recognized, especially when it comes to the formation of what we call a "sexual economy," based on unequal power and systematic sexual harassment, even though it is rarely explicitly acknowledged as a result of the fundamental authority relations at parks worksites. We then show the ways in which sometimes workers at different levels of the hierarchy resist the personalism and division of the workplace and then how these authority structures are both put in place by and make the management of the parks difficult for those who have to do it.

## Competition

The segmented workforce in parks is not only segmented along the formal lines suggested in chapter 2. When the Central Park Conservancy fired thirty-one workers in January 2009, it did so without warning. Said Francis, who worked as a maintenance technician and Foreman in Central Park for nearly six years:

> When they did the layoff, it was like *boom* they're gone, done. After how many years of working . . . People coming in, what's going on here? And fear in the eyes when they heard this happened. I saw people walking around, didn't know what to do or what to say or what to think or . . . it was like shock and awe.[2]

While regular parks workers bore this as a trauma, and suspected that many of the firings were due to the management's belief that the workers supported the unionization drive then underway, the management of the Conservancy presented the firings as having simply been necessitated by fiscal woes stemming from the financial crisis that erupted less than two years earlier. More important, there was a strong sense both among fired workers themselves, and even among allies of the union, that parks users, donors, and volunteers did not have a clear sense either of the blunt force of the firings or of the grievances that many workers bore against the Conservancy's management. A good many of those grievances were captured by Francis's view that management and lower-level workers did not work together:

> [I]t seems like it's a segregated company . . . You go to say hello to a supervisor and they turn *their* head like they don't want to know you. And then one day when they feel like saying hello, they'll . . . it's like a mind game. . . . I want it to be an integrated company, where everyone's working together. It's not like a prestige that you got a better position or whatever, it's networking together as a company. Sometimes I feel it's a bunch of cliques just working. It's not the right way to do things . . .

And yet, even if Francis describes what seems to be a rather unforgiving management style at the Central Park Conservancy, he does not

CHAPTER FOUR

describe anything that is fundamentally at odds with the general consequences of the division of labor in other parks workplaces, including public ones. Nor, for that matter, does he describe anything too different from many other workplaces in which less-skilled workers interact with others charged with more complex and administrative tasks. As the sociologist Randy Hodson points out, "In defending dignity and achieving self-realization, workers establish themselves as active agents with some control over their work-lives. Without some minimum control, without dignity, work becomes unbearable."[3] Where control and agency are curtailed, grievances against management disrespect and insults against workers' dignity follow.

Importantly, however, the structure of the division of labor in parks results in different ways in which workers exert everyday control over their work, including competing and cooperating with workers of the same or similar types. The division of labor contracts and the rough matching of work status to tasks means that workers experience competition (and cooperation) at the workplace quite differently, depending on where they are in the organizational hierarchy.

Harlan, the Supervisor we met in chapter 2, told us and our research assistants on more than one occasion about the way in which competition used to work among lower-level parks workers. During one interview, he reached for an old picture of a parks crew on which he served in the late 1980s. "Back then," they had competition for things like t-shirts, hats—little things. But it meant that there was an incentive to pick up more trash, do more work. Another time, he said, "I don't see it as it was fifteen, twenty years ago. Because at that time there was more competition. There was one position and you would have a hundred people for that; now you have one position with only ten people for that. We used to have fun competing. There was a reward at the end." In other words, even though there were more people potentially qualified to get promotions, the competition for picking up more trash, for example, was one that both motivated workers to work more and that reduced the tedium of the work. The competition itself became "fun." This is a lot like Michael Burawoy's famous observation about work games in a machine-tools factory in his landmark *Manufacturing Consent*.[4] And one important aspect of these games is that they are played among equals who have developed a sense of mutual trust. If they have not, it cannot be fun; it stops being a game.

But Harlan also misrecognizes the structure of the workplace, and hence, of competition, to some degree, though he does note that it has changed over the last twenty years. The people now picking up the garbage are not CPWs, and few new APSWs have been hired, especially since many districts now have CPWs who drive the light packers (naturally, for less money). Instead, the people picking up garbage—and even working with APSWs on the heavy packers—are mostly JTPs. To the extent that *they* compete, they do so with higher stakes and lower chances of success (the 100-to-1 ratio of lower- to higher-level parks workers Harlan cited was an exaggeration). The question is not one of promotion but of getting a full-time job, or getting the opportunity to work overtime, and making ends meet on very low incomes. Finally, JTPs compete with people with whom they have not been working long enough to develop trust.

In Central Park, we heard of a different kind of competition, one that more explicitly comes from above. Moses regularly worked with Jackson, and they regularly helped each other out. They complained that their supervisor wanted workers not to cooperate with each other:

Moses: But if we ask for, if a person asks for help, give them help! Now, but he don't want to do that. You gotta stay in your area. You can't help your fellow worker. Fuck him! So if my fellow worker is out on lunch, I'm not going into his section, because you told me you don't want me over there. What do you want? You want me to go over there, keep a check on his area, or not? What do you want?
Maud: Because they will ask you sometimes to go, to check . . .
Moses: Yes. We already know that! That's why Jackson and I didn't pay him no mind. If Jackson needed help, and my section, my area was pretty well in shape, I'd go over there and help him! I don't care what you say. He needs help!

The idea that one worker should blithely let another one—even a friend—fail at doing his job up to the expectations of supervision is typical of workplaces in which working together to get a job done is prized less than individualized evaluations. It also clearly reflects a management style that is geared toward undermining collective identification and action among workers, even when this might result in benefits to the park.

It was not just the fired workers from the Central Park Conservancy who told us this. In other ways, we found that individualization of workers and their being put into competition with each other was part of a more general discourse found even in the JTP orientation. As Star, a former JTP worker, told us about her experience in the mid-2000s:

Yeah, there was a lot of conflict amongst JTPs, because of gossiping and being such a small space that everybody worrying about each other's business, and just, and

CHAPTER FOUR

they tell you too, like keep to yourself, don't try to get too friendly with people, because they will put your business out . . . and that's with everywhere, but it seems that it manifests worse in this situation, because they talking about that girl, that girl, talking about this one, she stole this, they stole that . . . always something going.

That JTPs were told to keep to themselves recognizes that to a large extent, competition on the level of work-related tasks was secondary to competition around other matters. As we will see, below, much of this competition occurs within the favor system that governs a good deal of the JTP, WEP, and conservancy workforces.

### Sources of Authority

Moses, among the more outspoken Central Park Conservancy workers who was fired in January 2009, gave an example of what was ultimately an unspoken conflict with his manager that shows how authority is constituted at the workplace. Importantly, it does not matter whether one agrees or disagrees with Moses's or his Coordinator's approach. Instead, what is important is the question of legitimacy and whether it turns on official positions or the knowledge of the job.

John: Were you ever asked to do things that you refused to do, or you thought you shouldn't have to do, or you thought it was really other people's job to do or anything like that?
Moses: No. But my philosophy was this. If you ask me to do something, and I know it's wrong, I will do it, and then when it hit the fan, make sure you take that weight.
John: Like can you give an example of something that . . . ?
Moses: Well, let's see. If you ask me to take some barricades. Bethesda Fountain. You ask me to take five barricades and cut Bethesda Fountain off, OK? Fine. I'm gonna take five barricades, knowing five barricades is nowhere near nothing to cut all the entrances off to Bethesda Fountain. I know that. I'm gonna take five barricades—put it up on the entrance. OK? Now, I know that's wrong, but I didn't refuse the order to take the five barricades.
John: What would happen if you said, "Five barricades aren't gonna do it"?
Moses: Well, really, I don't think, nothing. But I would try to explain, but if you still told me to take five barricades, fine, I'll take five barricades. I would explain to you, "Five barricades is not enough to cut that off." "*I said* . . ." Done. I'll take five barricades. . . . That's it. Then I'm gonna leave. Then when you call me

again, tell me about the barricades, I said, "You told me to take five barricades and cut it off. I did. I didn't refuse no order. I didn't refuse what you told me. This is what you told me, this is what I did." "Did you know that was wrong?" "Yup." "Then why didn't you say something?" "Would you have listened to me? You ain't been listening to us. So I didn't say nothing." I knew it would come back to him. Somebody over the top of him would have jumped straight on it. Because it was not done, the work was not done. Normally, you have to use common sense. Ever since you've been there, you've been doing things wrong. We going by what you say. Who can you fault for that? Yourself. You can't fault the worker. You won't listen to the worker. You want it done your way. So we gonna do it your way, knowing it's wrong.

We found this clash of principles of authority everywhere. Recall that Harlan complained that supervisors drawn from areas other than the Maintenance and Operations unit of the Parks Department "didn't know how to clean a bathroom." On top of this, however, he emphasized the importance of higher-level workers passing on their knowledge of the job to those working under them: "Everything I learned, I learned from someone else."

Similarly, arguments among workers—including between JTPs and crew chiefs—can and often do occur after workers are on the job for several months and develop their own understandings both of the job and of the authority structures in the workplace. Often, these arguments turn on the question of who does how much work and to what standard. There is, on the part of lower-status workers, a strong feeling that higher-status workers, including CPWs and crew chiefs, sometimes leave the work to them. Samantha, a JTP in Queens, told us:

Samantha: We work with CPWs where they do no work. We end up doing all the work. We do all the work. And it's hard work. It's not easy work. They get the big bucks for doing nothing, right? I mean, everyone will tell you here, the guy that just came in . . . he's fifty-eight years old, he does more work than the CPW, three put together.
Maud: Really?
Samantha: Yes. He works from the time he comes in to the time he leaves. I always feel sorry for him.
Maud: Is he a JTP?
Samantha: Yeah, like us. And it's sad, because they know he works hard, they know he works good, but they like people like that. I work with George, because he's a good worker. He doesn't let you do everything. He helps. They have others who let you do everything.

CHAPTER FOUR

Recall Raymond from chapter 2, the Central Park Conservancy worker who complained that some of his supervisors had "soft hands" and that their degrees were not always suitable for understanding the work they were supervising. Raymond argued that knowing how to assist workers, to "stand by them and sweat with them," in fact put these managers at a disadvantage with upper management relative to their less hands-on peers. Raymond's complaint is a rebuke to the idea that managing is itself a set of skills that can be applied broadly without necessarily knowing about the work one is managing. Of course, there are common elements of organizations across contexts, and managers cannot always work alongside their subordinates. Raymond's complaint contrasts a factory model of management with a craft model based on apprenticeship and escalating responsibilities for the whole service provided, and in which the distance between supervisors and staff is reduced by joint work and experience. There is no reason to believe that municipal services should be like a factory and not like a craft.

As if to underscore the same point, but in the publicly managed parks, Harlan began to explain what happens when it snows in playgrounds jointly operated with schools:

But the main thing is [pointing to the phone] *this*. When the phone rings, these guys panic. And the principals call the Managers and start yelling, and the Managers call us and start yelling. But we just don't have the people, and we don't know how many people we'll have on a given day. Like today, we have five out of twenty-four JTPs. Prior to 1991—you had the Laborers. They knew how to get a job done, from A to Z.

In this situation, Harlan says, "I pick up a shovel."

This kind of legitimation of authority is repeated in daily interactions, too. During one of our visits to the park where Harlan's headquarters were, he joked with a Gardener, who was mopping and cleaning the bathroom. "You're paid too much to mop floors." The Gardener responded, "I've seen you pick up a shovel. I see you do work."

Similarly, Julia, a PS1 in a Manhattan park, clearly valued the reputation she had with the workers who work under her supervision. She told us

one of the best compliments, I consider it a compliment, is when I first came here, we had a water main break . . . so we had to call this other company to come in and everything, and one of the guys said, "This is the Supervisor over there. This is Julia," and the guy went to shake my hand, and he realized his hands were dirty, and . . . he pulled back, and my guy said, "It's OK, she gets down and dirty like us, you can shake her hand, dirty or not!" Like, OK, I'm cool. So that made a big difference.

Nevertheless, the dominant view of authority—from the point of view of successive parks commissioners—could not have been more different. Henry Stern, the commissioner under Mayor Ed Koch from 1983 to 1989 and again under Mayor Rudolph Giuliani from 1994 to 2001, explained his recruitment strategy to us by talking about hiring graduates from a range of colleges, including Ivy League and historically black colleges and universities, to work in parks:[5]

John: And what kinds of positions did you hire . . . ?
Henry Stern: We started paying $22,000. And they were assistants. They were supernumeraries, factotums, aides, assistants, analysts. Whatever we needed in the office.
John: So you brought them in for the office . . . Did they ever go out in the field?
Henry Stern: Yes. A lot of them were promoted, and some of them chose careers in the field, and some of them are park managers today. They got an internship and residency in the field. But the basic, we have very high standards, and they answered letters, they set up appointments, they . . . they acted as aides to the commissioner. I got a letter and I'd give it to them to answer, to make the correct decision for the situation. They had no park experience. So we ran the business. That was their real training.
John: And that was preferable to bringing people in from the field?
Henry Stern: We can't bring people in from the field. There was a reason they were in the field rather than in the house. And that is because that was their ability. They, we always wanted to bring people in from the field, and whenever we found one, we would encourage him or her. But there were very few.[6]

Similarly, Adrian Benepe, the commissioner under Mayor Bloomberg for the period for which we conducted the research for this book, described Stern's predecessor under Mayor Koch, Gordon Davis, as "brilliant," in part because

. . . he took guys, he took people who had degrees, graduate degrees, management, had been in various places . . . And they were pretty young when they started out, and they came out and he put them into the various borough commissioner jobs . . . So he did that. The other thing he did was appoint park administrators for Central Park and for Prospect Park, so Betsy Barlow and Tupper Thomas. Again, to sort of have one person in charge of a whole park and look at it holistically. Because otherwise in Central Park, you have the chain of command for maintenance and operations, another chain of command for say horticulture, and security . . . it's like, and nobody looking . . . nobody overseeing what kinds of capital projects get done. So the first time they had sort of a holistic view of how to run a major park. So he did that. I wouldn't be here but for his creation of the Park Rangers. Park Rangers didn't exist when he came in, and he created the Park Rangers. He wanted to have uniformed ambassadors to the public who would both for the first time in many years establish that there were some rules for how to use the park and also be a sort of very diplomatic ambassadors to the public.

To this day, Park Rangers and others hired during Gordon Davis's tenure as commissioner are highly placed in the Parks Department. The overarching idea is that management authority stems from a different skill set than is gained from the ground up at the worksite. Authority in this version stems from an overall ability to strategize around the needs of the park, to be a visible face of the organization to the public, and to manage workers according to the maintenance and operations needs of the park and to the perception of those needs by the public. To put it differently, the source of authority is a kind of power that may be imposed upon workers, rather than stemming from knowledge of the work itself. Because the knowledge required of this kind of authority is of a different order than the on-the-ground knowledge of the workers, it is understood to merit deference in its own right. Stern's suggestion—perhaps a little too strongly suggesting that mere workers cannot rise above their station—nevertheless indicates that one should not even expect regular parks workers to be able to develop holistic views of parks maintenance and operations, even if they have worked their way up through its various jobs.

### Paternalism, Favors, and Favoritism

One result of the two principles of authority present at parks worksites is that, frequently, workers—at whatever level—with one understanding of authority will experience the exercise of another kind of authority as essentially arbitrary. This is not a question of there being completely divided and insular normative communities of "bottom-ups" or "top-downs." Instead—and one can well imagine this from Moses's story of the barricades—those in authority will often experience the actions of those below them as pig-headed, short-sighted, or simply arbitrarily hostile. Those who pride themselves in knowing the work will question authority when it does not take workers' own knowledge into account, and they will often take issue with the constituted authorities for not treating workers with dignity and respect.

Nevertheless, there is arbitrary and there is arbitrary. It is one thing to give authority to supervisors and managers based on the assumption that it rests on a kind of holistic knowledge of management instead of on the practical knowledge of specific tasks. Indeed, the entire idea that one can learn management rests on this very idea. It is another thing altogether—though still frequently related—to encourage management practices that set the manager or supervisor so far above other workers in terms of their power in the workplace that management becomes an exercise in personal control over the workplace. Here, the decision to implement workplace rules of all kinds becomes idiosyncratic to the personal judgment manager him- or herself. Management often becomes the very opposite of the rational system overseen by holistic thinkers, instead a system of favors conferred by superiors on their subordinates. And workers often react to this in anger. In Central Park, Moses echoed the sentiment of others on his crew about his Coordinator:

Between him and I, it was personal. You know why? Because I wouldn't not bow down to him. I'm not bowing down to you. You don't know as much as me. And I'm older than you! OK? Let's put it there. I'm older than you! You not gonna treat me like this. I don't care what your title is or who you are, and I told him one time, the way you speaking to me, don't nobody speak to me like that but my mother and father, and the only person that can do it now is my mother, because my father's no longer here. So don't talk to me in that type of way. Simply fact. You see, the whole thing is, it got to the point with the Conservancy, there's no respect for the workers any more, especially among the Supervisors and the Coordinators.

Jackson told us:

And there was quite a few Foremens, one or two Foremens and a couple of Coordinators, Supervisors, that I didn't speak to, because when I first started, "Good morning! How you all doing?" Especially at 79th St. Yard, "Good morning, how you doing!" Martin, he wouldn't say nothing. Frank Reich, at first, he wouldn't say nothing. It got to the point where I'm being respectful, "Good morning, good morning," and they don't say . . . Well, you know what? I don't stand up to that. I ain't wasting my time.

CHAPTER FOUR

If paternalism involves "favors to win," some proportion of workplace relations, especially between supervisors and the irregular workers in the parks, is based on the personal exercise of power in conditions of extreme inequality. The perception of favoritism among workers is common, and the potential for abuse significant. The perception of favoritism existed among workers in the Parks Department worksites as well as conservancy worksites, frequently about the treatment of other workers and sometimes, too, about decisions made by worksite managers and supervisors about hiring and promotion.

In the Central Park Conservancy, among the fired workers we interviewed there was a strong sense that their Coordinator had gotten his promotion because he was at once vehemently anti-union, enthusiastic about finding fault with the crew, and—in their estimation—consequently close to his superiors. Their coworker, whom they expected to be promoted, had more years on the job (but was not the most senior among them), got along well with others, and was popular among the crew. A typical complaint came in Jackson's words:

Yeah, like I said, he got that position, what everybody [on the crew] felt [was] that he was not the right person for that position. He was not. The one person, if you gonna give that position to anybody, give it to the person that deserves it. All of us felt that was one guy that actually deserved that position. Bill deserved that position more than anybody. Bill deserved that position. But by this guy being your snitch, OK, let's call a spade a spade, by this guy being your snitch, you give him the position.

Another worker, who had not been fired, told us:

I'm at my wits' end at this place . . . I wanted fairness for everybody. When you have a crew that's supposed to be an integral part of Central Park and . . . you take preferences . . . you pick your favorites, and the people don't feel like they're treated that way. You can see in their eyes and the face, you know. . . . So that's how he got his position. Who's over me, and I was there longer than him. And I worked really hard! So he said to Ernest, it doesn't matter if you're the hardest worker in the park, if they like you, that's what matters.

This kind of favor system is exacerbated by the fact that Conservancy managers do not necessarily understand the system the way that at least some of the workers under them do. From both "above" and "below," we heard that workers were free to take issues they have with their supervisors to the human resources department or even to the top management of the Conservancy. The top managers of the park told us that they had an "open-door policy"; this was echoed even by workers who were fired or unhappy. And it was made clear to the workers again after the union drive started. One worker reported that the president of the Conservancy said, "My door is always open! If you need anything, mine and [the vice president's] door is always open! Just come right on in and tell us!" Nevertheless, where this personal openness occurs in an overall environment where workers do not necessarily believe that they are being treated equally, fear supervisors whom they think evaluate their work unfairly, and do not trust that things said in confidence will remain isolated from networks of managers, the effect may be to exacerbate the sense of threat, rather than mitigate it. If workers feel as if their pay levels and chances of promotion are dependent on the goodwill of a boss whose managers may or may not show goodwill, it makes for a distrustful and uneasy work environment. Seen from the other side, one top manager worried that "If we get a union here, I won't be able to treat my guys as individuals anymore."

Outside of Central Park, we also found allegations of favoritism. To be sure, Supervisors have a great deal of power, especially because of their roles in setting work schedules and evaluating workers. And it can be complex, from the point of view of workers. Samantha, the JTP in Queens who complained that CPWs often let JTPs do all the work, told us:

Samantha: Yeah. They have, it's like favoritism here. If you like me, then we best buddies. So this is favoritism. That's what I call it. And they have some CPW who have certain people they like, and certain people . . . there's a lot of people here that you not gonna like, because they don't want to work, or for whatever reason. So it's different. And if you like somebody—like, we have different crews for different people—then that's your buddy, because you work with them all the time. And that's what I call favoritism . . . Yeah, like, I don't belong with you, so you're not going to treat me the same way you treat your people, right?

Maud: Give me an example?

Samantha: People can come in . . . let's see. OK, let's say if I, someone works this weekend. And we have to work on a weekend, and you don't want to work on a weekend. Your crew chief is going to vouch for you. Oh, she cannot work on weekends because of x, y, and z. That's favoritism. If you have one person that you just want to hang out with . . . you going to do something for that person because that's your chief. And I don't like that, because the rules should be for everyone, not just for certain people.

CHAPTER FOUR

It is precisely the perception of uneven treatment, however, that makes the actual presence of it difficult to analyze. Another JTP from the same district told us the opposite, with the proviso that there is flexibility:

You work every other weekend. So basically, how it's set up is that you're supposed to have an off day within the week, just in case you have personal business that you have to take care of, you're always supposed to have that off day in the week. If it just so happens you would need an alternate day, you can work your day off and take another day that you need. So it works out. They really work with you, and it's really no complaint . . . Because everybody gets to work a weekend. Most jobs, there's some people that don't work weekends. But here, everybody works the weekends, whether you work one Saturday, one Sunday, but it rotates. So it works out for everybody. You don't want to work on Saturday, but you just gotta do what you gotta do.

The point here is that favoritism and personalism are versions of the discretion that inevitably falls to managers between the cracks of the rules that govern a workplace. The rules, alone, would make the workplace unmanageable. In order to supervise and to manage, the responsible staff has to improvise procedures. Nevertheless, improvisation can easily fall into abuse, particularly where the cracks between the rules open into chasms and managers are given too much power. Improvisation can appear unfair if people are treated differently, especially if it seems that different treatment is the result of different ability to advocate for one's interests, and especially if it seems as if greater ability accrues to those with personal connections to others, above them, whose access to status and to managers makes the difference. Even when there are good reasons to treat people differently—say, not to have to fire workers for excessive absences if accommodations can be made to their schedules—not everyone at a workplace will see these reasons or even agree with them.

At the same time, if one is in good favor with one's supervisors, or if Supervisors and Managers *choose* to be compassionate, they can make an enormous difference in the experience of some of the workers who are consigned to the bottom of the hierarchy. And it is appreciated. One JTP worker—just nineteen years old—after telling us about her absent parents, and the no-good father of her son, told us: "Because my life must go on. And me and my son have to eat, you know what I'm saying? So his father and everything else, I don't really care. I don't care. My son is beautiful. I don't care. *I have my Supervisors, if I need anything, my Supervisors is here, and if I need something, I talk to them, and if they can help me, they will help me and I know that."*

Much more important than scheduling in nonconservancy workplaces were questions having to do with overtime, extension of the JTP term, and the possibility of assignment to easier work. The first two, especially, related to the ability of JTPs to make ends meet and were therefore most closely linked to the different power, status, and financial resources JTPs and permanent workers had when coming into their relations at the worksite. Here, perceptions of favoritism were no less common and no less serious. Indeed, they were more so.

Danny, a former JTP we interviewed early in the project, was discussing the issue of getting overtime for special events when he began to mention favoritism at the park in Queens where he had been stationed on fixed-post.

Danny: Three shifts one day, you know, but we did overtime that day, there was a lot of gray shirts [City Seasonal Aides]. And like JTPs—comp time, overtime, we're not supposed to get that. We get that—it's really rare, you know—we supposed to get that at certain points in time, but they gave it to their favorites, whoever they sleeping with at the time, whoever they promise something to or they owe a favor to or whatever . . .

John: So . . . you mentioned that people got overtime depending on who they slept with and who they were sleeping with. Is that really going on?

Danny: Yeah!

John: And who is in charge of allocating the overtime, giving the overtime hours?

Danny: You had Supervisors, you had park Managers, you know, and then some that didn't even have nothing, they have nothing to do with it, they wasn't sleeping with nobody, but the people that wanted overtime for the upper folks, had to go to them to get overtime, and that was they friend . . . Those that was doing favors for other people was doing it. In fact, at the end, I was promised to get overtime with cutting grass, and because [the CPW I worked with] thought I was sleeping . . . sleeping with the other girl that he was trying to sleep with, he took me off the overtime shift. Like, literally he took my name off the list. And every time I went to check on the overtime, my name wasn't on the list because he kept thinking I was sleeping with that girl I was telling you about. I'm telling you, now it seems crazy, but . . .

. . . but five years later, a story broke in the New York *Daily News* about the suspension of two Parks Supervisors on Randall's Island, who held

CHAPTER FOUR

parties in a back room, where JTPs were encouraged to strip and pole dance. The *News* reported:

> The clandestine parties were held in a so-called "boom-boom" room at a city-owned facility on Randalls [sic] Island. And the seasonal workers who "got on the pole" were rewarded with additional work or permanent jobs, sources told The News. . . .
>
> There was never a direct order from [the supervisors] for the women to participate, according to the female staffers who took their complaints public. But the seasonal workers get asked back for jobs or offered permanent positions based on the recommendations of [the supervisors], the workers said.[7]

This sort of favoritism is well known in the department and arose more frequently in our interviews than we initially expected.

## The Sexual Economy of Parks Workplaces

We interviewed Star, the former JTP worker quoted earlier, quite late in our research. As with Henry, we found her through a referral from a poor-people's advocacy organization. Star had been through JTP in 2006 in the Bronx. When asked if there were any issues that came up with men and women working together, she told us

> Well, what I seen was, it was a lot of, promising of "Yeah, I can keep you in, I can get you in," and it seemed like these females was tempted by . . . "If I go with you, or you have more money than I at this point, so you either taking care of me in the lunch lines, or you taking care of me, buying me things, so I getting sneakers or buying me clothes or what, so thinking, I'm having a relationship with this man, I'm gonna have a better chance of getting hired than you."

Star's interview suggests that there is a lot more to sexual harassment in parks workplaces than the almost baroque type described in the *Daily News* exposé. The problem is that it is not a matter of one or two lecherous Supervisors—bad individuals—but of a workplace economy in which the severe poverty of a majority of women workers is brought into contact with the *relative* affluence and security of many male supervisors who have direct authority over decisions that can affect the ability of the women to get access to material goods and stability for themselves and their families. It is known that people with access to few other resources sometimes turn toward the exchange of sexual services for favors, but the peculiar expansion of WEP and JTP in the

Parks Department has led to the *expectation* on the part of many—including, apparently, POP trainers—that this will occur. The response is to assume that the JTP women will come into the workplace looking to hook up with a permanent employee and to warn them that this is a bad idea because, in effect, men are unreliable and only want one thing. Accordingly, a nineteen-year-old JTP in Brooklyn told us:

Because as they explain it to us in orientation, that we only here for six months, you know what I'm saying? And the supervisors, they see different people all the time. Your days off, like when you not there, somebody else is coming in, know what I'm saying? And a lot of the girls, they think that oh, they getting some attention from the supervisor, they try to get ahead or think they gonna get over or whatever, whatever their intentions are for it . . . I don't know, but nothing really good comes out of that. I mean, it's rare you gonna meet a supervisor, get married or something, I mean, lead on with that, but come on, what's the chances of that? So it would be a bad idea. Because then you think you're the girl, and then the next thing you know, it's another girl, and you wondering . . . but it ain't all about you, because you wanted to be somebody else. So imagine a supervisor that's been working for four years, and how many girls he's been with throughout that time. No. It's never a good idea to involve business with pleasure anyway. It's never a good idea. So those companies that do enforce the no-relation policy, I think that is a good idea, because it always brings conflict and problems.

Marie, a CPW in Manhattan, described a situation in the Bronx when she had been a JTP and a male CPW had started to rub up against her when showing her the "right way" to use a broom. In this situation—and in most others—the most immediate recourse for women who feel harassed is transfer to another district. We have not heard of women having faced particular problems in getting transfer requests honored, so it seems as if the Parks Department knows this is happening and deals with it by focusing the remedy on the victim, rather than on the perpetrator.

Many times, JTPs just try to avoid situations in which they suspect that supervisors will expect them to exchange sexual favors for better treatment or for the expectation that they will be hired (an unlikely proposition to begin with). An excerpt from an interview with Tanisha, a former JTP who was in Harlem from 2006 to 2007, explains:

John: Would you ever go on mobile?
Tanisha: I didn't like mobile, because we were told to go to other parks to clean up and I was told a few horror stories.

CHAPTER FOUR

John: So did you—were you able to say that you didn't want to go on mobile and avoid it?

Tanisha: No. The director actually didn't want me to go mobile.

John: Because?

Tanisha: Because of the horror stories.

John: What kind of horror stories?

Tanisha: I was told that some of the females were given the ability to have sex with the crew chiefs and stay in the park houses at individual parks, and didn't have to work.

John: Mm-hm.

Tanisha: So.

John: I mean, we've heard the same horror stories.

Tanisha: I did not want that possibility.

John: And did you have any sense that those horror stories were real and corroborated, or . . . ?

Tanisha: I saw a mattress, so I believed it.

John: A mattress. In a park house?

Tanisha: Yeah.

Another CPW—also in Manhattan—told us:

I used to work for a Supervisor [in Harlem]. I didn't get along with him. Things with these Supervisors, they're bad. Every day are going up to JTPs, trying to screw with them . . . There's a lot of that going on. Me personally, he sees me as a young guy, whatever, and he sees me sometimes, I come and I look nice or whatever, and he sees me as a threat. Let me tell you, this is a picture of my girlfriend. They're workers, they work with me, I don't want anything with them. Most of these girls have drug problems, or they on welfare. Like, what are they going to do for me? These guys, they don't care. Pretty much go for anything. The thing is, me and [the Supervisor] now have a good relationship, but he tells me about his little rendezvous with these girls. I don't want to hear about it. I just listen to him because he's my boss. I really don't want to hear about it. But I could use that against them if I wanted to, but I'm not.

The same CPW, however, also suggested that JTPs themselves will bring sexual harassment allegations against supervisors or other workers if the JTPs do not get what they are after. Referring to the movie *Disclosure*, in which a woman sues a man for sexual harassment, even though it is she who has harassed him, he says:

They actually want to do things with these people, and then if they don't get whatever they want to get, it will be like a sexual harassment. Mind you, if you already did any of that, it's not sexual harassment anymore. Because you did whatever you wanted to do. A person gets on their knees, you got on your knees voluntarily, it's not like he had a gun to your head, anything like that, then you gonna charge sexual harassment, how can you? . . . I mean, it's kind of like, Michael Douglas, almost like that.

While it does appear that sexual exchanges for favors do occur in the Parks Department with some regularity, it is also the case that JTPs and supervisors are widely understood to be equal parties in the exchange. Indeed, in *Disclosure*, the woman who sues her male victim for harassment is his boss.

Nearly nobody appears to acknowledge that the problem is a direct outcome of the *unequal* relations of domination at the workplace. Supervisors and Managers do not have the power to create workforces that can easily and predictably do their assigned jobs, but they do have the power to decide how the workplace is experienced by those below them. As both those who spoke about the sexual economy and the nineteen-year-old JTP suggested, they can have real power over the lives of JTPs, in large part because JTPs *cannot make a stable living in their jobs*. Added into the equation are layers of structural inequalities in workplace relations.

The age-old tropes of the sexually promiscuous African American woman and of the "madonna/whore" pair (the mother working for her kids as opposed to the promiscuous woman) get put together here with poverty, hard physical work, low pay, and the instability of a temporary appointment. If the sociological term of "social structure" has any meaning at all, it suggests the patterned, historically formed social arrangements that lead to sets of shared expectations about social interactions among people in specific types of social situations. It seems clear that the sexual economy of parks workplaces is based on the interaction between paternalist domination at the worksite and the broader structural inequalities that are present among workers at the worksite.

Thus, when, just after we were shut out of doing more worksite interviews, a top Parks Department manager with some oversight responsibility over POP denied to our faces that there were any problems with sexual harassment—she later mentioned generally that there was EEO training in the program—we were surprised that we would be taken for such fools and that Parks Department brass felt as if sexual harassment could not be publicly acknowledged. Even saying "It's a problem we're working on solving" would have been a good sign.

CHAPTER FOUR

**Pushing Back**

While there certainly appears to be some truth that women in JTP sometimes make advances toward men who work above them in the workplace hierarchy, this just points to the general proposition that within a highly structured environment, people still make choices—but these choices often reinforce the power relations rather than challenge them.

The agency of people maintaining the parks may be found most clearly, however, when they do things that resist the pressures of the workplace to carve out those moments of self-realization and control that are essential to dignity at work. At a very basic level, this often involves answering back to supervisors when they ask for something that the worker does not think is right, either for the accomplishment of the job or from a moral standpoint. But it can also involve calling in the union or, in the case of the Central Park Conservancy, supporting a union drive and refusing the implicit idea that Conservancy workers and municipal workers should be at odds (which, though not an official policy, is often suggested by supervisors, and certainly follows the justification of the Conservancy contract to run the park with its own, nonunionized staff).

The fired workers in Central Park told us repeatedly about confrontations with a Coordinator whose attitude toward them they experienced as an affront to their dignity. Francis, for example, told us:

And there's many times when [the Coordinator] would come out there, raining cats and dogs, he want to speak to you, he would call you over to the truck and open up the window less than an inch and talk to you through the window. He tried that with me . . . and I walked away. I said, "That's not happening. Either you getting out of the truck, or I'm getting in. You don't want to get out? Fine." I left. See, I know—excuse my language—I know that pisses him off. Because he can't control me. How do you get a person that comes from a drug program, put him in a supervisory position, and that supervisor treats the workers like it's a drug program? We told him one day . . . "[T]his is not a drug program. You not going to treat us like that."

For these workers, their support for the union drive was directly related to their perceptions of favoritism and to repeated slights against their dignity. They complained bitterly about being told not to help each other out, to let each other fail, and about their sense that their supervisor opposed any expression of independence on the job. Their reception to the union also gave expression to their perception that little separated Central Park Conservancy workers from regular city workers. Francis told us:

When I got with the Conservancy, as the years went on, I told the city guys, "You know something, I get along with y'all better than I do with the Conservancy workers." Because the city workers had a completely different attitude, OK? An attitude where they know we all in this park doing the same thing. Trying to keep the park clean, trying to maintain the park, trying to do this, trying to do that. But our biggest problem is the supervisors. They try to pit the Conservancy workers against the city workers. . . . He used to bad mouth them. "Oh, those city workers, they don't do nothing, this, that, the other, they left this, they left that . . ." We'd just look at him like he was crazy. Come on, we got to work with these guys!

To be sure, even city workers sometimes saw that Conservancy workers worked harder than they did. Keith, a current city worker in Central Park, told us:

There are some people who probably look at it like that, like Conservancy probably look at . . . us, as, being that we city, we lazy, whatever like that. Got nothing to do with being lazy. You gotta take your work ethics to a certain extent, because after a while your body be hurting . . . You want to keep constantly just getting out there, going crazy, going crazy, then what? I'm not going to pull my back out. I'm still young! I would do it to where, if I feel like my body say "It's over," it's over. I gotta take a break. I'll come back to it later.

But both Keith and Harlan, one of many Supervisors who had once worked in the park, tempered this observation with the idea that Conservancy workers do not have a union. Keith, who turned down an offer to work for the Conservancy, justified his decision: "Because one, they didn't have no union to back them up; two, they could fire you for any little reason at all." Harlan simply said, "But they have no rights."

A Foreperson in the Conservancy, however, told us that rights or not, Conservancy workers knew how—as workers do in many places—to catch a break when they needed it. Speaking of the summer after the firings, when workers throughout the park had to take some evening shifts every week, he told us:

I think this summer was maybe one of the toughest years for attendance, because people were just getting burnt out so easily. So I don't know, at least in our sec-

CHAPTER FOUR

tion, I think people calling out sick just because they were just flat exhausted and like, I know if I don't get enough sleep a couple days in a row, I just get run down and get a cold, like that kind of thing, and if you're constantly doing that, you're gonna get sick more, because you're not taking care of yourself, you're just worried about, "Have to get up! Go!" And you're not necessarily eating the best stuff, so . . . That's at least what I saw. I don't know if it's prevalent throughout the rest of the park, but yeah. It was definitely people taking off, like one day here or there, just to recuperate.

Nevertheless, the larger issue here is that while by all accounts Conservancy workers were not well received in the early years by municipal parks workers who saw their numbers dwindling and their work belittled by Conservancy management, by the time we did our interviews, support for the union and camaraderie between Conservancy workers and city workers was a sign of a kind of resistance to Conservancy management.

Outside of Central Park, we heard several stories about workers calling in the union to mediate conflicts. A good number of the complaints we heard about were about out-of-title work, and particularly about unpaid crew-chief work by CPWs. One Supervisor, who had once been active in the union, told us that he sometimes holds out a complaint form and says to a worker he has just asked to do out-of-title work: "I am *not* giving you this grievance form." Nevertheless, the choice *not* to grieve is more common and more consistent with the conduct of the park. As one PS1 explained to us about his days as a CPW supervising JTPs, "You want to make a good name for yourself. That's not a bad way to go about doing it. Got a lot of disgruntled people in this agency, and I didn't want to be one of those disgruntled people. I saw myself as trying to advance."

One area in which workers sometimes clearly went against the wishes of supervisors was in the matter of clearing homeless people out of the parks or getting them to follow parks rules about sleeping on benches and the like. Here, they both rely on a certain kind of "park sense" that goes against superiors' orders, and upon their own moral compasses. Harlan spoke of his Manager's wanting him to get a longtime homeless resident of a major park in his district to leave:

He's been living here forever. The manager wants them out. *I'm* not going to get rid of him . . . The guy argued back saying that he'd been here for years. And you have to tell him that he's not allowed to live there permanently, and he has to get out. And to tell the truth, most of what he had was just junk. He took what he could, 'cause he knew and I knew that he'd be back . . . The guy seems rational. Just poor.

He continued, saying that his Manager wants to bring a boulder up to seal off the cave where the man is living. "Where am I going to get the heavy equipment to bring a boulder up there? It's the City's problem . . . they should have the housing and services . . . Where is he going to go?"

Similarly, Marta, a former JTP PEP officer, told us that she would be given the job of clearing homeless people from parks as a punishment for speaking up: "Every time I would file about something, they would punish me, and give me homeless. That was my punishment. They thought that was my punishment. But they didn't know it worked for my advantage, because I just called my kids, to give them food." She detailed how she would call her children to bring homeless people food—since she could not be seen doing so—and recounted one episode with a partner to whom she was assigned.

Marta: It's like, no . . . so one day, this man, and he has a sleeping bag, and he's laying down on his sleeping bag, and one of the officers started hitting him with the nightstick, and I go . . .
John: Which officer? A PEP officer?
Marta: Yeah. And I go, "Hello? Why do you gotta do that?" "Like, he's sleeping, he needs to get up." I was like, "Excuse me sir? Could you get up?" He goes, "You don't gotta be that nice." I was like, "Do you know he's a human like you and me?" And I was like, "Sir, excuse me, are you OK?" He goes, "Yeah, I'm OK. I'm just tired." And I go, "Well, darling, could you get up and sit on the bench, please, because you can't be here right now." And he goes, "Oh, I was just trying to rest a little." And I was like, "Just get up and have a seat, please. Thank you, I would appreciate it." So he got up and sat down, but he was still, he was agitated, because the man was poking him, you know? How could you just be poking at a person? And . . . so I apologized for my partner, I apologized for him, because that's not a way of conducting himself, but I apologized for him. So he walked away, he was like, "You don't have to apologize for me," and I was like, "Well you know something? I have a problem with that. I really have a problem with that. Do you have a place for them to go? Because if you have a place for them to go, then you can throw them out. Otherwise, if you don't have a place or resources for them?" So he called my captain. He called my sergeant. So we had a meeting. You know. We had, so we all sat together, and I told my sergeant, "Look, I'm gonna tell you something. I have a problem with it. And if you need to fire me, you can fire me right now, but I'm not gonna do it. If I don't have a

CHAPTER FOUR

resource for them, if you're not gonna give me any pamphlets that I could call in an emergency number for them, if they need shelter or something, I'm not gonna throw people out of the park because you want me to throw them out of the park. Because . . . the commissioner wants them out of the park? No. Because the commissioner wants the parks to look nice? And no homeless people? We got a crisis of homeless people in New York City. Did you know that?" So he was like, "You know what? That's so true. Here." He gave me all these papers. He said, "Did you see this? These are all emergency numbers. Put it in your phone. Anytime that you see anything, you do it. You call for them, if they say 'Yes, I want something,' you go for it."

In spite of her supervisor's humane actions, Marta's story is also one of retaliation: she is given the job of getting rid of homeless people from parks (not one relished by many workers) as a punishment for filing grievances. Similarly, for every Supervisor who gives a grievance form to a CPW doing crew-chief work, there are others who will threaten the CPW with a transfer to a difficult district for speaking up. Plaintiffs in the *Wright v. Stern* discrimination lawsuit also complained about retaliation, which took the forms of being passed over for promotion or being moved to a basement. Saying "no" is not something done lightly.

**Initiative and Cooperation**

Unlike factory work, in which the product being made may be a source of indifference to the worker, whether because the worker does not necessarily see the consumer use the product or because the product is just part of a larger, more distributed commodity chain, parks maintenance, while certainly manual labor, is very much service work. Parks workers interact with the public at the worksite, and this interaction is the basis of a great deal of the pride they take in their work and the importance they ascribe to it. One JTP told us that she loves it when the people in the park introduce her as the worker who keeps everything so clean and that she takes special pride in spotless bathrooms. Even when they do not directly interact with members of the public, parks workers often talk about the importance of keeping parks and playgrounds safe for kids and families as a motivation for their work. Marie, a JTP in Queens, was effusive, though fairly typical: "I love it. I'm a kids person. I love it. Everything that I do for the park is not for me. It's for the park. The park is for the kids. The maintenance of the park, keeping the park clean, the bathroom clean, all for the kids. You can see the kids' smiles on their faces. All for the kids." Importantly, as with the former JTP PEP officer who called her kids to bring food for the homeless, or for Jackson and Moses in Central Park, who covered each other's areas when they needed help, workers—even at the lowest rungs of a hierarchy—will often take initiative and cooperate with each other in order to be sure that the work gets done.

This initiative and cooperation, while certainly reinforcing the mission of the department, does not necessarily reinforce worksite relations. We saw, earlier, for example, that Jackson and Moses's cooperation was a point of contention with their Coordinator, in large measure because it showed a kind of collective control over workplace decisions that cut the Coordinator out of the loop, however efficacious it may have been for getting work done. It also would upset an individual-level evaluation system in which getting "written up" was common for work left undone.

As in most jobs, cooperation and initiative on the part of lower-level workers is motivated by different things, whether the hope of permanent appointment, a promotion, a raise; loyalty to coworkers; or the inherent joy of doing something well, whatever it is. In parks worksites, workers often told us with pride about their development of knowledge of the job and of experience, that they can then apply themselves to their work. Ayline, a JTP in Queens we quoted earlier, told us that she had gotten to the point at which she trains other JTPs:

Mostly . . . I'm on Jeanette's mobile crew. Jeanette's right-hand person on mobile crew. Like if she drops us off and she says she needs this done, she'll tell me and I may have a crew with me, and we just do . . . I make sure that everything gets done. And basically, since I've been here the longest, I basically show the other JTPs how to blow the park, how to weed-whack, how to cut the grass, how to properly clean the bathroom, and things of that nature. How to recognize play equipment that needs to be repaired, things of that nature . . . Basically, I'm helping train them. I like to help out.

To be sure, this is an ideal situation for the Parks Department, in a way: A JTP who is paid far less than a CPW is doing work far beyond her title and is actually performing tasks that a crew chief, with APSW pay, is meant to be doing. And yet, as Harlan told us, his own practice in the park—and the advice he gives others—is to "do the job above yours" in

CHAPTER FOUR

order to increase your mobility within the department. Indeed, Ayline told us that she would like to continue to work in parks:

> I would keep in contact with the people I work with now, yeah, I definitely will. Just to see, because it's a six-month program. I'm hoping that within the six-month time I can get extended to stay on, and hopefully lead into a permanent position with the Parks Department.

The problem, of course, is that in the two years following the interview, the number of CPWs shrank from 1,386 to 980, and fewer than thirty JTPs were promoted into the CPW ranks. We do not know if Ayline was among the lucky few, but the chances were slim, at best.

The gap between what we like about our jobs and what we do not is probably the source of most of our complaints. The hope conferred by things we enjoy—the hope that we might enjoy more things about a job—clashes with the frustrations about those we do not, whether it is a supervisor, pay or benefits, certain tasks, favoritism, or the structural limits on mobility imposed by the organization itself. There are nearly always things to like about a job, though we did interview a few JTPs who disliked almost every aspect of it, or at least most of their coworkers and the work itself. On the other hand, most of our interviewees enjoyed working outdoors, enjoyed the variety of tasks that they were assigned to do, and enjoyed many aspects of interacting with the public. Jeannette, an APSW in Queens, was typical in her view of the joys of parks work, and in describing with humor the occasional discomfort:

> I enjoy working with people. It doesn't bother me to drive a truck. I'll do whatever they ask me to do. I don't have a problem with any of it. I enjoy my job . . . I like being outdoors. Who else gets to say they work outdoors and get to be out in the weather all day? Especially this time of year. But it doesn't bother me in the winter either. Getting soaked now and then doesn't help, you know . . . the other day my boss was calling me Aqua Woman because I was completely soaked. Because it was pouring out we had a park that the sprinkler system, the drain was flooded. It was covered in leaves. So it was like, when I walked in there, came up to here on me. And it was pouring out, so I was soaking head to toe. The next day my underclothes are still wet. So you know . . . but it didn't bother me to do it. You get a little uncomfortable, you get dry clothes, change your clothes, you go back to work. That's what I do.

Francis from Central Park, always eloquent, expressed much of the same thing but pointed to one crucial gap between the joys and frustrations of the workplace:

You're always interacting with people every day. You're always busy, on the move. You're getting work done. So you feel good at the end of the day that you did a day's work. I enjoy it. I enjoy it. But I just don't enjoy the negativity and disrespect. There's no reason for it.

Most workers suffer this gap between positive and negative aspects of their workplaces in relative silence. They may grumble to their coworkers but rarely speak up either for themselves or for others. Whether for fear of retaliation or because of a lack of identification with other workers, due to the difference in status among the many people at a parks worksite, we mainly heard about specific instances of individuals talking back to supervisors, or supervisors telling workers how to avail themselves of the union's help. Solidarity among workers tended to come in the form of cooperation and help in their tasks, but we found little in the way of stories of workers standing up for each other in the face of arbitrary discipline, supervisory mistakes, insults to their dignity, or sexual harassment or depredation. Only in Central Park, where we witnessed what would turn out to be an unsuccessful union drive, did we see this kind of collective endeavor, and most of the leaders of these efforts were fired. Even here, we found another lesson. When workers of different statuses do not work together in the same worksites—or only cross paths casually—it is easy for them to believe the worst about each other. For example, Mark, a Zone Gardener we interviewed in Central Park—one who was new to the park when the union campaign was underway and who was not pro-union—told us that he had a good rapport with the parks management, saying,

Mark: I work hard and I do my job. I don't have a problem with them. There's some guys who grumble and bitch and they're not the best workers, and I see the correlation there. And they seem to also be the ones who are very pro-union.
John: What kinds of things would there be to, I mean, union aside, what kinds of things do people grumble about when they grumble?
Mark: Pay. Some people don't think our benefit package is so great, whether it's the health, the dental, or the—we have an annuity as opposed to a pension. It's sometimes the conditions under which we work.
John: Like what sorts of . . . ?
Mark: Like, it's raining cats and dogs. Yeah. *You work in a park.*

It is true that several of the fired workers had blemished job evaluations, but many had been in the park so long that it is difficult to believe that they were consistently poor, if the agency could hire and fire at will. What is more, none of the workers we interviewed who were pro-union complained about rain, or even about any particular aspect of the work. Few even complained about the pay and benefits; the largest complaint was about having to suffer indignities and their supervisors' favoritism.

## Managing the Worksite

In spite of the abuses we heard about by supervisors at parks worksites —and certainly not excusing them—we conclude this chapter with the observation that in many respects, supervising parks worksites is among the hardest of the tasks we observed. It involves a kind of alchemy, by which supervisors attempt to make gold out of the chronic scarcity of supplies, the instability and material deprivation of the lives of a great proportion of their workforce, and the attendant absences, lateness, and unpredictability. Amid all of this, in the best circumstances and with the best—and nonpredatory—supervisors, they are getting evaluated constantly by the Parks Inspection Program, whose inspectors are trained *not* to take extenuating circumstances into account. In the meantime, they have to resolve conflicts among workers, respond to calls left by the public to operators in the city's 311 phone-in inquiries and complaint line, and, perhaps most important, manage the expectations of dozens of JTPs a year, who have to be motivated, evaluated, and yet also informed that their work for the parks ends in a maximum of six months.

Parks Supervisors, and Managers, are the link between parks worksites and the upper echelons of the department, both at the borough and the citywide levels. This means that they are positioned at the hinge of the principal contradictions of the parks maintenance and operations systems as we have described them, so far. Alvin, a Supervisor we met in chapter 2, gave a colloquy on having to be lenient with JTPs' attendance or lose useful hands in his districts. It is worth quoting his interview at length:

Let's say I have five people working today. OK? And let's say one of my guys comes in, and I smell alcohol on him, OK, for example, right? I have to make a decision. I can look the other way and pretend I didn't smell the alcohol on him, or send him home, which means I have one guy less to help me clean up. OK? Or I have the flip side, I have really really good workers, but they have a bad attendance record. I could fire the guy. After six absences, I could fire him. What do I do? I look the other way. Because this is a real good guy. But he has fifteen absences. If I fire him, then I'm down a really good guy.

In a system in which the rules governing work bear little relation to the satisfactory performance of the job itself, the rules themselves fail in practice. Thus, a significant space opens up for supervisory discretion—discretion about which supervisors themselves are not always pleased. Alvin continued:

And sometimes I feel bad for [the JTPs]. I'll say, listen, tell you what, it's going to be a holiday, you come in, a lot of times I'll look the other way. A lot of the time school's out. I'll say, you know what, bring your kids. Leave them here, let them play in the sprinkler. Because you gotta work. It's tough to have somebody pick between their kids and the job. I'm a father. My kids are grown now, but if my kids were four and five and I got nobody in the world to leave them, what am I going to do? So some of the time I'll say, don't tell nobody that you told [Alvin], because I'll say you're lying, don't tell them I said, but bring them there, I'll leave you in this park, make sure that they don't get involved in anything . . . What am I going to do? It's either that or lose the person, and maybe have to fire her because she has an excessive amount of absences. It's a tough juggling act. And they expect so much from us. All because of this . . . that's all they care about is the [Parks Inspection Program]. . . .

See, let me tell you, John, and this is something that I firmly believe in. The system is designed to fail . . . The reason . . . I've always said, they gotta make up their minds, the City. HRA, Human Resources Administration [the city's welfare department]. I have girls [JTPs] that come here, and they only work, out of a five-day work week, they only work sometimes two or three days. The other two or three days, they have training, GED; maintenance, the guys sometimes have carpentry . . . which is fine. That's fine. But they should make their minds up if they're going to be a priority for [Maintenance and Operations] because apparently they make such a big deal of the cleanliness. Now, if you give me ten people and half of them are out on any given date, then what are you leaving me to do? I have to clean 200 properties with sometimes fifteen, twenty people. It's hit or miss. So what does that do to the overall enthusiasm and motivation of the Supervisors? You're like, I can't clean 200 properties with three or four people, on any given day. It's not good for morale.

So it forces me to lower my standards. And it's a double standard, because my regular employees, I don't tolerate that from them. But I have to tolerate it from JTPs. So it's a double standard. And it's very evident. Because regular workers see what they get away with, and sometimes they throw it in your face, and say "How come . . . ?" "That's none of your business. I expect more. That's what—I expect more of you; you're a civil service worker."

This, of course, also makes his power seem more arbitrary, since he is exercising judgment independently, trying to make the whole system work, while also dealing with PIP and demands from *his supervisors* to do more with less. At the same time, more globally, it shows that he *cannot* treat JTPs as "regular" workers, because if he did, he could not do his own job. He *has* to exercise a kind of paternalist judgment in order to function properly.

Similarly, given the necessity for supervisors and managers to exercise a great deal of judgment about how to enforce policies and rules, both in City-managed and conservancy-managed parks, supervisors can either be helped or threatened by lower-level workers who develop a real sense of their jobs, and sometimes both. They are helped enormously because a JTP who develops a sense of ownership of a park and a clear sense of the work involved can be terrifically valuable. So can a conservancy Grounds Technician. The problem arises when the lower-level workers either have or perceive that they have greater knowledge of the work than the supervisor. Then, supervisors can be threatened, and if they do not know how to trust workers to do their jobs, they will find it difficult to manage in any way *other* than by demanding deference and resorting to favoritism.

It was clear, however, that where supervisors could either claim a long-time knowledge of the work or did not hesitate to "pick up a shovel," they gained more respect from workers than if they did not. Conversely, it is these same supervisors and managers who have the hardest time navigating the long-time culture of the department—and, to a large extent, the conservancies—in which the qualifications for supervision are widely understood to lie outside of a physical knowledge of the work itself. Furthermore, this very negotiation is often felt most immediately through the interactions between Supervisors and Managers, where Supervisors are somewhat more likely to have risen through the ranks of Maintenance and Operations than have Managers, who have sometimes made lateral moves within the department, and often from the Parks Enforcement and Recreation hierarchies within the agency.

Supervisors also have the ability to use their positions to promote cooperation and initiative on the part of the workers they supervise, even though the larger system within which parks workplaces exist is set up in such a way as to discourage it. The long-term failures of the City to offer promotional tests, corrected only because of a lawsuit, for example, meant that promotions could be done on the basis of favoritism, and the churning of welfare recipients through JTP and WEP does little to promote the sort of engagement with the work that would help keep parks maintained at an optimal level. Supervisors' discretion, then, supports the system's actual operation, even as it sometimes helps parks workers to resist its worst features, such as its officially inflexible treatment of JTPs—even amid its historical gutting of the earlier POP program benefits—and its treatment of homeless people as little more than nuisance objects to be removed from public view. Several supervisors—as we saw above—promote cooperation by working alongside their staffs, at least occasionally, to reduce the social distance created by the outsized power they are granted. Even when supervisors do not do this, they may find other ways, even if more consistent with a classic favors system, to try to reduce this distance. Alvin, again, gave us one example:

I know where I am in the hierarchy. I'm a Supervisor in the Parks Department. It's not like I work for the FBI. It's not like this is the NYPD. This is the Parks Department. My head is not so big that I'm not going to talk to you. I came from the ranks. . . . I started as a Park Service Worker. I was fortunate that I was able to study and pass the promotional test. There's a lot of my peers that started with me that have not been able to pass the test because they didn't study or they didn't apply themselves, you know what I mean? So I know where my place is . . . I'm not going to get involved in the white shirt [the uniform of the PS2]. I'm not like that. I relate to them, I say good morning to them, I joke around with them, I throw them pizza parties like for Christmas or for Labor Day; when the season's over, I do a barbeque for them. It doesn't bother me to relate to them. And why should it? I mean, I'm Hispanic myself, my wife cleans houses. My wife doesn't have like an office job that she . . . my wife cleans houses. She works hard for her money. So I'm not like, "I'm here and they're down here." Do you need to make them feel worse than they already feel? No.

Considered from another perspective, however, even Supervisors and crew chiefs who engage in the department's unofficial sexual economy or actively harass JTPs and WEPs are exercising their discretion in ways that pit them against official policy but that, arguably, also help the system to function as it does. Even this misbehavior helps to gain the compliance of some segment of the workforce, compensating for the fact that JTPs and WEPs may not be in the parks workplaces completely voluntarily. Similarly, in the Central Park Conservancy, strong opposition to the union and to any semblance of a collective voice among workers there—and the mass firing of thirty-one people without notice—reinforces the idea that the whole system runs on supervisory discretion and that whatever initiative and cooperation occurs must do so with the blessing of management. Although quite different from the sexual economy in the Parks Department, it is an expression, ultimately, of a more coercive approach to management that avoids the contradictory tugs of more consensual approaches. In other words, those elements of parks workplace relations that we are most inclined to dislike may be as much part of the way the system works as they are part of how it fails.

FIVE

# Public-Private Partnerships

In 1980, three years after the city's crippling fiscal crisis had officially ended, New York City's parks were in terrible condition. Large parks, such as Central Park and Brooklyn's Prospect Park—jewels of the city's parks system designed by Frederick Law Olmsted and Calvert Vaux—were widely understood to be dangerous, and vandalism and disrepair had claimed some of the parks' most widely recognizable features. The victorious "Columbia" astride her chariot on the marble arch at the entrance of Prospect Park had fallen over, almost in symbolic defeat. The Bethesda Fountain in Central Park—a neoclassical plaza designed by the firm McKim, Mead, and White, which also designed Columbia University's grand campus on 116th Street—had been stripped of paint and much of its ornamentation. Bryant Park, behind the New York Public Library, which was an "oasis" for office workers, host to flower shows, and a popular hangout for heroin users, had been reduced to what Mayor Edward I. Koch called "a public urinal."[1]

Within three years, each of these parks would be on its way to some form of private management through agreements with the Parks Department. Gordon Davis, parks commissioner under Mayor Koch, led a major effort to revamp the management of the city's parks system, including decentralizing and devolving significant management responsibilities onto borough commissioners, even while maintaining central control at the Arsenal. It also included experimenting with new forms of parks governance. Among these were privatization and empowerment of new "Parks Administrators" for Prospect and Central Parks, whose job included the founding and maintenance of nonprofit partners for the Parks Department to raise money for, and bring volunteers into, the parks. Bryant Park, by contrast, was almost wholly signed over to the Bryant Park Restoration Corporation—which has now become the Bryant Park Corporation—to revive and run, nearly on its own, with money raised primarily through charges levied on real estate owners in the park's vicinity.

In hearings before the city council in 2013, Veronica White, the parks commissioner for the last years of the Bloomberg administration (2012–2013), cited no fewer than twenty conservancies active in administering New York City's parks under contractual agreements. She distinguished these from "Friends of" groups (even though at least one conservancy uses the name "Friends of" and some groups use the name "conservancy" without having a formal maintenance and operating agreement with the City) that work in parks to coordinate volunteer activities and to raise funds, but which do not have management contracts. According to White, the terms under which the twenty conservancies operate are idiosyncratic to them; there is no standard management contract that even forms the basis for variations in each case.

Historically, this makes sense. It would seem difficult for the Bryant Park Corporation to draw on volunteer resources in a neighborhood that largely consists of office buildings, few residential buildings, and—at the time of its founding—strip clubs and porn theaters; it was similarly difficult for the Prospect Park Alliance to amass the level of philanthropic donations available to the Central Park Conservancy due to the tony surroundings of Central Park. Nevertheless, the Prospect Park Alliance has become expert in drawing on volunteers from the corporate sector, while Bryant Park has done as much as any park to intentionally configure space so as to draw the public into the park and to its concessions. At the same time, questions about the allocation of income generated by concessions (everything from hot dog and other food stands to bike and boat rentals to carousel rides) and special events, capital investments by the City, and the share of municipal employees doing the everyday work of maintenance are not obviously given by the location or history of the parks themselves. Instead, these are the outcomes of complex processes of bargaining, precedent setting, and performances of legitimacy among elites and the local state that have reshaped how parks are governed and that signal larger changes in the conduct of public administration.

## Public and Private in Urban Governance

This chapter moves "up" a level of abstraction from the previous ones. No longer at the level of the worksite exclusively, we now examine the organizational arrangements that shape how the worksites operate. The sociologists Elisabeth S. Clemens and Doug Guthrie, who have recently trained their attention on public-private partnerships, suggest that understanding these arrangements as they really are helps us to make sense not just of our contemporary forms of governance but also of the submerged alternatives, disagreements, contradictions, and areas of ambiguity that characterize them and are part of their formation. They write:

> Despite the fact that volunteerism, charity, and nonprofit organizations seem to be almost everywhere in public policy debates, it has been surprisingly difficult to conceptualize their role in American governance . . . Once relations among government agencies, voluntary or civic associations, and even private firms are placed front and center, their history is transfigured from the development of three distinctive domains to a process of contestation over the legitimacy of organizational forms, their respective jurisdictions, and their interdependencies.[2]

We share this objective in this chapter. By refocusing on questions of work relations at the end of the chapter, we do not take up other issues that have generally been rather more central to debates about privatization in parks, namely, those about how "public" public space is and what "public" even means in concrete, historical terms, when it comes to parks. Yet, from a larger perspective, the variety of public-private partnerships we discuss here begins to make the larger point we raised in chapter 1 about the different ways in which neoliberal urban governance takes hold. It is not only the imposition of market-based policies on previously social-democratic polities (as we might expect from "neoliberalism"), but also diverse arrangements of public-sector cuts, private investment, institutional accommodation, and "mission drift," alongside explicit projects for reorganization, that produce the range of new governance strategies we encounter.

### *Regimes and the Public-Private Boundary*

The distribution of "governance" between public and private agencies is by now a venerable topic of debate for students of urban politics. The debate turns around questions of how power is distributed, who decides what, and what kinds of policies are subject to what kinds of coalitions and with which kinds of players. For example, John Logan and Harvey Molotch's pioneering work in the 1970s and 1980s argued that place-based capital (real estate, utilities, local media, etc.) was most invested in the growth of their particular localities and that place-based capitalists routinely formed the core of urban coalitions. Others, like Mollenkopf, have distinguished between governing coalitions—also often called "regimes"—and electoral coalitions and have highlighted the importance of racial and ethnic coalitions for the latter, which set up some nonelite expectations for the former and often squeeze some concessions from the ongoing processes of intraelite bargaining.[3]

While theorists of urban regimes often talk about the informality of regime arrangements (by definition, one does not have to hold public office to be part of a regime, and networks and trust act as the glue that binds them), conservancies both make them visible—at least in part—and show the variety of ways in which the public and the private are intermixed in practice. To be sure, other bodies charged with governance do, too. Business improvement districts (BIDs) are organizations in a special district designated by the city government as being able to collect an assessment from business and property owners in the district. Typically, BIDs use the money these assessments raise to pay for enhanced private security services or street-cleaning services, which, in turn, enhance the area's appearance for prospective customers of their businesses. The visibility of local business leaders on the boards of BIDs makes clear the presence of private interests in governance and raises the question of whether they are, in urban planning professor Jill S. Gross's words, "the private sector in the public service, or the public sector privatized," neither, or both.[4] Gross further notes that even BIDs differ among each other: the larger, more centrally located ones are typically the focal cases for scholarship and theory about BIDs and their roles, but the ones in poorer areas, and in neighborhoods outside the central business district, will have different kinds of representatives on their boards, reflecting local entrepreneurs at least as much as representatives of global players in real estate, law, and philanthropy.

Parks conservancies overlap with BIDs but are distinct from them, even as they raise some of the same focal issues. Like BIDs, they expanded first in response to a crisis in public-service provision and municipal budgets in the 1970s and 1980s; they tend to have nonunion workforces; they have boards that include prominent leaders of place-serving businesses; and they differ from each other according to the neighborhoods in which they operate, even as the larger conservancies appear to be models. Conservancies, however, tend to have a far more explicitly public mission. Because they are not based on a voluntary tax assessment by local businesses, they are expected to have the care of "their" parks for the public benefit more clearly at the center of their missions. Conservancies also have many more organizational forms than do BIDs and, as Commissioner White pointed out, no standard relationship with the City. Moreover, conservancies and "Friends of" groups depend far more on volunteer labor and on municipal workers than do BIDs.

## Repertoires of Governance

Accordingly, conservancies enact distinct "repertoires" of governance involving different organizational forms, labor practices, and appeals to legitimacy. Scholars of social movements describe repertoires as clusters of performances including organizational forms and public claims, which develop in particular historical circumstances but that gain a kind of coherence that allows them to be used as templates for improvisation in new settings. For example, Charles Tilly notes that the particular political circumstances of Parliament's increasing centrality in Great Britain in the mid-nineteenth century led ordinary people to shift the ways that they protested. Tilly marks the birth of the "social movement" repertoire in the growing coherence of a set of performances—national coordination, marches, special-purpose associations, public claims to worthiness, unity, numbers, and commitment—that overcame the more localized and direct forms of protest that preceded it. The social movement form has persisted for more than 150 years, in multiple contexts, and yet is not enacted in *exactly the same ways each time* but, rather, is a "modular" set of templates for local action.

Students of urban regimes sometimes characterize them according to their main focus: for example, progrowth regimes concentrate on the growth of the central business district; caretaker regimes concern themselves with the maintenance of good public services; and redistribution regimes are rooted in neighborhoods outside the central business district and try to steer resources to them. Similarly, urban theorist Bob Jessop—cited in chapter 1—proposes that there are typical clusters of performances that characterize cities' approaches to governance, which he calls neoliberal, neocommunitarian, neostatist, and neocorporatist, based on the dominant organizational performances that are enacted. Treating these typologies as repertoires has the advantage of emphasizing their balance of coherence and fluidity, worrying less about whether the types are pure and more about whether and why certain performances cluster as they do and how repertoires are enacted in new contexts.[5] Further, treating them as repertoires calls to mind the ongoing interaction between movements and states that reconfigure them both, rather than treating them as templates to which conservancies, other public-private partnerships, or whole regimes must somehow adhere.

In what follows, we describe the growth of three distinct repertoires of blending the public and private in the operation of parks, though we also argue that these repertoires can be conceived as performances in a broader repertoire of urban governance. We trace the formation and operation of the best-known group, the Central Park Conservancy, the Prospect Park Alliance, and the Bryant Park Corporation, as contemporary exemplars of *civic, philanthropic,* and *corporate* conservancies. In them we find a rough distinction among the "performances" of organizational leadership, labor relations, and legitimacy. We then consider the more recent generation of conservancies and "Friends of" groups from the 1990s until today and show how and why, in spite of the prominence of the Central Park Conservancy and the philanthropic repertoire, the corporate and civic repertoires of Bryant Park and the Prospect Park Alliance have been greater influences on the new conservancies. In the next chapter, we consider some of the broader consequences of this development in New York City's governance.

### Emerging from Crisis

Gordon Davis remembers an "apple-cheeked" young woman, Tupper Thomas, interviewing for the job of Prospect Park Administrator. He was so taken with the optimistic—though perhaps naive—energy of Thomas that he hired her.[6] Yet Thomas, however young (she was thirty-five at the time), had experience supervising a staff of a hundred people, had worked in the Housing Department under Mayor John V. Lindsay in the early 1970s, and had a degree in urban planning. Thomas had first come to New York City in 1965 as a college student to work for Lindsay's campaign. Lindsay, a good-government, liberal Republican, was photogenic, a real supporter of civil rights, and an opponent of the machine politics of the Democratic Party. The city's labor unions supported the Democratic Party, as the previous mayor, Robert F. Wagner

Jr., had granted them provisional collective bargaining rights by executive order. Lindsay opposed them, too.[7] Yet Lindsay focused the imaginations of many young, idealistic, civil-rights-and-good-government-supporting liberals. Thomas, originally from Minnesota, joined the ranks of those seeking to contribute to public service in New York after Lindsay's victory.

Thomas, whom we interviewed shortly after she announced her retirement after thirty years as Prospect Park Administrator and twenty-three years as head of the Prospect Park Alliance, the nonprofit she and others founded in 1987, recalled her early days in the park:

Thomas: Basically my mandate was to bring Prospect Park back to the people of Brooklyn by doing the following things: I was to make better use of the Parks Department workforce . . . I was supposed to try to pull together resources from within the Parks Department to see how I could get the park better. Manage it better, run the place better, and to establish a private, fundraising organization.
John: Who was managing at the time?
Thomas: There was no one who had the authority to do everything. There was a Park Supervisor who was in charge of the uniformed staff. But he had no control over programs, he had no control over vehicle repair, he had no control over plumbers or electricians, he had no control over public access or press.

The press turned out to be important. Thomas further recalled being interviewed by Gabe Pressman, a fixture of New York City broadcasting, early in her time at the helm of Prospect Park:

On my first day on the job, he says, "So, this park is pretty run down, and it looks like nobody's going to bring it back. What makes you think you can?" . . . But what I had to learn a lot about was perception and how people perceive the park, which is that it was unsafe and horrible and awful. That was the perception, because there was nobody here. So you walked in the park, and it was dirty, and there's nobody there. So it felt unsafe. So I had to start calling the local papers and I just learned it, how do you deal with the press. And if they'd say "Oh, there was a rape over here, near Prospect Park," I'd look at the address and the area and it was like a mile and a half away! In New York, a mile and a half away is like . . . ! So I'd call and say "Hi!" [She smiles sweetly and waves with her fingers]. But also I found out if you feed people information, they like that, and so right away learning how to write press releases and have fun activities so people would just put their byline on our press release and we didn't have to worry. So we had to learn that kind of stuff first. And the theory we all had was that it would be very hard to raise private dollars until the park looked better, until some people went into it [and] the public [got] interested.

CHAPTER FIVE

Across the East River, Elizabeth Barlow—now known more widely as Betsy Rogers (her married name)—had been asked by Gordon Davis to become the administrator of Central Park. Rogers had a background in urban planning and design and had staked out a career as a historian and a writer. She became interested in parks as a volunteer with the Parks Council—a group now called New Yorkers for Parks—which had protested the dumping of landfill in the city's wetland preserves in the early 1970s, and she wrote a book, *Forests and Wetlands*, about parks such as Jamaica Bay and Pelham Bay. She then turned her attention to Central Park and wrote a book about Frederick Law Olmsted, the park's primary designer (who also designed Riverside Park and Morningside Park in Manhattan and Prospect Park and Fort Greene Park in Brooklyn, among others in New York City, and many others nationwide). Rogers's book, and her involvement with philanthropy in Central Park, both made her a prominent advocate for bringing the park back to its former state of beauty and connected her to networks of philanthropists—people like Iphigene Sulzberger, wife of the publisher of the *New York Times*, Brooke Astor, George Soros, and Richard Gilder—who would be early contributors to the restoration and improved management of Central Park. Rogers led a small nonprofit, the Central Park Task Force, and was interested in restoring the park's horticulture and physical features. Soros and Gilder's Central Park Community Fund raised money for maintenance equipment. In 1973, it commissioned a study of the park's management, carried out by E. S. Savas, which recommended centralized management under a single administrator and a "Board of Guardians" for the park.[8]

As part of a larger effort to decentralize authority in the Parks Department—he created borough commissioners, too—the parks commissioner, Gordon Davis, asked Barlow to become the administrator of Central Park, much along the lines that Savas suggested. Rogers recalled:

The Community Fund was focused more on park operations because management was so inefficient. Because the park was in such terrible shape physically, I was primarily interested in restoration design. We were, however, good friends since all of us were involved in the same mission: saving Central Park. Dick and George wanted the Task Force to merge with the Community Fund, and although this was in effect what happened, it only occurred after Ed Koch was elected mayor. Here is how it came about: Since I had a small office in the Arsenal, Gordon Davis, Koch's first commissioner, knew what I was trying to do. He also read the white paper I prepared for him detailing the history of Central Park and what was now happening to it. Then one evening I had him over for dinner, and it was then that he popped the question: "I want to create a position for you in my administration."

You have to realize what mess he had on his hands. He was trying to ship out the deadwood, the mistresses and the political hacks, and this was the beginning of decentralization of the parks management. I'm the first of the decentralized [system] of Parks Department management. Then came Tupper Thomas, administrator of Prospect Park, and the individual commissioners responsible for each borough.

In Central Park, Rogers set about unifying the volunteer efforts that were on the ground and, with Davis's support, founded the Central Park Conservancy, which combined the Central Park Task Force and the Community Fund. The Conservancy's goal was mainly to raise money for management improvements and the restoration of the park, largely in keeping with Olmsted's original vision. Rogers recalled:

The situation at the time was that, in spite of my new title as administrator, I had no real budget, and I knew that in order to raise money I needed to form a board of directors for the Central Park Conservancy. I knew also that I needed a chairman to help me form the board. Then one day I got a call from the director of the Beinecke family foundation. He told me that Mr. Beinecke and his wife had taken a walk in Central Park recently and seen a sign outside the dairy saying that it was in the process of restoration. When I went to call on him later at his office, he told me that he was stepping down from the chairmanship of his company and that they were moving back into New York from New Jersey. He said that since New York City was now their home and they lived just a block away from the park on 79th Street and also because his wife Betty was a gardener, the foundation planned to make gift of $25,000 to the park. It occurred to me then that possibly Bill Beinecke could be the chairman for the newly formed Central Park Conservancy. When I asked him to consider doing this, he said that he would think about it over the summer. In September, he, Gordon, and I met with the mayor, and he agreed.

I introduced him to Dick Gilder and a couple of other members of the Community Fund board as well as two of the existing members of the Task Force board. This became our nucleus. After that he took me with him to the offices of certain CEOs that he knew, and I introduced him to representatives of the philanthropists who were already interested in helping bring the park back to life. Gordon made sure that we reached out to prominent members of the African American and Hispanic communities. All in all, we created a board made up of people who had leadership positions in the city of one kind or another and knew that the health of Central Park was some kind of barometer for the health of New York City.

CHAPTER FIVE

Rogers herself had gotten some experience in raising money for the park with the Task Force. She wrote an article called "33 Ways Your Time and Money Can Help Save Central Park" and raised $25,000 in small donations. Larger donations followed: Richard Gilder gave a $17 million matching gift to the park in 1994; John Paulson, the billionaire private equity investor, gave $100 million in 2012. Yet a great deal of the fundraising remains small scale. In 2010, 42,000 people donated to the Conservancy.[9]

To the south of Central Park, behind the New York Public Library main branch on 42nd Street, sits Bryant Park. Stretching just two city blocks—from 42nd to 40th Streets—and occupying roughly half of the long block between Fifth and Sixth Avenues, Bryant Park is a crowded, bustling formal garden bordered by alleys of tall shade trees and focused on a grand fountain and central lawn. The east and west sides of the park have privately run restaurants, with those on the east more formal, sit-down restaurants and those on the west informal concessions at which one can buy sandwiches or coffee to enjoy at one of the park's many café tables. In the winter, the lawn is turned into a vast skating rink. On summer evenings, it is transformed into an outdoor movie theater. Year-round, on the west side, ping pong and *pétanque* are available, especially for the lunchtime crowd. For seventeen years, Bryant Park also hosted New York's Fashion Week, with access to the park restricted and enormous tents set up for fashion shows.

Like Central and Prospect Parks, Bryant Park was in parlous condition in 1980. In contrast to both, however, Bryant Park's administration was almost completely privatized all at once, with responsibility given over to a BID, the Bryant Park Restoration Corporation. The Bryant Park Restoration Corporation—now simply called the Bryant Park Corporation—instead asked the City to cede control over the park to it, and it managed the park and brought in activities to the park in such a way as to try to bring more people into it, just as Thomas had tried to do in Prospect Park. In the meantime, the Corporation worked on a redevelopment plan, much as Rogers and the Conservancy were doing. Unlike the Central Park Conservancy, however, the Bryant Park Restoration Corporation was given the right to shut down the park entirely for three years, between 1988 and 1991, in order to do a thoroughgoing redesign and renovation based on the ideas of successful park use promulgated by William H. ("Holly") Whyte, the noted urbanist, writer, and sociologist, who worked with the Corporation as a consultant.

The Bryant Park Restoration Corporation began as a project of the Rockefeller Brothers Fund, which was first interested in philanthropy directed at the Public Library. That the park abutting the library had become so dilapidated, so crime-ridden, and so druggy was a problem they sought to remedy. In addition to this, however, the Rockefellers, along with other owners of commercial real estate in West Midtown, sought to revive the area around Times Square, which had become notoriously seedy and lined with pornographic movie theaters. Time-Life's CEO, Andrew Heiskell (who was married to Marian Sulzberger, a daughter of Iphigene Ochs Sulzburger, who was among the philanthropists who first got the Central Park Conservancy going), became the first chairman of the Bryant Park Restoration Corporation, which hired for its CEO—who remains so thirty-five years later—a twenty-six-year-old Harvard Business School graduate named Dan Biederman.

Biederman, like Richard Gilder of the Central Park Conservancy, had strong convictions that public spaces such as parks would be better off run by private companies. But Biederman promoted the idea that BIDs—nonprofit companies backed by assessments from corporations with skin in the game—could be applied to parks and not just streets. The approach, more than simply a philanthropic one, expressly acknowledged that enlightened self-interest would be a powerful force in improving public infrastructure and services even while it greatly enhanced the value of the real estate in the area.

Ceding control over Bryant Park was controversial. As Jérôme Barth, the vice president of the Bryant Park Management Corporation and manager of the park, told us:

Our contract was signed when [the City of New York] had the least power in their history. They were on their knees. Massive crime . . . flight of white middle-class families to the suburbs, declining tax collections, racial riots, so a city that had become ungovernable. I don't know if you know the movie *Escape from New York*? In a lot of movies when you see New York completely derelict and in that one New York has become a prison camp, right? And that's what it was. New York was this jungle of graffiti and violence that nobody felt could come back. So the City was willing to try anything, and there were a few visionaries both in public service at the Parks Department and elected officials and financial business who said, "Let's get together. Let's draft something new." So they delegated [an] enormous amount of power to us to do this. And that's what made it possible . . . And to this day it remains. And they never did it again. They never gave it to anybody else. And yet a lot of other projects have been very successful, but nobody successful like us because, in part, the City has never given that to anybody else.

The extraordinary power granted to Bryant Park was not replicated, but it was not reined in, either, in spite of the fact that the contract to run the park is subject to renewal every five years. Even an advocate for at least partial park privatization, Henry Stern, testified that the power granted was excessive. At a city council hearing in 1997 on the subject of whether to grant a master contract to run Central Park to the Central Park Conservancy, the then-commissioner said:

. . . you know, I wish that we had this agreement with the Central Park Conservancy in effect in Bryant Park, because there is a park in which I believe there is an imbalance, and there is excessive private sector control. . . . Bryant Park, they keep all the concession revenues. All of it, which comes to the City in Central Park. They also have control over special events and charge for that. They also determine the opening and the closing of the park. So in great many issues of governance, the Central Park arrangement is superior to the Bryant Park arrangement, which may reflect different times. I mean, it's fourteen years later now.[10]

Yet it was Henry Stern who, in 1999, proposed that Bryant Park not accept even the small city subsidy that it had gotten as part of its contract since 1983. Stern told us:

What we did was we were supposed to contribute 250 [thousand dollars] a year, and then one day Giuliani just said, "Let's not. Let's save it." So we saved it. I mean, I thought, "How can he get away with it . . . the agreement . . ." That's why Giuliani's mayor and I wasn't. He just said, "Nah, enough. They're raising a million, they can raise a million and a quarter." They did. There were no complaints.

As Barth confirmed,

And he was right. We didn't need any more, and it was better for us, because it allows us to say, look, we're running without city money. We don't need the City, because that's what I see as the other part of the social compact. We can do things you couldn't do in Bushwick [Brooklyn], because you don't have the same density of population. But what it allows for the City to do is save money and spend it there. So they couldn't do what we do here, for a lot of reasons, but they can get resources away from the center and push them toward the edges. So everybody wins.

## The Development of Parallel Work Forces

By 1982, the Central Park Conservancy was in the process of planning a massive renovation of the park. From 1982 to 1985, it undertook a huge study of the park, such as had not been done since Olmsted designed it. A distinctive element of the plan, *Rebuilding Central Park: A Management and Restoration Plan*, was that it looked carefully at park use and circulation as well as capital needs. But it also emphasized *management*, a key concern of Soros and Gilder during the previous decade. Rogers spoke of *Rebuilding Central Park*:

If you look at the plan you'll see what was behind it. The reason it's called a management and restoration plan, with the word management first, is because we knew that it would be wrong to restore something if we didn't also build in a strategy for managing it. There were virtually no gardeners in the Parks Department at that time. Those lines had evaporated. Actually, I think there were three, who were headquartered in the Conservatory Garden, but they weren't working in the garden. Instead, as I remember, they were making the big Christmas wreath for the front of the Arsenal. In any case, three gardeners in Central Park couldn't possibly do all the horticultural work that needed to get done.

At the same time, the City had cut back significantly on hiring other kinds of Parks Department staff besides gardeners and had stopped backfilling positions in Parks when workers were fired, laid off, retired, or left for other jobs. There were not likely to be any more gardeners any time soon.

Our first fundraising effort was to support a staff recruited from degree-granting programs at the State University of New York or the New York Botanical Garden, people who were studying horticulture. In this way we were able to form a planting crew, a tree crew, and a restoration crew to repair or reconstruct such things as wooden bridges and masonry walls and steps. We called these employees interns because that way they posed less of a threat to the unionized city workers. Nevertheless, at the 79th St. Yard where the regular city park workers clocked in they were for the most part *persona non grata*. In fact, we had to install them in a comfort station in the Ramble where pesticides were kept in the basement. This was the beginning of a public-private parallel workforce in Central Park.

This "parallel workforce" grew, as we saw in previous chapters, to a point at which currently over 200 workers work for the Central Park

CHAPTER FIVE

Conservancy and fewer than twenty-five municipal employees remain in the park. Its creation in the context of the fiscal crisis is crucial to understanding its very possibility. As Rogers recalled, "When I started, the City had something called PEG program, Program to Eliminate the Gap, meaning that personnel cuts were being made by the City. Because of this the union could no longer say that a volunteer or outside worker was taking away the job of a union man." But it did not go down easy for many civil-service workers. Rogers describes an "us-versus-them" dynamic that developed between the Central Park Conservancy and the city workers, a dynamic she chalks up to the lack of effective management, patronage, and the fact that supervisors belonged to the same union as the workers who reported to them:

When you have the managers and the workers belonging to the same union, there isn't a lot of accountability, and there's no real work ethic with evaluations and promotions based on performance standards rather than employment longevity. According to union rules, workers could file a grievance if they were assigned what was called out-of-title work. To give an example of what the union regulations were in those days, it took three people to prune a tree. You had the climber, and then you had the groundsman who handed the climber the tools, and then you had the MVO, the motor vehicle operator. Men—there were no women field workers then—could simply show up for work and congregate in buildings such as the Wollman Rink and play cards and drink beer. The Parks Department headquarters in Arsenal was where City Hall sent people such as somebody's mistress or someone for whom they needed to do a political favor.

All of this came to a head when city workers refused on contractual grounds to clean up a large fish kill in the pond; the Conservancy got its workers to clean it up.

By the late 1980s, the number of Conservancy workers nearly matched the number of parks workers in Central Park. By the mid-1990s, the Conservancy's Zone Gardener system was in place and there was no "parallel" workforce anymore. There was a Conservancy workforce and a much smaller group of municipal employees consigned to two areas of the park and to collecting garbage on the packers.

Back in Prospect Park, Tupper Thomas followed Central Park Conservancy in setting up a nonprofit to support the park. For both administrators, this had been part of the expectations of the job when Gordon Davis brought them on. For Thomas, however, the process started in 1984, and the Prospect Park Alliance was announced in 1987, even as the City had begun hiring new employees in the Parks Department.

Because Prospect Park, unlike Central Park, was not ringed by some of the most expensive real estate in the world, the Alliance's fiscal capacity was not—and has never been—close to that of Central Park. It took Thomas nearly three years to pull together a board with sufficient financial clout to raise money—"the Beinecke family took pity on me and they found a friend of theirs who lived in Brooklyn"—so that they would not have to "do bake sales."

And we also used the name Alliance, and not Conservancy . . . Because we felt that [for] Brooklyn people, the word "conservancy" might seem too fancy. Hoity-toity. We were an alliance with the public, with the private sector, and we were the community, we were also people who could help to raise money.

In addition to this, however, the Alliance relied on an allocation of federal Community Development Block Grant (CDBG) funds, which were allocated to Prospect Park in the first year of Thomas's work there. The allocation remains in the city's CDBG budget thirty years later. The parallel workforce that the Prospect Park Alliance could support is much more of a *parallel* workforce:

So we were able to get started with this not-for-profit group as an *augment* concept. We would *augment* what the government can do, not *supplement*. And so over time, we were more and more in the supplement, as government has actually pulled out from lots of things they'd done. So more and more the not-for-profit parks people are actually supplementing. We weren't supposed to clean, we weren't supposed to raise money to clean the park or to buy a lawnmower or to clean the bathrooms. We were supposed to do programs that provided education at Lefferts Homestead and at the Boathouse because the Parks Department didn't have the resources. We had a natural resource crew to maintain natural areas. And over time, we have actually taken on outright almost all the concessions ourselves because no one would bid on or operate them well.

As Thomas told us, "I actually did not start the volunteer program until we had the staff to maintain the volunteer program, which is to me the most important thing: if you invite volunteers to come in, and you don't have somebody who's going to take care of them and lead them, it doesn't work." Moreover, the Alliance did its best to involve already-organized groups from the neighborhoods that surround the park.

And then we immediately started our volunteer effort and started to work on forming a community group, which would be our outreach to the community leaders, so they had more voice in operations. And that was very complicated. The Parks Department [has] a strong volunteer effort, but the involvement of the community in decision making is not natural for them. It was out of my sixties training that I believed in it, but it was a hard thing to get accomplished, and we sort of failed the first time around, by just allowing anybody to come to our meetings. Because then you always end up with two crazy people, and everybody else goes away, because they can't stand listening to them. So then we actually made it organizational. We had a cultural anthropologist work with us to help us figure out who the community was, and how to find the people representing those organizations, and so by 1997, ten years later, we finally had a strong community committee, which still meets.[11]

Unlike the Central Park Conservancy, then, the Prospect Park Alliance focused on volunteer efforts and community input in decision making and has hired its workers in a way such that the roles of Alliance and Parks staff are generally blended. Like Rogers, Thomas was at once the president of the nonprofit parks group *and* a city employee as administrator of the park (as are their respective successors, Douglas Blonsky and Emily Lloyd). But whereas in Central Park the Conservancy does not supervise city staff, in Prospect Park—which did not start off with as great an animosity toward the unionized workforce—the supervision is often blended in practice. Moreover, Prospect Park Alliance staff are concentrated in volunteer supervision, administration, and staffing the Alliance-run concessions such as the Tennis House, the Boat House, and the skating rink, while the Parks Department workers still attend to the rest of the park.

Philanthropic and corporate conservancies, such as the Central Park Conservancy and Bryant Park, which can raise their own revenues, also then have greater say over how maintenance and operations will proceed. The more civic conservancies, by contrast, cannot raise their own operating funds and therefore have less of this leverage, in no small measure because they rely to a far greater degree on the City's allocation of public workers for maintenance and operations than do corporate and philanthropic conservancies. The contrast becomes clear when we compare Dan Biederman's assessment of the stability and predictability of his workforce and Tupper Thomas's. Biederman told *Crain's New York Business*:

I like to do things without any public money. Our sanitation workers never leave voluntarily, and we know this is the best-paying job they can get. They start a little above the minimum wage, and they go up very quickly. We have guys in Bryant

Park who are making close to $20 an hour, plus benefits and overtime. We don't cap the salaries. That's still lower than what the city would have to pay for equivalent jobs because the [city] pension plans are so expensive. That's the genius of privatization.[12]

By contrast, Thomas spoke about staffing levels in Prospect Park, which are decided by the central administration of the Parks Department at the Arsenal in Manhattan. When asked if the Alliance would get as many JTPs in 2010 as they got in 2009, she answered "probably not." The Parks Department has to work directly with the Human Resources Administration, which runs the JTP program, and the Alliance cannot just call and say "Can I get five?"

## Anchoring Legitimacy

Clemens and Guthrie's suggestion that public-private partnerships involve "contestation over the legitimacy of organizational forms, their respective jurisdictions, and their interdependencies" rings true for those managing the parks, as well. Questions of legitimacy, of organizational form, and of jurisdiction are never far from the surface of criticisms of these partnerships. These questions are at the center of the conservancies' repertoires because the conservancies rely on their core sources of legitimacy to be able to mobilize the resources to pay for labor, in the case of Central and Bryant Parks, and to mobilize volunteers, in the case of Prospect Park. Establishing and reestablishing this legitimacy is an ongoing part of the work of the Conservancy management. Betsy Rogers explained:

What I had to learn was to slow down and do the community politics better. It was important for me to understand the importance of going to planning board meetings. This meant Board 7 on the West Side, Board 8 on the East Side, Board 10 in Harlem, and Board 5 south of 59th Street. Every single project we took to the community boards, the Landmarks Commission, and the Art Commission. And then we had to contend with the perception back then that the Conservancy was made up of a bunch of elitists who were attempting to privatize the park. Do you think the philanthropists want to just be the only ones to use it, or do you think they're really good-hearted people that want to have better playgrounds for kids, green lawns, no more graffiti? And yes they *are* dissed, and even Olmsted is sometimes characterized as an elitist. I really believe that Central Park is one of the great achievements of American democracy. It is the first purpose-built people's park in

CHAPTER FIVE

the world. The Royal Parks of London and the Tuilleries and Luxembourg in Paris were opened to the public, but Central Park was created to welcome everyone from the beginning. Oh dear, I have given you quite a little speech!

Philanthropy is central to the vision of the Central Park Conservancy. Its annual report contains pictures of fundraising events, putting key donors in the spotlight. Its rebranding in 2010—including a new logo and a new tagline, "Central to the Park"—also includes some appeals for broader-based giving. A banner reading "Your Green Keeps Our Green Greener" is probably the most explicit. Rogers's point is that the Conservancy's greatest source of resources is private philanthropy, and it does not feel as if it should apologize for it.

By way of contrast, the Prospect Park Alliance focuses a great deal more of its publicity on the "democratic vision." Every single photograph in its annual reports shows the faces of parks users, as opposed to roughly half of those in the Central Park Conservancy's. Thomas's "sixties training" and the reputation for danger of the park itself may have led her to seek out involvement from the park's neighbors, both as small-amount donors and as volunteers. Though Thomas talked about the importance of having wealthy people on her board to help raise money, and spoke about the importance of corporate donations (often done in tandem with volunteering), she kept returning to the volunteer programs as a very important resource:

Thomas: Sometimes I've met people who are in the social services volunteering, it's harder because . . . each day you have to come back and take care of that same person. But this way, you come in, you do the job, you see it gets done and it's better when finished, and you go home. So it satisfies that side of the volunteer attitude. People volunteer, as you know, for so many different reasons, and we have a regular crew of volunteers on Monday that always like to come in and clean up the garbage and stuff after a big weekend, and they have special areas that they like to clean, because they feel that we can't get to those areas, and they are not the most heavily used sections. And then we have a Wednesday group, two different Wednesday groups, one that works near the boat house and one at Grand Army Plaza, then we have a Thursday group that works wherever we need them, and many of those are also on the Monday crew . . .

Maud: So you have regular . . .

Thomas: Yes, those are regulars. And then we have a Saturday group that works in the mornings only. But we are developing more and more of those kinds of regular groups as well, so we almost have one a day.

John: So is that something pretty new that is really developing now?

Thomas: We just keep adding a little more here, a little more there, and keep making more things available, because so many people want to volunteer. And I think people are retiring earlier, people have alternate kinds of work schedules, so it's easier to volunteer. It is still a very middle-class, upper-middle-class activity, volunteering . . . and they come from all over, but I would have thought, if you'd asked, that they were all going to come from Park Slope. It's right here, it's a neighborhood that knows and gets volunteers. But no, they come from really all over the place, and it's really nice to see . . .

Note that Thomas was concerned that somehow even volunteering might be seen as elitist. There have been repeated criticisms of the Prospect Park Alliance that it has focused more resources on the west side of the park, toward the wealthier of its surrounding neighborhoods,[13] so even with the more civic partnership, the legitimacy of the key resource needs to be validated against the potential charge of elitism-through-privatization.

The question of legitimation was handled quite differently at Bryant Park. Barth explained that the Rockefeller Brothers—a philanthropy—gave Biderman his charge early on: "And they said, 'Well, we're going to give you some seed money, some basic money, to start, but don't come back for more. Figure it out. We don't want you to be always coming back for more.' And they had a natural antigovernment bias, so he really set out to run it like a business—like a not-for-profit—but like a business." Indeed, the Bryant Park Corporation's mission statement is clear on its multiple objectives:

The Bryant Park Corporation was founded in 1980 with a charge to reclaim Bryant Park for the people of New York City. Since then, the talent, dedication, and execution of the BPC board and staff has transformed the park into the greatest public space in the world. The ongoing mission of the BPC is: to create a rich and dynamic visual, cultural and intellectual outdoor experience for New Yorkers and visitors alike; to enhance the real estate values of its neighbors by continuously improving the park; to burnish the park's status as a prime NYC tourist destination by presenting a meticulously maintained venue for free entertainment events; and to help prevent crime and disorder in the park by attracting thousands of patrons, at all hours, thus fostering a safe environment.

The BPC is privately funded, and operates Bryant Park with private sector techniques and management methods. Working as agent for the City of New York, the BPC provides sanitation, security services, spotless restrooms, colorful gardens, and seasonal horticultural installations for the park, and maintains a lush lawn that is open to the public. The BPC also works with civic minded corporations and park

CHAPTER FIVE

patrons to offer interesting amenities, free educational programs, and free high-level entertainment for people of all ages. Careful selection and management of concessionaires ensures that park visitors have access to high-quality food and merchandise. As it strives to improve the park each year, the BPC pays close attention to other models and constantly seeks innovations, whether from its own staff or from outside, always with an eye on the ultimate goal: presenting the perfect park to the public.

As we will discuss in greater detail in chapter 8, the enhancement of real estate values is neither coincidental with, nor an afterthought in, well-managed parks. The Bryant Park Corporation, however, is unusually forthright in claiming this as a goal nearly coequal to its "ultimate" goal, "presenting the perfect park to the public." Even the ultimate goal sounds a great deal like a sales pitch; there is no question in the corporate model that what is good for the corporations is, ultimately, good for the public and vice versa. Elitism does not come into question because the park's conservancy is directly funded by ongoing assessments on businesses.

Bryant Park, which raises its money through a voluntary local tax and concessions, relies chiefly on its own workers for maintenance and operations. Prospect Park, both unable to raise the kinds of funds necessary to support a large maintenance and operations workforce and willing to work flexibly with volunteers, mixes its workforce; volunteers work side by side with Alliance workers, while the Alliance staff works with municipal employees and with the JTPs who do the bulk of the cleaning.

The Central Park Conservancy and its philanthropic model lies somewhere between the Prospect Park Alliance and the Bryant Park Corporation on this matter. Like the Bryant Park Corporation, the Central Park Conservancy has hired its own workers and prefers to rely on them. Unlike the Bryant Park Corporation, the Conservancy has proceeded since its founding with a corps of municipal employees, though their numbers have shrunk by more than 90 percent through attrition and replacement by the Conservancy's own employees. Apart from the APSWs who drive the garbage trucks and the Park Supervisors, however, the municipal employees are, and have been, segregated from the Conservancy's own workforce and not integrated into the Conservancy's zone system.

As we have seen, the Conservancy has been wary of unionized workers since its founding. Rogers, while recalling the early years, told us:

Until the Conservancy had an actual management contract with the City, there was a them-and-us kind of tension. You're going to think that I'm being very negative and very unsympathetic to unionized workers. That's unfair because many of them do work hard and are really good guys. But in the early days of the Conservancy, there *were* ones who were telling our privately funded workers, "Don't work so hard, you make us look bad."

Harlan, the Parks Supervisor quoted in earlier chapters, corroborated Rogers's view, even while qualifying it: recalling his time in Central Park in the early 1980s, he said that Conservancy workers did a lot more work than city workers did. "But," he added, "they had no rights."

Though the Prospect Park Alliance workers do not have a union either, the demand for one does not appear to have been as strong as it had been—at least among a segment of the workers—in Central Park (where demand still was not sufficient to trigger an election). Prospect Park Alliance's intermixing of workers—even to the point that the Alliance pays for several *municipal* workers—suggests that mixing union and nonunion workers did not represent as much of a threat to the organization as it did to the Central Park Conservancy.

Thomas pointed to a more consultative labor-management strategy that went far beyond an open-door policy, which she credited for her workers not responding to union overtures:

Thomas: But generally I think the Alliance staff have not felt the need for [a union]. We have a lot of built-in things to handle some of the problems that a union does. So we have an employee concerns committee; we have town hall meetings where you can bring up issues and questions; and we do a lot of that sort of thing. Which I think the Parks paid staff like too.
John: The Parks people that . . . ?
Thomas: Yeah, everybody goes to these meetings. So they all get to chat with each other then, and they get to bring up (issues) and then it's good, because they hear each other's problems, and the Parks guys certainly have more health benefits than the Alliance staff do, or, "Ooh, I have a dental plan! She doesn't!"
John: But then does it work the other way, that some of the Alliance employees say, "Why didn't we have better benefits?"
Thomas: Well, they do, and they understand that we try. Some of them have become Parks employees too.
John: Oh, they've gone over?
Thomas: Yeah. One or two people. But the Parks Department [hasn't hired in a long time].

CHAPTER FIVE

Similarly, one might expect that the Bryant Park Corporation would be more hostile to unions even than the Central Park Conservancy. Though administrators at both Bryant Park and Central Park spoke of being able to work with unions—in Central Park, the Conservancy has had to work with, and sometimes around, unionized workers for more than thirty years—both conservancies have had some experience in fending off union organizing drives. In Central Park's case, the drive we witnessed was the third in fifteen years. Bryant Park Corporation's sister BIDs largely parried attempts to organize in the late 1990s, though the maintenance staff of the 34th Street Partnership, also run by Daniel Biederman with the same staff as Bryant Park Corporation (but with a different board of directors), did vote to unionize. At the time, Biederman sounded the alarm. As the *New York Times* reported:

B.I.D. directors worry that unionization will compromise their ability to provide services efficiently and at low cost. Gretchen Dykstra, who runs the Times Square district, fears that inflexible union rules might prevent employees from carrying out many tasks, from sweeping streets to painting benches. Mr. Biederman says the wages the union is seeking (as much as $19 an hour for sanitation workers) will no longer allow districts to provide lots of service for little money. "That is what happened to municipal government," he said.[14]

Nevertheless, it is striking that this complaint is quite different than that of Central Park Conservancy directors, who focus far more on union rules and workplace relations: the story of the union workers' refusal of out-of-title work during the fish kill is part of Conservancy lore, and top staff prided themselves on what they considered an effective open door policy, where they can treat the workers "like individuals" and not according to the imposed rules of a contract. More than one top manager at the Conservancy similarly referred to the union organizers as "thugs" and "outsiders" who did not have the best interests of the workers in mind. The Conservancy's leaders see unions as being at odds with the philanthropic character of the Conservancy. If philanthropy is at least in part about "good-hearted people," unions are cast as *not* good-hearted, even if, and especially if, some of the workers are "really good guys." The discussion turns on moral distinctions, where for the Bryant Park Corporation, it turns on simple calculation of efficiency.

The calculation of efficiency also comes into play with respect to volunteers. Here, Tupper Thomas's concern, cited earlier, with being sure to have sufficient staff to run a volunteer program prior to starting is in stark contrast to Jérôme Barth's assessment that volunteers are "nightmares":

Barth: Because they're unreliable. They come in when they want to come in. You don't pay them, so you have no hold over them, right? As an employer . . . we make it very hard for people to volunteer for us, because we want to make sure that they're committed. We've had some great volunteers, but typically it's people that you come to know very much one on one, you have a job that's tailored to them, and you make sure that they stick to it. You can't rely on volunteers to run . . . It's like the Empire State Building. Would you run the Empire State Building with volunteers? No. You can't. You can't just do that. You have to be serious. So we can have volunteers in certain contexts, but that's it.
Maud: So like what? When do you . . . what kind of . . . ?
Barth: Someone from a business school recently. She had to do it, it was graded. It was great. Somebody from a university program. She did something very specific. . . . It's in a punctual way, just two hours a week, this or that . . . but you have to make it a privilege. And you want them in certain ways and not in other ways . . .
Maud: So they don't help with like maintenance or gardening or beautification of the park, right? And you don't have corporate volunteers, either?
Barth: They're useless. When the bank comes out . . . it's nothing. It's public relations. It has no practical impact on operations. It's a waste of time.[15]

## Divisions of Revenue

Repertoires form in contexts shaped by material resources. As Tilly points out, the premodern protest repertoire, in which grain seizures featured prominently, cannot be understood apart from rural economies with centralized market towns, grain silos, and periodic food shortages. The development of the social movement cannot be understood without expanding urbanization, growing ease of transport, and the rise of mass literacy.[16] Similarly, the rise of the corporate, philanthropic, and civic repertoires of parks maintenance are inextricably linked to the moment of New York City's postcrisis reinvention. Their divisions of labor and their claims for legitimacy endure through particular divisions of revenue with the City, which lend the conservancies different characteristic leverage with the City.

Summarizing the distinctions among park conservancy organizations, New Yorkers for Parks wrote in 2007:

CHAPTER FIVE

Some organizations, like the Central Park Conservancy, receive money from the City to hire staff, while others, like Madison Square Park Conservancy, pay the City as reimbursement for DPR staff assigned them. Some organizations, like Prospect Park Alliance, are given concessions in their park and keep some or all of those revenues; others, like the Central Park Conservancy, do not operate concessions but receive a payment from the City based on concession revenue generated in the park. The Bryant Park Corporation funds capital projects in the park, while the Prospect Park Alliance designs and manages capital projects funded by the DPR. Some parks are assigned staff employed and supervised by the DPR; some supervise DPR staff assigned to them, and others are heavily or solely dependent on staff they hire themselves.[17]

Melissa Mark-Viverito, the chair of the City Council Committee on Parks, in September 2013 asked Parks Commissioner Veronica White whether there was any possibility to standardize a template for conservancy agreements. Commissioner Veronica White replied that she, too, had found the variety of agreements mystifying when she first became commissioner. But then, longer-term Parks staff explained that the contracts

do look alike in that there are very common features in all the agreements. It's that the Parks Department approves every capital project, we determine and approve every concession; we make the rules. We issue every permit on parkland. So that's the common denominator for any agreement we have. But then, beyond that, the parks are very different and what the parks groups do are very different.[18]

Accordingly, within the general framework of governmental oversight, there is a great deal of actual variation among conservancy contracts. And as Jérôme Barth suggested, the power given to different conservancies to make decisions about what happens in the parks they manage or help manage varies a great deal, as well. While it is true that the parks commissioner is an ex officio member of more than seventy parks-oriented nonprofit organizations across the city—or because this is true—the actual level of oversight of conservancy activity is uneven. Moreover, though the Parks Department "makes the rules," it does so with a great deal of deference—particularly on more minor matters—to the administrators and conservancy staff with operational responsibility for the parks.

One measure of the relative power of a nonprofit organization vis-à-vis the City is the proportion of its operating funds it raises privately. In this light, it is ironic that Henry Stern, the parks commissioner in

1999, divested the City completely from supporting Bryant Park's operating budget since he had previously complained that the City had ceded too much power to the Bryant Park Corporation in its operating contract. Similarly, the Central Park Conservancy raises between 75 and 90 percent of its operating budget every year. It is conceivable that it could raise its entire operating budget privately. Nevertheless, Commissioner White told the city council in 2013 that:

> We expect the Central Park Conservancy to raise—and they do—the vast majority of operating funds for that park . . . I do think it's important that, as a public-private partnership, the City of New York continue to put taxpayer dollars into Central Park so that it is always a public-private partnership and it is not completely funded by a private entity.[19]

Recognition of the power that strong fundraising capacity gives a conservancy is central to the ways in which the Parks Department structures the contracts. On one hand, this capacity allows the City to spend some of its operating resources in other parks, but on the other hand, it means that the conservancies—most often in Manhattan—with a high capacity to attract funds from private donations or from concessions are increasingly indispensable to the City, which in turn gives these conservancies more negotiating leverage over the terms of the contract.

Similarly, partnerships of different sorts will vary in terms of how much they can keep of concession and special-events revenue. Only ten conservancies of the twenty with formal agreements with the City can keep any concession and event fees, and even here, the amounts relative to the overall operating budgets are not large. In Madison Square Park, for example, the Shake Shack, an "upscale" burger stand run by the Union Square Hospitality Group, which also runs more than a dozen high-end restaurants including some of the city's most sought-after reservations, had over $7 million in receipts, which threw off more than $570,000 in concession fees; a quarter-million dollars flowed back to the Madison Square Park Conservancy while $320,000 went into the city's general fund. For Madison Square Park, this represented less than 10 percent of its $3 million operating budget that year. Bryant Park, with an almost $8 million budget in 2012, generated $1.05 million in concessions alone, while generating more than three times that amount in restaurant rental and park user fees of various sorts. By contrast, until 2006, the more philanthropic Central Park Conservancy did not keep its concession revenue, as the Bryant Park Corporation did, and only then gained the right to keep half of the concession revenue after the first $6 million, but no more than $2 million a year. In its most recent renewal, the cap of $2 million has been removed in anticipation of higher revenues in its $58.3 million expense budget for 2013. Accordingly, it still shares the revenue with the City's general fund, but in an increasingly smaller proportion.

Prospect Park Alliance—perhaps surprisingly—has been granted a sole-source concession by the City in order to capture the lion's share of the revenues from its Lakeside Ice Rink and other concessions in the park. When the deal with the City was announced, the projected revenues were cast as being critical to replacing some of the more than $1 million cut over the five years from 2007 through 2012 in City support for Prospect Park. Nevertheless, for more "civic" conservancies, this is an anomaly—at least for now—since most other parks with these kinds of conservancies will not have the capacity to raise the capital funds—nor the space—for large concessions like ice-skating rinks.

## Newer Conservancies and Administrators

Prospect, Central, and Bryant Parks' management organizations and their involvements with the City exemplify civic, philanthropic, and corporate repertoires of governance. Though twenty organizations have formal management agreements with the Parks Department as of this writing, there are many other conservancies and "Friends of" groups that do not, and there are an increasing number of parks with Parks Department administrators whose briefs include the formation of *at least* supportive conservancies, if not full nonprofit management conservancies.

Among the conservancies are the more corporate, smaller parks— also surrounded by business and shopping districts they have helped to revive—such as the Madison Square Park Conservancy, the Union Square Park Conservancy, and the Friends of the High Line. Each has strong connections to surrounding businesses and each has, like Bryant Park, attempted to include restaurants or other eateries. Each, too, has its signature attractions. Madison Square Park has an ongoing public art program and the Shake Shack—an outlet of a mini chain of burger joints owned by famed restaurateur Danny Meyer, who also sits on the board of Madison Square Park. The High Line, an architectural gem built atop a repurposed freight railway trestle, is a public art installation in itself and offers often-theatrical views of buildings old and new that are being developed or redeveloped along its corridor. Further, along with high-end snacks offered around the Chelsea Market, with which it intersects, it has hastened the development of a restaurant and shopping area in the Meatpacking District and West Chelsea, which, even prior to the High Line's opening, was becoming an area known for dining, galleries, and nightlife.

In spite of their similarities, Madison Square Park and the High Line are woven into the Parks Department differently. Whereas Madison Square Park Conservancy's executive director has been hired as the park's administrator by the Parks Department, and, at least at the time of our research, the park was cleaned by a mix of Conservancy staff and JTPs overseen by a CPW and an APSW, the Friends of the High Line has almost Bryant Park–like control over the space and its all-privately-hired staff.

An example of a civic conservancy, mainly on the model of Prospect Park, has been given control over all of the parks in Brooklyn's District 1, covering the Williamsburg and Greenpoint neighborhoods. The Open Space Alliance for North Brooklyn organized originally in order to advocate for the upkeep of the district's largest park, McCarren Park, and nearby McGolrick Park, and sponsored summer concerts at McCarren Pool, one of seven enormous pools built by Robert Moses in the 1930s but, until its renovation and reopening in 2012, disused for decades. OSA's executive director also holds the position of administrator for North Brooklyn Parks and oversees the Parks Department staff, including, at the time of our research in 2009, about fifty JTPs and sixty-five WEP workers, a weekend crew of community service workers, about forty summer youth employees, occasional large volunteer groups through New York Cares, and a variable crew of volunteers in several parks. In addition to that, OSA deals with permits and events and supervises the regular Parks staff, including the recreation staff at McCarren Pool. Like the Prospect Park Alliance, OSA sometimes pays for Parks Department positions, as they had done with a seasonal CPW when we were interviewing workers there.

In Manhattan, the Riverside Park Conservancy is another example of a philanthropic conservancy, though it is one with fewer resources and staff than Central Park. Riverside Park is a multilevel sliver of a park that runs along the Hudson River in Manhattan from 59th Street to 181st Street—more than six miles—and that was designed, in part, by Olmsted, but also extended in parts by Robert Moses and then more recently in the wake of Donald Trump's apartment development between 59th and 72nd Streets in the 1990s and by Mayor Michael Bloomberg's parks expansion schemes in the 2000s. Riverside Park Conservancy's president is also the administrator, and the Conservancy has a mixed staff of privately hired Zone Gardeners and city workers. It also has a long-established volunteer program that combines a great deal of individual volunteer gardening and a teen program. Corporate groups also volunteer for the Conservancy. Like Central Park, however, Riverside Park can and does rely a great deal on its neighbors, who, for much of the park's length, live in some of the most expensive real estate in the city.

The portion of Riverside Park that runs parallel to the Riverside South development between 59th and 72nd Streets is maintained according to a funding formula that throws off payments from the development itself. Part of the City's agreement with the developer was that the development would pay for the park's development and perpetual management. A similar arrangement for management funds has been made in Brooklyn Bridge Park, a park jointly developed by the City and the state, with its own conservancy that includes representation from both governmental entities. A similar state-City-conservancy arrangement covers Hudson River Park, which runs along the Hudson for several miles south of Riverside Park, though the expected real estate development of old piers in the park has not yielded sufficient funds for the park's management.[20]

## Noncontractual Partnerships

In addition to the contractual public-private partnerships the City maintains with conservancies, there are hundreds of other noncontractual partnerships it has with conservancies and "Friends of" groups. Many of these are spontaneous groups of volunteers, the quintessence of civic organizations. Many of these volunteers are neighbors of the park in which they take special interest, and they get organized originally in order to counteract the effects of long-term maintenance neglect. Said one founder of a "Friends of" organization in the Bronx:

And we noticed that there was need for major cleanup if we ever were going to use it as an actual green space, because for so long it had just been neglected by the Parks Department and construction people would come and when they were done they would dump like tiles and brick and carpets and fences, and people would steal cars, they would drop like the spark plugs and brakes and wheels, and it was the craziest amount of stuff in this park ever. And on top of that, the community is a pretty heavy Latino community, so some of them practice Santería, which is a religion where you sacrifice animals, so sometimes you actually find like dead chickens inside of the park, and just things that don't make it so pleasant to go inside. So even today, the biggest struggle is changing the community's perception, because people for so long have known this to be the wooded area where people kill chickens and nobody should go in because it's dark and it's dangerous. So in 2007, we decided to do like monthly—every month we did a cleanup in the summer. So I think it was from May until November 2007 we did a cleanup every month, just to kind of get the park in a condition where we actually could use it. By 2008, we did the first cleanup, and we actually walked into the park, and we picked up like one bag, not even a whole garbage bag, but like a shopping bag full of stuff. So that kind of shows the usability increased, how people weren't using the park, and by then we had actually gotten the Parks Department to put a full-time staff in the park. They didn't have a staff in there at all.

Put differently, thirty years after the fiscal crisis that indirectly gave birth to the Central Park Conservancy and Prospect Park Alliance, residents in the Bronx were still dealing with the same kinds of management failures and neglect that had once characterized the city's "flagship" and "regional" parks—that is, the larger or more centrally located parks that attract tourists as well as locals. We heard similar stories in Queens, Staten Island, and the Bronx, where parks had been subject to illegal dumping and chronic understaffing.

In 1997, Henry Stern, the parks commissioner at the time, helped to set up the City Parks Foundation, a private foundation that could collect donations to fund activities in parks that was *not* itself a conservancy. Said Stern, "It was my idea that, 'Why should only Central Park [have recreation and private staff]?' Little parks want help with stuff like that. There should be a foundation to raise money for the public, the recreation programs at smaller parks, stuff like that." This effort then led directly into the formation of Partnerships for Parks. The logic behind it was to mobilize more than philanthropic money but also civic participation:

Partnerships for Parks is a project of the City Parks Foundation, and the . . . the joint project of City Parks Foundation and the Parks Department, and the idea was to recruit citizens. It's not a fundraising operation, but what do you do to get people to help, who don't have money, or not much money, who want to help? So that was Partnerships for Parks, where you get people to contribute their time and effort and form groups that would be support groups for particular parks.

CHAPTER FIVE

For most of the "Friends of" and noncontractual conservancy groups, the Partnerships for Parks is the main contact point between volunteers and the Parks Department. Partnerships for Parks has outreach coordinators in every borough who are, effectively, community organizers. They coordinate two large "It's My Park" days every year—one in the spring and one in the fall—and it is largely through these that they identify community groups and volunteer groups that might be willing to take a broader role in the upkeep of their neighborhood parks. It's My Park Day provides an opportunity for groups such as the one in the University Woods in the Bronx—but equally in Ives Pond in Staten Island, or Morningside Park in Harlem—to recruit volunteers to help out, even if it is just a few times a year. From there, the budding "Friends of" group can expand its activities. Geri, a volunteer, recounted:

Geri: I was the second grade teacher! And I was young and enthusiastic and, you know, I guess sort of fell into it. So from there what happened was as time went on, we did form Friends of [park], which now I run, which is a nonprofit, which is basically just for the [park]. It's to get programs for children. I get no pay, it's basically just for this community . . . And It's My Park Days would come, and I'd get volunteers from the children, hundreds of children would come . . .
John: With their parents?
Geri: Sometimes with parents, sometimes not.
John: So how old, when you say . . .
Geri: Pre-K through fifth grade. And also older brothers and sisters from the high school.
John: Did they come with their school?
Geri: With their school. The 650 children . . . So we would clean up the park and they would give us gloves and garbage bags and things like that, and . . . this is, you know, the kids were hungry and things like that, and I thought, "You know, we need to get funds, so when they do come, let's have snacks and drinks and a little prize," and then through the nonprofit we were able to slowly get grants to do things like that. So on It's My Park Day in October they go home with a pumpkin. On It's My Park Day in May, in April, they go home with, I don't know, Easter egg hunt. Or in June, we do a carnival. So they're working at the [park] and getting a special reward, so it's a very, very positive experience. And what happened in time is the children really took ownership of this community, and protect that pond. So as time went on, there is no illegal dumping [here].

The Partnerships for Parks has an annual budget of $4 million, split evenly between the Parks Department and the City Parks Foundation. Its staffs help to mediate the relationship between volunteer groups and Parks Managers and Supervisors, though there are also many groups that deal directly with the parks management staff without the intervention of the Partnerships for Parks. First Deputy Commissioner Liam Kavanagh described the role of Partnerships for Parks to the city council:

Part of the role of Partnerships for Parks is to organize all of these groups that support parks all over the city, and there are hundreds of them. I think the estimate is in excess of 600 or 700 groups that are friends groups, that have a working relationship with the Parks Department both on the local level, with the local park supervisors and managers, and through Partnerships for Parks, which not only supports them in their volunteer efforts, providing them tools and technical assistance, but Partnerships has a pretty well-developed program for helping organizations develop at the level that they aspire to grow to. So not every group wants to become a 501(c)(3), have tax exempt status, but some of them do. They want to be able to accept, you know, donations, you know, on behalf of their organization and have a more formal structure, and Partnerships helps them develop the capacity to do that, helps them to understand how to advocate on behalf of their park or the parks that they're interested in in a more broad-based way, outreach to elected officials, to foundations and things like that, so there are a number of steps that organizations can take if they want to take on more responsibility . . . The Partnerships for Parks maintains a database of all of the organizations that have signed up basically to support their local parks. It's a very active means of communication. Obviously, we keep in touch with them for events and activities. They offer workshops and programs throughout the entire year that are open to anybody who is enrolled in the Partnerships' network and we have outreach coordinators in each borough whose job is to maintain those relationships and contacts with the friends groups.[21]

## Repertoires as Models

In spite of the fact that the Central Park Conservancy is the paradigmatic conservancy and has been a model for parks-related public-private partnerships outside of New York City, the main model for organizing these partnerships is closer to Prospect Park's. The Partnerships for Parks' linking volunteers and neighborhood parks with the Parks Department, and helping to build both organizational capacity and volunteers' capabilities through training, suggests that the civic repertoire of public-private partnerships is the most widely pursued. And yet, even in New York City, the Central Park Conservancy has an outsized influence on how people think about conservancies and public-private

CHAPTER FIVE

partnerships, and especially their relation to the inequalities that exist among parks in terms of capital investment and maintenance.

Why does this matter? Repertoires—these clusters of ways of organizing, claim making, and interacting we have described—communicate ideas, including ideas about what is possible to do and what is possible to change. To the extent that Central Park dominates the conversation about conservancies, it is likely that the philanthropic repertoire will be widely understood to be *how conservancies act and what they are.* This, in turn, runs two risks: First, it can misrepresent both the work involved in maintaining the civic infrastructure for conservancies dependent on volunteering and the potentials for shifting goals away from a democratic conception of the public that is implied in the corporate model. Second, if the claims characteristic of the philanthropic model are amplified—that is, that philanthropy is the appropriate response to state failure and budgetary shrinkage—it can lead us to misapprehend the significant ways in which the local state itself has organized and is reorganizing the shift in the provision of this public service.

At the same time, the availability of alternative repertoires, such as the corporate one, provides ready reference for volunteers and others who correctly apprehend the ways in which the philanthropic model falls short in practice. In this sense, the three repertoires we have described also unite in a broader, more flexible repertoire, less moored to the particular times and locations of the "Friends of" groups' and conservancies' development.

## *The Centrality of Central Park*

The Central Park Conservancy is more than "central to the park"; it is central to discussions about conservancies. For Mike, a voluble and enthusiastic volunteer in Queens, Central Park is the reference point for all that works well. Speaking of Flushing Meadows-Corona Park, he drew on Central Park's experience to illustrate that park's conservancy's aspirations:

> The conservancy, that conservancy does not have any staff. So it's still growing, they haven't gotten the kind of funding and up to speed like Central Park, but that's one of our biggest hopes that [the conservancy] will become similar, but not exactly, like Central Park. But we want someone who will look out for the park from the community point of view . . . So they expect to get bigger and have more input, so they're planning for the future. But it'll be ten, fifteen, twenty years down the line.

He continued, mentioning some of the dangers of overformalization of private involvement with the park, and particularly that of workers' fears of displacement.

"Friends of" groups, they're less formal, and like I said, usually not incorporated, or not funded in any way . . . But they're still just as dedicated. Just a different form. Because once you start incorporating, there's a little more, there's reporting and stuff, and most of the friends groups just want to go out there and clean up, paint up, run an event. They don't want to be called in to the paperwork. But they will come in for training. We'll have a meeting every month where we talk about tree pruning, planting, how to get grants, how to retain volunteers, how to deal with parks staff, so you get what you need without alienating the staff. Sometimes they're a little protective. They're afraid we're going to take their jobs. Like we always said, "We don't want to take your job; we want to supplement what you're doing." So takes some time for people to understand that, though.

For his part, Henry Stern suggested that while Betsy Rogers was "the great leader of all this . . . an outstanding figure in parks in the last half of the twentieth century just as Robert Moses was in the first half," the Conservancy as a whole was "WASPy. And even the Jews in Central Park were WASPy. German Jews." For him, this meant that they were unconnected and not responsive to the needs of other parks to raise money as they had. He claimed that the Conservancy was not happy when he formed the City Parks Foundation and saw it as competition. And yet, he also supported the Conservancy and conservancies in general:

I supported them. I worked to bring them about. And welcomed them. And with the conservancies, they have to raise private funds to do whatever they want. But I support their fundraising efforts. And there were some people, socialists, who believe that the conservancies are no good because they mean that some parks will be maintained better than other parks, and therefore that's injustice, and we should not support some parks to a greater extent than others. My attitude, and the City took that position: If people want to pay their own money to make a park nice, I'm not going to refuse it, just because it's *only* Central Park . . .

Even for Jérôme Barth of Bryant Park, the conservancy model itself informs his outlook, even as a mirror image:

The . . . thing is the mindset and the background of the founder. The background is in private business and not in government. . . . And . . . our ideals. We have very

CHAPTER FIVE

high ideals and we are very curious. . . . Everybody else is a conservancy. They conserve. "The geniuses of the past have made it fantastic, and now us poor humble beings are going to try to maintain it." There's no conservancy here. It's a corporation. Yesterday was nothing. Tomorrow is everything.

## *Revenues, Legitimacy, and Alternatives*

The question of whether the parks as a whole are well served by letting "people who want to pay their own money to make a park nice" is put into greater relief when the same people have access to as much money as the people around Central Park have. In a city where levels of inequality are comparable to those in Brazil, there is every possibility that parks with access to enormous levels of private money will also be able to hire their own regular staffs, where other parks will mainly have access to city workers—in a context of long-term cuts in, and reorganization of, the workforce—and to a less reliable volunteer workforce.

Of particular concern to those troubled by unequal treatment of the city's parks, including some conservancies and "Friends of" groups, is the problem that some conservancies get to keep some or all of the revenue they raise through concessions and others do not. While for many parks concessions-based income is not likely to be significant, for others, it may be. Here, it is worth quoting the Friends of Dag Hammarskjold Plaza—a park opposite the United Nations campus in Midtown Manhattan, and a frequent site of rallies—on the perceptions of inequality that even active partners of the Parks Department can have:

Concessions are commercial ventures operating on public land, so at the very least, the park where the concession is located should derive some direct benefit. However, there's no direct benefit to parks except in a few cases where a contract has been negotiated between a powerful park conservancy group and the mayor's office.

We entered into our association with DPR through its Partnership for Parks program, which calls on the dedication of park lovers to voluntarily look after local parks. But the partnership, as it stands, puts the burden of upkeep on the community while DPR retains administrative control. The more powerful nonprofits like Central Park Conservancy, Bryant Park, and Madison Square Park have negotiated contracts between DPR and their organizations that define their relationship and responsibilities. Otherwise, it's a loosely defined arrangement.

Since Dag Hammarskjold Plaza was reopened to the public in 1999, we have provided park upkeep and beautification under the Partnership for Parks model, and now we know its limitations. It's unsustainable. Our directors serve as unpaid managers with no staff, entering into contracts with maintenance services and supervising volunteers to do work that DPR should provide.

Volunteers are a great asset but no substitute for professionally trained park workers. The most effective conservancies are those with paid staffs who have, through their contracts with the city, assumed a large degree of administrative control. Although most neighborhood park groups lack the resources to marshal the professional expertise and fundraising capability of the big conservancies, DPR continues to hold up Central Park and Bryant Park as models to emulate.

For our part, we would like to see our Partnership with Parks evolve into a relationship in which DPR provides the essential services, leaving Friends to focus on enhancements like park beautification and programming. That's how DPR characterizes the Partnership, but it's not the reality. Whenever we ask Parks to take on certain maintenance tasks, the answer is predictable: insufficient manpower—can't you raise more money? Which brings us back to concession reform: let the funds from concessions on public parkland provide a direct benefit to our parks and make the process of awarding bids more transparent.[22]

Further, one could plausibly make the case that conservancy or no, the richer the area, and the better organized and educated a park's neighbors, the better the general condition of parks will be. The reason for this is that so much of a park's infrastructural health relies on funding secured by local city council members. The combination of increased access to knowledge of the system, ability to financially support candidates, and—crucially—the paucity of competing needs in a district means that richer neighbors will be able to create the requisite pressure to retain fixed-post CPWs in their playgrounds or to replace the play surface in their playgrounds while poorer neighbors settle for mobile crews and rubberized play surfaces that become dangerously hot in the summer sun.

Nevertheless, even if conservancies and "Friends of" groups are not the *cause* of unequal treatment of parks users, they certainly compound the tendencies toward inequality, and do so proportionately to the management responsibility they take over their parks. This, in turn, raises a question about the ways in which the City encourages the formation of public-private partnerships and its role in promoting inequality in the name of promoting a general increase in the resources available to parks. For example, Gordon Davis's logic in appointing Parks Department Administrators for larger, regional parks such as Central Park and Prospect Park has now been extended not just to other large parks, such as Rockaway Beach, but also to collections of geographically close parks, such as Northern Manhattan Parks; to whole districts of hundreds of Parks Department properties, including playgrounds and planted street medians ("Greenstreets"), such as District 1 in North Brooklyn; and even to small, commercially active parks such as Madison Square Park. The city subsidy involved in supporting staff positions that either run a park jointly with a private conservancy or that may eventually form such groups suggests that whether the conservancies end up conforming more to corporate, philanthropic, or civic models, the answers to questions that arise over their "legitimacy of organizational forms, their respective jurisdictions, and their interdependencies" with the City depend strongly on the ways in which the Parks Department and the conservancies negotiate their institutional boundaries and manage accountability. It is to these questions, and to the larger issue of emerging forms of "the state," that we turn in the next chapter.

SIX

# Institutional Boundaries, Accountability, and the Integral State

With more than 29,000 acres, equivalent to 14 percent of the land in New York City, the Parks Department works with civic-minded partners to augment services in parks across the five boroughs. These partners act as cheerleaders and benefactors of particular parks, and they play an important role in the success of the city's parks through their collaboration with the Parks Department.

The largest role our partners play is in cultivating and engaging volunteers who give their time, energy and enthusiasm to care for parks throughout the city . . .

Our not-for-profit partners serve to augment the work of the men and women of the Parks Department and do not replace city services or authority. It is the Parks Department that sets all the policies for all New York City parks regardless of any public-private partnership that might support a park. It is the Parks Department that approves every capital project, determines and approves every concession on park land, and issues every permit affecting park land. These facts often are misunderstood, and it is important to recognize that while the Parks Department coordinates closely with its partners and gratefully accepts all assistance, it does not cede its authority to determine policy or activity on city property.[1]

Speaking at a city council hearing on public-private partnerships in the fall of 2013, Parks Commissioner Veronica White addressed council members' concerns that private conservancies held outsized power in parks where they are active and that the public-private partnerships joining the city and the conservancies directed an inequitable level

CHAPTER SIX

of resources to conservancy-run parks, to the detriment of other parks and playgrounds. Though she claims that the Parks Department "does not cede its authority to determine policy or activity on city property," what this really means in practice is not straightforward.

The public-private partnerships presented in the previous chapter are premised on the close cooperation and coordination of governmental and nongovernmental organizations. Sometimes this coordination is made official in contracts. New York City's Parks Department has formal management agreements with twenty conservancies. It also has "hundreds" of informal agreements with "Friends of" groups and conservancies. Whether formal or informal, the point of these partnerships is to work together on a common mission, and the justification of the public-private partnership is found in the idea that government and nonprofits can and must work in complementary ways, where nonprofits provide supplemental resources where government comes up short *and* adds a measure of civic engagement and virtue. In testimony to the city council in 2013, Sarah Nielsen, the newly minted administrator for Washington Square Park in Greenwich Village and the executive director of the Washington Square Park Conservancy, claimed:

> The dual role ensures that the work of the conservancy group is closely aligned with the actual needs of the park. The conservancy can bring together neighbors and develop a community of supporters for the park as volunteers, as eyes on the park and as advocates. The Parks Department will continue to manage the park and make all policy decisions related to the park. Conservancy goals are in line with the Parks Department's to keep the park clean, safe and beautiful.[2]

Here, Nielsen is responding to an ongoing concern among some people who take an active interest in their parks' maintenance. Unlike Daniel Biederman of the Bryant Park Corporation or Richard Gilder, the philanthropist and founding board member of the Central Park Conservancy, cited in previous chapters, these people, who are often leading members of smaller conservancies or "Friends of" groups, do not want private groups to take over the maintenance of parks. They, too, agree with the desirability of the supplementing of parks operations. But as Brad Taylor of the Friends of Morningside Park testified at the same hearing, "[I]f there are private dollars coming in we should make sure that those private dollars are supplementing the public dollars and not supplanting them."[3]

In the last chapter, we made two related observations: First, the blending of private and public authority has become a regular feature of urban political studies, as "regime theory" posits various combinations of private and public interests that combine into different regimes, in which elites bargain, usually, at least, for the right to develop the city as they wish. Second, we suggested a somewhat more fluid metaphor—repertoires—drawn from the study of social movements, as a means of understanding the particular clusters of ways of organizing and talking about park management and maintenance that constitute civic, philanthropic, and corporate repertoires of parks governance. If the last chapter contrasted the repertoires stemming from the three first large conservancies, this chapter zooms out and considers the developing governance repertoire as a whole. It asks how the state *integrates* the corporate, civic, and philanthropic repertoires and their actors into the larger complex of parks maintenance and does so in the face of considerable, and growing, criticism.

### The Neoliberalizing Integral State

Starting from Brad Taylor's concern about the private supplanting the public in terms of dollars and authority, we propose that instead we recognize—as regime theorists do—that both come together in what the early-twentieth-century Italian Marxist Antonio Gramsci called the "integral state." The "integral state" was Gramsci's way of talking about the state as more than a coercive organization, but rather as a unity between the basic coercive functions of government and its more expansive civil and moral aspects, and the organizational forms this takes. Well before—but also beyond—regime theorists, Gramsci understood that the integral state meant two things: First, that civil society and the state work together, not so that one cannot distinguish between the government and nongovernmental organizations but so that their actual functions intermix in the act of governing; and second, that the particular forms of the integral state produce and rely on distinct ideas—even ideologies—that legitimate the governing projects of those in power. It is "the entire complex of practical and theoretical activities with which the ruling class not only justifies and maintains its dominance, but manages to win the active consent of those over whom it rules."[4] Gramsci thought of the *act* of integrating the state as one of "passive revolution," or the gradual transformation of potential challenges into support for the regime's project.

And what is this project? It is, as we suggested in chapter 1, *neoliberalism*. To say this, however, opens up a can of worms. There is broad agreement that neoliberalism has to do with the primacy of individual property rights in public policy and that, accordingly, there is a preference for market- or market-like mechanisms to take care of the distribution of goods and services. But there has been an enormous debate in academia over the term, and we do not want to revisit all of that debate here. Key positions revolve around definitions of neoliberalism as a free-market philosophy pitched against the welfare state; as an attack on collective action from below; as a bid for class power by an ascendant class of financial capitalists; as the "hollowing out" of the state's functions; and as a mode of regulating the capitalist economy. There is much to recommend each of these, and most are not mutually exclusive. We want to distinguish our use of the term, however, from those that treat neoliberalism as a free-market philosophy first, that only subsequently gets put into practice. To be sure, the philosophical roots of neoliberalism have been traced and its initial exponents' political activities studied. And yet, as Neil Brenner and Nik Theodore have argued, neoliberalism is best understood not as an ideal to which one or another political practice approaches but rather as it "really exists," in *already* hybrid forms.

Others make the point even more sharply. They insist that it is better to speak of *neoliberalization*—a process—rather than neoliberalism. Jamie Peck and Adam Tickell, in an influential article, argue that we can distinguish between "roll-back" and "roll-out" moments: the former refers to points at which older state-mediated social relations are crushed, and the latter refers to points at which new, more market-based programs (or hybrids) are established. We could apply "roll-back" neoliberalization, for example, to the process by which disinvestment from the Parks Department was compounded by the loss of staff, and even by broadbanding and a switch to mobile crews as the foundation of the maintenance workforce. We could apply "roll-out" neoliberalism to the establishment of the Bryant Park Corporation, or even to the Central Park Conservancy.

And yet, as we will show in this chapter, moments of "roll back" and "roll out" are mixed together. Moreover, as Bob Jessop has argued, much as we have in the last chapter, even if the tendency of states has been toward more private- and market-based policies, neoliberalism only exists as an ideal type; in reality, it is always mixed with "flanking" mechanisms that could be grouped into ideal types—or better, repertoires—corresponding to more communitarian, corporatist, and statist policy strategies according to the ruling elites' needs to balance their ability to accumulate capital and to legitimize their rule.[5] Accordingly, while the foundation of the Central Park Conservancy *could* be seen as a moment of neoliberalizing "roll out" following the decimation of the parks workforce during the fiscal crisis, it could also be an instance of ongoing "roll back" of public workers' jobs and power, and one, moreover, that relies on philanthropic initiative—a peculiar exercise of class power—more than on market-based mechanisms. In what follows, we return to the public-private partnerships we mapped out in the last chapter, to examine the ways in which they advance the neoliberalizaton of the parks workforce via three distinct moves. First, the partnerships actively blur lines of accountability by combining rollback and roll-out dynamics in their staffing, promoting "flexibility" and making it difficult to dislodge this new configuration of the state. Second, they make a permanent state of scarcity seem inevitable and natural, through claims that the conservancies are needed to "supplement" a chronically underfunded Parks Department, and suggest the public sector is sclerotic. Third, they reinforce elite control of parks by publicly extolling the civic virtues of volunteering and philanthropy.

**Blurred Lines**

Even in the integral state, one can still distinguish between the "government" and "nonprofits"—they are not the same thing. But when it comes to understanding the ways in which organizational roles, authority, and accountability overlap in practice, these distinctions are more difficult to identify clearly.

The blurring of institutional boundaries and accountability is perhaps best captured by the double-sided business card we received from a Park Administrator in an outer-borough park and the email address on it. The card was green and white; on the green side, beneath the green leaf Parks Department logo, the administrator was named as such, and as an employee of the New York City Department of Parks and Recreation. The white side was dominated by the logo of the park conservancy of which the same person acts as executive director. The email was the same on both sides of the card: it was a "parks.nyc.gov" address. Conversely, the Parks Department website is no longer a ".gov" address; instead, it is www.nycgovparks.org, an address that typically signifies a nonprofit organization. This, in turn, suggests a rearrangement of priorities, from the location of parks governance in the *government* to its location in a hybrid, integral governance model, in which nonprofit organizations are central players. The business card was a tangible and condensed representation of a set of arrangements that has become typical of the public-private partnerships: the appointment of administrators for specific parks as Parks Department employees, while also having these administrators serve as the executive directors of a nonprofit park conservancies, links public and private park agencies at the head. A clear division of labor between the two is thus difficult to achieve.

The matter goes beyond hiring shared administrators. Nonmanagerial program staff also mixes together in ways that blur accountability, with publicly sourced salaries for private, nonprofit staff and staffs of some groups that are partially paid through private and public sources. As one employee of Partnerships for Parks told us, "Half of the staff (at Partnerships for Parks) is Park-paid, half is CPF (City Parks Foundation). The director . . . Half his salary is paid by the Parks Department and half by CPF." The same employee had a "parks.gov" email address, as do the roughly thirty-five employees of the Partnerships for Parks. Similarly, in Prospect Park, we were informed that the Volunteers in Prospect Park (VIPP) program office "is city employees working for the Alliance. The staff is paid by the City, but it's run by the Alliance." Lines between public and private initiative also blur when the nonprofit-but-publicly-initiated Partnerships for Parks organizes and advocates for new "Friends of" groups and encourages them to become more involved in their parks' maintenance and operations.

From the point of view of most workers at the workplace—whether in conservancy-run parks or not—organizational boundaries are not particularly salient. When we interviewed volunteer coordinators at one conservancy-administered park, it was striking that workers did not necessarily know which of their coworkers were city workers and which were conservancy workers. Even in Central Park, where the lines between the city workforce and the Conservancy workforce are reinforced by assignment to distinct zones and a shared history of competition and displacement of city workers, both some supervisors and lower-level workers in each organization reported working well with each other and for the shared goal of improving the park's appearance for its users.

As much as they may seem blurred, however, the institutional boundaries do not disappear. They become more clearly visible again during times of crisis. Such was the case, for example, when the Central Park Conservancy fired more than thirty workers in January 2009. Then, for all the shared goals, whether you were on one side or another of the public-private boundary made all the difference in whether you were at risk of losing your job. Moreover, it determined *how* you could lose your job: without notice, with severance pay linked to agreements not to litigate, and without the chance to seek employment elsewhere in the Conservancy. The larger impression of partnership fostered by close working relationships among workers, and for which the shared goals of parks care pushes the salience of institutional boundaries into the background, results in a shock to workers when it is breached. This breach was the principal source of the expressions of injured dignity widely expressed by the fired Central Park Conservancy workers we interviewed. But we should not forget the source of the very distinctions that are subject, in happier times, to being blurred: here, we find the celebration of the neoliberalizing "flexibility" in management of a private, nonunion workforce apparent since the founding of the Conservancy and periodically given new life in proposals to privatize more of the parks workforce.

## Supplementing and the Naturalization of Scarcity

The idea that conservancies exist to supplement what the Parks Department does is important in several ways. First, it acts as a *defense* of public work by asserting that the Parks Department, a public agency accountable to the public, ultimately through the mayor, remains in control of what is an admittedly complex system rife with informal agreements about basic issues such as parks maintenance and use. The defense of the public interest could be seen in the last chapter in former Parks Commissioner Henry Stern's claim that the Bryant Park Corporation had been ceded too much control over the use of the park. But as parks such as Bryant Park become at least partial models for Manhattan conservancies, and as conservancies work to attract more upscale food options for visitors than the once-ubiquitous New York "dirty water dog,"[6] an explicit defense of public control answers a small but growing chorus of doubters.

When we interviewed Commissioner Benepe in 2011, he reinforced the claims of public control. He cited the Parks Inspection Program as a key element of this:

Well, they get inspected like any other park. So PIP ratings apply. So a section of Central Park is just as likely to fail as a section of a park in the Bronx, because the inspectors are looking at it in the same way. And often it does. If they go into the Ramble in Central Park and all the paths are [in terrible shape] they're going to fail

CHAPTER SIX

it . . . So the PIP inspections are one way to hold them accountable. Then there are deliverables within the contracts that say, "You have to maintain up to these standards" . . . Generally speaking with the Conservancy, they're going to be able to hit those standards. But still we don't count on it, so we do PIP inspections.

Furthermore, like his successor, Commissioner White, Benepe emphasized the City's policy-making supremacy:

And finally and most important, those groups don't set policy. They don't set policy for events. They don't set policy for rules and regulations. The City sets the policy and we have the final say in everything. So in general, it isn't the Central Park Conservancy saying, "We want to have a big concert." It's the City saying, "We want to have a big concert"; the Central Park Conservancy just has to deal with it. And then they don't like the fact that they have to clean up after the concert, but they don't have a choice in that. So the only way these partnerships work is if the City has the final say in everything. And we have many—six or seven—arrangements that are actual contractual arrangements with a nonprofit group, and all of those contractual relationships are subject to being terminated at will by the city. So if we don't like the way someone's doing something, we have the ability—we could end it tomorrow.

Closely related to this assertion of ultimate control is the idea that with the public agency at the center of the parks system, conservancies are there as *necessary additions* to public efforts. Here, in partial contrast to the ways in which volunteers and JTPs (or WEP workers and community service sentencees) are portrayed by Parks officials as "extra help," and their importance to maintenance played down to some degree, conservancies appear as extra help that is, nevertheless, fundamental to the system as a whole. This ambivalent "fundamental supplement" works rhetorically to make a chronic lack of resources appear as a natural outcome of a neutrally functioning system of resource allocation, and more immutable than it would be if it were acknowledged as a result of specific political decisions. Henry Stern gave a more thorough-than-usual account of this logic, which we heard expressed by Commissioner Adrian Benepe on several occasions, as well:

I had a theoretical reason why Parks gets screwed budget-wise. One is that it's not a uniform service, like firefighters. Two, it's not considered an essential service. No one will die. Three, it's because it's not a modular service. For example, if you cut transit by 10 percent, you have 10 percent fewer trains. Cut Parks by 10 percent, they clean, the mow the lawns every two weeks instead of every week. So it's . . .

Four, there was no law that you have to have park services. The way that there [are] laws requiring fire services. There's no union contract that requires certain levels of service the way there are with other unions. There are union collective bargain agreements where part of the collective bargain agreements obligates the city to do certain things. There are no such obligations. And there are no court decisions. There are court decisions for the homeless and for this and for that, and every special interest group representing some people with some mental or physical—what used to be called defects, but are now called differences, or special needs—go before some judge, and the judge will order the city, regardless of the consequences or cost, to provide a certain service level, that [otherwise] is a violation of the constitutional rights. So Parks has none of those. It has no constitutional standards. It has no statutory standards. It has no labor union standards. And it has no judicial standards. So in all these areas, Parks comes up short.[7]

The political scientist Deborah Stone writes that complex causal stories "are in some sense analogous to [stories of] accidental or natural cause. They postulate a kind of innocence, in that no identifiable actor can exert control over the whole system or web of interactions. Without overarching control, there can be no purpose and no responsibility."[8] Stern's account of the complexities of Parks' "getting screwed budget-wise" suggests that the underlying economic conditions of the Parks Department are subject to almost inevitable reduction. And yet, within this complex background of inevitable *lack of economic control*, the Parks Department is still *programmatically in control*, as Commissioners White and Benepe argue. Conservancies *add* to the public, *quantitatively* by bringing resources and personnel and *qualitatively* by bringing advocacy for parks within the system that, but for this advocacy, might shortchange them even more. Conservancies do not subtract anything.

Commissioner Benepe encapsulated the quantitative elements of this supplemental but fundamental role played by the conservancies by answering whether any contracts had, in fact, ever been terminated:

We have done it with some nonprofit organizations that were running recreation centers, where they were not providing service. So we had to. So it's been done. So far, the groups like the Central Park Conservancy, the Prospect Park Alliance, have done a really good job. And you know, people will say, "Oh, you're privatizing the park, and when you gave the contract to Central Park Conservancy, why'd you give them a sole-source contract? Why didn't you want to see if someone else wanted to do this?" And our response is, "Well, anybody who wants to compete, the line forms to the left. Anyone who wants to of their own volition raise thirty million dollars of private donations a year to pay to maintain a public park, have at it! We'll give you another park!"

Prompted by an associate, Benepe went further, expounding on the effects of having privately paid conservancy workers in the parks: "Right. We don't have to put city workers in Central Park. We can use city workers in other parks. It's a great thing. It's like having an extra ninety million dollars in my budget to have these private groups."

Here, the rhetoric *is* quite similar to the rhetoric surrounding volunteers (at least some of whom are recruited by conservancies, in any case): volunteers are doing an extra job that public workers would not be able to do. They are called in to paint benches and fences and to clean areas that regular workers do not have time to clean in the normal, under-resourced run of things. Conservancies bring *extra* resources that help the Parks Department go beyond what it would normally be able to provide. That the normal situation is one in which resources are chronically scarce is itself rarely questioned.

The qualitative aspects of supplementing the Parks Department are captured first in Washington Square Park Administrator Sarah Nielsen's claim that "the conservancy can bring together neighbors and develop a community of supporters for the park as volunteers, as eyes on the park and as advocates." These are qualitative elements of the civic engagement that conservancies and "Friends of" groups foster that, presumably, the Parks Department and government as a whole cannot. The Partnerships for Parks website similarly says, "Ultimately, our work supports a culture of collaboration among people and government that recognizes that parks are vital centers of community life."[9]

Importantly, in this set of ideas about qualitative supplements to the Parks Department's work, there is an underlying, implicit view of government as a bloodless bureaucracy, incapable of responding to real people's aspirations for public lives and public spaces. The partnerships bring in new blood to revitalize governmental functions and, in so doing, reinforce the *distinction* between the *government* and *civic life* even as they blur it. Even if, in this view—different, again, from the view that parks should be fully given over to private management for reasons of efficiency—government agencies *can* manage larger, complex systems relatively efficiently, these agencies still require civic guidance from engaged citizens about their goals. Recounting the formation of Staten Island's Greenbelt Conservancy, Steven Cain, its executive director and the park's Administrator, told a City Council Committee on

Parks hearing that the people involved "were motivated not by money or acclaim but only by standing for the good and the right. They are the forerunners of the Greenbelt Conservancy. Our current board members share their deep appreciation for and commitment to open space, environmental education, and preservation."[10] Similarly, Commissioner White told the committee a version of the origin story of conservancies and "Friends of" groups:

Most of the groups, it's an evolution. I mean the Central Park Conservancy didn't have an agreement with the Parks Department for its first seventeen years, so it evolves. It's like I went to the park and I pick up after my kids and then I say to Larry, "Why aren't you picking up after your dogs?", and then Liam says, "I don't have any time but I'll give you some money for some tulips." This is literally how it starts, and then we in the Parks Department have a much more systemized approach now, so . . . the Partnerships for Parks . . . teams go out and they cultivate that, and they're like, "Wow, there's three people that are interested in making this park better. Can we help out?" And then we outreach to them, but it doesn't usually start with the Parks Department employees so much as it's a combination. It's people in the community paying attention and saying, "How can we make things better?"[11]

Though this story plays down the history of the Parks Department's active encouragement of volunteering from the 1970s on, and though it soft-pedals the development of a "more systemized approach" via the creation of the Partnerships for Parks by the Parks Department, it puts civic-minded individuals at the center of policy development, individuals whose everyday moral virtue steers government in the right direction.

Former Commissioner Adrian Benepe emphasized the other qualitative contribution of public-private partnerships that often is cited in literature about them. Echoing his successor's emphasis on long-term civic engagement, he also mentions the private partners' tendency to bring in new management strategies:

The vast majority of parks are supported exclusively by public money, as they should be. While private contributions are important to local parks, even more crucial is the role that the citizen-led boards play as perpetual park guardians. Mayors and city councils and park commissioners (and their budgets) come and go, but citizens make sure the cities keep up their investment in parks. Public-private partnerships also bring entrepreneurial management techniques and creative funding mechanisms to park stewardship.

CHAPTER SIX

## Supplanting the Parks Department and the Fear of Privatizing Accountability

The role of parks conservancies in New York City is increasingly questioned, however, and often by those who would like to believe in the continuation of the Parks Department's autonomous authority but who have lost faith in it, in the face of considerable institutional blurring of the sort we have just described.

The doubts form a constellation that is almost a mirror image of the official discourse of civic-minded supplementation of public action. A wide range of people—from union activists to parks advocates—have raised concerns about the alienation of accountability from the public and an increasingly elite orientation of parks programming and control by elites of parks use. In this context, they are more likely to question the moral virtue of administrators of park conservancies and likely to question the wisdom of getting into long-term agreements with conservancies, especially at a point at which many parks are not in the same kind of parlous condition that Central Park was in during the late 1970s. In short, these critics worry that private organizations *supplant* public initiative and accountability as public-private partnerships develop, rather than help or support ongoing, fully public endeavors.

Concerns that conservancies may supplant government support for parks is broadly consistent with concerns about the "retreat" or "hollowing out of the state" under neoliberal capitalism and the opening of public enterprise to private capital accumulation.[12] To be sure, critics are not saying that the Parks Department has completely retreated or is actually irrelevant to running the parks. But they are concerned with what they identify as the tendencies expressed in the public-private partnerships the City has initiated and that increasingly favor the relatively wealthy over the relatively poor.

### *Accountability*

From the point of view of parks "watchdog" organizations, the claim that conservancies can be the "eyes on the park and advocates" is problematic. For these groups, conservancies may be the source of deficits in public accountability and in a creeping lack of transparency in the Parks Department's operations. There are more "moderate" and "militant" versions of this criticism, represented broadly by New Yorkers for Parks (NY4P) and New York City Parks Advocates (NYCPA), respectively. NY4P is the most recent iteration of a venerable parks advocacy organization known as the Parks Council from 1970 until 2002, and before that it had several names going back to its founding in 1908. True to its Progressive Era roots, NY4P is interwoven with the same elites that form the boards of several conservancies, and especially the Central Park Conservancy.[13] Like Progressive Era advocacy organizations, it is founded on the principle that the development of expertise on parks—on a wide range of issues, including maintenance and operations but also parks use—is the key to effective advocacy for equitable and efficient government. For example, it issues periodic "report cards" on parks, which often vary from the Parks Department's own findings through its Parks Inspection Program, and usually rate parks less well than the department does. Nevertheless, it also goes to some lengths to praise the department's efforts to improve operations and suggests ways in which funding for parks might be improved. As such, it maintains good relationships with the Parks Department even when it is critical of it.

By contrast, NYCPA is a smaller, scrappier operation, largely run by a single former professional photographer and journalist, Geoffrey Croft. Croft has been involved in parks for twenty years, having founded a nonprofit to run a photography and youth program in a park in Manhattan's Yorkville neighborhood and having worked as a researcher for the Parks Council. He has visited every park property in the city and never spares the Park Department criticism. Unlike NY4P, NYCPA has a much more strained relationship with the department.

Both groups, however, have expressed concern over the inequalities in parks maintenance between parks in wealthier and poorer neighborhoods and concern that the array of arrangements between the City and conservancies and "Friends of" groups is insufficiently transparent. NY4P has largely taken the position held by the Parks Department that the source of inequality in parks conditions is not the result of conservancies as such but rather an effect of a general shortage of personnel and a capital funding system based in discretionary allocations to city council members that systematically favors richer neighborhoods' parks.[14] Nevertheless, NY4P has argued that the system of public-private partnerships should learn from "best practices" of existing partnerships in the Park Department's orbit and that a more uniform template for new and renewed contracts should be developed. Tellingly, this template includes some items that we had earlier been told characterizes all conservancies:

[A]ll agreements should require that the DPR commissioner and relevant borough commissioner are ex officio members of the organization's board; they actually don't all require that right now, to ensure DPR involvement in decision making. In addition, community committee such as that for Prospect Park should be required to ensure public input. Third, all organizations' 990 tax filing should be available in one place on the DPR website. I was glad to hear the commissioners think about doing that. Ideally, DPR would also require organizations to report their financial information annually in a more simplified consistent form that would be posted on its website.[15]

At the same time, NY4P is less concerned with some elements of the blurring of the institutional boundaries between the Parks Department and conservancies. It describes the system of dual appointment of park administrators and executive directors of conservancies as a "belt-and-suspenders approach," which "means there are more checks and balances for these parks than for the rest of the city's parks."[16]

New York City Parks Advocates, on the other hand, has argued much more vociferously that the blending of conservancies and the Parks Department sets up intense conflicts of interest, since conservancies are still, in effect, contractors for the City, and that the entire system of public-private partnerships supplants public control and accountability of parks. NYCPA's Croft described the parks system to us as a "tale of two cities" and testified to the city council that:

Experience with public-private partnerships over the last thirty years has proven that the private subsidization of individual parks, however well intentioned, has created an enormous gap between the haves and the have-nots while ignoring the real problem that our parks are not funded as an essential government service. It helps to ensure different or no parks for different people, discourages the government from maintaining the parks, and substitutes private decisions on the funding and the upkeep for accountable, transparent decisions regarding these precious public lands that can be changed by the public itself.[17]

Croft expanded on this theme in an interview we conducted with him in 2009, using a poignant example:

[M]ost of our surfaces are so compacted or they're completely [eroded]. So you go to these ball fields, and you would basically have child labor. I've gone up to parks where they have children literally spending hours and hours and hours cleaning up the field because, and you'll have, I'm pretty sure last year in the Bronx . . . these kids are out there working the field, and I look and it's kind of like a chain gang, you know. And again, I'm not opposed . . . I love working the field, and that's great. But for these kids to *play* in their field, these guys are out there for six hours, right? And I have the coach tell me that the park worker's really nice, he came and helped the kids water, and . . . that is really nice, you know? That is really nice. But then I went back and picked up my records for how many workers are in that district and again, there's nobody. So then, for these kids to [play], they have to maintain their own field. So now we have dozens of these situations where they are paying private contractors. And I know that's a union issue, they're looking at these public-private partnerships. But yes, on the ball fields themselves, in the springtime for instance, for baseball, they come and dump one pile of clay and that's it. There's no other maintenance. When you work for Central Park, you could have literally a half a dozen workers working on one field, working, preparing those fields. One field. And that's what you have. So you don't have that in any other park like that. So that's, again, it shows a huge discrepancy. So now, in the next month you'll see in Central Park and those types of organizations putting together their crew. Now, not only do they have dedicated ball field crews—so again, twenty-eight fields, twenty- eight dedicated—then they have what they're calling Grounds Technicians, they have their Zone Gardeners, these are all people dedicated with the express purpose to deal with those issues. So they have the staffing and the personnel, so that's why . . . it's not hard to understand why wealthy people want to have a private parks department. There's also people in the Central Park Conservancy who'd like to take over the [role of the] Parks Department. I mean, that's long known.

Others, too, are concerned with the supplanting of authority and accountability of public institutions with private ones. There are ongoing conflicts—including in court—about the involvement of conservancies and "Friends of" groups in changing park uses. Where "Friends of" groups have strong involvement from local business improvement districts, as in Union Square Park and Madison Square Park, there is the added danger of the commercialization of public space. When this occurs, the "belt-and-suspenders approach" to the double employment of Parks and conservancy staff makes potential conflicts of interest even clearer. Importantly, as the New York *Daily News* reported, no other agency in the city government has as many employees with this double employment arrangement as the Parks Department has, according to the city's Conflict of Interest Board.

In 2009, in response to increasing concern about the accountability of parks conservancies—in part, due to a plan by the Randall's Island Sports Authority to subsidize its operations through exclusive use agreements with New York City private schools—the city council passed a law requiring conservancy boards to have at least one director who lives or has a business in the council district in which the park in question lies. The city council member from that district would appoint the director.

*Elite Control*

Conservancy critics also are concerned about the possibility that parks fall increasingly under control of local elites, both because rich people can, through private donations, buy access to decision making on the private boards of nonprofit organizations and because events and amenities catering to elite tastes will have positive feedback in generating support for parks. Marlena Giga, a longtime PEP officer, gave the following testimony to the city council hearing, apparently contradicting Commissioner White's testimony that the Parks Department makes all the decisions about what happens in parks.

During my fourteen years, I've worked in all five boroughs and I've had the opportunity to see first-hand what various conservancies and park partnerships groups have done. In the worst case scenarios, they divide the parks into a state of being able to pick what laws are enforced, what types of concerts are heard, what types of sports are played, the designs of the park recreation centers, and prohibiting the public access and how the money will be spent in that particular park. . . . I have witnessed in Van Cortlandt Park in the Bronx only accommodating Riverdale schools and schools that are able to pay for permits that take up the entire playground or running track, making it nearly impossible for neighborhood children to use. I have also witnessed the diversity of the concerts of the past in many parks diminish to nonminority entertainment, making the park not friendly to the locals. This is happening in many parks. The conservancies are also able to make up their own signs which are different from the park rules and regulations and the laws of New York City.[18]

Further, NYCPA has publicized the controversy surrounding the group Save Union Square's efforts to protect that park's colonnaded pavilion from becoming an upscale restaurant for the most active six months of the year. It has argued against the bids that real estate developers have made to gain control over parts of the city's parkland in exchange for agreements to pay for maintenance. Though NYCPA has criticized these deals, it has been no less sparing of nonprofit organizations from wealthier neighborhoods, like the West Side Soccer League, that are able to pay for permits for the exclusive use of playing fields in parks during peak hours. Once again, NYCPA worries that the Parks Department promotes this in order to compensate for woefully inadequate budgets: "The city continues to try and abdicate its responsibility by entering into these public-private agreements that officials are not only allowing but actively encouraging. They are increasingly resorting to these pay-to-play funding schemes."[19]

Concerns about elite control of parks, moreover, extend beyond NYCPA. At the lengthy New York City Council hearings about public-private partnerships in 2013, Brad Taylor, of the Friends of Morningside Park, brought up the question of PEP officers:

Conversely though . . . we can't let the public funds chase the private funds, and I just want to bring up one example which has been bandied about a lot which is the PEP officers. You know, we're in a thirty-acre park. We have one PEP officer and, you know, Parks has tried hard but often these PEP officers are allocated based on who can provide private funding for them. And it really becomes an inequitable situation.

I'm also on the community board in West Harlem, and we heard from John Herrold [that] the two-acre West Harlem Piers Park gets $500,000 from Columbia. That funds four PEP officers. This is basically a two-acre park. Morningside has one PEP officer for thirty acres. I mean if they were an equitable system, Morningside would have 60 PEP officers. So we really need to make sure that, you know, these public resources and these people are—maybe paid by conservancies but they're, you know, they're trained on the public dollar, you know, their benefits are public—you know, they are allocated based on public need.[20]

In order to mitigate the directive force of "outside" money in the parks in the conservancy system, Brooklyn State Senator Daniel Squadron proposed a bill that would require 20 percent of the revenue collected by conservancies with operating budgets over $5 million to be paid into a common pool that would help other parks with less capability of raising funds.

Squadron's bill provoked a backlash among large conservancies, which worried about losing needed revenue and alienating donors. Tupper Thomas said that if the bill were passed, the Prospect Park Alliance would lose up to fifteen of its staff. Holly Leicht of NY4P said that it would produce too little revenue to matter if that revenue were to be spread among parks. Former Commissioner Adrian Benepe supported these arguments, adding that

Forcing private donations to local parks to be spread to other parks flies in the face of the spirit and motivation behind philanthropy. The uniquely American tradition

CHAPTER SIX

of large-scale charitable support for the arts and culture, higher education, the environment, and other causes is a foundation of this nation precisely because people have the choice to donate for things they personally care about. The quickest way to kill philanthropy is to mandate how and where our hard-earned dollars go. Imagine a donor to cancer research being told that twenty percent of her contribution is being reallocated to another disease.[21]

And yet parks advocates, such as Cathryn Swan, a blogger, champion of Washington Square Park, and opponent of its emerging conservancy, take issue with Benepe's characterization in his piece's title that "citizen involvement" in parks is under attack:

> People are not against "citizen involvement" in our public spaces and in our alleged democracy. They are against handing off control of our parks to the highest bidder. The public does not want to see a few parks being prioritized over others. Parks are our commons and we should all be equal there.

In an article in the *Huffington Post*, Swan cites Jim Walden, an attorney for several neighborhood groups fighting Parks Department partnerships with conservancies and private developers. Echoing—but from the opposite perspective—Benepe's point about philanthropy, Walden told a radio host that

> development corporations and conservancies don't have the same transparency, visibility, sunlight that a city agency would [in theory]. . . . From a pure public policy perspective, as long as the private interests that are contributing to the park understand that it's no different than making a charitable contribution, once you give the money, you're done. . . . There wouldn't be a problem. . . . The problem is control. With the private money coming into the park, there is some giveaway of control that ultimately allows a foot in the door, ultimately resulting [in] the park either changing, shrinking, or going away completely.[22]

## Modes of Integration

The dual privatization of public services and publicization of private associations[23] we find at the heart of the Parks Department's governance did not happen instantly, but rather developed incrementally over a period of the nearly forty years since New York City's fiscal crisis in the 1970s. We have already noted, for example, the distinction between the appointment of parks administrators under Commissioner Gordon

Davis in the early 1980s—targeted to large, regional parks—and today, when the jointly hired administrator who is also executive director of a nonprofit conservancy may be in charge of a park merely three square city blocks in size, however intensively used. Even as NY4P has called for some greater lesson learning and standardization based on these arrangements, the crucial point is that these very different partnerships have developed "pragmatically" over time and reflect different points in the perceived needs of these parks, fiscal position of the department, and strength of nonprofit partners.

## *Pragmatic Flexibility*

The pragmatic development of public-private partnerships did not develop in a political vacuum. If we look at their growth and change since the fiscal crisis years, we see that these partnerships were, at the outset, underwritten by a fairly thoroughgoing antistatist ideology, rooted largely in a view that public workers enjoyed too much power. Through the intervention of philanthropists such as Richard Gilder and academics like E. S. Savas, the Central Park Conservancy developed into a paradigmatic public-private partnership with a significantly anti-union bent. Even though this anti-union bent has not completely characterized other conservancies, Central Park became a model upon which other conservancies have either been based, or, more commonly, *justified*. Recounting a community board meeting about the Washington Square Park Conservancy, Swan wrote:

At the Parks Committee meeting, Manhattan Borough Parks Commissioner Bill Castro also appeared. He invoked a fear-mongering note: We don't want Washington Square Park to be like Central Park in the 1970s.

Community member **Georgia Seamans**, speaking against the Conservancy (feeling it was not sufficiently scrutinized) said in response: "**Washington Square Park in 2013 is NOT Central Park in the 1970s.**" To compare the two shouldn't even be relevant—but Castro did, using it as a scare tactic to get the Board to approve of a private body with what amounted to an unspecified level of control [bold in original].

And while there is little question at the moment of most conservancies hiring their own staffs in large numbers, Commissioner Benepe was forthright in his assessment that the conservancy staffs that do exist add significantly to the headcount of employees dedicated to parks maintenance, putting the total of conservancy workers citywide at 1,500 (a figure that is on the high end of many estimates we encountered).

The main point, however, is that the philanthropic-corporate-civic triad of conservancy types outlined in chapter 5 enables the public-private partnership–based approach of the Parks Department to be flexible and pragmatic and to build coalitions not just to politically support its reorganization of governance, but also to carry it out and embody it. In so doing, it cements these new partnerships in place, making the public-private partnerships relationships of *necessity* rather than choice. The thought of conservancies *not* getting their contracts renewed is almost impossible. Though the city comptroller, John Liu, refused to sign off on Central Park Conservancy's contract renewal in June 2013, on the basis that he thought that the City had given away the rights to too much concession revenue, he was derided by the Bloomberg administration as both engaging in a publicity stunt for his own mayoral campaign and reaching beyond his jurisdiction in the strong-mayor system enshrined in the city charter.

### *Philanthropic Neoliberalism and Neoliberal Philanthropy*

Commissioner Benepe's comment that existing conservancies like Central Park's are uniquely able to mobilize the resources needed by parks squares with a new vision of the relationship among private capital, the government, and civic engagement. Continuing his opposition to Senator Daniel Squadron's conservancy revenue-sharing proposal, he kept returning to the importance of the autonomy of philanthropy for his vision of "democracy":

> If we said to the Brooklyn Museum, "You know you've done a great job fund-raising, but you know, we're gonna take 10 or 20 percent of your money and reallocate it to the Queens Museum, because they haven't done quite as good of a job of fund-raising," or "Jennifer Raab has done an extraordinary job raising money for Hunter College, and you know what, let's take some of that $40 million she brought in this year and reallocate to the Bronx Community College because they need the money more . . ." That's not the way democracy works. They're both public institutions. One raises money, the other doesn't as much.

In this vision, philanthropy is so central to the operation of public institutions that it is allowed to operate without significant public direction. If, indeed, the Parks Department makes all the important policy decisions, as both of Mayor Bloomberg's parks commissioners insisted it does, then one of the key decisions it makes is to give philanthropy fairly free rein in return for the department's ability to keep attracting more of it. It is defined as democratic precisely because it involves the respect of philanthropists' individual choices of where to direct their largesse. This conflation of individual choice and democracy is common in neoliberal discourse and casually normalizes the coincidence of economic and political power.

Of course, in broad strokes, none of this is new or particular to the post-1970s era. As David Wagner and others have amply shown, philanthropy in the United States has long favored the power of the wealthy over the poor: from the "friendly visits" of judgmental charity workers to the homes of the poor to the central place of philanthropic foundations in the "nonprofit-industrial complex," the role of the wealthy in directing social provision and in the corresponding stinginess of state-allocated social provision in the United States is clear. Still, state-led provision has often also been carried out in ways that reflect the economic wishes of at least some capitalist elites. As Frances Fox Piven and Richard A. Cloward argued in their 1971 classic *Regulating the Poor: The Functions of Social Welfare*, the state only grants more expansive benefits in the face of social disorder and the—temporary—dissolution of the legitimacy of elites' work-enforcing moralism in the wake of large-scale economic dislocation and crisis.

And yet, what *does* strike us as different, here, is the extension of the logic of elite control via philanthropy to public provision for *all*, for a basic public service, and one that even helps define "public space," rather than for the poor only. This suggests something of a reconfiguration of forces. Georg Simmel, one of the founders of modern sociology and author of short, quirky essays about social "forms," wrote of a metaphorical shift that suggests how this reconfiguration of forces might inform our understanding of the way the neoliberal integral state works. Contrasting "The Bridge and the Door," he wrote:

If in the bridge the moments of separation and connection behave in such a way that the former appears to be more of a natural thing, and the latter more of a human thing, with the door both penetrate to the same extent into human activity, *as* human activity. On this depends the richest and most vital significance of the door as against the bridge. It is also disclosed by the fact that, while it makes no difference in which direction one crosses a bridge, there is a total difference of intention between going in and going out of a door.

CHAPTER SIX

We can extend this analogy to the discussion of public and private in the integral state. If public and private association are seen as fully distinct—almost naturally distinct—realms, rendered in a great deal of literature as the "state" and "civil society," then public-private partnerships are a method of "bridging" between the two and thereby enabling a meeting in the middle of the bridge, so to speak, of the representatives of the two realms. On the other hand, to see the distinction between public and private as being mediated by a "door" is to focus on the boundaries that people make themselves and on their ordering of space, understood as physical space or, more metaphorically, as social space. If we understand the public-private partnerships as doors instead of bridges, we have to understand that the spaces that we typically assign to "the state" or "government" on one hand, and "civil society" or "private enterprise" on the other hand(s),[24] are and have been given different boundaries at different times, with different doors—meeting points—between them. This, then, opens up the specific public-private partnerships we see in the parks to a broader inquiry that discusses what we have, until now, been calling "institutional blurring" as *new attempts at boundary formation* and investigates the development of larger-scale processes of which these new boundary-forming attempts are part. Thus, along with the privatization of public service, we have a concomitant *publicization of private service*,[25] which both makes privatization possible and undergirds at least some of its legitimacy.

## *The Rational and the Moral State*

If neoliberalism celebrates the individual over the collective, its proponents have nevertheless found that public policies that privilege individual initiative must be legitimated from the perspective of public-service provision and from a moral perspective, as well. As Daniel Cohn has pointed out, postcrisis demands for a return of public services in the 1980s required a new consensus on the role of the state. This new consensus—always short of the neoliberal ideal—has focused on what has become known as the "New Public Management," or NPM. NPM emphasizes the separation between politics and administration and encourages public managers to operate entrepreneurially within broad constraints established by goals set by politicians. Services can then be measured and assessed according to clear criteria that match the politicians' goals. In this way, politicians become valued for their CEO-like management capacity, and by having their deputies meet the goals that they set.[26]

The Bloomberg administration in New York City was clearly influenced by NPM, as was the Giuliani administration. The institution of the Parks Inspection Program, and later, the institution of ParkSTAT, biweekly meetings of park managers at which they are called to account for inspection failures, closely mirrors the application of a similar system in the Police Department during Giuliani's mayoralty and has a close analog in Mayor Bloomberg's (and other education reformers') advocacy of frequent testing of students and performance-based pay for teachers.

The institution of New Public Management techniques does not mean that the state is in retreat. Indeed, the governmental agency—the Parks Department—still has a great deal of accountability. If, for example, you are injured by a falling tree branch in a park, the City will most likely be a respondent in any civil lawsuit, regardless of whether there is a conservancy. And even if PIP is imperfect in catching violations or unevenly applied, all parks have to submit to it. At the same time, Park Managers in districts with conservancy-managed parks, and even with parks with a significant volunteer presence, must answer for work done by people they do not directly manage.

The other side of the card, so to speak, of the rationalism of NPM is something that many observers of neoliberal policy making miss, namely, the activation of a strong moral discourse emphasizing civic responsibility and engagement. This discourse of civicness helps to establish a kind of middle ground between the Parks Department, which mainly speaks the language of complementarity, in which philanthropies and volunteers are a crucial adjunct to a public agency still very much in charge, and conservancy critics concerned about privatization. Nobody dislikes volunteers, and nobody publicly questions their widespread presence in the parks; the only real doubters about the value of volunteers are found among Parks Department workers and managers themselves—and they are not part of these policy discussions.

In Simmel's terms, the promotion of volunteering and civic engagement would seem to be a bridge between the polarized camps. Except that if we look more closely, what appears as a bridge is more like a door. It is impossible to separate the growth of civic discourse from the larger privatizing strategies of the Parks Department. Telling in this regard is Commissioner White's testimony to the Parks Committee hearing about the founding of conservancies:

In all cases, it has been civic-minded individuals within the public, private, and nonprofit sectors that have taken the initiative to step forward and engage with local

CHAPTER SIX

parks, improving the quality of life throughout New York City. Most notable are Betsy Barlow Rogers and Tupper Thomas, city employees and the first Administrators of Central Park and Prospect Park, respectively, who founded the Central Park Conservancy and the Prospect Park Alliance....

While it is quite clear that both Betsy Rogers and Tupper Thomas *are* civic-minded, the way that Commissioner White tells the story effaces the facts that the Central Park Conservancy was set up as a way to wrest control of the park from a Parks Department bureaucracy that the Savas report blamed for the park's ruin and from the public-sector workers it—and others—blamed for their lack of care. It further conceals the fact that even according to Thomas, Commissioner Davis hired her with the charge to set up the Prospect Park Alliance, a project that took several years to accomplish even after she was brought on as the park administrator. However civic-minded the two individuals are, they were not the sole sources of initiative for the private administration of parks services. That came from the department itself.

Understanding the promotion of civic engagement as a "door" allows us to see how the discourse of civic engagement mediates between the increasing reliance on private philanthropy to fund park operations and ongoing concern for the public interest, almost as a common denominator of both. Even guests of the Standard High Line, a posh hotel built around the High Line and "growing up with it," are told that two dollars of their room bill (which can run past $400 per night) will be donated to Friends of the High Line unless they opt to withhold it. Similarly, COFFEED, a new kiosk in Bryant Park—which pays concession fees to the Bryant Park Corporation—is described on Bryant Park's website:

COFFEED allows patrons to give back, while they get caffeinated, in more ways than one. Their coffee is fair-trade, brewed from single-origin beans roasted locally in New York City. Their juices, sandwiches, and baked goods are made by hand in their Port Washington facility. To top it off, COFFEED donates a portion of each day's earnings to local charities. Your parkside java will taste a little richer when it's helping those in need.

The linkage of the consumption of luxury goods with civic engagement is but the commercial extension of the appeal to civic virtue that lies amid the organization of philanthropic and volunteer efforts to support the parks.

Through the lens of the integral state, neoliberalization appears both as a project of elite control and, within that, as dependent on a discourse of pragmatic flexibility and a strong, even sometimes progressive, morality. As we also see—and will develop even further in the next chapter—it also rests on a strong moral discourse. As sociologists Eve Chiapello and Luc Boltanski noted for France, the combination of managerial flexibility with the real social critique of state-led hierarchies typical of the late 1960s led to a celebration of individual potential and decentralization as a "new spirit of capitalism" weaves together organizational and moral strands in the regulation of work, in particular, and of society more generally. In a similar vein, anthropologist Andrea Muehlebach, writing about civic engagement and the neoliberal state in Italy, notes that the "Italian state has in the last three decades sought to mobilize parts of the population into a new voluntary labor regime—a regime that has allowed for the state to conflate voluntary labor with good citizenship, and unwaged work with gifting."[27] In both, the generation that came of age in 1968, and that sought to upend the stifling bureaucracy of the state in favor of more decentralized, civic initiative, has been crucial for the advance of a neoliberal project that many in that generation nevertheless find politically unpalatable. In the Parks Department's discourse of supplementation rather than supplanting of public control, and in its official resignation over the control philanthropists wield over specific park budgets, we find a similar distaste for the very privatization that the Parks Department's policies promote.

As we turn, in the next chapter, to looking more closely at the construction of volunteer and unwaged work in the Parks Department, we will see that neoliberal political projects—involving the privatization of state services, the reduction of worker power, the accumulation of wealth from previously more socialized areas of responsibility—organize through coalitions of sometimes unwitting bedfellows, drawn together by a common vocabulary of citizenship and service. We therefore miss something important if we treat these dynamics as a simple imposition by privatizing state elites tout court. We also miss something if we simply treat neoliberalism—and, certainly, the leaders of conservancies—as the object of moral outrage or opprobrium. Specifically, we miss the ways in which people help to create and justify these neoliberalizing moves through their efforts to keep the parks clean and enjoyable places to be, whether through volunteering, philanthropy, or performing their daily jobs.

SEVEN

# The Politics of Free Labor: Visibility and Invisibility

"We have one thing the private companies don't have: free labor."

This is how a top manager in the Department of Parks and Recreation ended his story about the department's effort, in 1996, to privatize park maintenance in several areas. That year, Commissioner Henry Stern began a pilot privatization project for maintenance of several parks districts in Queens, as well as for the "shops"—the machinery-maintenance units—in all the boroughs. For a year, the parks districts were cleaned by a private, for-profit landscaping company, apparently to a good standard and for less money than regular parks workers would cost. Several of the shops were contracted out, and remain so. Nevertheless, one thing saved the privatization project from continuing and expanding in the boroughs: WEP. The City's workfare program—the Work Experience Program—had, by then, expanded under Mayor Giuliani to twice its size in the pre-Giuliani era, and nearly 4,500 of the 21,000 WEP slots were in parks. Stern had used workfare workers before, during Mayor Koch's tenure, and one of his deputies at the time went on to be Mayor Giuliani's point person in expanding the program. As the senior manager told us, after a year, it was clear that for the relatively unskilled tasks of parks maintenance, privatization was not cost-effective when compared to workers who performed unpaid labor.

The senior manager's candor was offered without much apology, even if some higher-level parks officials talk about WEP as a necessary, but not optimal, solution to staffing problems. Sociologists Steven Vallas and Christopher Prener[1] have argued that it is not only the short-term dynamics of efficiency that drive the radical segmentation of labor markets, but rather that in order to understand these changes in labor markets, we must also understand the discursive politics that underlie the policy changes that, in turn, enable them. In other words, we need to ask what kinds of justifications, whether moral or practical, the neoliberalizing integral state, in its diverse composition, offers for its practices in restructuring labor markets.

In this chapter, we contrast four faces of free labor—volunteers, workfare and JTP workers, and out-of-title work—to show how a justificatory vocabulary of citizenship and service emerges from efforts of the Parks Department and nonprofit partners at once to use free labor and to manage the way others see it. Put differently, we are interested in how the processes of *using* free labor and *legitimizing* it come together and grow apart according to the program that produces it, who talks about it, and who uses it. In so doing, we examine here the ideological production of the integral state.

We emphasize two main points about this ideological production. First, it involves managing the visibility of unpaid work. Managing the visibility of unpaid work means, by turns, denying that the work being done is itself valuable or critical to the goal of maintaining the parks, euphemizing the work as being less like unpaid labor than it might otherwise seem to be or emphasizing the allegedly nonwork aspects of the activity, or making a spectacle out of the work or workers as exemplary in some way.[2]

The term visibility management invokes the feminist idea that some labor (traditionally household labor and "care work") was invisible *as work* on a broader cultural basis, where even some women did not recognize reproductive labor as work, and invisible to analysts of work, whether sociologists of work or economists, because of the difficulties this labor presented for established means of assessing value. Arlene Kaplan Daniels,[3] for example, wrote of the "invisible careers" of women in the volunteer labor force, and recent scholarship on care work—caring for children, family members, the aged, the infirm, and so on—amply shows the ways in which visibility and invisibility of work and workers can operate together; care workers are clearly visible to us—they pervade nearly every corner of our adult lives—but they are less visible *as workers* in labor law, less visible to unions as genuine workers, and their work "feminized" and denied as being *real* work, especially when care workers demand similar treatment as other workers from their employers.[4] Frequent euphemization of the wage-labor, employer-employee relation into the metaphor of family may coincide with genuine feelings of affection but may also coincide with hidden antipathies and coercion.[5] In the governance of park maintenance, denial, euphemism, and spectacle are all part of a process that unites visibilization and invisibilization of unpaid or poorly paid labor. This is done through three principal means: the production of a powerful rhetoric of citizenship and reciprocity, the coding of workers through clothing, and the composition of work crews.

The second point about the ideological production of the integral state is that, as we will see, even critics of free labor tend to talk about their objections in the hegemonic language of reciprocity and citizenship. And even when they contest the dominant denial of some workers' status *as workers*, they often do so with reference to an unmet expectation of reciprocity from the state. In other words, the ideological production is neither complete nor consistent in its effects. It is constantly contested with reference to workers' experiences at every level, even while forming the basis of their claims. This means, as well, that when these contradictions threaten to become unruly—when, for example, they spill over into the consciousness of parks workers who *could* file grievances or supervise "free labor" differently—the *coercive* aspects of the state become more evident. Moreover, we see that the strategies for mobilizing free labor form a spectrum from coercion to consent that are unevenly applied across social hierarchies.

### Giving Back: Mobilizing Reciprocity

One common aspect of the work of workfare workers, JTPs, volunteers, and even community service sentencees—diverse a group as they are—is that each, in its way, is cast as "giving back" to the community. Each does so in similar ways, though important differences exist (as we saw in chapter 3, where we noted that volunteers almost never are asked to clean toilets). Nevertheless, the most important differences lie in how politicians, Parks Department managers and workers, volunteers, nonprofits, JTPs, and WEP workers talk about and understand this giving back and how a common—albeit ambiguous—discourse of civic-mindedness can mask, and even help reproduce, extreme inequalities.

Giving back and the language of reciprocity works differently depending on whether one is forced to be at the worksite—as are WEP workers, community service sentencees, and, to a different degree, JTPs—or whether one is there voluntarily. That this maps onto disparities in wealth and income nearly goes without saying, but it produces a distinction in the meanings of reciprocity itself, as the wealthier volunteers reciprocate the favor of fortune and the poor "reimburse . . . the community for the aid received."[6] For one, giving back permits their claim to ownership of their community, for the other, it forgives their debt to it.

## WEP Workers and the Language of Reciprocity

When the Work Experience Program expanded in 1995 under Mayor Rudolph Giuliani, the mayor, his aides, and a great number of sympathetic commentators—from columnists to welfare recipients themselves—often used the language of reciprocity to justify the program. Richard Schwartz, the mayoral aide in charge of expanding the program, and who had previously worked with a similar program in the Parks Department under Henry Stern in the 1980s, claimed that saving money with the program was not a foregone conclusion. Instead, "[t]he factors within our control are building integrity and a philosophy of reciprocity, and that is regardless of the financial payoff."[7]

Mayor Giuliani was more expansive: In an address to a business lobbying group in 1998, he linked the idea of reciprocity directly to democratic citizenship:

We're honoring the meaning of the social contract, which is one of the foundations of democracy: for every benefit there is an obligation, for every right there is a duty.

The fact is when the City's welfare rolls are rising, and the social contract is being neglected, that's not something to celebrate. That's the sign of a City moving in the wrong direction. That's retrogressive. . . . The City's workfare program, which is a fundamental component of our welfare reform efforts, asserts that basic social contract. It says that in order to receive benefits or a paycheck you must work. Since it began in March of 1995, New York City's welfare to work program has grown into one of the largest and most successful of its kind in the nation. . . . To shift from dependence to independence—to return work to the center of New York City life—we have to do this, and more. . . . Everyone, with very few exceptions, is subject to the universal work requirement. That's not a penalty. That's a truly compassionate answer, because it begins to give people the gift of their own independence.[8]

CHAPTER SEVEN

Ten years after this speech, in the midst of our interviews, however, we found fairly little praise for WEP in the Parks Department, and not just because of the logistic problems it posed for supervisors. Far more common was the view that WEP was little better than slavery. Jerry, a Job Training Program participant in Brooklyn, juxtaposed his criticism of WEP with his own understanding of reciprocal obligation:

I'm a maintenance man by trade, understand? Used to work in the World Trade Center, both towers. I was there for the cleanup. Basically, I know the stuff that they do. And you know, to me, it's giving back to the city, but the city doesn't give back to you. You understand?

What I wanted to say is, OK, now you have another program is called WEP, so after you finish the six months [in JTP] and you go on to public assistance, the first thing they gonna tell you is to go work for WEP. Now, to me, and I'm gonna say this, this is not slaves! We not slaves! You not going to pay somebody $68.50 [the biweekly welfare cash benefits for single adults] to come work in a park. I mean, how much work that person gonna do? You understand what I'm saying? So now he's used to making $10, but now you telling him to go work for free. So you telling him to be a slave, in other words.

But it was not just disgruntled JTPs who considered WEP in this way. May, a retired social worker and a volunteer in a Brooklyn park, also said, "I do not consider folks who have to work off their welfare checks to be volunteers. Because that's more like slavery." And even the top administrator responsible for the JTP program favorably compared JTP to WEP, saying that "We prefer to pay people".

The idea of reciprocity dies hard, though. It is also implicated in ideas that paying taxes and working entitle people to citizenship—at minimum, the right to have rights. And this, even to WEP's critics, becomes a way of drawing distinctions not just among city programs for the poor but also among welfare recipients and workers themselves. Jerry, for example, criticized JTP for raising expectations only to put people back in workfare, but he did so with these distinctions in mind.

You don't give somebody a taste of work and they doing it . . . I'm not saying for everybody, I'm talking about me. I'm a worker. And I don't care, I'm a worker. I will go as far as $7.15 an hour. I started at American Airlines at $7.15, and by the time I was finished, I was making $22, and that was on my own sweat. Nobody gave me nothing. It was my workability. And the same thing comes to these parks. It's my workability that gets me the overtime that's $14 an hour. They not just going to give that to anybody. Every day. So you have to think about, what am I doing. And

I never see the overtime. Say . . . so I'm pulling my weight. And I'm strong with it. But it doesn't make no sense to me. I mean, the working and training, it makes a lot of sense, in that aspect. But the other aspect, it doesn't make no sense, because you telling them to go back to where they came from! And if they coming from welfare, they going back on WEP! They going immediately to WEP! So how are you helping these people? The only thing you're doing is putting them in a circle.

Even for Jerry, then, the most righteously incensed critic of WEP we interviewed, the basic justification for WEP—that it fostered norms of reciprocity, citizenship, and independence—could sneak into his critique. The superiority of JTP to WEP, for example, had to do with whether the worker himself or herself merited the right to even a temporary job because of "workability."

To others in the Parks workforce, however, the distinctions between WEP and JTP were far less apparent, and these distinctions were seldom made, in no small measure because they were not forced to be in the workforce as were WEP workers. From borough chiefs of operations to crew chiefs, we found that parks workers often confused WEP and JTP, especially if they had been working in the department for a long time. One telling example came from the highly ranked manager quoted earlier, who credited "free labor" with keeping parks maintenance in the public sector. Just prior to saying this, he said that "JTPs saved the Parks Department," even though the period he was discussing was five years before the program started. He had meant WEP.

The fact remains that as long as WEP remains on the books, as long as people can move from being WEP workers to JTP workers and back without much of a break in between, and as long as WEP and JTP are both part of the "welfare-to-work" universe of programs, working in either program will carry with it both the assumption on the part of others that one has not worked before and the association with a kind of forced reciprocity.

### *Community Service: Reciprocity as the Price of Freedom*

The idea of forcing reciprocity and repairing citizenship through labor is, of course, at the heart of the practice of assigning those convicted of misdemeanors to work in community service placements. As the New York State Department of Criminal Justice Services defines them, community service programs "provide the courts with a means of creating a meaningful sanction for non-violent offenders who will return, through unpaid supervised work, an established amount of service to the community, as 'payment' for the harm caused by their criminal behavior."[9]

Because community service sentencees are sometimes blended in with other groups on work teams—whether on mobile crews with WEP workers or JTPs or in volunteer days—and because they are only deployed in certain districts and at the discretion of the district Manager, they do not generally attract a great deal of attention from other parks workers. Nevertheless, in the districts in which they are used, they are a constant presence, and one that needs to be managed, as indicated in earlier chapters. Sometimes this management is accomplished through the threat of jail. Said one Manager: "The parents have actually come to me, said, 'you sent my son home,' and I told them why, and they smacked their kid in front of me and said, 'Whatever this man wants you to do, you do. It's either that or you go to jail.'"

The fact that the primary objective with community service has to do with restoring citizenship through punishment distinguishes it from other types of unpaid labor used by the parks, but the distinction is not complete or categorical. Parks workers in any position did not comment on the fact that community service workers, who had broken the law, were put to the same tasks as JTPs, WEPs, volunteers, and even some CPWs, who presumably had not done so. Instead, when there were no conflicts, adult community service workers became largely invisible, blending in with the rest of the workforce and not too worthy of comment. Like volunteers, especially, community service sentencees were not considered to be integral to the workforce even though they sometimes make up the bulk of the staff working on a given day, at least in some part of the districts that accept them. Further, like volunteers, the number of community service workers who show up at a given district to be assigned fluctuates a lot. As Alan, a PS1 in Brooklyn, told us, "No, it's not something you can count [on]. The objective is to try to get done what we need to get done with what we already have, and everybody else is extra and that's great."

### *Volunteers, Giving Back, and the Ownership of "Community"*

According to the Parks Department website, "Volunteering in New York City parks is a great way for New Yorkers to give back to their communities. You can join community groups, participate in recreational programming, or work in the parks planting and maintaining the city's greenspaces." Beyond this larger, official pronouncement, as we saw in chapter 5, the Parks Department, along with its nonprofit arm, the

New York City Parks Foundation and the Partnerships for Parks, is extremely active in trying to start volunteer organizations and to formalize a network of volunteers both to do maintenance and operations work, and also to run special programs and recreation activities in the parks. Moreover, both the Parks Department and private conservancies draw on corporate volunteering and large, annual or semi-annual events such as "It's My Park" days to constantly renew their volunteer corps.

We found that many volunteers in the parks also defined their activity at least in part as "giving back." Typical were expressions such as May's, a retired social worker who volunteers with a crew in a Brooklyn park: "After having appreciated and enjoyed the park for many years, I figure it's time to give something back to it, so there's the satisfaction of helping out with something that you think is important. What's not to like?" To others, the link is simply self-evident: "Since 1955. A volunteer, giving back."

In addition to "giving back," there are other rewards: many are not exclusive to volunteers, but some are more typical of them. May, again, articulated a common set of elements:

It's exercise. I love being outdoors. There was this cute little article in the *New York Times* about how fresh park air is good for you, and I don't think it's true but I like to believe and certainly enjoy it. It makes me feel better to be out doing things than to be indoors doing things. I like the companionship. I like my fellow volunteers and some of the Parks Department people that work with us. So it's . . . social.

It is with admiration—and some irony—that May also indicated that there were some who "gave back" more than others. Speaking of one of her number, "As I said, I only come once a week. There are several people who come more than once! [He] comes so much, he's almost an employee! An unpaid employee!"

For volunteers, giving back generally means something different than what it means for poor people who enter WEP and JTP; and it means something different, again, for graffiti writers, turnstile jumpers, and other people guilty of violations and misdemeanors. Frank, a borough-level manager, with decades of experience in the department, made distinctions among the volunteer capacity across boroughs and neighborhoods: "Yeah, Manhattan had much more volunteer base. I think it comes down to economics, too. They can afford to give back. When I worked in the Lower East Side [a poorer area], we didn't have many volunteers, but the short time I was in Riverside Park [among the

CHAPTER SEVEN

richer areas of Manhattan], you had a wealth of volunteers, so it was a different animal."

Nevertheless, the issue of citizenship and community involvement, whether *restored* or not through volunteer labor, comes across clearly in our interviews. With volunteers, in contrast to WEPs, JTPs, and those put to work by the courts, this often comes with a sense of ownership. Ownership refers to the sense of an entitlement to intervene as an *individual* in what happens in the parks. But it also entails a kind of responsibility to the community, one that echoes Parks Department and Partnerships for Parks' promotional material that speaks of parks as being "community parks" (often with volunteers making this point). There is, to be sure, no inherent contradiction between individual (it's *my* park) and community-oriented justifications of volunteering. Indeed, the idea of the individual giving back to the community, with the community and the individuals who compose it "owning" the park, is a fairly common, liberal understanding of community.

Another way of understanding this is that by casting volunteers as "owners" of the park, the rhetoric of Partnerships for Parks invites interventions of a proprietary sort; "Friends of" organizations, in effect, "adopt" parks as their own and often feel entitled to report to Parks Department managers on matters pertaining not just to parks conditions, but also to other parks workers. The contrast, therefore, with JTPs, WEPs, and community service workers is stark. Repaying a debt—whether for training, welfare benefits, or crime—casts them as debtors; volunteers, given a kind of rhetorical ownership of parks, are released from this debt and only "give back" insofar as they are contributing to their *community*. Where volunteers are concerned, the *state*—the public sector—is held at a distance, creating an image of community *against* the state. This image, which is tied to Alexis de Tocqueville's observations on nineteenth-century American civic life (and which retains a great deal of rhetorical force in the United States), at once masks the intensive organizing of volunteers by the Partnerships for Parks and conservancies that we noted in chapter 5 and privileges the voices of the whiter, richer, and older group that composes the majority of regular parks volunteers over those of both the regular workers and those cast, in their way, as debtors.

For regular volunteers, the contrasts between public and community ownership and between the kinds of "giving back" that pertains to different sorts of workers can be quite clear. For example, Jay, a volunteer at a Queens park, told us, in effect, that because of systematic failures in the public sector, the voluntary sector had to step in:

[T]hey really need to continue pushing and working with volunteer organizations, because I think that budgets are not going to open up, and I think that people are not going to be able to donate money. Even corporations are less able to donate money. But people will and can and should donate time, then. This is part of the conversation we've had in the past with state parks . . . I can't guarantee that we're going to be able to get hundreds of thousands of dollars and millions of dollars or whatever, but I can bet you that I can get a couple hundred volunteer hours . . .

For her part, Carole, leader of a downtown Manhattan "Friends of" group, spoke about her entitlement to intervene and praised the institutional creation of a forum—regular meetings with the borough commissioner—in which these interventions by volunteers could be heard and processed:

We've had crew chiefs who've come here, and all they do is sit around, and they set an example for the JTPs that, "Oh, I can sit around too." And that's what you get. They'd just be sitting around. And I would bitch and moan and bitch and moan and most of that bitching and moaning happened before we started these operations meetings. So I'd be calling supervisors that I know and everything, but their hands are somewhat tied. But if you bring it up at the operations meetings, you can push it further. It's all communication. Having this dialogue is really a good thing. So I'm glad that the commissioner started that.

Carole came back to this theme later: "I have called and complained about many workers. They just sit around don't do anything. They sit in the house . . . and believe me, I'm not going to volunteer and put my extra hours in if the people who are getting paid aren't doing their job."

The idea that public workers—and even those who are coerced into being at the worksite—are not doing their jobs, and further, that volunteers have a proprietary right to be attracted to park work, was crystallized in Susan's—the director of a Brooklyn park—description of how she scrupulously separates volunteers from WEP workers:

Susan: Actually, I asked my staff to make sure that when they were organizing a volunteering event, there were no WEPs around . . .
Maud: Really?
Susan: Because honestly, they were really terrible. I love my staff [here]. Employees here are respectful of each other, they respect the community. They work when they're supposed to work; they aren't on the phone shouting insults. The staff I saw in the other park made me sick. Because . . . why is it that the big shot at a large corporation who makes $250,000 a year takes a day off to clean up the

leaves in the park, while the person on welfare is sitting on the bench doing nothing? What's that about? It's horrible. It's really bad form. I can't ask a guy to come and work for nothing when someone who is paid by welfare is sitting there doing nothing. We have a large enough park to make sure of that.

If volunteers are led to make their work equivalent with that of others—and especially that of JTPs, WEP workers, and community service workers—it destroys morale and works against the very objective of creating reliable, permanent volunteers amid an otherwise contingent and often-temporary labor force.

By encouraging volunteers and by setting up the organizational infrastructure to attract them, the City creates a privileged class of unpaid workers. By virtue of the fact that they are constructed as freely giving their time to the cause of civic involvement—with Partnerships for Parks, the Parks Department, and conservancy groups seen merely as facilitators—volunteers can be used to do the work that regular employees once did, even as parks managers and volunteers lament shrinking budgets. Said Jay, the Queens volunteer,

Especially in this kind of time, I think that . . . the City is very good about dollarizing volunteer hours. I mean, they have a—that's the whole Partnerships for Parks, the whole program is set up to funnel and work through that whole process of saying, "You know what? Every volunteer means that this many hours worked, if we had to pay 20,000 extra staff, would be this much money, and we don't have that much money, so this means the parks are in OK shape . . ." And not that the staff is not doing their job. It's just the sheer volume of it is too much for a reduced staff or for a staff that can't grow to grow with the spaces and with the programs.

Further, individual volunteers, or volunteers with park-coordinated "teams," are often lauded for taking a kind of entrepreneurial initiative. In Prospect Park in Brooklyn, for example, official appreciation of volunteers extended to one man described in a Parks Department publication in 2003 in terms explicitly reminiscent of private property: "[He] has even adopted a section of this park—the Vale of Cashmere—as his own. He has taken personal responsibility for this site, picking up trash, emptying the trash cans, and weeding. He takes care of the park as though it were his own backyard."[10]

Similarly, managers often spoke in our interviews of individuals, usually older, to whom they effectively gave over the management of one or another piece of a park, from the Rockaways to Manhattan. In some instances, the Parks Department or a local "Friends of" group—

working with the Partnerships for Parks—would recognize these efforts either through remuneration (the gardener would be hired to work on a part-time basis) or through naming. "Paul's Park" in the Bronx and "Carmen's Garden" in Prospect Park refer to particularly energetic volunteers who adopted these areas "as their own." The rhetoric here is important to mark, since it is the combination of free will ("voluntarism") and the image of taking care of *private property* that makes these efforts exemplary. A public worker who exerts the same care for the park in her daily rounds is just doing her job, and the JTP who does the same is, regrettably, not usually able to be kept on.

The symbolic making of volunteers' contributions permanent resonates with the larger project of making volunteer labor a regular and reliable part of the parks. As May, the Brooklyn volunteer, described her work group in terms of age, she also described the ideal volunteer: "Late fifties on up range. Which is a good volunteer. I mean, I've watched us, and I've watched some of the college students, and they can heave more stuff, but in terms of just constancy and keeping at it and doing it and getting the job done, I think it's not a bad age. If you're looking for volunteers, you want us." Responsibility and constancy are underlying values attributed to property owners, as well as to good volunteers. By fostering, both institutionally and rhetorically, the idea that regular conservancy and Friends of the Park volunteers are the ideal volunteers, the Parks Department and its ancillary organizations build a workforce in that image.

There are, however, numerous ways in which this project is incomplete. First, although constancy and reliability are often attributed to owners of property, they are not the sole preserve of owners. Indeed, we also heard from several supervisors that volunteers that take too much initiative and too much ownership can be trouble. As Henry, a Supervisor, told us, "Sometimes it could be a help. Sometimes not . . . Like [imitating a volunteer] 'We need four trucks of wood chips so we can do our thing. We need pitchforks and we need gloves and . . .' You need a lot of stuff to volunteer, don't you? What *we* need is for you to just do what you gotta do without bothering us and let us do operations." Similarly, Frank, the borough manager quoted earlier, reflected on his earlier days as a district Supervisor:

I used to argue with the volunteers, because we'd dump woodchips *here*, and they'd wanted them across the path *here*. But you're going to bring them forty feet in the wheelbarrow off the path, so it doesn't matter if it's six feet off where you wanted them! . . . A lot of volunteers seem to like to establish a garden, plant bulbs, and then move on. And then somebody has to inherit the maintenance of that. So it's nice, if you have a volunteer group that wants to come out, do a nice planting, but also come out every week and water it and weed it and mulch, it is much better than somebody who just comes out twice a year and . . ."Oh, why does it look like crap?" "Oh, well, have you been here since you planted it?"

Accordingly, there is a tension with volunteers about those who are constant *enough* and those who are not, and between those who *actually* take ownership over their work and those who use the rhetoric and *feel* entitled without actually understanding the work.

Furthermore, the tension between individual and community-oriented ideas of ownership on one hand, and a more public conception of ownership on the other, is one that volunteers often understand, though not in these terms and not always with an understanding that volunteer labor is part of the system. Nevertheless, sometimes volunteers' own exposure to the parks allows them to make connections: Jesse, a volunteer in the Bronx, reported that he "became a parks greeter about two years ago. The position just opened up. It was a position before, they just fired everybody. Yeah, because they was paying them $14 an hour. So they ran out of funds, like I said again: That's a program that was eliminated like other programs, I could mention them, because you just don't know about them until they're gone."

A further way in which the production of "good" volunteers is incomplete lies in the reports by many volunteer coordinators that the growth in volunteering is linked to more people having time to put in volunteer hours after having lost jobs or after their businesses have had to cut back their operations. This, again, pertains mainly to wealthier volunteers who may have some financial buffer that allows them to volunteer. Nevertheless, the encouragement of a kind of ownership and entrepreneurial spirit in volunteers can also lead some volunteers to think about themselves as potential public managers: As Carole, the "Friends of" coordinator from Manhattan, told us, the fortunes of her sales career were uncertain: "I don't know how much longer I'm going to be . . . it's really—it's difficult. So networking with the Parks Department and other people isn't such a bad idea. Even though nobody's hiring right now. But you never know."

Until now, we have focused on the regular volunteers. For volunteers, the line between freedom and compulsion, ownership and debt, gets blurrier when extended to different sorts of volunteers. About a quarter of the high schools in New York City have community service requirements for graduation, and volunteering in parks is a common activity.[11] Similarly, corporate volunteering can be quasi-compulsory, as it is often linked with "team building" and is therefore an activity that combines claims to citizenship both for the corporation (which uses volunteering to tout its commitment to the "community") and for the employee, who must be a good team player, who is obliged to participate in her or his community, even though this participation may be compulsory.

## Managing Visibility

The language of reciprocity helps to justify the widespread use of free labor in the parks and, in its complexity, also helps to draw and further undergird distinctions among different kinds of workers, typically drawn from different classes. It combines the euphemization of free labor as "giving back," the occasional playing down of the contributions of volunteers, and the frequent praise—and even official commemoration—of volunteers' contributions, sometimes offered in contrast with public workers' alleged laziness. Beyond this discourse, however, we also found concrete management practices that employed and reinforced distinctions among free or low-cost laborers in the parks. The provision (or nonprovision) of uniforms and the organization of work crews were other ways in which the Parks Department manages the visibility of free laborers, employing a similar mix of denial and display of value and virtue for distinct kinds of workers.

### *Clothes Make the Worker*

As with many city employees who work outside of office buildings, parks workers wear uniforms and are given an allowance to purchase them (the allowance has, since at least the 1950s, been inadequate and forces workers to spend out-of-pocket on their uniforms). As with most uniforms, the parks uniform conveys rank. Top management does not require uniforms—they are akin to the civilians in control of the military. PS2s wear white shirts and greenish pants, PS1s wear brown shirts and greenish pants, APSWs and CPWs wear either gray t-shirts or dark blue work shirts. All have the department logo.

Since the 1990s, WEP-worker activists and advocates had, among their many complaints about the program, the lack of uniforms for WEP workers. This put WEP workers more visibly in a subordinate position, both because their regular street clothes would get especially

CHAPTER SEVEN

dirty, given the job they were doing, and because they were issued protective green or orange vests, which visibly marked them as WEP workers but were also identical to vests worn by prisoners on work-release programs or by community service sentencees. This has not changed. It is still impossible to distinguish whether a mobile crew is composed of WEP workers or community service workers, other than by the general—and unreliable—rule of thumb that WEP workers are more likely to be younger women and community service sentencees are more likely to be younger men or teens (and that, at the time of this writing, there are fewer WEP workers than community service workers). WEP-worker activist groups such as Community Voices Heard now display the vests themselves in demonstrations making explicit the vests' intent (figure 7.1).

The Parks Opportunity Program and the JTP position were founded in large measure in response to agitation for "real jobs" by WEP-worker advocates. JTPs were given a uniform—a royal blue shirt, also with the parks department logo, with STAFF emblazoned on the back. In many respects, of course, this is an improvement over WEP, but it is ambivalent. Because JTP is linked to welfare and its stigma, we encountered at least two JTPs who had somehow gotten their hands on gray shirts, which they sometimes wore over, or instead of, their blue ones. Moreover, the blue shirts could have other significantly negative consequences for visibility management, as Danny, a former JTP, explained:

Danny: Every time we would go somewhere it was other gray shirts, or somebody that was a CSA [City Seasonal Aide, a seasonal, but not JTP, position]. Because CSA had gray shirts, they always refer to JTPs as a negative thing . . . And every time we went somewhere, it got to the point, I started wearing my [gray] shirt because they were referring to JTPs as a negative thing. "Oh, you driving that trailer like you're a JTP! Oh, you raking the grass like you're a JTP!" And it was insulting to the point that anybody that had a blue shirt on that would be among all these people with gray shirts, they would feel uncomfortable for whatever reason. My thing is, yeah, don't refer to them a JTP! I'm a JTP but that doesn't mean I'm not a human. I can do the same job you do if not better, you know? But you been here for fifteen years, and you know you got the knack for it, whatever. That was the thing. JTPs was always a form of insult. You know, "Look at that JTP walking down the street, blueback!"
John: Blueback?
Danny: Yeah, JTPs, blueback . . .
John: I never heard that before. Blueback.

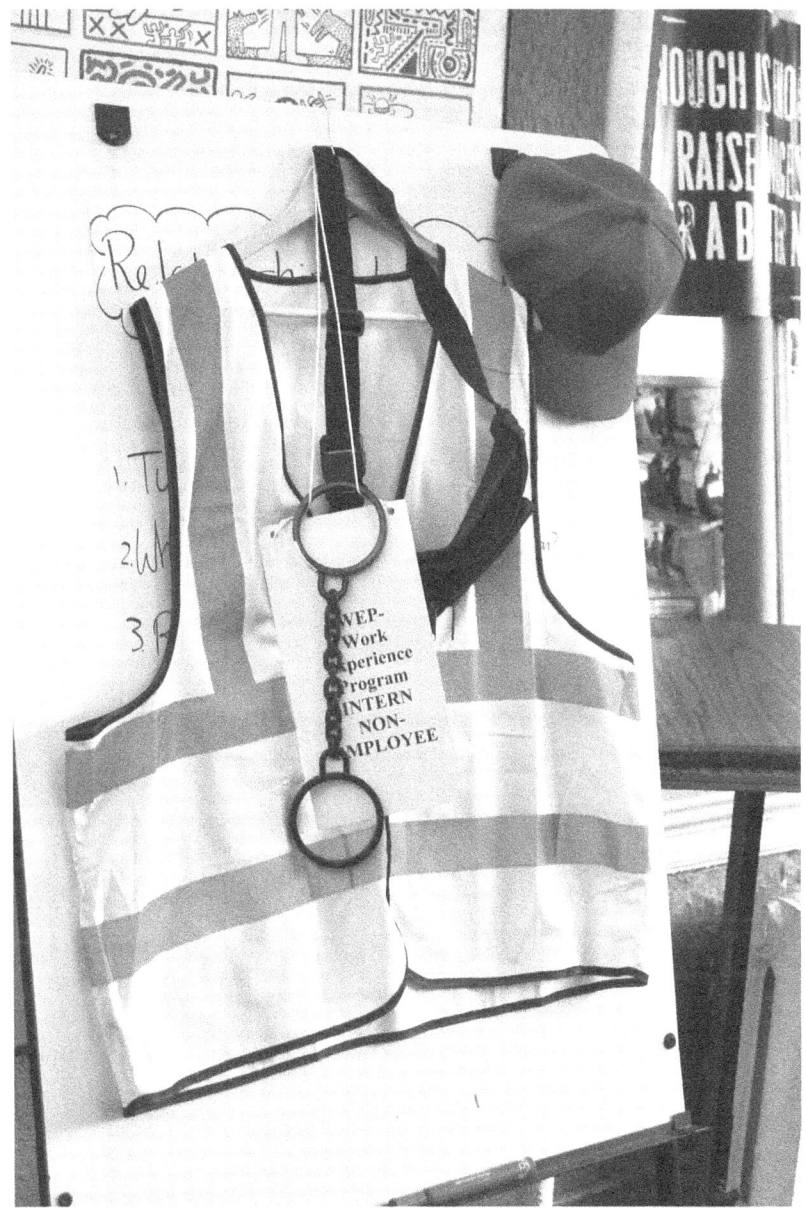

7.1  A WEP vest and ID badge identified specifically as a "non-employee," paired with irons. Community Voices Heard presented it to former welfare commissioner Robert Doar during a demonstration, with a sign reading "WEP Humiliation Gear." He did not accept it.

CHAPTER SEVEN

Danny: Rookies . . . And these people would get drunk and be belligerent to other people and whatever girl that comes their way wearing a blue shirt—they won't hit on the people that got the gray shirts, but they'll hit on the blue shirts, because they know the blue shirts, they don't know better, and all the people with the gray shirts, they already dealt with this before they got there, so . . .

That the JTP uniform makes it clear that JTPs are staff and not simply incidental to the park's maintenance workforce reinforces a good deal of what the full-time staff told us about JTPs' importance. But for some park workers, the blue shirt marks JTPs as different and inferior—and as likely marks for harassment and exploitation.

On the other end of the spectrum, volunteers also often get shirts, though this is most true in privately run parks with conservancies. In Central Park, for example, regular volunteers for the Central Park Conservancy also get shirts, close in appearance to those worn by regular conservancy staff but with VOLUNTEER written in large letters across the back. For long-term volunteers, this is certainly a badge of pride; one is not obliged to wear the shirt while volunteering. Margaret, a volunteer who works with May in Brooklyn, touched on the importance of the shirt:

And it can also be useful, a useful little tidbit, that so often when we work in the park, so often, I would say two or three times, when people see us, not when we're doing weeds, as it were, but raking, or whatever it is, people who are walking by would say thank you! Because we wear these shirts, a lot of us, and it's obvious that we're volunteers. They say, "Gee, thank you." In other words, the public is aware that there is a volunteer corps here doing work in the park.

For corporate volunteers, a t-shirt with the corporation's logo on it—and often the name of the volunteer program of the corporation—*is* something of a uniform; everyone, or nearly so, on corporate volunteer teams will wear the same t-shirt. It is an opportunity for the corporation to display its good citizenship, just as it is a way for individual volunteers to do so. It is also, of course, part of the team-building and internal identity-building exercise that corporate volunteer days so frequently are.

*Composition of Work Crews*

We have already alluded to the composition of work crews and their frequent segregation. It is important to highlight that this segregation accomplishes several things at once with respect to the visibility and invisibility of unpaid labor. First, it insulates volunteers from learning about the dynamics of the workforce in the parks. For the most part, volunteers reported working separately from other, regular workers and showed little particular interest in the composition of the workforce, other than concern that it not be whittled down to nothing. But this also means that volunteers are insulated from any kind of advocacy on behalf of their erstwhile coworkers. Solidarity is impossible if volunteers do not know of some of the problems that JTPs and permanent workers face on the job.

Second, the segregation of work crews means that JTPs are most likely to be sent to work with other JTPs, with WEP workers, or with other nonmarket laborers, such as community service sentencees. This, in turn, shows JTPs—the backbone of the Parks Department maintenance workforce—that they have not, in fact, "risen above" the circumstances from which they came. It is doubtful that this is intentional, but it is clear that by keeping JTPs with JTPs, WEP workers, and community service, and volunteers with volunteers with volunteers, the department is reinforcing what Charles Tilly called "categorical inequality."[12]

Third, and perhaps most important to the Parks Department and to conservancies, is that the segregation of work crews reduces the extent to which volunteers might be uncomfortable socially with working in the parks. That many Managers, Supervisors, and even CPWs and crew chiefs did not see a real distinction between WEP workers and JTPs suggests that the park director Susan's concern about upsetting the wealthier, hard-working volunteer with the presence of a potentially lazy, poor—and overwhelmingly black—welfare-to-work worker is likely more pervasive than a view expressed in a single interview.

It must be said, however, that all of this can be justified from an operational standpoint. Especially when JTPs, community service sentencees, and WEP workers are *required* to be at work as a condition of fulfilling the obligations of their respective programs, it makes a certain kind of sense to keep them together as a core maintenance workforce and to do the same with volunteers; further, volunteers of different sorts are often kept apart because regular volunteers have a different level of experience and trust with regular workers than do corporate volunteers out for a team-building day or the occasional volunteers who come out during the Partnerships for Parks' biannual "It's My Park" days.

CHAPTER SEVEN

## Coercion and the Extraction of Value from Visibility Management

A final important aspect of the politics of free labor in the Parks Department is what might be called its "double management." On one hand, those most frequently charged with overseeing the implementation of free labor are themselves regular Parks Department employees: they make judgments about the composition of work crews, coordinate volunteer days, decide whether and how community service sentencees will be deployed, and so on. On the other hand, the work of supervising unpaid and low-wage labor in the parks is often done out of title or in ambiguous areas of workers' job descriptions. By civil service regulations, out-of-title work should be compensated at the pay of the higher title; accordingly, if it is not, the increment between the lower-title pay and the higher-title pay is a different kind of "free labor," albeit even less visible than the other kinds we have described so far.

Our discussions with district Supervisors and Managers suggested that they feel the pinch of a reduced permanent labor force particularly in the problem of how to allocate staff to the mobile crews that now form the basis of their districts. As one Supervisor told us, with resignation: "We improvise a lot. I am pretty fortunate to have two districts. I use equipment and personnel from [one district] and vice versa. Some of my workers cover both districts. They do not have to do it. But it is what it is and they understand that. When there were a lot of people, they would have complaints, but they understand now."

In discussions with management staff in one borough, these issues were clarified further. We interviewed Gary and Wanda, who together have forty years' experience in the department between them:

Gary: Each title has a job spec, and some of them are a little gray as to what you can do, so there's always an issue, occasionally . . . There are occasional issues where things have been talked about, they're doing out-of-title work . . . Like an out-of-title is more like getting a CPW to drive a vehicle. That's an out-of-title . . . if somebody works in a different district, it probably wouldn't qualify.
John: Right. Or a CPW who's basically a crew chief but hasn't gotten the . . .
Gary: Right, that would be more of the out-of-title stuff that you would get. Somebody looking for a salary adjustment for doing work outside of their title. And that's probably one of the most frequent . . .
Wanda (reentering the room): I don't know what you're talking about, but just what I'm overhearing, one of the cases that we might have would be a CPW who is

taking out JTPs, and then all of a sudden they're saying, well they're supervising the crew, so they deserve the different . . . they deserve to get crew chief money. But meanwhile they're really just working with that, working alongside them, not supervising them. So that would be something that *they* would say was out of title.

Whether or not a particular case involved out-of-title work, we heard many of the same complaints as Wanda mentioned. We also witnessed JTPs supervising summer youth workers in a Brooklyn Park and heard Marybeth, a former JTP, offer this account of her work in a Harlem park:

John: So, and because you were there for six months, you said you were supervising, you did some supervision of the community service? What did that entail?
Marybeth: That just entailed taking them to the amphitheater, which was directly attached to the building, take them to the amphitheater, have them clean up the amphitheater area. They would take all day to do it, so . . .
John: And the crew chief wasn't doing that? He would delegate that to you?
Marybeth: He would delegate that to two of us, myself and a young lady named Samantha. Because we were more responsible.

The more normal set of circumstances, however, involved CPWs who had not been promoted to crew chief. Jeremy, one CPW we interviewed, also said that the definition of what constituted "supervising" JTPs was slippery. He described a normal day, which involved picking up JTPs at the district headquarters and driving them to various scattered sites in the district, working alongside them to clean up garbage, and moving on to the next site. Making the distinctions among crew chiefs and CPWs and APSWs, he told us:

Honestly, the only thing different between CPW and APSW is that they get to drive heavy equipment. They get to drive big packers. Like, I can drive the mini-packer. They drive big packers because they have a [commercial driver's license]. Other than that, it's pretty much fair game. A CPW's not supposed to take out the crew. They're just supposed to drive. They're not supposed to tell the JTPs what to do.

Further, he recounted his having been transferred to his current district: "I asked why, and they just said they needed me out here. But, oh, actually, I think it's because there was a crew chief here that died. So they need another person." And yet, as Wanda indicated—and other Supervisors did, as well—the line between supervising and passing on

CHAPTER SEVEN

orders from supervisors is blurry. Alvin, a Supervisor, affirmed that "There is a chain of command," and, therefore, a good deal of the time that CPWs *think* they are supervising, they officially are not.

At other points, the distinction between taking out a van and taking out a pickup truck governed whether or not a worker would get the crew-chief pay differential. Yet, as we have seen in previous chapters, districts struggled to maintain work crews big enough to make it matter which vehicle conveyed them to their worksites. In these cases, the actual work done by crew chiefs or CPWs barely mattered. In other cases, crew chiefs would take out a smaller crew on a pickup truck because the van was broken.

In other words, the distinction between crew chiefs and CPWs—however it might legally stand up in an out-of-title grievance—is often one without a difference. That the crew chief position was negotiated—after a lawsuit from the union—in order to recognize new duties for CPWs seems to be a fact that has largely gone forgotten.[13]

So why don't CPWs grieve more often? We put that question to Jeremy, who responded: "I mean, I could go to the union and grieve it and all that, but the part about that is, as soon as you grieve it, they blackball you and they send you to a bad district. And that's how it goes." Though not too many of our interviewees directly mentioned fear of retaliation, it must be said that fear of management was a thread running through our fieldwork, whether in publicly run or privately run parks. In spite of the supervisor's contention, quoted earlier, that "everybody understands" the challenges of keeping up high standards of cleanliness and repair in the midst of chronic understaffing, and his contention that they don't have to do out-of-title work, it was clear to us that even if individual supervisors were willing not to abuse the rights of CPWs and others, this sense of pitching in and being a team player only went so far. And it did so for several reasons.

First, whether because of out of a sense of complete resignation that other, more "necessary" city agencies have priority over parks in their claims on the budget, or because of a pride in lean management, the system for managing Supervisors and district Managers discourages these workers from asking for too many more resources from the department. Biweekly, borough-wide meetings of managers and upper-level Supervisors (PS2s and PPSs) reinforce the idea that PIP inspections and performance guidelines are important no matter the level of staffing and no matter the equipment available. As Alvin, a friendly and open supervisor, told us, "Listen, I'm not going to tell the commissioner, 'Wow, I didn't have enough people.' They don't want to hear that. My job as a PS2 is to find resources." Supervisors and Managers whose districts have parks that fail inspections can be humiliated in front of their peers, at meetings that were modeled on the Police Department's much-touted "CompStat" system. ParkStat, a geographically enhanced maintenance and operations database, enables top managers to identify problem areas in their boroughs, but as often as not, this does not result in a greater—or even consistent—level of resources.

Second, the Parks Inspection Program lowers the morale of Supervisors as inspectors, usually in CPW civil service titles, can go over their heads to report problems to their Managers. In a joint interview with two supervisors in Brooklyn, Henry and Jasmine, they told us:

Henry: Like we do our inspections and then they have other inspectors who come around, and they see something wrong, they'll send immediate attention to our manager, and we have to fix it right way. But if I put in immediate attention to the shops, it doesn't get taken care of right away. And we're Supervisors and they're pretty much CPW titles for inspection. So for me it's a little bit disrespectful. If they're all on the same team, we should be working together, and we're pitted against each other . . .
Jasmine: It'd be nice, too, that when they see something they call the district . . .
Henry: And let us know . . .
Jasmine: Right.
John: Instead you go through all that . . .
Henry: Go to the manager, go to the big bosses? Come to us.

Henry, who expressed frustration in chapter 3 with these work orders getting priority while his own languished, identifies this situation both as a breakdown of the teamwork that is a cornerstone of the department's rhetoric and as an infringement of his own autonomy to make managerial decisions. This dynamic inevitably flows down the chain of command. With pressure on Supervisors to meet priorities and standards that they do not control come efforts to cajole CPWs to do work that is not, strictly speaking, in their job titles. It makes the rhetoric of teamwork harder to sustain at the district level, too.

Third, the fear of retaliation is real and pervasive. It is not just about complaining about out-of-title work. Instead, it is about *any* infraction of rules or any clash with supervisory personnel. As we have mentioned, during our fieldwork, Parks Department workers were, in general, barred from speaking to the media. In Central Park, too, pages of nondisclosure forms accompanying volunteer applications, and the very real absence of union protections (such as they are), suggested a

CHAPTER SEVEN

management style in both public and private parts of the parks system that reacted poorly to criticism.

But in addition to fears of retaliation, there is the problem that defining out-of-title work is slippery business, even though it is clear that for most commonsense definitions of the term, CPWs do a great deal of training and supervising JTPs, and JTPs often show other, more temporary workers how to do their jobs. This, together with the problems of managerial credibility and the eroding sense of cooperation in the department, leads to a default to coercion as the legitimacy of the management of free labor in the parks is increasingly questioned by those charged with carrying it out.

## Legitimizing the Contradictions of the Neoliberalizing Integral State

The integral state manages its unpaid labor force by means of the rhetoric of reciprocity and the management of visibility, underpinned by the blunter force of economic coercion, when the legitimacy of the extraction of free labor is questioned by the people from whom it is demanded. The various pieces of visibility management, however, work together. It is easier to sustain the justifications of free labor, the claims of reciprocity, the humiliation of workfare, and the like if the workforce is segregated. Figure 7.2 shows the two axes along which this segregation works; together, they make it harder to question the overall system of ideological justifications, because the larger sets of relationships are difficult to see from any particular point in the field, even if some people suspect their outlines.[14]

That the ideological work of the rhetoric of reciprocity and "giving back" and the segregation of work crews does not always work is as important as the fact that it often does. Along with Gramsci's conception of the integral state, his idea of a contradictory consciousness allows us to think about the ways in which words and deeds, speech and practice, can mix uncomfortably in the implementation of a broadly neoliberal parks management program. In many respects, we see that the terms people use to describe free labor in parks sometimes contradicts their experience and certainly contradicts the rhetorical efforts of park management to justify its use. This "practical" consciousness sometimes breaks through the normal ways of speaking about welfare-to-work program participants, community service workers, and even volunteers. But even when it does break through, this practical con-

# THE POLITICS OF FREE LABOR

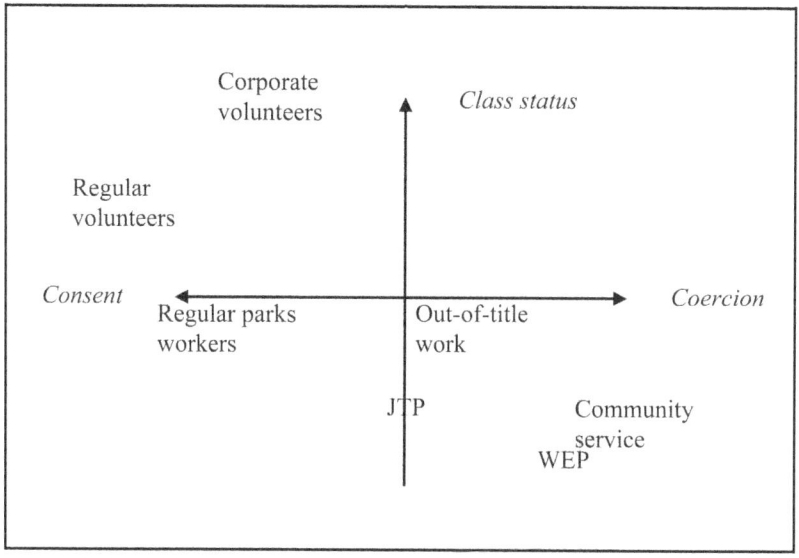

7.2  Two axes of segregation of the free labor force

sciousness can be difficult to articulate, as when Jerry, the JTP worker, denounces WEP as slavery even while saying that WEP would be bad for *him* because he is a *worker*—but that this does not apply to everyone. We see this again, where May, the volunteer, also says that WEP is like slavery but does not see her own volunteer labor as something that is related to the dissolution of the ranks of regular workers in the parks. We see this, as well, in the troubled ways in which parks workers both praise and complain about volunteers. It is not simply that volunteering—or JTP, WEP, or community service—is complex enough to attract multiple possible evaluations, to be seen differently by people in different positions, and the like. It is rather that the *larger picture* of austerity, workforce segmentation, privatization, and increasing reliance on free labor is difficult to articulate because each category of free labor and each segment of the labor force carries with it a set of justifications that is both durable and exists beyond the confines of the Parks Department itself. Moreover, people develop deep theoretical and emotional attachments to these justifications as they fuse, however awkwardly, with their daily practice. It is simply often too hard or too painful to make visible what we know, on some level, to be true.[15]

Here, for the people who maintain the parks, then, the deflection of these larger questions about how the workforce is composed in favor of considering the relative virtues of volunteering, of workfare or welfare-to-work training programs, or of community service means that it is difficult for them to imagine making common cause to improve their conditions of work, their workplaces, and parks maintenance itself. This ideological accommodation to austerity is always incomplete, as we have shown, but we can call it an accommodation to austerity *precisely because* this accommodation is always in question, even if its contours are not well recognized, and this questioning is often suppressed by institutional measures of coercion.

In the next chapter, we look more closely at the larger picture of parks maintenance and neoliberal governance by the integral state. Having discussed the workers, the workplace, the institutions of parks management, and the politics of free labor, we can now consider the historical, economic, and political changes that have animated them and have been, in their turn, reinforced by them.

EIGHT

# Valuing Maintenance, Valuing Workers

## Marge and Nora

Marge is over seventy years old. As she tells her neighbor, pointing her finger to a building on the outskirts of the park, she lives in one of those beautiful urban castles that overlook the park in one of the wealthiest neighborhoods in the city. Marge is the doyenne of this small group of twenty volunteers who, for the most part, meet up several Saturdays a month at one corner or other of the park to "beautify" it. Around her neck she wears a plastic ID with big letters that read "volunteer," next to her picture and her name. She wears work gear from head to toe and tells me in a rather dry tone that you don't show up for gardening in a pair of sandals. "There's a lot of poison ivy here," she says as she points to poisonous plants I have a hard time recognizing. This is the only time she will speak to me during the three hours of "team" work during which, with the help of gloves and garbage bags, we set out to rid a portion of this prestigious park of weeds, dead plants, and scattered paper. Aside from newcomers and those walking past and who are not part of the group, Marge seems to know everyone here, and David, the director of volunteer programs at the park who oversees us all morning long, treats her with consummate respect.

Nora is in her thirties and lives alone with her son. She has been in the Job Training Program for a few weeks. Her job is to clean one of the buildings in this Brooklyn park. When she has finished cleaning inside, mainly the public restrooms, she moves outside to con-

CHAPTER EIGHT

tinue her work, equipped with a pair of little metal tongs that allow her to grab paper, bottles, and other trash littering the lawns and playgrounds. She says she prefers to work alone, that she is a loner and that she has more control over her work this way. She used to be a cashier at Staples, the office-supply chain, but then lost her job and went back to welfare, and they sent her here. When I ask her if this is the first time that she has done maintenance work, she replies "Yes," before adding: "Yeah, first time. Well, I can't really say first time. First time I'm getting paid for it. Because I do it at home. I clean at home . . . I have that down pat. But first time I'm getting paid for it, and first time I'm doing it in a vast area." During our interview, which takes place in a small area set aside for staff, a few people come and go and a woman even takes a seat at our table and eats next to us while Nora tells me about daily hassles and the usual arbitrary ways of welfare services. When we leave the room, one of the conservancy supervisors calls out to me and asks me what I am doing there. Nora replies that I was interviewing her. The supervisor then asks if I obtained the approval of Nora's Parks Supervisor prior to conducting the interview. Nora says yes, that I spoke with Kelvyn last week, which is true. And yet I feel tense as I leave, and I cannot help giving my contact info to Nora and insist that she get in touch if there is any problem. Nora smiles; she seems to be used to all this.

These write-ups from Maud's field notes from early in our research (fall 2008) reveal a good deal of the dynamics we have discussed in previous chapters. In the broadest sense, these two women share the fact that their work is often seen by supervisors as "extra" or supplementary to the main work done by "regular" employees, and sometimes seen as "saving" the department. Both owe their work in the park to the expansion of workfare and volunteer programs in the wake of the 1975 fiscal crisis and the large-scale layoffs of city workers that took place at the time, and again in the early 1990s. Otherwise, these two women seem to be opposites in every way: age (seventies/thirties), social class (high/working), skin color (white/black), and choice and remuneration of work (volunteer/JTP). Marge also contributes money to the conservancy that maintains the park, while Nora is paid about $9.50 an hour, from a combined purse of state and federal welfare funds. Moreover, Marge is treated with deference and respect, apparently feeling no compunction about being arch with newcomers, while Nora is frequently interrupted and quizzed and has apparently gotten used to being treated with a baseline level of disrespect.

## Not *Just* Saving Money

In addition to their being valued and devalued, respectively, on the level of social interaction at the worksite, Marge and Nora also have a different relation to the possibility of extracting value from their work. To be sure, Nora is paid—though her wage will likely be inadequate to raise her and her son out of poverty or near-poverty—and Marge is not. But if Marge owns her apartment—which is likely—she realizes a significant premium on the value of her real estate for living next to the park. Nora, on the other hand, is likely to rent her apartment. If it were near the park in which she works—and it is not—it also would carry with it a premium on its value, but it is value that would accrue to her landlord, not to her.

Marge and Nora open up a larger set of questions to which previous chapters have only partially alluded, most importantly, *Why do parks need to be cleaned, and why are they cleaned as they are?* We could certainly *imagine* the parks *not* being cleaned as much or as well as they are. Indeed, in poorer neighborhoods, as a whole, this is not a great feat of imagination, and for other New Yorkers older than twenty-five, they need only to dip into their memories. We can also imagine a system of cleaning that does less to damage the morale of regular municipal workers, that respects the spirit and not just the letter of civil service titles, that relies less on unpaid or poorly paid labor, and that does not encourage the concentration of racial minorities in poorly paid, temporary positions, and clear the path for sexual harassment of subordinate workers. *Why*, then, do we have the system we have?

If we consider Marge's and Nora's positions a little more deeply, we recognize that one frequently cited answer to these questions is incomplete, if still true, namely, that the current system saves money and is cheaper to run than a system that relies less on free and low-wage labor. There is no question that this is important, as we will discuss in more detail below. But *as* important are the facts that, as the premium on Marge's real estate holdings suggest, there is money to be *made* from well-maintained parks and not simply money to be *saved*. Moreover, in the contrast between how they are treated by park managers, we can see that the way we organize park maintenance work reinforces categorical social hierarchies and inequality, legitimating a set of grossly uneven and unequal social relations. These two forces at the heart of the parks maintenance system—supporting the private accumulation of wealth and reinforcing and legitimating social hierarchies—are always at work together. Sometimes they work in mutually reinforcing ways, and sometimes they work at cross-purposes. When they reinforce each other, they *discipline* the poor, *regulate* the workforce, and *fortify* the wealthy. When they are in contradiction with each other, they suggest the possibility of alternative paths for policy.

In the rest of this chapter, we look more closely at the production of value in parks maintenance and its accumulation by real estate owners and businesses, and the increasing importance of private gain as a justification for public spending on parks and park maintenance. We then turn to the cracks that have opened up in the current system and point to the ways in which the workforce changes we have documented are implicated in these ruptures. They include public arguments about concessions, PEP officers, conservancies, and the general level of cleanliness of parks; the arguments themselves are driven by the unevenness of social hierarchies, which are in turn reinforced through policies that privilege some people more than others. They also include an occurrence that our research did not anticipate, and that happened after we began to write our book, namely, that in 2013, the Parks Department hired more than 420 full-time, year-round workers. At first, it would seem that everything we have described so far in this book points in the opposite direction: The Department of Parks and Recreation has, for forty years, been a virtual laboratory for innovations in driving down the costs of public employment by mobilizing various forms of low-paid and unpaid labor. Why, especially at a period of low ebb in the power of municipal unions, and amid repeated mayoral warnings of the unsustainable costs of public-sector workers and their benefits, should Parks suddenly gain authorization for a 15 percent hike in its full-time payroll? The answer is complex, because some of the staff has been hired on a permanent basis and some on a temporary, but renewable, basis; it is an attempt to balance the real needs of a parks system for a predictable and stable maintenance corps, and the managerial desire for flexibility.

Understanding the ruptures leads us into the final section, in which we consider the larger implications of our research for urban policy and politics and for our understanding of neoliberalism and the integral state. We focus on the more abstract version of the idea raised in the contrast between Marge and Nora, that accumulation and legitimization are key functions of the state and that they are contradictory, working in some tension with each other. Out of these contradictions arise potentials for change. We conclude by identifying some of these potentials.

## Parks and the Promise of Profit

### *Real Estate Values*

In 1872, the Board of Commissioners of the Department of Parks reported that the value of real estate parcels in the Twelfth, Nineteenth, and Twenty-Second Wards of New York City (Manhattan, at the time) had increased from $26 million to $186 million since 1856, when the City had finished purchasing the land for "The Central Park." Eleven years before this stunning Board of Commissioners report, in 1861, a New York State Senate report was equally gleeful, even though the park would not be fully completed until after the Civil War:

> Although the Committee do not think it proper for municipal corporations to purchase lands on speculation, yet it cannot be concealed that the Central Park has been, and will be, in a merely pecuniary point of view, one of the wisest and most fortunate measures ever undertaken by the City of New York. It has already quadrupled the value of a large extent of property in its vicinity.

In many respects, the story has changed little. Though the historian Matthew Gandy writes that pecuniary concern for real estate value was "consistently played down" among the "cultural elite" who advocated for Central Park's development in the 1850s, these financial concerns "were decisive."[1] In 2009, the Central Park Conservancy commissioned a report from the research firm Appleseed, Inc. on Central Park's contribution to New York City's economy. Of the report, ten pages—the longest chapter—are devoted to the premium on the price of real estate of proximity to the park. Appleseed, Inc. finds that in 2007, real estate in the direct vicinity of Central Park enjoyed an 18 percent premium, or $17.7 billion, in value over other, comparable Manhattan real estate not immediately adjacent to the park. This premium enables the real estate around Central Park to be worth, in aggregate, more than *half* the value of *all* Manhattan real estate in 2007, before the Great Recession.[2] All told, Appleseed, Inc. estimated that "City tax revenues related to Park operations, visitor spending and increased real estate values totaled more than $656 million in 2007—an amount roughly equal to the total annual cost of the entire Parks Department."[3] What of other parks?

There are several outstanding examples that suggest that the dynamics of Central Park are not unique. Bryant Park Corporation's mission statement includes a charge to "enhance the real estate values of its neighbors by continuously improving the park."[4] A study done by New Yorkers for Parks in 2002 confirmed that they had succeeded when they agreed to set up the business improvement district that funds the park through assessments: "Financially, the City and local business owners made a sound investment. The entire neighborhood has become more desirable, with commercial rental values increasing up to 225%, far outpacing increases in nearby buildings not adjacent to the park."[5] Ten years later, when office vacancy rates in midtown Manhattan hovered over 11 percent, rates around Bryant Park were a negligible 3.8 percent, producing an average premium of more than 23 percent on rent per square foot ($78.29 vs. $63.40).[6]

The effects of real estate value enhancement in the area around the High Line are no less impressive, in no small part because of speculation on the available buildable lots in its vicinity. Writing in 2010, Alison Gregor of the *Times* reported: "At the height of the market, the price of properties next to the High Line may have soared as high as $400 a buildable square foot, but current prices are roughly $200 a buildable square foot."[7] Just *two years later*, as the final stretches of the railway line and surrounding land were acquired by the City and the various zoning approvals passed, a developer paid $800 per buildable square foot, a record price for the Chelsea area of Manhattan.[8] Similarly, working with the Regional Plan Association, the Friends of Hudson River Park commissioned a study in which it sought to quantify the differential between the value of Greenwich Village properties before and after the 2003 opening of the park to the public. The study found that there was likely a 20 percent premium—worth nearly $200 million—attributable to the park, and which had not been evident in the years prior to its opening.[9]

New Yorkers for Parks' 2002 study, *How Smart Park Investment Pays Its Way*, found that in the six parks they studied intensively, real estate values in the neighboring areas increased significantly, carrying a premium of up to 40 percent for neighborhood parks. To the extent that parks with significant new investment were located in poor areas, the effects were diminished, as would be expected. Nevertheless, even for smaller parks outside of Manhattan, there still exists some enhancement to real estate values from parks with new investment.[10]

Indicating the benefits for real estate of investment in parks is not—as we will see—just a way for us to understand the ways in which public parks maintenance creates and safeguards private value; it is also a way for parks advocates and the city government to reassure property owners that their own contribution to surrounding parks—whether through philanthropy, BID assessments, or requirements from zoning upgrades—is a good investment. It is also a way to reassure developers that they can "do well by doing good" when they agree to reserve funds for the perpetual care of parks built as part of larger residential and commercial development deals, such as Riverside Park South in Manhattan, developed as part of Donald Trump's Trump City.

*Parks as Commercial Generators*

When Adrian Benepe touted Central Park's role as an economic engine, he emphasized the money that came back to the city's coffers in revenue and taxes. To be sure, the increased value of real estate generates significant property tax revenue and transfer fees (when it is sold). But Benepe was surely referring primarily to revenue that the Central Park Conservancy collects through its concessions and sales taxes generated by these concessions, as well. As we discussed in chapter 5, Central Park's contract with the City requires it to pass half of its concession income to the municipal government (Bryant Park does not have that provision). Furthermore, Central Park, like the High Line, is a significant tourist magnet, and thus counts, in a sense, as an "export" product for New York City's economy. The vast majority of the city's hotel rooms that go for more than $400 a night are within blocks of Central Park, and the park has a significant impact on tourism-generated revenue.

The High Line and Bryant Park have pioneered upscale concessions, sometimes in partnership with celebrity chefs. Madison Square, too, has a partnership with the Shake Shack—a burger joint that inspires nearly cultlike devotion and long, snaking lines through the park at peak hours—and for several months a year, across the street, the local BID (run by the same people who run Bryant Park) hosts a food fair with mid-priced food concessions from the "artisan" food scene. This food fair, which also visits Herald Square, has prices that are out of reach for the working-class customer of the average hot-dog vendor or Halal food cart, but it is packed with both New Yorkers and tourists at nearly all hours of its operation.

In the winter, Bryant Park turns its lawn into a skating rink and hosts a holiday shopping village of temporary stalls that ring the lawn. In the summer, too, food kiosks on the park's western end and restaurants on its eastern end give a considerable amount of the park's space over to commercial activity. As a generator of commercial income, the

CHAPTER EIGHT

park's potential is probably nearly maximized in all seasons, short of turning it into a full-time mall.

## Doing Well by Doing Good

The tax revenue generated by parks' commercial and real estate value is significant enough that parks advocacy groups like New Yorkers for Parks—and the former commissioner Adrian Benepe—emphasize the economic benefits of parks in published materials and speeches. If the *budgetary* calculus of parks maintenance and capital investment puts it behind the essential municipal services such as fire and police protection, the *economic* calculus can put it on a more equal footing as a generator of income.

The audience for such claims is comprised by city decision makers, and especially the mayor, who proposes the annual budget, *and* private companies, which might donate to conservancies. The important point is that a broad justification for parks maintenance now lies in the generation of private profit, cementing growth strategies as the principal solution to budgetary shortfalls. It is a significant internalization of the logic of collective action, in which public goods can only be provided given state provision for selective incentives for those in the position to produce them. You do not need to be a Marxist to recognize that the condition of providing public amenities has become whether or not private accumulation of significant value can be generated as a driver—rather than a simple by-product—of public goods.

Importantly, then, the justification for parks maintenance as a profitable enterprise is consistent with—and even contingent on—a larger view of public budgeting and the public enterprise it funds that suggests that *public* sources of budgetary income will forever be insufficient and that therefore, the public benefits of parks are only to be had through generating private profit with public resources. Even New Yorkers for Parks, which always argues for greater parks maintenance funding, and even for greater parity in the distribution of maintenance money and effort across the city's parks system, plays this card. When they do, they subtly elide the distinctions between public and private, in ways that—like former Parks Commissioner Adrian Benepe's comments on democracy in chapter 6—show the "integral state" to have taken hold even in the claims of advocacy groups. Note how "higher real estate values" are put on an equal footing with true "public goods":

As a public good, these recreational and contemplative spaces are open to all residents and visitors to enjoy. Everyone benefits to some extent from New York City's parks, whether through recreation, cleaner air, or higher real estate values, and so it is in the public's best interest to keep our parks in healthy operating condition.[11]

The difficulty with this approach is that it skirts, at least to a large degree, the problem of distribution of resources, not just their growth. Small parks and playgrounds—the bulk of Parks Department properties, the most dispersed of them, and in many respects, the most challenging to cover and clean "deeply"—do not have much revenue-raising potential. New Yorkers for Parks clearly recognizes this. Writing of such parks in the same report on alternative funding models for parks, they note:

> At the other end of the spectrum, many neighborhood parks suffer from inconsistent funding and deferred maintenance. Additionally, a growing body of evidence suggests that the benefits of parks accrue to a greater extent to landowners in close proximity to parks. . . . Owners benefit from higher land values, higher commercial and residential lease rates, and lower tenant turnover. These owners are benefitting from public investment; as a result, there may be some justification in trying to assess a tax on this incremental financial benefit.

The trick would be to attach this tax assessment to funding for other parks. It is an interesting proposition, especially in light of the resistance both New Yorkers for Parks and former Commissioner Benepe displayed in response to State Senator Daniel Squadron's proposal for a pooling of a percentage of conservancy funds from successful conservancies to help other parks. One can equally imagine, however, that tax assessments on the value increment for real estate in proximity to well-maintained parks could be structured in such a way as to be shared with the relevant conservancies, with less money available for redistribution. This would be akin to the driving principle behind the Bryant Park model and would likely make the whole arrangement more palatable to those being taxed. While it does suggest that we recognize the importance of public investment in the creation of privately accumulated value, it does not automatically solve the distributional problem for parks with little potential to be monetized.

CHAPTER EIGHT

## Producing Value through Maintenance

If well-maintained parks have the economic benefits their proponents say they do—and there is clear evidence to support this—the question is whether we can specify how value is produced through maintenance. It is not simply that value is extracted from *rents from land ownership in proximity to a valued park*. To be sure, that is a large part of the story. But it is a story that has to be supplemented with the value produced by the *labor of maintenance*, which keeps the land valuable. Accumulation of this value is indirect—rarely, if ever, are the real estate owners the employers of the labor of parks maintenance—but works in multiple ways. It is uneven, flexible, and opportunistic. It is uneven because the mode of value generation and accumulation works differently and with different results according to a park's geography and its place in the overall system of parks. It is flexible in that this unevenness is marked, too, by different strategies: here, by replacing unionized labor with unpaid labor, thereby *enhancing* the paid labor force, even while moving it off the public's books, in order to maximize the value potential of the park. It is opportunistic in that there seem to be few patterns set in stone according to whether a park is managed publicly or privately: park employers and managers follow different strategies according to what kinds of workers are programmatically and physically available.

We can compare the basic ways in which value is realized through maintenance by contrasting the strategy of labor displacement with the strategy of mobilizing development through the commodification of maintenance. In the first case, value is captured by *saving* money on the labor process of maintenance, typically in parks without high premiums for surrounding real estate holdings and in playgrounds. This can happen in three ways, none of which generates a great deal of value directly but is instead important for other reasons.

Displacing regular city employees with cheaper or unpaid workers such as WEP workers, JTPs, or volunteers drives down the per-hour cost of labor, with the savings felt in the city budget. To be sure, there are some costs associated with supervision; to the extent that both volunteering programs and welfare-to-work programs of any kind are administered off the worksite, they cost money. Nevertheless, at least with welfare-to-work programs, federal and state mandates suggest that these costs would exist in any case. The budgetary savings, both in hourly wages and in health and pension benefits, multiplied out by thousands of workers can be significant. If the parks are maintained at a reasonable standard with a "standard" workforce half the size it once was, the savings are obvious. At the same time, however, the privately captured *value* of the maintenance is less straightforward, beyond the political value that accrues to those politicians who can claim credit for efficient public management (and then, perhaps, like Rudolph Giuliani or Richard Schwartz, turn the reputation fed by this credit into lucrative consulting contracts or programmatic subcontracts).[12]

Table 8.1 summarizes three ways in which the value of well-maintained parks can be accumulated privately. The first way is that premiums still exist for real estate in proximity to parks that are maintained well in spite of the casualization of their labor force. To the extent that those premiums exist, maintenance of the parks is likely a factor in their generation. The reduction in the price of maintaining the parks, then, simply means that the difference in the cost of the producing the thing of value—here, a well-maintained park capable of having spillover effects on real estate rents—is reduced, and its value reallocated to profit. The logic of New Yorkers for Parks' idea of dedicating a portion of the premium in the real estate transfer tax due to proximity of the taxed property to parks toward park maintenance is not simply that *public investment* helps to create private value but that the form this public investment takes, that is, capital investment *and labor*, results in private accumulation.

The second mechanism for capturing value from the changes in the treatment of workers has to do with the effects of these changes as they multiply throughout the public sector. The conversion of the maintenance labor force into the myriad labor contracts described in chapter 2 generates larger effects on the price and conditions of labor

Table 8.1 Summary of mechanisms of private value extraction from parks maintenance

|  | Real estate premium and reduction of labor costs | Public-sector labor reform | Speculative disinvestment and reinvestment |
|---|---|---|---|
| How it works | The value of the initial investment, which is generally credited with producing the real estate premium, has to be maintained. Reducing labor costs reallocates part of the value to profit. | Park maintenance gets cheaper on a per-worker basis and this innovation spreads to other agencies. | Geographically uneven undermaintenance creates new opportunities for real estate premiums upon reinvestment |
| Example | Madison Square Park | WEP | McCarran Park, Brooklyn |

227

itself in the public sector. Where unions are on the defensive; where concerns about contract enforcement trump those concerning the creation of categories of secondary-labor-market jobs and nonmarket labor contracts; where public managers can and do increasingly avoid bargaining over contracts; and where public managers publicly treat civil service rules as if they were meant to be broken—here, the price of a worker's labor power decreases, and the difference accrues to the private accumulation of the taxpayer. Of course, the increment of value, if distributed across taxpayers, cannot be big. Nevertheless, it is important to remember that what has happened in parks is an often more extreme version of what happens across the public sector and that in New York City, the public sector employs more than 300,000 people.

The third way that value is captured in the labor-displacement strategy is less intuitive, but important nonetheless. The basic idea is that speculation on property value involves a complex dance in which the timing of investment—*and disinvestment*—is critical. Parks came to look as they did in the 1970s because it was a smart business decision for many landlords to walk away from housing in poor neighborhoods across the city: the city had hemorrhaged more than 600,000 jobs in the 1960s, many of them solid, unionized working-class jobs. The result was that millions of New Yorkers had trouble meeting the monthly rent. With an aging housing stock, landlords often calculated that it was better to cut their losses than to maintain the properties and pay property taxes. The city's tax receipts fell. And in many neighborhoods, parks and other amenities fell into disrepair. This *disinvestment*, however, both made the remaining valuable investments *more* valuable (good investments were scarcer) and cleared the way for future *reinvestment* on new bases in some of the areas that had become run down. Central Park (and especially the north end, near Harlem), Bryant Park, and Prospect Park all speak to parks reinvestment facilitating gentrification, even as the new residents of formerly run-down areas support these conservancies through contributions and philanthropy. But in a grotesque mirror image of the first basic process of accumulation through proximity to a well-maintained park, it can also be the case that *decreasing maintenance* can set the stage for speculation on new capital infusions and reinvestment—and greater profits—down the line *and* maintain the value of well-maintained parks and their neighboring real estate without undue competition. Accordingly, we should understand the labor market segmentation and creation of high-turnover unpaid and poorly paid labor in parks as being both geographically uneven—it hits some parts of the city harder than others—and part

VALUING MAINTENANCE, VALUING WORKERS

of a larger complex of investment and disinvestment decisions on the part of the Parks Department that has closely followed the potential of parks to become lucrative generators of value in their own right.[13]

Figure 8.1 moves beyond the money-saving basis of labor displacement. It illustrates the circuits by which some (limited) labor displacement combines with other value-generating dynamics to put parks maintenance in the middle of much more complex and lucrative circuits of value extraction, as it facilitates both the commercial and the speculative and rent-generating premiums of the larger or tonier parks with private conservancies. Here, albeit in the context of the city's prime park—which, over time, developed its surrounding areas into prime real estate—we see this process in its full magnitude. Central Park Conservancy, it should be emphasized, has to keep running as an organization and has to balance its books. It is not funded by a tax surcharge on surrounding properties, as is Bryant Park, and it keeps roughly half of the concession money it generates. Maintenance labor costs are the single highest line item in the Conservancy budget, and therefore it has to keep these costs from spiraling in order to meet its mission. Its costs for maintenance labor run slightly lower on a per-

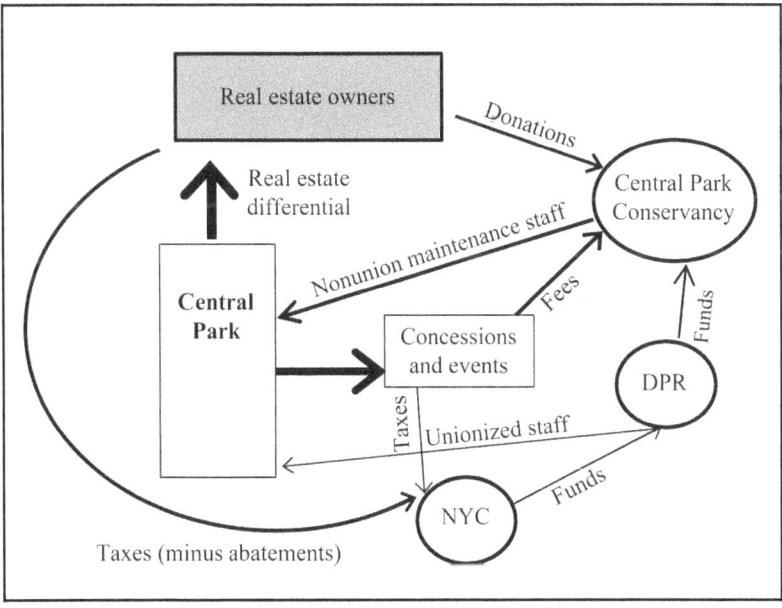

8.1  Circuit of value extraction, Central Park

CHAPTER EIGHT

person basis than would the equivalent costs in DPR, though it gets more than $5 million in subsidies from the agency a year. And yet, as noted before, the real money is to be found in the staggering premiums to real estate value.

No metrics exist to measure the extent of the premium that maintenance produces for parks, and an Ernst & Young study in 2002, done in conjunction with New Yorkers for Parks, found that net of capital improvements, only 45 percent of parks they sampled in New York produced a real estate premium at all. Nevertheless, there are parks that appear to produce premiums well in excess, in percentage terms, Central Park's. Ernst & Young suggest, moreover, that where parks do not produce premiums, the lack of a long-term maintenance plan might be partly responsible for this failure. Similarly, Appleseed, Inc., in a report written for the Central Park Conservancy in 2007, showed that for Central Park, the premium on values increased over time. They conclude:

> There are several factors that could have contributed to the more rapid appreciation of property values close to Central Park. But it is logical to infer that proximity to the Park has over time become more attractive at least in part because the Park itself has become more attractive. Rising values around the Park thus reflect the cumulative impact of 25 years of investment in Park facilities, infrastructure and landscapes—in improved maintenance and greater safety—and in more extensive programming and services for Park users.[14]

Even if a small portion of the real estate premium were due to good maintenance—let's say, 5 percent (which is probably low)—the *maintenance premium* would have been nearly $120 million in 2007 for Central Park alone.

## Moments in a Process

Of course, beyond these three principal ways in which parks maintenance and the reconfiguration of the parks workforce generates privately accumulated value, there is another—related to the second and third elements in table 8.1, namely, what Harvey calls "accumulation by dispossession" and what Sites, following Marx, calls "primitive globalization."[15] In short, it involves the uprooting of previously existing social relations in order to develop the means of production in a new system. The decision to not replace retiring or transferred DPR employees in Central Park beginning in the 1980s is one indication of this. So, too, is the closing of Bryant Park for renovation and the transferring of responsibility for the park to the Bryant Park Restoration Corporation. Both explicitly uprooted civil service and union rules in ways that allowed a new workforce to be brought in that could manage the park in the ways envisioned by their new masters. Harvey points out, however, that the litmus test for the success of these dynamics is less whether they generate profits in the short term, and far more whether they succeed in building class power for the ascendant class. These processes, accordingly, can and should be seen in light of the growing importance of the finance, insurance, and real estate industries in New York City beginning in the 1960s and their particular prominence in the post-crisis era.

None of these processes are mutually exclusive. They are moments in a larger process that unfolds unevenly across the city. Not all parks have conservancies and none will generate the revenues or have the spillover effects of Central Park. Some parks, however, will generate significant concession profits, and yet others—even whole districts—will be left to struggle with basic services and infrastructure, only to see investment increase as gentrification takes hold in the neighborhood at large, in part because of the political power that the new residents bring with them.

## Contradictions and Cracks in the Edifice

If parks maintenance opens a window onto broader dynamics of capital accumulation, extraction of value from the labor process, and contests over class power, it does so in a way that reveals the conflicts and cracks in the edifice of neoliberal governance as much as it shows neoliberalism's creativity, resilience, and adaptability. These conflicts and fissures are evident in four specific areas: the point of consumption of parks around issues of cleanliness, safety, concessions, and the perceived privileges of conservancies; the hiring of more than 450 workers in 2013 and more in 2014; the reliance on capital funds for replacing undermaintained infrastructure; and the continuing invisibilization of the contradictions of park maintenance and cleaning work.

### *The Point of Parks Consumption*

From the point of view of parks users, there are costs associated with the different types of accumulation strategies. To have a local park be one that has compromised cleanliness for a cheaper workforce, or safety because of a redeployment of PEP officers, is to tangibly experience the unevenness and inequality of contemporary New York City life—and its administration. This experience has led to hearings about the deployment of PEP officers in the city council, as we saw in chapter 6, and to charges—substantiated by groups as diverse as New Yorkers for Parks and the New York City Parks Advocates—that the smaller "neighborhood" parks, particularly in working-class areas of the outer boroughs, are relatively neglected. Without significant commercial potential and rich neighbors, both because of what their neighborhoods' characteristics are and because of what they are *not*—i.e., tourist attractions—they fight, when they have the capacity, to retain the year-round, fixed-post City Seasonal Aide or City Park Worker assigned to their playgrounds. They are often unsuccessful in the face of growing needs for steady personnel in the district as a whole.

On the other hand, the embrace of conservancies can be a little too warm for some park users. New Yorkers for Parks and the Regional Plan Association, in spite of their advocacy for alternative funding mechanisms for park maintenance, also recognize that "Commercial activities can diminish the park experience and can price some members of the public out of the park. . . . Putting private uses on public lands raises issues of accountability and governance."[16] These issues arise in many parks—Bryant Park being, perhaps, the quintessential case, where even parks commissioners have complained about the Bryant Park Corporation's outsized power to govern and program the park, and where food concession prices have steadily risen as vendor contracts have turned over. Yet even if these problems have gained public attention on and off in the last thirty years, they came to a head in the last years of the Bloomberg administration. Then, the push to form conservancies in the face of the recession—both to enhance the value-producing capacity of certain parks and to move their care off budget—accelerated. Washington Square Park, in Manhattan's Greenwich Village, was one park at the epicenter of these dynamics.

Washington Square is the southernmost of a line of parks, including also Madison and Union Squares, originally cut out of the relentless grid of the 1811 Commissioner's Plan of Manhattan. First a Potter's Field, and then a parade ground, it is now surrounded by the buildings of New York University and is its symbolic heart as well as that of Greenwich Village. With a large marble arch on its north side, at the beginning of Fifth Avenue, it is about six square blocks and similar in size to Madison Square Park. Though it has a playground, its focal feature is a fountain, which had been—before relocation and redesign beginning in 2008—in the exact center of the park and was the site of street performances. Other areas of the park had been almost continuously used by musicians and their impromptu audiences since at least the 1950s, when the park was the epicenter of Bohemian life in the Village. NYU's expansion in the neighborhood beginning in the 1960s has also been unrelenting. It took over the factory loft buildings on the east side of the park (one of which was the site of the infamous Triangle Shirtwaist Factory fire of 1911, a tragedy that led to the establishment of workplace health and safety regulations) to turn them into classrooms and faculty offices. The park itself remains a tourist attraction but also is heavily used by locals, whether they are students, parents with children, chess players, elderly bench sitters, or buskers.[17]

In 2007, the Parks Department announced a multiyear renovation of the park, which closed it, in pieces, from 2008 until 2014. Among the aspects of the redesign was the moving of the fountain from the center of the park to being in line with the arch. The rationale for this was aesthetic, as well as explicitly oriented to tourism: if the fountain were relocated, tourists could take pictures of both of the park's main features at once, composing shots through the arch to the neoclassical fountain beyond. Not all neighborhood residents were thrilled at the redesign and the loss of their park space for years, and some raised complaints about the redesign itself. A "Save Washington Square Park" committee formed and tried—but failed—to halt the development. At roughly the same time, NYU announced plans for a significant building project in the neighborhood that generated notable opposition and that finally was blocked in 2013 by a judge's ruling that the plan illegally took away public park space without the proper regulatory measures.

Against this backdrop, when Washington Square Park reopened in full, it did so with its own Administrator. A group of four neighbors, including a well-known actor's wife, formed a "Friends of" group that, with the help of the administrator and the Manhattan borough commissioner's office, quickly morphed into the Washington Square Park Conservancy with little in the way of other significant public input. The Conservancy board shortly expanded to include celebrity chef Mario Batali, who maintained a gelato cart concession in the park, and several corporate lawyers with residences around the park. The Conservancy raised money for a $25,000 supplement to the administrator's Parks Department salary and secured a half-million-dollar gift from

NYU. Though it denied publicly having any plans for a license agreement with the Parks Department, both the way that the Conservancy was forming—hewing closely to a pattern that most often leads to such agreements—and e-mails secured by the local activist and blogger Cathryn Swan suggested otherwise. Then, in December 2013, the hot-dog vendor in the park got notice that his concessions would not be renewed, even though Batali's gelato cart, an "artisanal" ice-cream sandwich cart, and a longtime Indian *dosa* cart would be renewed. The hot-dog vendor had already been moved—by the Parks Department administrator, allegedly at the behest of the Conservancy and at the suggestion of the architect who had redesigned the park—in order that he not get in the way of tourists' pictures of the arch. The banishing of the hot-dog vendor—still the quintessential representatives of "popular" foodways in the city (though they have largely been supplanted by Halal food carts)—raised the alarm, and newspapers began to give coverage to the opponents of the conservancy. Small rallies in support of the hot-dog vendor got press coverage. The hot-dog vendor himself complained about losing hundreds of dollars a week if he were relocated. In the "zeitgeist" that had already formed around the election of a more populist city government led by Mayor Bill de Blasio in 2013, the banishing of the hot-dog vendor was a bridge too far.[18] The concessions were renewed.

The appearance of discord over the role of conservancies, after they had been aggressively touted and expanded under mayors Giuliani and Bloomberg—for twenty years—resulted in the suggestion of a "tax" on successful conservancies by State Senator Daniel Squadron and—given their opposition to this—an alternative suggestion of a real estate premium tax dedicated to park maintenance by New Yorkers for Parks. The conservancy tax is less far-reaching than the real estate premium tax. A conservancy tax would redistribute funds from successful conservancies (e.g., Central Park, with its $100 million gift from hedge-fund manager John Paulson) to parks with less or no fundraising potential. New Yorkers for Parks objected that this would spread around too little money among too many parks. In either case, however, there is a growing sense that the successful model of parks maintenance through conservancies has reached a limit of its *political* acceptability, in large measure because of the inequalities it reinforces in the lived experience of urban public space, and in part because the populist mood of the aftermath of the 2008 financial crisis has cast into doubt the motives of the philanthropists who direct the conservancies.

## Contradictions and Moral Hazards in the Workforce

In 2013, the City hired more than 420 full-time Parks Department workers, including 81 PEP officers, more than 250 maintenance workers, and more than 40 pruners. In 2014, budget plans suggested that more workers would be hired. While this bucks the trends we have been discussing so far, it is important to see this as a recognition of the limits of the workforce strategy undertaken by successive administrations for at least two decades—and, in some ways, for more than three.

New Yorkers for Parks expressed these limits in a report in 2013, writing that

> when you scratch below the surface and look at trends across park features, it becomes apparent that the Parks Department is caught in a property management version of "Whac-A-Mole": in order to address one problem, resources must be pulled from another area, causing a new problem to arise in that area. Bottom line: the Parks Department simply does not have sufficient resources to keep up with the endless demands of maintaining the City's 29,000 acres of parkland—including the more than 3,600 acres spotlighted in this report.[19]

These limits began to appear in several ways: First, after years of improvement, park cleanliness ratings started to drop, even if slightly, according to DPR's own figures. Second, the capital budget for the Parks Department had been growing for years. Much of this had to do with new parks creation, especially under Mayor Bloomberg. But some of the capital budget, and a good deal more capital money spent through city council members' "member items," or special allocations for their districts, went into overhauling parts of parks that might not have needed systemic repair had they been properly maintained in the first place.

The application of capital budgets to replace undermaintained infrastructure is only one small step removed from simply paying for maintenance out of capital, rather than operating funds. Though the small step affords the City legal protection—according to the accounting standards to which the New York City budget has been held since the 1970s' fiscal crisis—the fact that it *is* small encapsulates a significant irony. The first chapters of this book discuss the devastating cuts to the Parks Department and municipal workforce in general during the fiscal crisis of the 1970s and, later, the fiscal pressures of the early 1990s. In the 1970s, in particular, the fiscal crisis consisted, in part, of the City paying its bills by rolling over short-term debt: in other words, it was

CHAPTER EIGHT

paying for operations through borrowing in the capital budget. This is something like paying for groceries on a credit card and paying the credit cards with other cards. It is not sustainable.

During the fiscal crisis of the 1970s, the Wall Street banks that had marketed New York City's bonds decided that the problem the City faced was one of "moral hazard." Moral hazard is a term economists use to describe what happens when a valued good is made too easily available. Their answer is that it gets taken for granted, abused, and overused. According to New York's creditors, credit was too easily available for the City, and rather than getting its costs in line with its revenues, it was abusing the credit markets by continuing to borrow. The crisis broke when the banks stopped marketing New York City's bonds and demanded payment on the bonds that had reached maturity, leaving the City no way of making payroll. The administration of President Gerald Ford, led by Treasury Secretary William Simon, a former head of municipal lending for the Salomon Brothers investment bank, refused the City aid and deepened the crisis. The rationale was explained by Ford's press secretary, Martin Tolchin: The City, he said, was like "a wayward daughter hooked on heroin. You don't give her $100 a day to support her habit. You make her go cold turkey." While federal loan guarantees finally helped to pull the City out of its crisis, its conditions were stark: tens of thousands of layoffs of city employees; charging tuition at the City University of New York; public transportation fare hikes; closing of hospitals, clinics, and publicly funded day care centers; and the temporary suspension of budgetary authority by New York City's elected government in favor of an Emergency Financial Control Board appointed by the governor. Moreover, all of this was only possible because of a massive infusion of investment money from the city union's pension funds, which bought risky bonds to fund the City's operations.

If, in the popular narrative of the fiscal crisis, New York City's extensive welfare-state apparatus was like an addictive narcotic, too easily available and cheap, going "cold turkey" was accompanied by many efforts to reduce the costs of running the city. Some of the most elastic of these costs—in spite of widespread unionization—were labor costs. Most of what we have discussed in this book stems, at least in part, from this: the call put out by Mayor Beame in 1975 and 1976 for volunteers to help keep the city running; the formation of the first conservancy in Central Park; the formation of alternative funding mechanisms for Bryant Park's renovation and management; the stark cuts in the number of basic park maintenance staff and the broadbanding of maintenance titles; and the use of welfare recipients as cheap or free labor.

And for a while, it worked well enough. Parks maintenance not only recovered, but improved over its previous levels. A whole new set of workforces—private, workfare, volunteer, transitional—cropped up where there had previously been civil servants. Profits from concessions soared. The real estate premium for proximity to parks did, too.

Nevertheless, as the hiring of nearly 500 full-time workers in two years suggests, the neoliberal governance of parks may have produced a moral hazard of its own. The continual exposure to free or cheap labor, and workers with a diminished set of workplace rights, was too tempting for DPR and its private partners and the level of maintenance had begun to slip. The instability of the very labor force that DPR created, relying on JTPs and community service sentencees; on WEP workers, sometimes, and deferred maintenance frequently; and on curtailing opportunities for advancement leads to widespread absenteeism and, increasingly, complaints by the park-going public and politicians that the allocation of this workforce across the city is skewed. Like any good subject to the moral hazard, the parks workforce was overstretched and used badly.[20]

That deferred maintenance was a result of this moral hazard means, too, that the replacement of park infrastructure was possible, for a while at least. The problem is that since many of the capital funds to fix parks and playgrounds comes from city council members' budgets, parks funding necessarily competes with other priorities in a council district, thereby reinforcing inequality. For poor districts, where parks are more likely to be undermaintained and less likely to have conservancies with the ability to raise money, other priorities, such as funding health centers and day care providers, often take precedence over a park infrastructure or beautification project. In many such districts, as the Great Recession compounded years of already dire employment and social-welfare problems, the priority of basic survival crowded out park improvement on the public agenda and deepened the effects of deferred maintenance and understaffing. For richer districts, the opposite was true. The result is an ironic replaying of the logic of the fiscal crisis: we still pay for maintenance from capital funds, but we hide it better. We wait until maintenance is no longer relevant, and buy new, and pay far more in the long run for this than we otherwise would.

And yet, even this hard-learned lesson has only been partially internalized in the department's practice. Except for the PEP positions, these positions were not "baselined" in the budget. That is to say that the jobs are *temporary*, even if year-round, full-time civil service jobs, because the city council must specifically renew their funding every year. Only the mayor can baseline an item in the budget, and this has not happened, in spite of the city council's urging. In this way, through the budget rules in a city with a "strong mayor" system, flexibility in the workforce can still be maintained. Accordingly, though it is a big advance in many ways to get the department staffed-up with CPWs and Climbers and Pruners again, it is an advance that is precarious as long as it must be revisited annually in the budget.

## *The Limits of the Contradictions*

Despite the fact that the inequalities of parks funding and services began to be a political problem for the Bloomberg administration at the end of its time in office, and despite the efforts at redress by the de Blasio administration, the problems only appear in politics from the point of view of *consumption* of the park, with the production of maintenance remaining largely invisible. The politics of park funding is defined from the perspective of park users: whether a park is underprotected by PEP officers, undermaintained by mobile crews, or unequally maintained relative to a conservancy-administered park in a neighboring community, the problem is still seldom seen as one of inequality and exploitation *within the workforce*. The moment of a park's *use* is seen as essentially distinct from the moment of the park's *maintenance*.

In most respects, our presentation in this book is guilty of the same conceptual separation. But we have bent the stick in the opposite direction, focusing on the workers who maintain the parks and the systems for its maintenance, precisely *because* we see park use and park maintenance as inextricably linked. We have sought to make visible the development of a neoliberal model of park maintenance and management from the point of view of the workers because we cannot separate the way in which the parks generate and reinforce inequality at the point of consumption from the way that they do so at the point of their production as an everyday good in the city.

Thus, the different ways that ideas of "citizenship" are mobilized in the cases of Marge and Nora; the complaints Harlan has about supervisors who do not rise through the ranks and do not know the work of maintenance; the difficulties some supervisors have with volunteers and the perpetuation of the idea that volunteers and JTPs are "extra help"; the absenteeism among JTPs; the chaos in scheduling that WEP brings to parks worksites; the feeling among JTPs, WEPs, and the occasional volunteer, alike, that WEP is akin to slavery; the vigorous resistance to unionization by the Central Park Conservancy; and the lack of "deep cleaning" by mobile crews: all of these are integral to the experience of the park, even if parks users do not know it.

And they should not know it under normal circumstances. Indeed, even many of the workers in the parks are unaware of the conditions under which others who tend to the parks' maintenance work. Part of this is a result of the geographic unevenness of park maintenance—corporate volunteers are unlikely to share shifts with mobile JTP crews cleaning outer-borough playgrounds—and part of this is a result of segregation among several kinds of workers, such as that which we saw with volunteers and WEP workers.

## Back to the Neoliberalizing Integral State

It is difficult to overstate the importance of the contradictions in parks maintenance work and its relationship to profit-making (the bare rudiments we have been able to sketch out here, given the increasingly complex financial relationships that underlie urban real estate). These contradictions' importance lies in their helping us to build a picture of contemporary neoliberal governance from the ground up, and to understand—even with a fairly small domain in the orbit of a single city agency—the range of ways in which coalitions or "regimes" in the integral state cohere and change.

As a range of social theorists attest, what Jamie Peck and Adam Tickell call "roll back" and "roll out" of neoliberal policies can be more or less mixed with *non-neoliberal* policies and supported by coalitions that are *not* dominated by advocates for neoliberalism. For Jessop, governing coalitions can be more "neostatist," "neocorporatist," or "neocommunitarian" as well as neoliberal, according to the policy preferences and styles of their core members. Similarly, Peck argues that neoliberalism draws "on an increasingly wide range of (often co-opted) social actors" and "must always cohabit with others." Like urban regime theorists who focus on bargaining about policies among urban elites—often real estate owners, but also, at least potentially, nonelite groups that have managed to organize effectively enough to control blocs of votes or other resources—these theorists suggest that policies are still somewhat more malleable than some theorists of neoliberalism might claim. On the other hand, he also argues that all the other modes of politics *tend toward neoliberalism*. That is to say that those political modes that favor

CHAPTER EIGHT

redistributionist state programs; those that favor the collaboration of diverse groups of organized interests in a city; and those that attempt to regulate local social and economic relations through local, more democratic solutions exist in a period defined largely by neoliberalism applied at a planetary scale and will thus *tend* to be subsumed to its program.[21]

Thus, the questions of change and coherence arise more forcefully. On the question of change, we have to ask whether neoliberalization has reached such a level of dominance that it cannot be displaced. On the question of coherence, we still have to ask why it is that coalitions that *end up* supporting neoliberalization have cohered and supported it as they have.

Even when vigorously contested, neoliberalism has some element of path dependence: once existing social relations were largely rolled back in the period of the fiscal crisis, it was difficult to reestablish them, and what replaced them was often compatible with a larger set of neoliberal policies. We can see this with the layoffs in the fiscal crisis of the 1970s and again, later, with the layoffs in the early 1990s under the Dinkins administration. The first set of layoffs was followed by the broadbanding of entry-level maintenance titles, which reduced internal mobility for workers and gave managers the ability to "do more with less." It was also followed, with a lag of several years, by the founding of the Central Park Conservancy, the Bryant Park Corporation, and the Prospect Park Alliance, and the hiring of maintenance staff at the former two. The second set of layoffs was followed by roughly ten years of increasing reliance on WEP workers (who, it turned out, were less expensive than workers for contractors), the vast expansion of the volunteer programs in the parks, and the eventual formation of the POP program and the JTP title.

Each of these developments required arm twisting and even the creation of organized allies where none existed before. But they also required alliance building among people and groups that do not necessarily share political views or a commitment to neoliberal principles. As a result, we regard an "ideal" neoliberalism as a distraction: in its place, we see a set of compromise positions, wherein a variety of organized social actors have promulgated ideas and speech that, while perhaps not neoliberal in intent, are readily co-opted; or they share some goals or analyses of actively neoliberalizing elites; or they identify opportunities to win at least partial victories in their limited domains by making common cause—or at least peace—with policies that "roll out" in ways that secure more power for (primarily) FIRE-sector elites.[22]

Often, coalition partners seek to be *pragmatic* and *apolitical* in solving problems—such as welfare dependency, shrinking public budgets for park maintenance, failing schools, and so on—even while being essentially compatible with state policies that privatize public goods, reduce and disorganize the power of workers, promote increasing inequality, and enhance the ability of capital to secure profits and rents from newly mobilized or remobilized property. In other words, in the name of solving real problems whose contours have largely been defined by neoliberalizing policy elites in and out of government since the 1970s, a disparate set of groups and individuals *act* in ways that tend toward neoliberal solutions.

As a result, we have found in our research that the combination of "roll-back" and "roll-out" moments in neoliberal park-maintenance policy making has resulted in a varied landscape. The more community-oriented Prospect Park Alliance, bearing the influence of Tupper Thomas's 1960s liberalism, works closely on volunteer projects with the investment bank Goldman Sachs, dubbed the "vampire squid" of Wall Street; closely intermingles the duties of Alliance-hired and City-hired staff; and leaves a portion of the park to be tended almost exclusively by volunteers. The Open Space Alliance for North Brooklyn extensively used WEP workers—those most often understood by themselves and others as being most akin to slaves—in spite of its self-understanding as a progressive organization in a progressive neighborhood. In fact, its founding director was not clear on the differences between WEP workers and JTPs. Even in Central Park, where Betsy Barlow Rogers was principally concerned with restoring the park to the beauty of Olmsted's design and its role as a democratic oasis, the neoliberal influence was significant in the founding of the Central Park Conservancy and in its subsequent animus toward unionization. And in districts where resources had simply been withdrawn over time, leaving them to be maintained with mobile crews of JTPs, WEPs, and community service sentencees, we find managers who approach the shortage of staff with increasing frustration or resignation. But we also find activist organizations and unions extolling the relative virtues of JTP over WEP, even while JTPs are as vulnerable to sexual harassment, discrimination, and abuse as the workfare workers whom they often replaced and alongside of whom they sometimes worked.

"Really existing neoliberalism," then, takes its shape from the coalitions and alliances that enable it. Far from being a state based on "the destruction of collectives," or even on the destruction of "all collective structures that could serve as an obstacle to the logic of the pure market,"[23] we can see that the neoliberal state's particular features rely on the legitimacy of the collective institutional actors that uphold it, even grudgingly. Thus, in 1996, when the Giuliani administration found that it could do even better than contracting out park maintenance to private-sector firms by impressing WEP workers into service, it relied on the active acquiescence of District Council 37. When the Parks Department uses community service sentencees to staff its mobile crews, it does so in part because alternative sentencing activists and advocates have successfully pressed for the state to punish low-level offenders without putting them in jail. Even antipoverty advocacy groups sometimes soft-pedal the endemic problems with JTP because it *still* represents a better alternative to WEP. And "Friends of" groups across the city, many of which press for increased funds for park maintenance, still become part of a system that relies more heavily on volunteer labor for basic maintenance than many such groups would like. Thus, the role of these groups is *contradictory*; they are neither destroyed as advocates for alternatives to "the logic of the pure market" nor fully co-opted into the integral state. Rather, the very fact that their co-optation is *partial* helps to lend legitimacy to the entire arrangement, as if it were simply a rational, pragmatic compromise among groups with somewhat equal power. It gives the illusion of pluralism.

## *Legitimation and Accumulation*

The contradictions that face parks advocates and volunteers have to do with several aspects of the parks system but are also manifestations of more basic tensions of governance, such as that between the enjoyment of the park and the prioritizing of programming-for-revenue and real estate value, and between the necessity of governments to gain revenue and thus support accumulation and the same governments' claims to represent the interests of the whole population. This basic tension between accumulation and legitimation is seen across public policy areas.

There are many ways to address this basic contradiction. One of the most common is to insist that government be efficient. Since the Progressive Era, which accompanied the rise of the robber barons and extreme levels of inequality, arguments for efficiency have been central to public administration, and with them, the argument that *politics* creates inefficiency. Since the 1980s, the so-called New Public Management has reiterated these claims in ways that span partisan politics. Many scholars argue that New Public Management favors measurement and testing, privatization and contracting out of public services, and the application of various market mechanisms to enhance privatization. Like their Progressive Era precursors, advocates of New Public Management are reflexively against unions in the public sector, in large part because they argue that unions inject a "special interest" and politics into otherwise neutral public administration. These ideas, sometimes taken together and sometimes separately, suffuse public policy today; they can be seen equally in parks as in sanitation, education, health care, and even policing.[24]

Because of the ethic of civic-minded philanthropy—and it is important to add that claims for its importance are not based in cynicism—the "attack on collectivities" under neoliberal and New Public Management practices can usually be more passive than active. As we suggest in earlier chapters and with the figures of Marge and Nora in this one, "giving back to the community" comes in philanthropic and workfarist versions that are sufficiently distinct from each other as to make solidarity between those who "give back" through their work extraordinarily difficult to conceive, much less organize. Civicness can be rooted in a distrust for the bureaucratization of the state and trust in the natural efficiency of volunteer initiatives. It can be rooted in the moral imperative to "give back," especially when the scarcity of resources becomes taken-for-granted common sense. Claims to citizenship and worth can likewise be rooted in claims to be industrious—even in the context of onerous working conditions—and in claims that others are not. Here, multiple versions of citizenship and civicness can be recruited into the integral state upon a political and cultural terrain in which philanthropy, volunteering, and coercive work have long histories of coexistence. Andrew Carnegie's *Gospel of Wealth* (1900), drawing on Protestant sources, did not limit to the upper classes alone the obligation to serve the community through work: "Those who do not have surplus means can at least donate part of their time, which is usually as important as money, and sometimes even more so."[25] If in Carnegie's Gilded Age, the governing projects of an integral state were at once economic and political, strategic and moral, it is no less true in our own.

Even if there is a long-term, cultural idiom that is compatible with neoliberalism and that affects how neoliberal policies look, there is still a *process* of neoliberalization that unfolds over time. As the feminist philosopher Nancy Fraser has argued, the extended rollout of neoliberal policies can shift the ground on which legitimation claims are based. Thus, by the time of Mayor Bloomberg's third term in office, conservancies and parks advocacy organizations began to play down

CHAPTER EIGHT

the philanthropic aspects of park support and instead began to justify park budgets on the basis of the rents and profit differentials of good parks maintenance. As a way to try to overcome the tension between accumulation and legitimation, this rhetoric seeks the legitimation of public investment through appeals to accumulation, in addition to a general but limited appeal to reciprocity. Even the New Yorkers for Parks' idea to dedicate a portion of real estate transfer taxes on the premiums generated by proximity to parks is based on "giving back" a very small portion of the return that property owners actually receive. Moreover, if this does not involve a *new* tax, it is simply a fancy way of getting the same money out of the general fund. Amid historic levels of economic inequality, this appeal makes sense if one takes as a given that the public has now simply become a supplicant in the face of plutocratic wealth. The intertwining of park advocacy organizations and conservancies with the economic elite of the city makes this form of limited reciprocity more appealing to these groups. It is another example among many of the response to the crisis of neoliberalism that erupted with the financial crisis of 2008 being a doubled-down neoliberal policy.[26] This dynamic also feeds into the generation of relatively high levels of inequality *within* conservancies and *between* conservancies and DPR, as conservancy CEOs make higher salaries than does the parks commissioner and conservancy-run parks' administrators get a significant bonus paid by the conservancy, while front-line maintenance staff tends to be paid less than their equivalents in DPR. As the *Times* reported in 2009, speaking of Robert Hammond, the executive director of the Friends of the High Line:

Mr. Hammond's salary [$250,000], found in the organization's tax filings, falls short of that of Douglas Blonsky, president of the Central Park Conservancy and administrator of the 843-acre park. He earns a salary of $364,000 a year. But Mr. Hammond's salary is considerably greater than his counterpart at the 526-acre Prospect Park in Brooklyn and about $45,000 more than the city's parks commissioner, Adrian Benepe, who oversees about 1,700 parks, playgrounds, and other recreation facilities.[27]

A similar problem arises where new parks, such as the new addition to Riverside Park and the joint state-City Hudson River and Brooklyn Bridge Parks, are meant to be self-sustaining. This means that as real estate is developed on parcels next to—or, in some cases, in—the park, a set fee must be paid in perpetuity for the upkeep of the park. In this way, real estate developers are compelled to pay for the park's maintenance. On the other hand, it means that the government has decided that public park land and its use will depend on development and the success of the developer in throwing off sufficient funds to maintain the park. In some parks, this has worked; in others, such as Hudson River Park, it has run into problems, and a rezoning of adjacent areas to allow for larger buildings (and, therefore, more sellable space) has been proposed in order to generate enough money for park maintenance. Even Commissioner Benepe, who helped to expand this model, told a panel in 2011:

The risk . . . is if you become dependent on that revenue, then you start to exploit the parks as much as you can for that revenue. I think the risk is that if a lot of our budget is dependent on how much revenue we bring in, that will start to turn the parks into a cash cow. We have a little bit of that now. We have some parks where revenue stays in the parks. As a long-term model it's hard to say. Is it a good model or a bad model? I suppose that depends on who's in charge, who's running things, and how much oversight there is.[28]

## Exploring Alternatives

If the financing for parks maintenance is increasingly tied to development and commercial activity in the parks, the public's claim on control of the parks decreases correspondingly to the degree of direct public investment in them. Without a mechanism for redistribution, as with other neoliberal policies, parks maintenance under this system preserves public control over the assets in the worst condition, with the fewest resources to maintain and improve them. In the absence of adequate funding for parks maintenance, the burden this creates for the public sector also creates pressure to reduce the pay and rights of the people cleaning the parks. In these circumstances, repeated in various ways throughout the public sector, public workers' interests are cast as inimical to those of the public at large.

What if we did *not* conceive of public workers' interests as hostile to those of the public? What if that did not apparently increase the public's tolerance for the unpaid, compulsory labor of workfare, for the displacement of regular workers, and for the sexual harassment of JTPs?

We have shown that attacking the stability of employment, the rights of workers, and public control over parks maintenance is not responsible for deep and stable improvements in park maintenance and is at least partially responsible for growing inequality among the parks.

CHAPTER EIGHT

If we are right about this, we raise the question: Who *should* clean our parks?

*Political Change*

In the mid-1950s, as park workers rallied to secure union rights from the recalcitrant commissioner Robert Moses, they sought rights that other workers, in the private sector, enjoyed. It took until 1968 for New York State's public workers to gain anything close to the rights of "regular" private-sector workers. As the right to collectively bargain was won by militant strike action by several unions (Welfare Department workers in 1965, transport workers in 1966), it is perhaps no surprise that they were denied the right to strike in the new regime, subject to tough but enforceable penalties. Just seven years after the new public-employee labor regime was established, the fiscal crisis broke in New York, unleashing a wave of layoffs and, as we have shown, neoliberalizing innovations in public administration that have accumulated toward the current situation in which the question with which we opened the book, "Who cleans your park?," can be answered in myriad ways, with most touching on one form or another of coerced, unpaid, or contingent labor.

We cannot, however, have nostalgia for a seven-year period. Even the period before 1968, when rights were not well established but workers were more likely to strike and win concessions, is no source of nostalgia. They struck because they were routinely exposed to unfair and arbitrary management and had poor wages and benefits relative to what they could and would eventually bargain. From the point of view of parks workers, even those, like Harlan, who point to periods of greater camaraderie and motivation to get promoted, there is no Golden Age.

In 2014, a new city administration came into office in New York City, led by Mayor Bill de Blasio. The mayor and the key members of the city council were drawn from the "progressive" wing of the Democratic Party and more publicly concerned with equity than any of their predecessors since before the fiscal crisis of the 1970s. The same city council member who, as head of the Parks Committee, held hearings during Mayor Bloomberg's tenure on inequities in the parks system became the powerful speaker of the city council. The council quickly promulgated new rules for the allocation of discretionary capital funds to council members. These have been a key source of funds for capital projects in parks, and now they will be at least partially allocated according to the level of district needs. Moreover, the first budget under

Mayor de Blasio featured an $80 million capital investment for "neighborhood parks" and additional money for increased park maintenance staff. Further, the new administration is unenthusiastic about WEP and has committed to phasing it out, not just in the Parks Department, where it has waned in use, but citywide. Nevertheless, the coalitions organized in favor of the current system of park maintenance, and municipal government as a whole, remain strong.

*Cleaning the Parks Beyond Parks*

A central premise of this book, announced in chapter 1, was that the work and workplace dynamics we found in parks are a version of similar dynamics that are unfolding throughout our economy. Our accounts of labor-market segmentation in chapter 2 share much in common with accounts of segmentation elsewhere. Our findings about broadbanding share a great deal with other accounts of employers seeking greater "flexibility" in the face of restricted budgets or profits. Our findings that, in spite of these dynamics, workers continue to take a great deal of pride in their work and find meaning in it; that their criticisms of their work environments often have to do with perceptions of unfairness and the promotion of people to supervisory roles who do not understand the work done by those lower down in the hierarchy; and that workers in lower labor-market segments are prone to abuse and harassment, sometimes in ways that dovetail with their understandings of how to survive in these workplaces—all of these have ready analogies beyond the parks workplace and, indeed, beyond the public sector.

Parks, furthermore, had the "virtue" of assembling many different kinds of labor contract to a single job—parks maintenance—even as they variously shared or differed in specific tasks within it. Because of the variety, however, it is very difficult, without sustained study, to know what you are seeing if you walk into a park. Sometimes, you can see volunteers, clearly in their volunteer t-shirts. And yet, even here, you might not know whether they are regular volunteers in the park or more occasional corporate volunteers, or whether or not the park has a conservancy and an established volunteer program. Even in the midst of the significant complexity in the allocation and deployment of labor in the city's parks that this book has shown, we have spared the reader some of it. It is not obvious to a park-goer what is a City park, what is a State park, and what is a jointly administered park. It is not obvious to a park-goer the difference between a public plaza created from the intersection of zoning regulations and private development—certified by the Parks Department but maintained by the private developer—and a park created from a traffic island or a "greenstreet." It is no more evident to your average park-goer why the Doe Fund, Inc. has a contract to water the plants in the traffic island in the middle of Broadway (the Broadway Malls) or who the Broadway Mall Association is—the private group that manages this park property—and why the malls are maintained by a mix of Parks Department workers, JTPs, community service sentencees, and private staff supplied by a nonprofit service program for people with mental disabilities.

Indeed, even an inside observer has an extremely partial view. This fact means that most of the labor arrangements in the parks—what they are and how they have changed—are largely invisible to parks workers themselves. For workers, then, holding politicians to account for deteriorating working conditions in the park is made all the more difficult, since solidarity among the various types of workers is that much more remote.

Again, many of these same problems are present in private-sector workplaces, especially when global commodity chains and just-in-time production mean that workforces that produce commodities can be dispersed around the world and combine highly skilled and remunerated work and conditions of near slave labor all in the production of a single complex product. The problems also exist in local-serving service industries, though here the issues of degraded working conditions and, often, low wages are perhaps more amenable to political and community organizing, as witnessed by local ordinances against wage theft and a national movement to raise the minimum wage substantially.[29]

Yet once the public sector is added to the equation, we more explicitly open up questions about the specificity of parks as presumptive public spaces, about their governance and the accountability of private actors that become, essentially, part of a reformed state and that are at least partially shielded from accountability from both the public and, in many meaningful ways, from their nonunion workforces. The public nature of parks—a public good from which no one, in theory at least, can be excluded—further raises questions about how park maintenance is funded and, therefore, how concessions are chosen by conservancies and approved by the Department of Parks and Recreation, and even how parks fit in with larger policies on land use and real estate development, and the balance of public and private interests there, as well.

Parks are, therefore, revealed to be a kind of hybrid, public-private good in the first place. The *uses* of the park may mostly be nonexcludable (though the dependence on concession income often excludes increasing numbers of people from its equal use), but the *exchange value* of the park can be privately appropriated. That money can be made on the basis of good park maintenance—which we all enjoy in myriad ways—focuses our attention on the dynamics of labor, rents, and the possibilities for social solidarity in ways we find provocative. It also focuses our attention on the different ways in which we understand the demands of being a good citizen.

Like the beginning student of literature who might resist picking apart and analyzing a well-loved story, we nevertheless find our experience of the parks enriched. We can no longer look at parks in the same way.

We walk into a park and ask: "Why has the concession changed?" "Why has (or hasn't) the garbage can been emptied before 11 a.m.?" "Why are the stairs in this park in abysmal condition and the walks in terrible need of edging, while the stairs in the park I was just in are in tip-top shape?" "Who are the people cleaning up the picnic over there, and why are they wearing reflective vests but not park t-shirts? Are they WEP workers? Community service sentencees?" And if we could peer behind doors, we might ask "What is this mattress doing in the park house?"

Because once you know something, you are no longer innocent; asking these questions then leads to hypotheticals. What would a park maintenance system look like that made sexual harassment exceedingly difficult to get away with? What would a park maintenance system look like that did not rely on a decades-long campaign to undermine the working conditions and rights of workers as the only answer to efficiency? Can we imagine a parks maintenance system that incorporates the insights of longtime workers about the craft of maintenance? Can we think about what it would take to build sufficient solidarity among various sorts of workers so that volunteers could join forces with JTPs or conservancy workers to protest workplace abuses?

As we conclude the drafting of this book, another New York summer—the sixth since we started—has begun to bloom, after a tough winter with record snowfall. The fountains are on (someone had to turn them on, someone has to shut them off), kids are sliding on the jungle gym (someone had to inspect it for safety), pools and beaches are open (and regular staff are pulled from their districts on step-ups to maintain these), concerts are beginning (someone will likely get paid overtime), and so on.

Who cleans it? Who should?

# Afterword

Qualitative research—and academic publishing—are slow processes. Add to this the birth and growing-up of children, managing a transatlantic collaboration, and the inevitable pressures of other work, and all of a sudden eight years elapse between the initial fieldwork for this book and its release. In the summer of 2015—seven years since the beginning of our research, and four since we left the "field" (with a little prodding from the Parks Department!)—we decided to do several follow-up interviews to see what, if anything, had changed.

We had reason to believe that *something* had. In 2013, Mayor Bill de Blasio was elected on a platform of redressing the staggering inequality that had developed in New York City. Parks, as well as welfare-to-work programs, were part of his vision. There was also a new city council speaker, Melissa Mark-Viverito, who had been the chair of the Parks Committee and who had chaired some of the contentious hearings about PEP officers and conservancies from which we quoted in earlier chapters. District Council 37 had a new leader, Henry Garrido, who had become a critic of conservancies (and contracting-out work more generally). And the Department of Parks and Recreation had a new commissioner, charged with bringing the mayor's vision of equity into the core of the department.

We were also interested in double-checking our initial research on several issues, most significantly that of sexual harassment and the sexual economy about which we wrote. Little is written about this elsewhere, and still less links this to the general subordination of certain kinds of work contracts in the workplace. We have had several reviewers—including one for the manuscript for this book—who doubted our evidence and suggested it was more hearsay than anything else (despite our efforts to document its prevalence). But more broadly, we were interested in whether our observations about the integral state and what might be called the "neoliberalism with a human face" about which we wrote remained in place in the wake of what had been widely considered a significant political transformation.

What we found both confirmed much of our research and confirmed our idea and hope that *some* things could—and did—change.

**Sexual Harassment**

We certainly got confirmation about our claims regarding sexual harassment. In contrast to our first time interviewing top Parks Department officials, when responses about men and women working together in the context of JTP, especially, were evasive at best, this time, we heard a great deal about how the department had elevated the issue of sexual harassment to the highest priority. The article from 2013 that we cited about a park-house party at which women in JTP were asked by Supervisors to strip—a story broken by the *Daily News*—was a turning point. Both top Parks brass and the new executive director at DC 37 told us that the training had become more intensive for JTPs and for supervisors, and Parks officials told us that multiple routes were now available to report and investigate harassment and that top officials meet regularly with the Equal Employment Opportunity officer to review and expedite pending cases. Even without prompting, Tupper Thomas—who came out of retirement from the Prospect Park Alliance to run New Yorkers for Parks—told us of several incidents at Prospect Park, including one involving a JTP whose allegations were not initially taken seriously by her Parks Department Supervisor.

All stressed the importance of due process and suggested that resolution of these cases can take a while. So while it still exists, and known harassers remain in places, it is acknowledged widely as a significant problem. As Thomas suggested, however, the real problem lies in the status and power difference among the workers:

It would be much more the whole issue that you need a permanent, very solid workforce that is there all the time, that grows and learns and goes through the process. And that's what we're promoting. Obviously, you can use this core of people; it's a good training program . . . but it shouldn't be 70 percent of your cleaning force. It's just not going to work for the agency in the long run.

## WEP and JTP

And in some ways, the agency seems to be moving more in the direction of *desegmenting* its workforce, though this is incomplete for a number of reasons. WEP is virtually gone—again—from Parks. Nobody seems sorry to see it go. Top Parks officials corroborated the complaints of managers about the irregularity of WEP workers' hours and the general preference for JTP. But other agencies, such as the Department of Sanitation and the Department of Citywide Administrative Services, still use WEP workers. They will not for long, however, as the de Blasio administration has decided to phase WEP out by 2016 and replace it with a public-sector apprenticeship program run by DC 37. This brought together the union with antipoverty activists and the new welfare commissioner, Steve Banks, who had spent the thirty years prior to his appointment as a Legal Aid attorney—and was for some time the head of the agency—suing the City on behalf of welfare recipients and other poor New Yorkers. In this program, welfare recipients will get prevailing wages for work they are doing for the City and have a chance at new job openings.

JTP is also changing. With prodding from the new leader of District Council 37, the de Blasio administration announced raises for the lowest-paid city employees. The DC 37 leader pointed to Mayor de Blasio's support for raising the minimum wage to $15 an hour—a position pushed by the mayor's key labor allies in the Service Employees' union. He reasoned that many city workers do not get comparable pay, and suggested that the mayor did not want to look like a hypocrite. And that the mayor probably did not want low-income, African American women in his union showing up with signs calling him a hypocrite at his speaking engagements. JTPs and other low-wage city workers got roughly two dollars an hour more, without having to reopen contract negotiations.

Two things should be said about this: First, bringing JTPs up to $11.50 an hour still represents a pay cut relative to the wage at the start of the program in 2000. Then, the wage was $9.38, which would be closer to thirteen dollars an hour in 2015 dollars. Yet, relative to the Bloomberg administration's pay cuts—first to $7.50 an hour, and then up to $9.21—it represents an inflation-adjusted gain of over a dollar an hour. The wage is set to rise to $15 an hour in 2018.

Second, the raise brings the JTP wage much closer to that of CPWs and to basic parity with City Seasonal Aides. This means that the "carrot" of further employment that provides an incentive for JTPs—or that acts as a subtle "stick"—is less effective. As one high-level Parks Department administrator said of the $11.50 wage: "So normally, if someone comes into the parks who's JTP, you say 'OK, the next step is this.' Now the next step isn't really all that much."

Interestingly, however, even as JTPs' pay is coming closer to that of "regular" Parks employees, the program treats them less as simple labor and more as "clients." When we interviewed Parks staff, they were in the midst of a transition to a more individualized case-management program, for which they had brought on new staff to POP as "career counselors" who are given individuals to help and track through the program and into training and further employment. This leads to some tension between the two visions of the JTP in practical ways. On one hand the POP program keeps encouraging JTPs to take on new classes and training—even at the cost of missing more time in the districts—and on the other, the Parks Supervisors are saying "I need you here."

Further, the new pay scale means that the education and training parts of POP take on new importance, since JTP workers—many of whom do not have a high school diploma or GED—are loathe to leave the Parks Department into new jobs that routinely pay less. As Liza Erlich, the director of POP, told us: "The $11.50 is great because it helps to stabilize them in terms of their path forward. But we have to do a lot of managing the conversation around it."

## Community Parks and Equity

The cornerstone of the de Blasio administration's new approach to Parks—and its link to the administration's greater focus on equity—is the Community Parks Initiative, or CPI. For the CPI, the City identified small parks that had gotten virtually no capital improvement for twenty years and that were in significant disrepair. These were mainly in low-income communities, which makes sense, given that, in the absence of a steady capital budget for parks, most capital investment in small parks had to be done with city council "member items." In poor communities, lots of other needs compete with parks for these funds, and parks are often neglected. The CPI will rebuild thirty-five parks across the five boroughs and make capital improvements in many more. In addition, it has dedicated increased maintenance to these parks, and has involved Partnerships for Parks to try to build up "Friends of" groups and to bring in recreation and programming to the parks.

The CPI designates several "zones" across the city—focusing on dense, poor neighborhoods that are still growing—comprising fifty-five neighborhoods. Not coterminous with parks districts, these zones serve as a cross-district means of sharing resources such as maintenance crews.

The CPI—the department's "first major equity initiative," at $130 million in capital funds—stands in contrast to the focus on capital investment in larger parks during the Bloomberg administration. Though in its final year the Bloomberg administration allocated a small, flexible capital budget for Parks, and also had historically included some money for smaller parks, it remains the case that its focus was on larger parks, and many of the areas targeted by the CPI were, quite simply, neglected. The capital budget for Parks was subsumed into the CPI under de Blasio. And though more maintenance workers were allocated to CPI zones, the fact that these new workers were not baselined raises the possibility that, in the future, the City will continue to pay for under-maintained parks through the capital budget, a problem we have indicated in earlier chapters.

### The Politics of Conservancies and the Integral State

One thing we expected to find—and did—was some tension between the de Blasio administration and the conservancies. As a candidate, de Blasio had voiced some support for the approach championed by State Senator Daniel Squadron to levy a kind of tax of up to 20 percent on wealthy conservancies' revenues to redistribute to other parks. Tupper Thomas described real trepidation among conservancy leaders when de Blasio was elected as well as an unwillingness on the part of the Parks Department to meet with them as a group. Though de Blasio moved off his support for the Squadron proposal and in fact asked less of several conservancies than they might otherwise have been willing to offer, his Parks Department is still trying to require conservancies to contribute *something*, whether expertise or funds, and to use these, especially, for the CPI. Accordingly, the design office in Prospect Park was asked to redesign a playground in a CPI zone; Central Park has expanded its citywide programs for technical assistance and training of horticulture, lawn-care, and other workers, and continues its contribution of maintenance crews to the Historic Harlem Parks.

Above all, we see a shift in the balance of forces between the conservancy side and the government side of the integral state. Parks officials talked about conservancies realizing that "this is a new world," and this world seems much more like one of arm's-length relationships than one in which the commissioner would convene conservancy leaders several times a year in his office. At the same time, the de Blasio administration does not want to get rid of the conservancies and the whole public-private system. Indeed, it treats them as a permanent feature of the landscape. It does, however, want to show—at least symbolically—that the private partners are subordinate to a larger system that is more focused than the partners are on equity.

Whatever tension there is between conservancies and the new Parks Department administration is more symbolic than tangible in everyday practice. Since our study concluded, the new appointment of an administrator caught our attention, in part because the administrator's jurisdiction comprises four parks in three districts in Harlem (Marcus Garvey, Jackie Robinson, Morningside, and St. Nicholas). The Historic Harlem Parks show, if nothing else, a kind of regularization of the integral state, even amid what might be called the *de-neoliberalizing* moves in the employment conditions of JTPs. The Historic Harlem Parks' Administrator, Arnyce Foster-Hernandez, is, like other administrators, a Parks Department employee. Unlike other administrators, she is not the director or president of any "Friends of" groups. In fact, part of her role is to support the Friends of the Four Historic Harlem Parks, which, having once formed the Historic Harlem Parks Coalition, had drifted away from each other. Foster-Hernandez's task is less directly about maintenance: this is the main task of the Parks Supervisors and the rest of the maintenance hierarchy in the districts, and there is little indication that the Historic Harlem Parks will enable the "Friends of" groups to hire their own workers in the near future. Instead, she handles a great deal of programming and dedicates a lot of time to attracting resources—both public and private—to the parks. This may mean taking advantage of being "public" in order to get a free projector for a summer film series, and it might mean organizing a meeting of African American real estate developers to brainstorm about what improvements they would like to see in the parks under her jurisdiction (and, possibly, to contribute money to the fund for the Historic Harlem Parks).

Foster-Hernandez indicated that her first priority was to raise half a million dollars for a three-year commitment for PEP officers and gardeners. Without this commitment of private funds, public PEP officers could not be allocated:

Foster-Hernandez: That's what Chelsea Piers does. The West Harlem Piers does. Riverside does it. Hudson River Park, Madison Square Park, Battery Park City.
John: So they are paying, they're contracting with the Parks Department.
Foster-Hernandez: Yes. I have to do the same thing. Even though I'm a Parks employee.
John: You can't just say, "I need more PEP officers"?
Foster-Hernandez: I mean I can make phone calls if I'm in an emergency. I can call them. But I can't keep them there. I need them there for sixteen hours a day, two shifts a day. Every single day . . . Two on one shift and two on the other shift. And I just can't do that. They can't just give it to me that way. Because everybody wants that, you know! If they are not contracted for a specific site, they have to spread themselves throughout the city to other sites as well as mine. So that's my goal, parks enforcement and gardeners. The next sixteen, eighteen months, that's what I want to see happen.

With the normalization of internal contracting for PEP officers by entities directly set up by the Parks Department that must raise private money, our understanding that parks governance must be understood *integrally* makes more sense to us than ever. Beyond PEP officers, private funds can also purchase gardening services, which for the Historic Harlem Parks can mainly be mobilized otherwise either through the horticulture training program for JTPs based in Morningside Park or through corporate volunteering. In any case, our discussion with Arnyce Foster-Hernandez suggested something we had not put together before, namely, that the baselining of PEP officers enabled the Parks Department to have a greater pool of officers it could provide—for a fee—to conservancies but that this is not yet done with gardeners or others more clearly in the Maintenance and Operations chain of command.

**Equity vs. Equity**

We leave this phase of the project—for as we wrote earlier, we cannot look at the parks without thinking about how they are maintained and by whom—with a mix of hope and frustration. We are, of course, encouraged by the new administration's commitment to equity and real strides in raising pay and addressing some of the worst aspects of the decades-long subordination of the Parks labor force. Much of this entails regaining ground that was lost during the two previous city administrations, rather than effecting a larger-scale improvement. But regaining this ground should not be dismissed, least of all for the people who work for the Parks Department. Further, one can hope that this leads conservancies to raise their pay, as well, though it is also possible to imagine subsequent mayors either reducing pay again—as Mayor Bloomberg did in 2004—or relying ever more on private, nonunion, and less remunerated conservancy staff. This becomes even more plausible when we consider that the CPW, Gardener, and Pruner lines were not baselined in the budget.

Further, there is much to applaud about the CPI. Equity for all park users should be a guiding principle for the Parks Department, and the very fact that there were small parks that had been largely neglected for twenty years is testimony to the fact that this principle has not been honored. At the same time, there is another sense of the word "equity" that haunts the potential of these projects, namely, the monetary value of real assets. As we indicated in the last chapter, well-maintained parks generate real estate premiums, and these can sometimes be more threatening than nice parks are welcoming to residents of poor areas. Tupper Thomas told us:

You know, in Prospect Park, that the usership is still pretty low-income. But the low-income community has moved further and further away from the park. So there is this whole fear in lower-income communities that if you fix up the park it'll get "too nice." And all of us in the parks world are nervous wrecks about this because we don't want people to feel that way. So my theory is that every park should be nice, and then it's not going to make a difference. Parks need to have more money allocated for staff by the administration.

It's a hopeful thought. It addresses the potential to redress the unevenness of park development, at least to some degree. At the same time, we find it difficult to be sanguine. The mayor has signaled his intention to rezone areas of the city that are still low-income areas but are "still growing" in order to accommodate the city's housing needs. Like his predecessor, however, the plans for greater density—while really benefiting from having neighborhood parks—do not include plans for sufficient affordability for the low- and moderate-income users, among whom are likely to be city workers, JTPs, and their families. The residents of these neighborhoods have cause to worry. It will not be the well-maintained parks that push them out, but these parks will doubtless become an adjunct to still larger dynamics that threaten them. Nearly all areas of the city have become ripe for real estate speculation and development in an age in which the financialization of real estate assets (exactly that which was behind the housing "bubble" of the mid-2000s) draws in a global pool of investors. Any and every area, no matter its history of neglect, can become a kind of "export" product for the city, in a way that only those touristic areas around Central Park and other centrally located parks could earlier. If the greater equity in pay and in the distribution of park resources is subsumed into the equity of real estate investors, the progressive vision of the city will have won a Pyrrhic victory, indeed.

# Acknowledgments

This book represents the culmination of a research project begun in 2008, conducted largely in New York but with writing and discussion sessions in Paris, as well. It would never have happened at all without a suggestion on the part of the urban sociologist Nicole Marwell that Maud look up John's work; Nicole connected Maud's interest in the work of volunteers with John's interest in the work of workfare workers. It was a fruitful connection.

Along the way, we have had many interlocutors about the project and have received a good deal of material, moral, and intellectual support, and people have opened doors, or kept them open. A partial list, with apologies to any omissions, includes: Debbie Becher, Natalie Benelli, Anne Bory, Vince Boudreau, Kendra Briken, Hillary Caldwell, Neil Calvanese, Susan M. Chambré, Bruce Cronin, Edgar DeJesus, Daniel DiSalvo, Volker Eick, Bernard Friot, Henry Garrido, Pavel Gerardo, Elisabeth Hill Gest and Christophe Gest, Matthieu Hély, Ruth Horowitz, Marilyn Hoskin, Bill Kornblum, Barbara Leopold, David Meacham, Ruth Milkman, Delphine Naudier, Richard Ocejo, Evelyn Seinfeld, Lewis Steel, Leslie Paik, Betsy Rogers, Penny Ryan, Henry Serrano, William Sites, Greg Smithsimon, Frédéric Viguier, Sondra Youdelman, and the colleagues from IDHES and from IES who discussed some early presentations of the text.

Students who served as research assistants at various points in the project include Kenn Vance, Marcela Gonzalez, and Samantha Halsey, who did interviews, transcriptions, and coding, as well as research on several legal cases; Andrew Miller, who coded many interviews and did important background analyses of several parks districts; Charlesworth Mabheka, who compiled a useful archive of news reports about parks; and Joseph Alston and Patrick Fitzpatrick, who provided early assistance and insights. Shoshanna Seid-Green did brilliant, punctual, and affordable transcriptions of the interviews.

Thanks are also due Kyle Adam Wagner, Caterina MacLean, and Doug Mitchell from the University of Chicago Press, who shepherded us through the publication process and encouraged us not to lose hope. A wonderfully helpful review was provided by an anonymous reviewer.

Our research and writing, and our trips to do so, would have been impossible without the love and support of Keren Osman, Maya Osman-Krinsky, and Adam Osman-Krinsky, as well as Frédéric Joubert, Mathis Joubert, and Clara Joubert. Mano Joubert joined us partway through the project but did so in high style. John's parents, Robert and Carol Krinsky, have been encouraging throughout and helpful with contacts. John's parents-in-law, Roman and Miriam Osman, have been no less encouraging and have warmly welcomed Maud into their home on numerous occasions. Maud' s parents, Jean and Renée Simonet, as well as her larger family and friends tribe, have been incredibly supportive in keeping such a vivid interest and a strong faith in this "New York parks" project through all these years.

Several research grants also helped us get our work done. Funds from the NSF (grant #0848590), PSC-CUNY (grant #64722–00), and IDHES-CNRS were indispensable. On multiple occasions, Lissy Wassaff, Gregory Wehrner, Regina Masterson, Ana Delgado, Candice Baptiste-Sexton, Tricia Mayhew-Noel, and other staff at the City College Office of Research Administration worked through documents that were critical to our getting and maintaining funding.

Finally, our deepest gratitude goes to the workers at all levels, and across the parks system, whom we interviewed and who remain anonymous, and especially to the borough and district Supervisors and Managers who facilitated this work. Without you, there would be no research. We hope our work redeems your gift of time, energy, and trust.

Any mistakes of fact or judgment are, of course, our own.

# Notes

CHAPTER ONE

1. We have changed the name, and all the other names of interviewees. Sometimes we have changed the gender or borough of work of our interviewees as well (where doing so would not, in our judgment, affect the interpretation of what is being said). Both changes are meant to make it more difficult to discover the real identities of particular speakers. This is part of our protocol for the protection of human research subjects and was a condition of our interviewees' granting of consent to us to conduct and publish the findings of the interviews. In addition, anyone quoted with their real names had an opportunity to review the quotes in question and to withdraw their consent to be the named speaker in this work.
2. See, e.g., Alan Finder, "Decline of Tenure Track Raises Concerns," *New York Times*, November 20, 2007; "Most Presidents Favor No Tenure for Majority of Faculty," *Chronicle of Higher Education*, May 15, 2011.
3. See, e.g., Trebor Scholz, ed., *Digital Labor: The Internet as Playground and Factory* (New York: Routledge, 2013).
4. See, e.g., Ross Perlin, *Intern Nation: How to Earn Nothing and Learn Little in the Brave New Economy* (New York: Verso, 2012).
5. See Marc Doussard, *Degraded Work: The Struggle at the Bottom of the Labor Market* (Minneapolis: University of Minnesota Press, 2013); David Weil, *The Fissured Workplace: Why Work Became So Bad for So Many and What Can Be Done to Improve It* (Cambridge: Harvard University Press, 2014); see also Guy Standing, *A Precariat Charter: From Denizens to Citizens* (London: Bloomsbury, 2014).

NOTES TO CHAPTER ONE

6. Robert Yin describes "critical cases" as those that can, through a single case, "confirm, challenge, or extend" established theories. See Robert Y. Lin, *Case Study Research: Design and Methods* (Thousand Oaks, CA: Sage, 2009), 47.
7. Joshua Freeman, *Working-Class New York: Life and Labor Since World War II* (New York: The New Press, 2002). For versions of theories of "rolling back" and "rolling out" phases of neoliberal policy development, see Neil Brenner and Nik Theodore, "Cities and the Geographies of 'Actually Existing Neoliberalism,'" in *Spaces of Neoliberalism: Urban Restructuring in North America and Western Europe*, ed. Neil Brenner and Nik Theodore (Malden, MA: Blackwell, 2002), 2–32; Jamie Peck and Adam Tickell, "Neoliberalizing Space," in *Spaces of Neoliberalism*, 33–57; William Sites, *Remaking New York: Primitive Globalization and the Politics of Urban Community* (Minneapolis: University of Minnesota Press, 2004).
8. Placard pictured in Roy Rosenzweig and Elizabeth Blackmar, *The Park and the People: A History of Central Park* (Ithaca: Cornell University Press, 1992), 487.
9. Rosenzweig and Blackmar, *The Park and the People*, 488. Also see Jewell and Bernard Bellush, *Union Power and New York City: Victor Gotbaum and District Council 37* (New York: Prager, 1984), 47–61. The Bellushes recount that the parks workers' union's paper trumpeted the headline "Who Built This Union? Bob Moses!"
10. See, e.g., Clarence N. Stone, "Looking Back to Look Forward: Reflections on Urban Regime Analysis," *Urban Affairs Review* 40, no. 3 (January 2005): 309–41; John Hull Mollenkopf, *A Phoenix in the Ashes: The Fall and Rise of the Koch Coalition in New York City Politics* (Princeton: Princeton University Press, 1992).
11. See, e.g., Arlene Kaplan Daniels, *Invisible Careers: Women Civic Leaders from the Volunteer World* (Chicago: University of Chicago Press, 1988); Danièle Kergoat, "Division Sexuelle du Travail et Rapports Sociaux de Sexe," in *Dictionnaire Critique du Féminisme*, 2nd enlarged edition, ed. Helena Hirata, Françoise Laborie, Hélène Le Doaré, and Danièle Senotier (Paris: Presses Universitaires de France, 2004), 35–44; Jules Falquet, "La Règle du Jeu: Repenser la Co-Formation des Rapports Sociaux de Sexe, de Classe et de 'Race' dans la Mondialisation Néolibérale," in *Sexe, Race, Classe: Pour une Épistemologie de la Domination*, ed. Elsa Dorlin (Paris: Presses Universitaires de France, 2009), 71–90; Susan Leigh Star and Anselm Strauss, "Layers of Silence, Arenas of Voice: The Ecology of Visible and Invisible Work," *Computer Supported Cooperative Work* 8, no. 1 (March 1999): 9–30; Pamela Herd and Madonna Harrington Meyer, "Care Work: Invisible Civic Engagement," *Gender and Society* 16, no. 5 (October 2002): 665–88. For a general conceptualization of domestic labor as *theoretically* invisible, see Lise Vogel, *Marxism and the Oppression of Women*, 2nd edition (New York: Haymarket), 192–93. On the political history of the "employee," see Jean-

Christian Vinel, *The Employee: A Political History* (Philadelphia: University of Pennsylvania Press, 2013).
12. A small literature exists on unions and nonprofits, indicating the tensions that confront mission-driven nonprofits and unions when workers try to organize to protect or improve their pay and working conditions. See, e.g., Rick Cohen, "Unions and the Nonprofit Workforce: A Few Considerations," *Nonprofit Quarterly* (August 8, 2013), http://nonprofitquarterly.org/2013/08/08/unions-and-the-nonprofit-workforce-a-few-considerations/; Jeanne B. Peters and Jan Masaoka, "A House Divided: How Nonprofits Experience Union Drives," *Nonprofit Leadership and Management* 10, no. 3 (Spring 2000): 305–17; Eduardo R. C. Capulong, "Which Side Are You On? Unionization in Social-Service Nonprofits," *New York City Law Review* 9 (2005–2006): 373–404.
13. Maud Simonet, *Le Travail Bénévole: Engagement Citoyen ou Travail Gratuit?* (Paris: La Dispute, 2010); other exceptions include Andrea Muehlebach, *The Moral Neoliberal: Welfare and Citizenship in Italy* (Chicago: University of Chicago Press, 2013); and Nina Eliasoph, *The Politics of Volunteering* (Malden, MA: Polity Press, 2013).
14. Though Marcela speaks Spanish as a first language, only one interview was conducted in Spanish. Two interviews in the study were conducted partially in French.
15. The Arsenal is the name used for the main office for the Department of Parks and Recreation (DPR). It is located in Central Park.
16. Rosenzweig and Blackmar, *The Park and the People*.
17. Oliver Cooke, *Rethinking Municipal Privatization* (New York: Routledge, 2008). Cooke's work is a heavily theoretical economic analysis of privatization based on the case of Central Park, but it lacks specific detail on workers and working conditions.
18. We are indebted to Colin Barker for this metaphor of the process of abstraction.
19. E.g., Arne Kalleberg, *Good Jobs, Bad Jobs: The Rise of Polarized and Precarious Employment Systems in the United States, 1970s-2000s* (New York: Russell Sage Foundation, 2011).
20. See, e.g., David M. Gordon, Richard Edwards, and Michael Reich, *Segmented Work, Divided Workers: The Historical Transformation of Labor in the United States* (New York: Cambridge University Press, 1982); also Jamie Peck, *Work-Place: The Social Regulation of Labor Markets* (New York: Guilford, 1996).
21. An exception is Hazel Conley, "Modernisation or Casualisation? Numerical Flexibility in Public Services," *Capital and Class* 30, no. 2 (Summer 2006): 31–57.
22. E.g., Donald Kettl, *The Transformation of Governance: Public Administration for the Twenty-First Century* (Baltimore: Johns Hopkins University Press, 2002); also see Tania A. Börtzel, "Organizing Babylon: On the Different

Conceptions of Policy Networks," *Public Administration* 76, no. 2 (Summer 1998): 253–73.

23. See, e.g., Peck, *Work-Place*, and his *Workfare States* (New York: Guilford, 2001); Jennifer Wolch and Michael Dear, eds., *The Power of Geography: How Territory Shapes Social Life* (New York: Routledge, 1989); a more general statement of the links between the regulation approach and a geographically inflected Marxist political economy can be found in Bob Jessop, "A Neo-Gramscian Approach to the Regulation of Urban Regimes: Accumulation Strategies, Hegemonic Projects, and Governance" in *Reconstructing Urban Regime Theory: Regulating Urban Politics in a Global Economy*, ed. Mickey Lauria (Thousand Oaks, CA: Sage Publications, 1997), 51–74. Feminist geographers range farther afield from the regime-theoretical concepts themselves but are centrally concerned with the way that public and private interests intertwine, particularly in the "fleshy, messy" business of social reproduction, and how "public" and "private" are themselves constituted with respect to state and economic power. See, e.g., Cindi Katz, "Vagabond Capitalism and the Necessity of Social Reproduction" *Antipode* 33, no. 4 (2001): 708–28; Liz Bondi, "Gender, Class, and Urban Space: Public and Private Space in Contemporary Urban Landscapes," *Urban Geography* 19, no. 2 (1998): 160–85.

24. Antonio Gramsci, *Selections from the Prison Notebooks*, trans. and ed. Quintin Hoare and Geoffrey Nowell Smith (New York: International Publishers, 1971), 267; also see Jessop, "A Neo-Gramscian Approach." We prefer this more open-ended term to another quite evocative one, "the shadow state," coined by the geographer Jennifer Wolch, which focuses more on the contractual relationships between nonprofit service providers and governments (which is, of course, part of the story here, as well). See Jennifer R. Wolch, *The Shadow State: Government and Voluntary Sector in Transition* (New York: The Foundation Center, 1990); see also Ruth Wilson Gilmore, "In the Shadow of the Shadow State," in *The Revolution Will Not Be Funded: Beyond the Non-Profit Industrial Complex*, ed. INCITE Women of Color against Violence (Boston: South End Press, 2009), 40–52. Also see Stephen Rathgeb Smith and Michael Lipsky, *Nonprofits for Hire: The Welfare State in the Age of Contracting* (Cambridge: Harvard University Press, 1993).

25. On the early history of public sector unions, see Joseph E. Slater, *Public Workers: Government Employee Unions, the Law, and the State, 1900–1962* (Ithaca: Cornell University Press, 2004); for New York's public unions, see Mark H. Maier, *City Unions: Managing Discontent in New York City* (New Brunswick: Rutgers University Press, 1987). An important difference between public and private workers is that like agricultural and domestic workers, public workers were exempted from the National Labor Relations Act of 1935, which established the institutions and procedures of collective bargaining and union certification. Parks workers' activism in the 1950s helped to expand bargaining and labor rights in New York City,

but these rights, and regular collective bargaining regimes, were achieved piecemeal, state-by-state, throughout the 1960s and 1970s. The dependence on state-level laws for public sector labor relations means that they can be undone more easily than they can be in the private sector, as the wave of anti-union legislation in Indiana, Wisconsin, and Ohio late in the first decade of the twenty-first century shows.
26. See, e.g., Daniel DiSalvo and Fred Siegel, "The New Tammany Hall", *Weekly Standard* (October 12, 2009); see also Daniel DiSalvo, *Government against Itself: Public Union Power and Its Consequences* (New York: Oxford University Press, 2015).
27. See Bob Jessop, "Liberalism, Neoliberalism, and Urban Governance: A State-Theoretical Perspective," in *Spaces of Neoliberalism*, 105–25; see also Peck and Tickell "Neoliberalizing Space"; Brenner and Theodore, "Cities".
28. See, e.g., Kim Moody, *From Welfare State to Real Estate: Regime Change in New York City, 1975–2007* (New York: The New Press, 2007); see also Miriam Greenberg, *Branding New York: How a City in Crisis Was Sold to the World* (New York: Routledge, 2008).
29. See Loïc Wacquant, *Punishing the Poor: The Neoliberal Government of Social Insecurity* (Durham: Duke University Press, 2009); also see Joe Soss, Richard C. Fording, and Sanford F. Schram, *Disciplining the Poor: Neoliberal Paternalism and the Persistent Power of Race* (Chicago: University of Chicago Press, 2011). Soss, Fording, and Schram significantly point out that racialized neoliberalism is also paternalistic—the state tries to enforce behavior—in a way that complicates the "market logic" of neoliberalism but is also compatible with it.
30. See Francis X. Clines, "City Layoffs Hurt Minorities Most," *New York Times*, February 20, 1976, 69; see also Roger Waldinger, *Still the Promised City? African-Americans and New Immigrants in Postindustrial New York* (Cambridge: Harvard University Press, 1996), 226.

CHAPTER TWO

1. Personal communication from Deputy Commissioner Robert Garafola, October 6, 2010. In contrast, the full-time year-round workforce was, in fiscal year 2010, 41 percent white, 31 percent black, 20 percent Hispanic, and 68 percent male.
2. Weil, *The Fissured Workplace*.
3. We are indebted to Evelyn Seinfeld and the staff at the Research and Negotiations Department at District Council 37 for their assistance in providing archival documents from this period.
4. Sylvia Hutchins, quoted in Bill Schleicher, "Parks Union-Busting: Who's Doing the Work," *Public Employee Press*, October 4, 1991, 4–5; Vito Locasio, quoted in "Union Decries Brutal Slashes in Parks Budget," *Public Employee Press*, December 13, 1991, 10.

NOTES TO CHAPTER TWO

5. Robert Caro, *The Power Broker: Robert Moses and the Fall of New York* (New York: Vintage, 1975), 7.
6. New York City Community Board 4, "Statement of District Needs, FY2006" (New York: Department of City Planning, 2005), http://www.nyc.gov/html/mancb4/html/budget/statement_fy06.shtml.
7. See e.g., Waldinger, *Still the Promised City?*, 233; also Sewell Chan, "City Settles Parks Bias Suit for $21 Million" *New York Times*, February 26, 2008. The principal impetus for offering more civil service exams and complying more closely with the law was the *City of Long Beach v. Civil Service Employees Association* decision in May 2007, in which New York State's highest court ruled that provisional employees were not entitled to tenure under a negotiated union contract and that they should only be hired for nine months in a provisional title. New York City as a whole employed nearly 30,000 provisionals at the time, and the Parks Department, specifically, has used a lot of provisional employees. This includes employees with a civil-service rank and title who are working in another job title as a provisional. We met several Parks employees in this position. See Lisa Colangelo, "City Provisional Worker Rules," *New York Daily News,* June 10, 2008.
8. See "Plaintiffs' memorandum of opposition to defendants' motion for summary judgment," in *Wright, et al*. v. *Stern, et al.*, United States District Court, Southern District, 01-CV-4437, 11–16.
9. See, especially, Peck, *Work-Place*.
10. Chris Tilly and Charles Tilly, *Work Under Capitalism* (Boulder: Westview, 1998), 171.
11. Ibid., 170.
12. The layoffs in Parks, however, targeted the Laborers Local 924. Longtime writer on municipal union politics and editor of the *Chief/Civil-Service Leader* Richard Steier suggests two reasons for this: First, most of the workers in Local 924 were older; this was the local that first took on Robert Moses in 1954 and some of the members were still working thirty-seven years later, with correspondingly higher pay than other union members in the Parks maintenance workforce. Second, the local had gained the enmity of Victor Gotbaum, the former executive director of DC 37, because it took the side of its former leader, Jerry Wurf, in a union leadership battle in the early 1980s. Gotbaum retired in 1986, but his wife, Betsy Gotbaum, was parks commissioner under Dinkins, and Steier suggests that he advised her on where to effect the layoffs. Several interviewees suggested this, as well. See Richard Steier, *Enough Blame to Go Around: The Labor Pains of New York City's Public Employee Unions* (Albany: State University of New York Press, 2014), 240–41.
13. City of New York Office of the Mayor, *Mayor's Management Report, Fiscal Year 1998* (New York: City of New York, 1998).

14. For a more complete account of WEP-related policy development, see John Krinsky, *Free Labor: Workfare and the Contested Language of Neoliberalism* (Chicago: University of Chicago Press, 2007).
15. See, e.g., Maier, *City Unions*.
16. Richard Gilder, "Set the Parks Free," *City Journal* (Winter 1997).
17. Doussard, *Degraded Work*, especially chapters 2, 3.
18. Peck, in *Work-Place*, especially, insists on the actual variation in labor-market segmentation according to place- and time-dependent regulation.

CHAPTER THREE

1. Natalie Benelli, *Nettoyeuse: Comment Tenir le Coup Dans Un Sale Boulot* (Zürich: Éditions Seismo, 2011).
2. Everett C. Hughes, *Men and their Work* (Glencoe, IL: The Free Press), 1958; also see Randy Hodson, *Dignity at Work* (New York: Cambridge University Press, 2001); and see Luis L. M. Aguilar and Andrew Herod, eds., *The Dirty Work of Neoliberalism: Cleaners in the Global Economy* (Maldon, MA: Blackwell, 2006), which makes the case, inter alia, that cleaners' experience of inequality is intensified because the office buildings in which they work exhibit such wealth next to the squalid slums in which they live.
3. Benelli, *Nettoyeuse*, 39.
4. Lisa Foderaro, "Training to Spot Tree Decay is Urged for Park Workers," *New York Times*, May 30, 2012.
5. Mayor's Office of Operations, *Mayor's Management Report 2012* (New York: The City of New York: September 2012), 54, http://www.nyc.gov/html/ops/downloads/pdf/mmr0912/0912_mmr.pdf.
6. Quoted in Foderaro, "Training."
7. Quoted in William Glaberson and Lisa Foderaro, "Neglected, Rotting Trees Turn Deadly," *New York Times*, May 13, 2012.
8. See http://www.treesny.org/about.
9. Foderaro, "Training"; Glaberson and Foderaro, "Neglected, Rotting Trees."
10. See New Yorkers for Parks, *The 2012 Report Card on Large Parks*, report, http://www.ny4p.org/research/report-cards/rc-largeparks12.pdf; also see "New Yorkers for Parks, Councilmembers Lander, Mark-Viverito, and Oddo decry Parks Department budget cuts," press release (June 4, 2012), http://www.ny4p.org/advocacy/advocacypdf/budget060412.pdf.
11. See Krinsky, *Free Labor*, 18–19.
12. Independent Budget Office, "Analysis of the Mayor's preliminary budget for 2013," report (March 2012), 37, http://www.ibo.nyc.ny.us/iboreports/march2012.pdf.
13. Richard Gilder, "Set the Parks Free." It is curious that this "fish story" formed the justification for expanding the nonunion workforce in the parks, since a 1993 fish kill in Westchester County (a close-in suburb of New York City) was the justification for the expansion of workfare in the

NOTES TO CHAPTER FOUR

county. See Krinsky, *Free Labor*, 13. In both cases, dying fish seemed to call forth the necessity of a more pliable workforce.

CHAPTER FOUR

1. Nicolas Jounin, "Loyautés Incertaines: Les Travailleurs du Bâtiment entre Discrimination et Précarité" ["Uncertain Loyalties: Construction Workers between Discrimination and Precarity"], PhD diss. (Paris: University of Paris VII-Urmis, 2000), 432, translation by the authors.
2. Our interviewees further noted that in earlier meetings between Conservancy management and workers, they were assured that there would be no layoffs. This was technically true; although the Conservancy claimed financial hardship, the dismissals were firings, not layoffs, and dismissed workers were not to be called back at the point at which new staff were required and able to be paid.
3. Hodson, *Dignity at Work*, 4.
4. Michael Burawoy, *Manufacturing Consent: Changes in the Labor Process under Monopoly Capitalism* (Chicago: University of Chicago Press, 1979).
5. Stern acknowledged that the recruitment at HBCUs was largely unsuccessful, due in part to the relatively low wage that DPR was offering. He also mentioned that two alumni of the "Class Of" program became deputy mayors under Michael Bloomberg.
6. The language of "field" makes some sense, but when juxtaposed to "the house," it gets troubling for rather obvious historical reasons, and in light of the racially segmented workforce that became more so under Stern. In a deposition connected with the *Wright v. Stern* discrimination lawsuit, Mark Rosenthal, the dissident union leader of the Motor Vehicles Operators Local 983 (the DC 37 unit that represents APSWs), "counted 3 African-Americans and 2 Hispanics among the 61 highest-ranking and middle-management employees at Parks in 1998. . . . He also described how African-Americans and Hispanics [sic] members of the local union were being bypassed by lower level Caucasians as a result of not receiving promotions to PS and PPS positions, stating his belief that 'Stern was running a plantation'" (see "Plaintiffs' Memorandum in Opposition to Defendants' Motion for Summary Judgment," 37–38). Given Stern's language, Rosenthal's is not surprising.
7. Ginger Adams Otis, "Female Parks Department Workers Stripped for Permanent Jobs, More Work at Raunchy Holiday Parties: Sources," *New York Daily News*, May 29, 2013.

CHAPTER FIVE

1. Dave Madden, "Revisiting the End of Public Space: Assembling the Public in an Urban Park," *City and Community* 9, no. 2 (June 2010): 187.

2. Elisabeth S. Clemens and Doug Guthrie, "Introduction: Politics and Partnerships," in *Politics and Partnerships: The Role of Voluntary Associations in America's Political Past and Present* (Chicago: University of Chicago Press, 2010), 2–3.
3. See John R. Logan and Harvey L. Molotch, *Urban Fortunes: The Political Economy of Place* (Berkeley: University of California Press, 1987); John Hull Mollenkopf, *A Phoenix in the Ashes: The Fall and Rise of the Koch Coalition in New York City Politics* (Princeton: Princeton University Press, 1992).
4. Jill Simone Gross, "Business Improvement Districts in New York: The Private Sector in the Public Service or the Public Sector Privatized?" *Urban Research and Practice* (2013): 1–19.
5. George Steinmetz suggested a connection between regulation and repertoires in "Regulation Theory, Post-Marxism, and the New Social Movements," *Comparative Studies in Society and History* 36, no. 1 (January 1994): 196, note 29; see also Jessop, "A Neo-Gramscian Approach"; John Krinsky, "Neoliberal Times: Intersecting Temporalities and the Neoliberalization of Public-Sector Labor Relations in New York City," *Social Science History* 35, no. 3 (Fall 2011): 381–422.
6. Kareem Faheem, "Returning Prospect Park to the People" *New York Times*, April 5, 2010.
7. Lindsay's campaign in 1965 emphasized his resolve to stand up to the city's labor unions. He was, in consequence, greeted on his first day in office in 1966 by a transit strike, led by the voluble leader of the Transport Workers Union, Mike Quill. Facing a shutdown of the city, Lindsay backed down and granted the TWU most of its demands. Lindsay would face several more public-sector strikes during his tenure, including the 1968 teachers' strike, prompted by the firing of several teachers from the Ocean Hill-Brownsville school district, which had recently been decentralized as part of Lindsay's plan to enhance "community control" and ally himself with the demands of African Americans. That the vast majority of the teachers' union at the time was Jewish made the strike a flashpoint of racial tensions and was the clearest expression of a growing rift in the black-Jewish core of the city's liberal coalition that had been in place since the New Deal. The teachers' strike took place just as the new state public labor relations law—called the Taylor Law—came into effect, but the teachers were able to escape its consequences for the most part. DC 37's leader, Victor Gotbaum, had threatened a general strike over the Taylor Law provisions (which contained enforceable antistrike provisions) but never followed through. In 1971, DC 37 led several locals out on strike in protest of the state legislature's refusal to take up pension improvements that had been part of the collective bargaining understanding with the city. Promising the "biggest, fattest, sloppiest strike" in the city's history, Gotbaum led sewage plant workers and drawbridge operators to the picket lines; raw sewage ran into the rivers and key bridges were shut down at

rush hour. The public backlash against the union was severe, and the workers lost. Gotbaum never again led a strike. See Joshua B. Freeman, *In Transit: The Transport Workers' Union in New York City, 1933–1966* (Philadelphia: Temple University Press, 1989); Jerald E. Podair, *The Strike That Changed New York: Blacks, Whites, and the Ocean Hill-Brownsville Crisis* (New Haven: Yale University Press, 2002); Maier, *City Unions*.

8. Emanuel S. Savas, *A Study of Central Park* (New York: Columbia University Center for Government Studies, 1976).

9. Jason Sheftell, "Central Park: The World's Greatest Real Estate Engine," *New York Daily News*, June 3, 2010.

10. "Transcript of the Minutes of the Committee on Finance (Held Jointly with) Committee on Parks, Recreation, Cultural Affairs and International Intergroup Relations (August 25, 2007)" (New York: Legal Ease Reporting Services, Inc.), 27, 73.

11. All the elected officials with districts around the park, as well as about forty different community organizations identified by the elected officials, could come to meetings of the Prospect Park Alliance Community Committee. This committee discussed and prioritized capital and operational plans, as well as ways to help people use the park better. They were involved in day-to-day management decisions in which people on the Alliance board were not involved.

12. Quoted in Annie Karni, "Private Park, Meet Private Partnership." *Crain's New York Business* (April 7, 2013), http://www.crainsnewyork.com/article/20130407/REAL_ESTATE/304079979.

13. Some of this may have to do with the fact that capital improvements were first seen on the west side of the park, closer to Park Slope and other wealthier neighborhoods. The east side of the park, closer to poorer neighborhoods, waited much longer for renovations. See, e.g., Michael Brick, "A Park Pretty for the Rich Yet Run-Down for the Poor: Prospect Park Overseers Direct Money to Make East Side More Like the West," *New York Times*, May 27, 2004.

14. Andrew Jacobs, "Neighborhood Report: Manhattan Up Close; Street Fight: Unions vs. B.I.D.'s," *New York Times*, March 24, 1996.

15. Mr. Barth, contacted more than five years after this interview, and no longer at Bryant Park, indicated that he would be less radical in his rejection of volunteering and took a more pragmatic and contextual approach: "I would adjust my comments in the following way: I believe that every park is different and that volunteering, or other management issues, will have different answers in different places, and for good reason. I do believe that it is necessary to clearly identify tasks that are onerous for staff to perform, either because of scale or irregularity or sheer annoyance and difficulty. A group of screened, committed, and trained volunteers is best. Volunteering for the organization should be a privilege and bring great satisfaction to the person volunteering their time and efforts as they can

then be sure of the value of their work and of the fact that their involvement is special." Personal communication, January 28, 2016.
16. E.g., Sidney Tarrow, *Power in Movement* (New York: Cambridge University Press, 1994); Charles Tilly, *Popular Contention in Great Britain, 1758–1834* (Cambridge: Harvard University Press, 1995).
17. New Yorkers for Parks, *Making the Most of Our Parks* (New York: NY4P, 2007), 13.
18. Transcript of the Minutes of Committee on Parks and Recreation, New York City Council, September 17, 2013, 35.
19. Committee on Parks and Recreation, transcript, 46.
20. See, e.g., Theresa Agovino, "Hudson River Park gets financial lifeline," *Crain's New York Business*, November 14, 2013.
21. Committee on Parks and Recreation, transcript, 32–33.
22. Friends of Dag Hammarskjold Plaza, "Concession Reform: Why It Matters," http://www.hammarskjoldplaza.org/news_article2.html.

CHAPTER SIX

1. Committee on Parks and Recreation, transcript, 13.
2. Ibid., 210–11.
3. Ibid., 202.
4. Gramsci, *Selections from the Prison Notebooks*, 244.
5. There is a key difference between treating neoliberalism as an "ideal" and an "ideal type." An ideal type is a historically informed abstraction, generated by sociologists for the purposes of comparison. It assembles what appear to be critical properties held in common by many examples of a phenomenon.
6. A "dirty water dog" is a hot dog sold from a pushcart. It gets its name from the fact that the hot dogs are heated and kept in a tub of hot water.
7. Interview with Henry Stern, April 7, 2011.
8. Deborah A. Stone, "Causal Stories and Policy Agendas," *Political Science Quarterly* 104, no. 2 (Summer, 1989): 289.
9. Partnerships for Parks, website. Accessed January 13, 2014.
10. Committee on Parks and Recreation, transcript, 155.
11. Ibid., 50.
12. E.g., R. A. W. Rhodes, "The Hollowing Out of the State: The Changing Nature of the Public Service in Britain," *Political Quarterly* 65, no. 2 (April 1994): 138–51.
13. For example, emeritus directors of NY4P include Ira Millstein, a board member of Central Park Conservancy and its counsel, and Richard Gilder. Iphigene Sulzberger, the heiress of the *New York Times*, was an early leader of the Parks Council beginning in the mid-1930s and an early supporter of Betsy Rogers's efforts at the Central Park Conservancy in the late 1970s.

NOTES TO CHAPTER SIX

14. Until 2013, nearly all the capital funding for parks came through "member items"—discretionary funds allocated to city council members. The problem with this is that in poorer districts, there are many competing needs, and park improvement often does not rise to the top of the list of the most pressing. Further, this means that park improvement projects take a long time, as smaller amounts of money than are needed are set aside to accumulate over time.
15. Committee on Parks and Recreation, transcript, 127.
16. Ibid., 125.
17. Ibid., 137.
18. Ibid., 134–35.
19. Ibid., 140.
20. Ibid., 205–6.
21. Adrian Benepe, comments at "Talking transition: an open conversation about NYC's future," video, http://new.livestream.com/talkingtransition/NYC.
22. Cathryn Swan, "Privatization of the Commons in Bloomberg's New York, Part II—Who Has the Control?" *Huffington Post*, April 26, 2013, http://www.huffingtonpost.com/cathryn-swan/new-york-parks-privatization_b_3112139.html.
23. See Matthieu Hély, *Les métamorphoses du monde associatif* (Paris: Presses Universitaires de France, 2009).
24. Who couldn't use a third hand, from time to time?
25. See Hély, *Les métamorphoses du monde associatif.*
26. For a good over view of NPM, see Daniel Cohn, "Creating Crises, Avoiding Blame: The Politics of Public Service Reform and the New Public Management in Great Britain and the United States," *Administration and Society* 29, no. 5 (1997): 584–616.
27. Muehlebach, *The Moral Neoliberal*, 6.

CHAPTER SEVEN

1. Steven Vallas and Christopher Prener, "Dualism, Job Polarization, and the Social Construction of Precarious Work," *Work and Occupations* 39 (November 2012): 331–53.
2. See Emmanuel Renault, "L'invisibilisation du Travail et ses Echos Philosophiques (The Invisibilization of Work and its Philosophical Echoes)." Lecture in the colloquium Work or the Experience of Necessity, organized by the University of Nantes (October 9–10, 2009), http://www.univ-nantes.fr/1255505116582/0/fiche_document/.
3. Daniels, *Invisible Careers.*
4. Indeed, the development of employment law in the United States exempted domestic workers (as well as agricultural workers and, for different reasons, public-sector workers) so that a sector dominated by African

Americans at the time would be deprived of basic labor rights. See, e.g., Ira Katznelson, *When Affirmative Action Was White: An Untold History of Racial Inequality in Twentieth-Century America* (New York: W. W. Norton, 2005).
5. Christelle Avril, *Les Aides à Domicile: Un Autre Monde Populaire* (Paris: La Dispute, 2014); see also Evelyn Nakano Glenn, *Forced to Care: Coercion and Caregiving in America* (Cambridge: Harvard University Press, 2010).
6. Sylvie Morel, *Les Logiques de la Réciprocité: Les Transformations de la Relation d'Assistance aux États-Unis et en France* (Paris: Presses Universitaires de France, 2000), 20.
7. Quoted in Esther B. Fine, "Workfare Not Just a Program to Save Money, Adviser Says," *New York Times*, January 13, 1995.
8. Rudolph W. Giuliani, "Address to the Forum Club: Restoring the Centrality of Work to New York City Life," *Archives of Rudolph W. Giuliani* (March 25, 1998), http://www.nyc.gov/html/records/rwg/html/98a/forumclb.html.
9. New York State Department of Criminal Justice Services, "Alternatives to Incarceration (ATI) Programs," website, http://www.criminaljustice.ny.gov/opca/ati_description.htm.
10. "Many Hands Make Prospect Park Shine," *Daily Plant*, March 6, 2003.
11. Volunteering as a requirement for graduation has not yet become citywide policy, but it has been proposed; cleaning parks is one often-cited example of possible service opportunities. See Kathleen Lucadamo, "Councilman Proposes Community Service Be Required for High School Graduation," *New York Daily News*, January 19, 2009.
12. Charles Tilly, *Durable Inequality* (Berkeley: University of California Press, 1998). Tilly suggests that the layering of categories of identity whose boundaries mark unequal access to socially valued resources results in "categorical inequality," which, in turn, becomes durable as the categories reinforce each other.
13. The negotiation of the position also occurred in the context of the fraudulent contract vote held for the DC 37 master contract for 1995–2000. This, too, is frequently forgotten.
14. See Pierre Bourdieu, *Outline of a Theory of Practice*, trans. Richard Nice (New York: Cambridge University Press, 1977), 106.
15. And this is no less true for us; we do not pretend that contradictory consciousness is just what affects our poor, benighted research subjects! As researchers and teachers in workplaces that are in many respects not so different from parks, where adjunct lecturers and graduate students without job security and with extremely low pay do work in jobs that might once have otherwise been available to them as a career, we may grumble, but we soldier on in the belief that what we are doing has its own reward and justifications well beyond the vicissitudes of the workplace.

## CHAPTER EIGHT

1. Matthew Gandy, *Concrete and Clay: Reworking Nature in New York City* (Cambridge: MIT Press, 2002), 84.
2. Appleseed, Inc., *Valuing Central Park's Contribution to New York City's Economy*, report (New York: Appleseed, Inc.), 42, http://www.appleseedinc.com/wp-content/uploads/2013/12/Valuing-Central-Parks-Contributions-to-New-York-Citys-Economy.pdf.
3. Appleseed, Inc., *Valuing Central Park*, 9.
4. See http://www.bryantpark.org/about-us/mission.html.
5. New Yorkers for Parks, *How Smart Parks Investment Pays Its Way*, report (New York: New Yorkers for Parks, 2002), 3, http://www.ny4p.org/research/other-reports/or-smartinvestment.pdf.
6. Alison Gregor, "Bryant Park office rents outperform rest of Midtown," *New York Times*, October 2, 2012.
7. Alison Gregor, "As Park Runs Above, Deals Stir Below," *New York Times*, August 10, 2010.
8. Katherine Clarke, "Shvo's High Line Deal a 'Make-or-Break' Second Chance," *Real Deal*, May 28, 2013, http://therealdeal.com/blog/2013/05/28/shvos-high-line-deal-a-make-or-break-second-chance/.
9. The Regional Plan Association, *The Impact of Hudson River Park on Property Values*, report (New York: RPA, October 11, 2008), http://www.rpa.org/article/impact-of-hudson-river-park-on-property-values.
10. New Yorkers for Parks, *How Smart Park Investment Pays its Way*.
11. New Yorkers for Parks, *Supporting our Parks: A Guide to Alternative Revenue Strategies*, report (New York: New Yorkers for Parks, 2010), 1–2.
12. John Krinsky, "The New Tammany Hall? Welfare, Public Sector Unions, Corruption, and Neoliberal Policy Regimes," *Social Research* 80, no. 4 (Winter 2013): 1087–118.
13. David Harvey notes that rentier capital has been ascendant since the 1980s, feeding into the imposition of neoliberal policies, as the rate of profit from manufacturing and services has fallen and investment in "productive" sectors of core economies has become comparably less secure. For a brief example of this thinking, see David Harvey, "The Right to the City," *New Left Review* 53 (September-October 2008), http://newleftreview.org/II/53/david-harvey-the-right-to-the-city; see also his *Rebel Cities: From the Right to the City to the Urban Revolution* (New York: Verso, 2012), 22–25.
14. Appleseed, Inc. *Valuing Central Park's Contribution*, 46.
15. See David Harvey, *A Brief History of Neoliberalism* (New York: Oxford, 2005), 159; also Karl Marx, *Capital, Volume 1: A Critique of Political Economy*, trans. Ben Fowkes (New York: Penguin Classics, 1992), chapter 26.
16. Regional Plan Association, *On the Verge: Caring for New York's Emerging Waterfront Parks and Spaces*, report (Spring 2007), http://www.rpa.org/pdf/waterfrontparksreport.pdf, 10. See also New Yorkers for Parks, *Support-*

*ing our Parks: A Guide to Alternative Revenue Strategies*, report (June 2010), http://www.ny4p.org/research/other-reports/or-altrevenue10.pdf, 25.
17. A visit in June 2014 suggested that there were fewer pot dealers than there had been before. There is a new park house on the south side of the park that doubles as a police substation.
18. See Bob Master, "The Zeitgeist Tracked Down Bill de Blasio," *Nation*, December 26, 2013.
19. New Yorkers for Parks, *Report Card on Large Parks, 2012* (New York: NY4P, 2013), 1.
20. It is noteworthy that at least until recently, social policy arguments based on the moral hazard tended to be used as a bludgeon against the poor; even early analyses of the financial meltdown of 2007–2008 often cited irresponsible homeowners taking on irresponsible levels of mortgage debt, rather than emphasizing the irresponsibility of banks that issued the debt and marketed it as if it were good, knowing that they were likely to be bailed out if anything went awry.
21. Jessop, "Liberalism, Neoliberalism, and Urban Governance."
22. See Nancy Fraser, "Feminism, Capitalism, and the Cunning of History," in *Fortunes of Feminism: From State-Managed Capitalism to Neoliberal Crisis* (New York: Verso, 2014), 209–27.
23. Pierre Bourdieu, "The Essence of Neoliberalism," *Le Monde Diplomatique* (December 1998), http://mondediplo.com/1998/12/08bourdieu.
24. See, e.g., Natalie Benelli, "Sweeping the Streets of the Neoliberal City: Racial and Class Divisions Among New York City's Sanitation Workers," *Journal of Workplace Rights* 16, no. 3–4 (2011–2012): 453–74; see also Michael Fabricant and Michelle Fine, *Charter Schools and the Corporate Takeover of Public Education: What's at Stake?* (New York: Teachers College Press, 2012). For a clear expression of anti-unionism in the public sector, see DiSalvo, *Government Against Itself.*
25. It is both by working—"by multiplying one's talents"—and by serving the community through work that we can repay the debt we owe to the Creator, according to the parable of the talents (Matthew 25:14–30), a key text of the Protestant ethic. See Simonet, *Le Travail Bénévole*, 63–64; also see Anne Bory, "De la Générosité en Entreprise: Mécénat et Bénévolat dans les Grandes Entreprises en France et aux Etats-Unis" (PhD diss., University of Paris I–Panthéon-Sorbonne, 2008).
26. Philip Mirowski, *Never Let a Good Crisis Go To Waste: How Neoliberalism Survived the Financial Meltdown* (New York: Verso, 2014).
27. Serge Kovalevski, "With High Line's Success, Dual Rewards for Executive," *New York Times*, August 25, 2009. By 2011, Hammond's compensation as executive director and CEO had risen to $317,600 according to the organization's Form 990.
28. Quoted in Dan Rosenblum, "Is the Revenue-Generating Park a Good Thing? Commissioner Benepe Says, 'It Depends on Who's in Charge,'"

*Capital New York*, August 11, 2011, http://www.capitalnewyork.com/article/politics/2011/08/2945592/revenue-generating-park-good-thing-commissioner-benepe-says-it-depe.

29. See, e.g., Doussard, *Degraded Work*.

# References

Agovino, Theresa. "Hudson River Park gets financial lifeline." *Crain's New York Business.* November 14, 2013.

Aguilar, Luis L. M., and Andrew Herod, eds. *The Dirty Work of Neoliberalism: Cleaners in the Global Economy.* Malden, MA: Blackwell, 2006.

Appleseed, Inc. *Valuing Central Park's Contribution to New York City's Economy.* Report. New York: Appleseed, Inc., 2013. http://www.appleseedinc.com/wp-content/uploads/2013/12/Valuing-Central-Parks-Contributions-to-New-York-Citys-Economy.pdf.

Avril, Christelle. *Les Aides à Domicile: Un Autre Monde Populaire.* Paris: La Dispute, 2014.

Bellush, Jewell, and Bernard Bellush. *Union Power and New York City: Victor Gotbaum and District Council 37.* New York: Prager, 1984.

Benelli, Natalie. *Nettoyeuse: Comment Tenir le Coup Dans Un Sale Boulot.* Zürich: Éditions Seismo, 2011.

Benelli, Natalie. "Sweeping the Streets of the Neoliberal City: Racial and Class Divisions Among New York City's Sanitation Workers." *Journal of Workplace Rights* 16, no. 3–4 (2011–2012): 453–74

Bondi, Liz. "Gender, Class, and Urban Space: Public and Private Space in Contemporary Urban Landscapes." *Urban Geography* 19, no. 2 (1998): 160–85.

Börtzel, Tania A. "Organizing Babylon: On the Different Conceptions of Policy Networks." *Public Administration* 76, no. 2 (Summer 1998): 253–73.

Bory, Anne. "De la Générosité en Entreprise: Mécénat et Bénévolat dans les Grandes Entreprises en France et aux Etats-Unis." PhD diss., University of Paris I Panthéon-Sorbonne, 2008.

## REFERENCES

Bourdieu, Pierre. *Outline of a Theory of Practice*. Translated by Richard Nice. New York: Cambridge University Press, 1977.

Brenner, Neil, and Nik Theodore. "Cities and the Geographies of 'Actually Existing Neoliberalism.'" In *Spaces of Neoliberalism: Urban Restructuring in North America and Western Europe*, edited by Neil Brenner and Nik Theodore, 2–32. Malden, MA: Blackwell, 2002.

Brick, Michael. "A Park Pretty for the Rich yet Run-Down for the Poor; Prospect Park Overseers Direct Money to Make East Side More Like the West." *New York Times*, May 27, 2004.

Burawoy, Michael. *Manufacturing Consent: Changes in the Labor Process under Monopoly Capitalism*. Chicago: University of Chicago Press, 1979.

Capulong, Eduardo R. C. "Which Side Are You On? Unionization in Social-Service Nonprofits." *New York City Law Review* 9 (2005–2006): 373–404.

Caro, Robert. *The Power Broker: Robert Moses and the Fall of New York*. New York: Vintage, 1975.

Chan, Sewell. "City Settles Parks Bias Suit for $21 Million." *New York Times*, February 26, 2008.

City of New York Office of the Mayor. *Mayor's Management Report, Fiscal Year 1998*. New York: City of New York, 1998.

Clarke, Katherine. "Shvo's High Line Deal a 'Make-or-Break' Second Chance." *Real Deal*, May 28, 2013. http://therealdeal.com/blog/2013/05/28/shvos-high-line-deal-a-make-or-break-second-chance/.

Clemens, Elisabeth S., and Doug Guthrie. "Introduction: Politics and Partnerships." In *Politics and Partnerships: The Role of Voluntary Associations in America's Political Past and Present*. Chicago: University of Chicago Press, 2010.

Clines, Francis X. "City Layoffs Hurt Minorities Most." *New York Times*, February 20, 1976, 69.

Cohen, Rick. "Unions and the Nonprofit Workforce: A Few Considerations." *Nonprofit Quarterly*, August 8, 2013. http://nonprofitquarterly.org/2013/08/08/unions-and-the-nonprofit-workforce-a-few-considerations/.

Cohn, Daniel. "Creating Crises, Avoiding Blame: The Politics of Public Service Reform and the New Public Management in Great Britain and the United States." *Administration and Society* 29, no. 5 (1997): 584–616.

Colangelo, Lisa. "City Provisional Worker Rules." *New York Daily News*, June 10, 2008.

Conley, Hazel "Modernisation or Casualisation? Numerical Flexibility in Public Services." *Capital and Class* 30, no. 2 (Summer 2006): 31–57.

Cooke, Oliver. *Rethinking Municipal Privatization*. New York: Routledge, 2008.

Daniels, Arlene Kaplan. *Invisible Careers: Women Civic Leaders from the Volunteer World*. Chicago: University of Chicago Press, 1988.

DiSalvo, Daniel. *Government against Itself: Public Union Power and Its Consequences*. New York: Oxford University Press, 2015.

DiSalvo, Daniel, and Fred Siegel. "The New Tammany Hall." *Weekly Standard*, October 12, 2009.

Doussard, Marc. *Degraded Work: The Struggle at the Bottom of the Labor Market*. Minneapolis: University of Minnesota Press, 2013.

Eliasoph, Nina. *The Politics of Volunteering*. Malden, MA: Polity Press, 2013.

Fabricant, Michael, and Michelle Fine. *Charter Schools and the Corporate Takeover of Public Education: What's at Stake?* New York: Teachers College Press, 2012.

Falquet, Jules. "La Règle du Jeu: Repenser la Co-Formation des Rapports Sociaux de Sexe, de Classe et de 'Race' dans la Mondialisation Néolibérale." In *Sexe, Race, Classe: Pour une Épistemologie de la Domination*, edited by Elsa Dorlin, 71–90. Paris: Presses Universitaires de France, 2009.

Finder, Alan, "Decline of Tenure Track Raises Concerns." *New York Times*, November 20, 2007.

Fine, Esther B. "Workfare Not Just a Program to Save Money, Adviser Says." *New York Times*, January 13, 1995.

Foderaro, Lisa. "Training to Spot Tree Decay is Urged for Park Workers." *New York Times*, May 30, 2012.

Fraser, Nancy. "Feminism, Capitalism, and the Cunning of History." In *Fortunes of Feminism: From State-Managed Capitalism to Neoliberal Crisis*, 209–27. New York: Verso.

Freeman, Joshua B. *In Transit: The Transport Workers' Union in New York City, 1933–1966*. Philadelphia: Temple University Press, 1989.

———. *Working-Class New York: Life and Labor Since World War II*. New York: The New Press, 2002.

Friends of Dag Hammarskjold Plaza. "Concession Reform: Why It Matters." http://www.hammarskjoldplaza.org/news_article2.html.

Gandy, Matthew. *Concrete and Clay: Reworking Nature in New York City*. Cambridge: MIT Press, 2002.

Gilder, Richard. "Set the Parks Free." *City Journal*, Winter 1997.

Gilmore, Ruth Wilson. "In the Shadow of the Shadow State." In *The Revolution Will Not Be Funded: Beyond the Non-Profit Industrial Complex*, edited by INCITE Women of Color against Violence, 40–52. Boston: South End Press, 2009.

Giuliani, Rudolph W. "Address to the Forum Club: Restoring the Centrality of Work to New York City Life." Archives of Rudolph W. Giuliani, March 25, 1998. http://www.nyc.gov/html/records/rwg/html/98a/forumclb.html.

Glaberson, William and Lisa Foderaro. "Neglected, Rotting Trees Turn Deadly." *New York Times*, May 13, 2012.

Glenn, Evelyn Nakano. *Forced to Care: Coercion and Caregiving in America*. Cambridge: Harvard University Press, 2010.

Gordon, David M., Richard Edwards, and Michael Reich. *Segmented Work, Divided Workers: The Historical Transformation of Labor in the United States*. New York: Cambridge University Press, 1982.

REFERENCES

Gramsci, Antonio. *Selections from the Prison Notebooks*. Translated and edited by Quintin Hoare and Geoffrey Nowell Smith. New York: International Publishers, 1971.

Greenberg, Miriam. *Branding New York: How a City in Crisis Was Sold to the World*. New York: Routledge, 2008.

Gregor, Alison. "As Park Runs Above, Deals Stir Below." *New York Times*, August 10, 2010.

———. "Bryant Park Office Rents Outperform Rest of Midtown." *New York Times*, October 2, 2012.

Gross, Jill Simone. "Business Improvement Districts in New York: The Private Sector in the Public Service or the Public Sector Privatized?" *Urban Research and Practice* (2013): 1–19.

Harvey, David. *A Brief History of Neoliberalism*. New York: Oxford, 2005.

———. *Rebel Cities: From the Right to the City to the Urban Revolution*. New York: Verso.

———. "The Right to the City." *New Left Review* 53 (September-October 2008). http://newleftreview.org/II/53/david-harvey-the-right-to-the-city.

Herd, Pamela, and Madonna Harrington Meyer. "Care Work: Invisible Civic Engagement." *Gender and Society* 16, no. 5 (October 2002): 665–88

Hély, Matthieu. *Les métamorphoses du monde associatif*. Paris: Presses Universitaires de France, 2009.

Hodson, Randy. *Dignity at Work*. New York: Cambridge University Press, 2001.

Hughes, Everett C. *Men and their Work*. Glencoe, IL: The Free Press, 1958.

Independent Budget Office. "Analysis of the Mayor's preliminary budget for 2013." Report. March 2012, 37. http://www.ibo.nyc.ny.us/iboreports/march2012.pdf.

Jacobs, Andrew. "Neighborhood Report: Manhattan Up Close; Street Fight: Unions vs. B.I.D.'s" *New York Times*, March 24, 1996.

Jessop, Bob. "Liberalism, Neoliberalism, and Urban Governance: A State-Theoretical Perspective." In *Spaces of Neoliberalism: Urban Restructuring in North America and Western Europe*, edited by Neil Brenner and Nik Theodore, 105–25. Malden, MA: Blackwell, 2002.

Jessop, Bob. "A Neo-Gramscian Approach to the Regulation of Urban Regimes: Accumulation Strategies, Hegemonic Projects, and Governance." In *Reconstructing Urban Regime Theory: Regulating Urban Politics in a Global Economy*, edited by Mickey Lauria, 51–74. Thousand Oaks, CA: Sage Publications, 1997.

Jounin, Nicolas 2006. "Loyautés Incertaines: Les Travailleurs du Bâtiment entre Discrimination et Précarité" ["Uncertain Loyalties: Construction Workers between Discrimination and Precarity"]. PhD diss., University of Paris VII-Urmis, 2000.

Kalleberg, Arne. *Good Jobs, Bad Jobs: The Rise of Polarized and Precarious Employment Systems in the United States, 1970s-2000s*. New York: Russell Sage Foundation, 2011.

Kareem, Fahim. "Returning Prospect Park to the People." *New York Times*, April 5, 2010.

Karni, Annie. "Private Park, Meet Private Partnership." *Crain's New York Business*, April 7, 2013. http://www.crainsnewyork.com/article/20130407/REAL_ESTATE/304079979.

Katz, Cindi. "Vagabond Capitalism and the Necessity of Social Reproduction." *Antipode* 33, no. 4 (2001): 708–28.

Katznelson, Ira. *When Affirmative Action Was White: An Untold History of Racial Inequality in Twentieth-Century America*. New York: W. W. Norton, 2005.

Kergoat, Danièle. "Division Sexuelle du Travail et Rapports Sociaux de Sexe." In *Dictionnaire Critique du Féminisme*, 2nd enlarged edition, edited by Helena Hirata, Françoise Laborie, Hélène Le Doaré, and Danièle Senotier, 35–44. Paris: Presses Universitaires de France, 2004.

Kettl, Donald. *The Transformation of Governance: Public Administration for the Twenty-First Century*. Baltimore: Johns Hopkins University Press, 2002.

Kovalevski, Serge. "With High Line's Success, Dual Rewards for Executive." *New York Times* August 25, 2009.

Krinsky, John. *Free Labor: Workfare and the Contested Language of Neoliberalism*. Chicago: University of Chicago Press, 2007.

———. "Neoliberal Times: Intersecting Temporalities and the Neoliberalization of Public-Sector Labor Relations in New York City." *Social Science History* 35, no. 3 (Fall 2011): 381–422.

———. "The New Tammany Hall? Welfare, Public Sector Unions, Corruption, and Neoliberal Policy Regimes." *Social Research* 80, no. 4 (Winter 2013): 1087–118.

Lin, Robert Y. *Case Study Research: Design and Methods*. Thousand Oaks, CA: Sage Publications, 2009.

Logan, John R., and Harvey L. Molotch. 1987. *Urban Fortunes: The Political Economy of Place*. Berkeley: University of California Press.

Lucadamo, Kathleen. "Councilman Proposes Community Service Be Required for High School Graduation." *New York Daily News*, January 19, 2009.

Madden, Dave. "Revisiting the End of Public Space: Assembling the Public in an Urban Park." *City and Community* 9, no. 2 (June 2010): 187.

Maier, Mark H. *City Unions: Managing Discontent in New York City*. New Brunswick: Rutgers University Press, 1987.

"Many Hands Make Prospect Park Shine." *Daily Plant*, March 6, 2003.

Marx, Karl. *Capital, Volume 1: A Critique of Political Economy*, translated by Ben Fowkes. New York: Penguin Classics, 1992.

Master, Bob. "The Zeitgeist Tracked Down Bill de Blasio." *Nation*, December 26, 2013.

Mayor's Office of Operations. *Mayor's Management Report 2012*. New York: City of New York: September 2012. http://www.nyc.gov/html/ops/downloads/pdf/mmr0912/0912_mmr.pdf.

## REFERENCES

Mirowski, Philip. *Never Let a Good Crisis Go To Waste: How Neoliberalism Survived the Financial Meltdown.* New York: Verso, 2014.

Mollenkopf, John Hull. *A Phoenix in the Ashes: The Fall and Rise of the Koch Coalition in New York City Politics.* Princeton: Princeton University Press, 1992.

Moody, Kim. *From Welfare State to Real Estate: Regime Change in New York City, 1975–2007.* New York: The New Press, 2007.

Morel, Sylvie. *Les Logiques de la Réciprocité: Les Transformations de la Relation d'Assistance aux États-Unis et en France.* Paris: Presses Universitaires de France, 2000.

"Most Presidents Favor No Tenure for Majority of Faculty." *Chronicle of Higher Education,* May 15, 2011.

Muehlebach, Andrea. *The Moral Neoliberal: Welfare and Citizenship in Italy.* Chicago: University of Chicago Press, 2013.

New York City Community Board 4. "Statement of District Needs, FY2006." New York: Department of City Planning, 2005. http://www.nyc.gov/html/mancb4/html/budget/statement_fy06.shtml.

New York City Council. "Transcript of the Minutes of the Committee on Finance Held Jointly with Committee on Parks, Recreation, Cultural Affairs and International Intergroup Relations." August 25, 2007. New York: Legal Ease Reporting Services, Inc.

———. "Transcript of the Minutes of the Committee on Parks and Recreation." September 17, 2013. Ardsley, NY: World Wide Dictation.

New Yorkers for Parks. *How Smart Parks Investment Pays Its Way.* Report. New York: New Yorkers for Parks, 2002. http://www.ny4p.org/research/other-reports/or-smartinvestment.pdf.

———. *Making the Most of Our Parks.* New York: New Yorkers for Parks, 2007.

———. "New Yorkers for Parks, Councilmembers Lander, Mark-Viverito, and Oddo Decry Parks Department Budget Cuts." Press release, June 4, 2012. http://www.ny4p.org/advocacy/advocacypdf/budget060412.pdf.

———. *Supporting Our Parks: A Guide to Alternative Revenue Strategies.* Report. New York: New Yorkers for Parks, June 2010. http://www.ny4p.org/research/other-reports/or-altrevenue10.pdf.

———. *The 2012 Report Card on Large Parks.* Report. New York: New Yorkers for Parks, 2012. ttp://www.ny4p.org/research/report-cards/rc-largeparks12.pdf.

New York State Department of Criminal Justice Services, "Alternatives to Incarceration ATI Programs." http://www.criminaljustice.ny.gov/opca/ati_description.htm.

Otis, Ginger Adams. "Female Parks Department Workers Stripped for Permanent Jobs, More Work at Raunchy Holiday Parties: Sources." *New York Daily News,* May 29, 2013.

Peck, Jamie. *Workfare States.* New York: Guilford, 2001.

Peck, Jamie. *Work-Place: The Social Regulation of Labor Markets.* New York: Guilford, 1996.

Peck, Jamie, and Adam Tickell. "Neoliberalizing Space." In *Spaces of Neoliberalism: Urban Restructuring in North America and Western Europe*, edited by Neil Brenner and Nik Theodore, 33–57. Malden, MA: Blackwell, 2002.

Perlin, Ross. *Intern Nation: How to Earn Nothing and Learn Little in the Brave New Economy*. New York: Verso, 2012.

Peters, Jeanne B., and Jan Masaoka. "A House Divided: How Nonprofits Experience Union Drives." *Nonprofit Leadership and Management* 10, no. 3 (Spring 2000): 305–17.

Podair, Jerald E. *The Strike That Changed New York: Blacks, Whites, and the Ocean Hill-Brownsville Crisis*. New Haven: Yale University Press, 2002.

Regional Plan Association. *The Impact of Hudson River Park on Property Values*. Report, October 17, 2008. http://www.rpa.org/article/impact-of-hudson-river-park-on-property-values.

———. *On the Verge: Caring for New York's Emerging Waterfront Parks and Spaces*. Report, Spring 2007. http://www.rpa.org/pdf/waterfrontparksreport.pdf.

Renault, Emmanuel. "L'invisibilisation du Travail et ses Echos Philosophiques (The Invisibilization of Work and its Philosophical Echoes)." Lecture in the colloquium Work or the Experience of Necessity, organized by the University of Nantes, October 9–10, 2009. http://www.univ-nantes.fr/ 1255505116582/0/fiche_document/.

Rhodes, R. A. W. "The Hollowing Out of the State: The Changing Nature of the Public Service in Britain." *The Political Quarterly* 65, no. 2 (April 1994): 138–51.

Rosenblum, Dan. "Is the Revenue-Generating Park a Good Thing? Commissioner Benepe Says, 'It Depends on Who's in Charge.'" *Capital New York*, August 11, 2011. http://www.capitalnewyork.com/article/politics/2011/08/2945592/revenue-generating-park-good-thing-commissioner-benepe-says-it-depe.

Rosenzweig, Roy, and Elizabeth Blackmar. *The Park and the People: A History of Central Park*. Ithaca: Cornell University Press, 1992.

Savas, Emanuel S. *A Study of Central Park*. New York: Columbia University Center for Government Studies, 1976.

Schleicher, Bill. "Parks Union-Busting: Who's Doing the Work?" *Public Employee Press*, October 4, 1991, 4–5.

Scholz, Trebor, ed. *Digital Labor: The Internet as Playground and Factory*. New York: Routledge, 2013.

Sheftell, Jason. "Central Park: The World's Greatest Real Estate Engine." *New York Daily News*, June 3, 2010.

Simonet, Maud. *Le Travail Bénévole: Engagement Citoyen ou Travail Gratuit?* Paris: La Dispute, 2010.

Sites, William. *Remaking New York: Primitive Globalization and the Politics of Urban Community*. Minneapolis: University of Minnesota Press, 2004.

Slater, Joseph E. *Public Workers: Government Employee Unions, the Law, and the State, 1900–1962*. Ithaca: Cornell University Press, 2004.

REFERENCES

Smith, Stephen Rathgeb, and Michael Lipsky. *Nonprofits for Hire: The Welfare State in the Age of Contracting*. Cambridge: Harvard University Press, 1993.

Soss, Joe, Richard C. Fording, and Sanford F. Schram. *Disciplining the Poor: Neoliberal Paternalism and the Persistent Power of Race*. Chicago: University of Chicago Press, 2011.

Standing, Guy. *A Precariat Charter: From Denizens to Citizens*. London: Bloomsbury, 2014.

Star, Susan Leigh, and Anselm Strauss. "Layers of Silence, Arenas of Voice: The Ecology of Visible and Invisible Work." *Computer Supported Cooperative Work* 8, no. 1 (March 1999): 9–30.

Steier, Richard. *Enough Blame to Go Around: The Labor Pains of New York City's Public Employee Unions*. Albany: State University of New York Press, 2014.

Steinmetz, George "Regulation Theory, Post-Marxism, and the New Social Movements." *Comparative Studies in Society and History* 36, no. 1 (January 1994): 196.

Stone, Clarence N. "Looking Back to Look Forward: Reflections on Urban Regime Analysis." *Urban Affairs Review* 40, no. 3 (January 2005): 309–41.

Stone, Deborah A. "Causal Stories and Policy Agendas." *Political Science Quarterly* 104, no. 2 (Summer 1989): 281–300.

Swan, Cathryn. "Privatization of the Commons in Bloomberg's New York, Part II—Who Has the Control?" Huffington Post, April 26, 2013. http://www.huffingtonpost.com/cathryn-swan/new-york-parks-privatization_b_3112139.html.

Tarrow, Sidney. *Power in Movement*. New York: Cambridge University Press, 1994.

Tilly, Charles. *Durable Inequality*. Berkeley: University of California Press, 1998.

———. *Popular Contention in Great Britain, 1758–1834*. Cambridge: Harvard University Press, 1995.

Tilly, Chris, and Charles Tilly. *Work under Capitalism*. Boulder: Westview, 1998.

"Union Decries Brutal Slashes in Parks Budget." *Public Employee Press*, December 13, 1991, 10.

Vallas, Steven, and Christopher Prener. "Dualism, Job Polarization, and the Social Construction of Precarious Work." *Work and Occupations* 39 (November 2012): 331–53.

Vinel, Jean-Christian. *The Employee: A Political History*. Philadelphia: University of Pennsylvania Press, 2013.

Vogel, Lise. *Marxism and the Oppression of Women*. 2nd ed. New York: Haymarket, 2014.

Wacquant, Loïc. *Punishing the Poor: The Neoliberal Government of Social Insecurity*. Durham: Duke University Press, 2009.

Waldinger, Roger. *Still the Promised City? African-Americans and New Immigrants in Postindustrial New York*. Cambridge: Harvard University Press, 1996.

Weil, David. *The Fissured Workplace: Why Work Became So Bad for So Many and What Can Be Done to Improve It*. Cambridge: Harvard University Press, 2014.

White, Veronica. Testimony to New York City Council Parks Committee, September 17, 2013. Video at 00:26.25. http://legistar.council.nyc.gov/MeetingDetail.aspx?ID=262116&GUID=CE79FEAA-2C34-468D-A39F-ABD9960C5817&Search=.

Wolch, Jennifer R. *The Shadow State: Government and Voluntary Sector in Transition*. New York: The Foundation Center, 1990.

Wolch, Jennifer, and Michael Dear, eds. *The Power of Geography: How Territory Shapes Social Life*. New York: Routledge, 1989.

# Index

Page numbers in italics indicate figures and tables.

accumulation of capital, 24, 178, 224–28, 231; by dispossession, 230; and legitimation, 170, 191, 219–20, 242–44
Administrator. *See* Parks Administrator
alternative sentencing. *See* community service sentencees
Arsenal, the, 16, 131, 138, 143, 147, 263n15
Associate Park Service Worker, 27, 30, 61

Banks, Steven (HRA commissioner), 252
bathrooms, 15, 27, 51, 62, 68–69, 77–80, 82, 85, 87, 98, 105–6, 122–23, 145
Beame, Abraham (mayor, 1974–77), 236
Benepe, Adrian (parks commissioner, 2002–12), 43, 89, 107, 244; and conservancies' role, 173–77; and economic benefits of parks, 223, 245; position on philanthropy, 183–84, 186–87, 224–25
Biederman, Daniel (Bryant Park Corporation), 141, 146, 152, 168
Blackmar, Elizabeth (*The Park and the People*), 18
Bloomberg, Michael R.: administration, 107, 132, 187, 238, 243, 254, 268n5; Central Park Conservancy contract, 186; conservancies and, 232, 234; expansion of parks, 157, 235, 254; inequality, 238, 246; Job Training Program, 40–41, 252, 257; Million Trees Program, 56, 90; New Public Management and, 189
Boltanski, Luc (*The New Spirit of Capitalism*), 191
broadbanding, 38, 63, 70, 170, 236, 240, 247; definition, 27–28; implications of, 29–31, 35–36
Bronx, the, 14, 34, 85, 91, 114–15, 158–60, 173, 180, 182, 203–4
Brooklyn, 8, 14, 24, 26, 33, 42, 46, 53–54, 57–58, 60, 62, 71–73, 76, 86, 88–90, 115, 131, 137–38, 142, 145, 157–58, 166, 183, 196, 198–99, 201–3, 208, 211, 213, 217, 227, 241, 249
Brooklyn Bridge Park, 158, 244
Bryant Park, 6, 24, 46, 50, 63, 92, 131, 132, 136, 140–42, 146–47, 149–52, 154–57, 163–65, 168, 170, 173, 190, 221–25, 228–29, 231–32, 236, 240, 270n15
Bryant Park Corporation, 132, 140, 168, 170, 240; concession contracts, 150, 155, 170, 232; control over park, 155, 173, 232; corporate repertoire, 136,

287

INDEX

Bryant Park Corporation (*continued*) 149–50, 152, 154–56; and real-estate value, 190–91, 221–22. *See also* Bryant Park Restoration Corporation

Bryant Park Restoration Corporation, 6, 24, 46, 63, 132, 140–41, 231

Burawoy, Michael (*Manufacturing Consent*), 102

business improvement district (BID), 6, 78, 134, 181, 222

Carmen's Garden (Prospect Park), 203

Central Park, 1, 18, 63, 70, 72, 82, 87, 131, 164, 173–74; as an economic engine, 223, 228–31, 256; as an indicator of city's health, 139; real estate value, 221, 228–31; storm damage, 93. *See also* Central Park Conservancy

Central Park Conservancy, 1, 18, 21, 51, 59, 123, 140, 141, 145, 168, 244; assistance to other parks, 255; city workers and, 50, 59, 97, 119, 144, 172; contract to manage park, 50, 142, 154, 174–77, 186; contrast in maintenance with other parks, 181; division among workers, 13, 125, 128–29; entry into study and, 8, 10, 12–13; firing of thirty-one workers (2009), 13, 99, 101, 125, 128–29, 172–73; funding, 7, 95, 132, 155, 158, 234; influence of, 161–65, 181, 185; management, 47–50, 59, 72, 82–83, 89, 97, 99, 103–4, 106, 109–11, 118, 143, 173–74, 263n17; neoliberalism and, 170–71, 186–87, 240–41; and New Yorkers for Parks, 179, 271n13; origins, 5, 24, 46, 107–8, 131, 138–40, 190, 236; parallel private workforce, 48, 50, 63, 97, 143–44, 150–51; philanthropic repertoire, 136, 146–48, 150, 157, 159, 186–87; pride and satisfaction among workers, 48, 124–25; tree care, 89, 92; unions and, 12–14, 16, 97, 125–26, 128–29, 144, 150–52, 185, 239; volunteer program, 1, 8, 10, 16, 46–47, 50, 82, 208, 213; Women's Committee, 88; zone system, 16, 47, 50, 84, 89, 94–95

Chiapello, Eve (*The New Spirit of Capitalism*), 191

circuits of value extraction, 229

citizen involvement, 159, 176, 177, 184

citizen pruners, 55, 91, 92

Citizens' Budget Commission, 32, 34

citizenship, 191, 193, 194, 195, 196, 197, 198, 200, 205, 208, 238, 243, 249

City Parks Foundation: origins, 159, 163; Partnerships for Parks and, 14, 52, 159–60, 172, 199

City Park Worker (CPW), 1, *11*, 33, 49, 56, 58, 61, 105, 111, 113, 209; broadbanding and, 27–30; conservancies and, 51, 94–95, 157, 165; numbers of, 39, 65, 86–87, 96, 100, 103, 124, 232, 253, 257; out-of-title work, 31, 120, 122–23, 210–14; promotions, 15, 43–44, 65, 122; sexual economy and, 113, 115–16; step-ups, 30–31, 59, 96, 120; tasks of, 2, 40–42, 56, 62, 65, 68–69, 71, 78, 96, 81, 83–85, 88, 92, 100, 103, 210–14; uniform, 1, 205; wage, 28, 94, 103, 198, 238

City Seasonal Aide (CSA), 11, 40, 41, 43, 44, 46, 96, 113, 206, 232, 253

civic discourse and mission, 3, 21, 22, 24, 149, 167, 168, 171, 176, 177, 178, 189, 190, 191, 194, 200, 202, 243. *See also* citizenship

civic engagement, 12, 55, 159, 168, 176, 177, 186, 189, 190, 191, 202

civic repertoire, 136, 146, 149, 153, 156–57, 158–59, 161, 166, 169, 186

civic service, 3, 8, 12, 14

civil service, 5, 21, 41, 43, 45, 47, 50, 63, 94, 127, 213, 238; efforts to undermine; 5, 23, 25, 29, 31, 34–36, 64, 194, 228, 231, 266n7; promotions through, 27, 34–35, 70; rules, 22–23, 29, 46, 69, 100, 210; step-up promotions and, 59; titles, 27–30, 219

civil service examinations, 27, 29, 34–36, 59, 65, 94, 266n7

"Class Of" program, 35, 107, 268n5

cleaning, 33, 51, 54, 57–58, 62, 84, 98, 106, 123, 144, 145, 148, 158–59, 160, 175–76, 180, 211, 217–18, 219, 246, 247, 249; bathrooms, 27, 62, 68–69, 77–80, 82, 87, 97–98, 105, 194; "deep cleaning," 33, 53, 74, 81, 94, 225, 239; garbage and litter, 33, 70–71, 81–82. *See also* cleanliness; fences; leaves; painting; Parks Inspection Program; trees; weeds

cleanliness, 7, 81, 168, 220, 231; and economic value, 219, 225–28, 257–58;

288

pride in, 122–23; and staffing, 33, 127, 212, 232, 235. *See also* Parks Inspection Program; real estate
Clemens, Elisabeth (*Politics and Partnerships*), 133, 147
Climbers, 30, 90, 92, 235, 238, 257. *See also* Pruners
community service sentencees, 2, 7, 21, 23, 26, 30, 56–58, 62, 63, 70, 96, 100, 157, 174, 206, 209, 210, 211, 214, 215, 216, 237, 241, 242, 248, 249; citizenship, 194, 195, 197–98, 200, 202; composition of work crews, 51, 56, 58, 61, 94, 198, 206; conflicts with, 57
Community Voices Heard, 12, 206–7
competition (workplace), 30, 60, 100, 101–4, 172
concessions, 134, 140, 146, 150, 190, 249; contract terms, 132, 154–56, 164–65, 186, 229; debates about, 220, 223, 231–34, 237, 248
consent, 22, 102, 169, 194; procedures in interviews, 261n1
conservancies, 10, 78, 88, 158, 218, 238, 247; accountability, 154–55, 181–82, 189; city workers and, 58, 95, 176, 249; civic discourse and, 176, 184; concessions, 164–65, 234; dual employment of staff, 171, 181–82, 185; funding of, 7, 155, 166; growth of, 60, 162–63, 185; legitimacy of, 145, 167–68, 183–84, 186–87, 189; maintenance resources, 77, 82, 176, 185–86; management contracts, 132, 153–54; Partnerships for Parks and, 158–59, 164–65; reform of, 181–83, 186–87, 225; salaries of leaders, 244; supervisory discretion in, 100, 104, 110, 128; types, 154, 157, 163–64, 166, 186; volunteers in, 55, 202–3; workers in, 7, 11, 75, 78, 89, 100, 172, 185–86. *See also* Central Park Conservancy; Madison Square Park Conservancy; Prospect Park Alliance; public-private partnership; Riverside Park; Washington Square Park
Cooke, Oliver (*Rethinking Municipal Privatization*), 18, 263n17
cooperation (workers'), 102, 122–26, 128, 129, 130, 214
Coordinator, 47–48, 104, 109–10, 118, 123

corporate repertoire, 136, 146, 150, 153, 156, 158, 162, 166, 169
crew chief, 1, 28, 41, 51, 56, 59, 61, 64, 70, 71, 78, 81, 83, 105, 111, 116, 123, 197, 201, 209, 212; definition, 30–31; negotiation of position, 212, 273n13; and out-of-title grievances, 31, 120, 122, 210–11; sexual harassment and, 116, 129; step-up promotions to, 59
Croft, Geoffrey, 85, 89, 179; testimony, 180. *See also* New York City Parks Advocates

Daniels, Arlene Kaplan, 193
Davis, Gordon (parks commissioner, 1978–83): management changes in Parks Department, 108, 131; and Park Administrators, 6, 107, 131–32, 136, 138, 139, 144, 165, 185, 190
de Blasio, Bill (mayor, 2014–), 234, 238, 250; Community Parks Initiative, 246–47, 253–54; ending the Work Experience Program, 252; position on conservancies, 254–55; raising wages, 252–53, 254
degraded work, 38, 248
Department of Parks and Recreation (DPR): access to, 10, 16–18; broadbanding in, 29–35, 63, 170; capital funding and improvements, 63, 94, 159, 178, 228–29, 235–38, 253–54; changes summarized, 63, *64*, 65–66, 70, 250; civil service and, 27–28, 33–35, 63, 97, 210, 266n7; employees, *11*, 13, 28, 88, 143; funding, 7, 51–52, 64, 77, 170–71, 174–75, 225–26; hierarchy, 126, 129, 138–39, 144, 146, 191; management approach, 99, 108, 110, 114, 129–30, 178–79, 189–90, 212–13; non-employee workers for, 60, 192–93, 195–205, 209, 210, 218, 242, 247–48, 252–53; organization of, 11, 21, 30–31, 94, 95–96, 247–48; partnerships, 11, 14, 21, 51, 60, 62–63, 88, 95, 97, 131–32, 137–39, 141–47, 154–61, 164–66, 167–78, 180–91, 192–93, 233–34, 254–57; segmentation of workforce, 36, 39–46, 62–63, 170, 228–29; sexual harassment, response to, 114–17, 129–30, 251–52; significance of, 2, 69; staffing levels, 7, 26, 31, 51–52, 63–64, 81, 85–86, 90–91, 95–96, 123–24, 143–44,

## INDEX

Department of Parks and Recreation (DPR) (*continued*)
147, 151, 170, 179, 220, 228–29, 235–38; training programs, 40, 42–44, 55–56, 58–59, 75, 89, 91–92, 161, 163, 256; volunteers, 52–55, 60, 91, 146, 161, 177, 189, 198–205; youth programs, 58–59
dignity, 5, 45, 102, 109, 118, 125, 173
Dinkins, David N. (mayor, 1990–93), 39, 64, 240, 266n12
dirty work, 28, 69–70, 73, 80, 87, 97–98
District Council 37 (DC 37), 12–14, 30, 63, 242, 250, 252, 266n12, 269n7, 273n13. *See also* union drive; unions
Doussard, Marc, 38, 60

edging, 74, 75, 82, 249

favoritism, favor system, 15, 99–100, 108–14, 124, 126; managerial discretion and, 31, 47, 128–29; and paternalism, 104; resistance to, 118; sexual harassment and, 113–17
fences, 32, 34, 47, 53, 81, 82–84, 87, 96, 158, 176
financial crisis (2008), 7, 8, 234, 244; firings of Central Park Conservancy workers and, 13, 95, 101, 172
fiscal crisis (1970s), 26, 131, 188, 218, 231; broadbanding and, 29, 30; echoes of financial aspects, 235–37; foundation of conservancies and "Friends of" groups, 5–6, 24, 46, 134, 136, 144, 153, 159, 171, 184, 185; layoffs during, 25, 240, 246; mobile units and, 32, 39; neoliberalism, 4, 24; workfare and nonmarket work, 39, 45
fiscal crisis (1990s), 39, 64, 235, 240
fissured workplace, 29, 38, 60
Fording, Richard C. (*Disciplining the Poor*), 265n29
Foreperson, 11, 47, 48, 101, 119
Fort Greene Park, 58, 138
Fraser, Nancy, 243
Friends of Dag Hammarskjold Plaza, 164–65
"Friends of" groups, 58, 60, 88, 135, 136, 156, 158, 162, 233, 255; definition, 46; inequality and, 163–65, 179, 181–83; origin story, 177; Partnerships for Parks and, 46, 52, 55, 65, 160, 172, 176, 200, 254; role of, 52, 53, 82, 132, 168, 176, 200–203, 242
Friends of the High Line, 244
Friends of Morningside Park, 168, 183

garbage, 9, 10, 47, 50, 52, 53, 61, 69, 70–72, 74, 78, 82, 95, 96, 102, 103, 144, 148, 159, 160, 202, 211, 217, 218, 249
gardening, 52, 55, 69, 87–89, 91, 153, 158, 217, 256
Gilder, Richard: advocacy of privatization, 97, 141, 168, 185; founding of Central Park Conservancy, 47, 138–39, 143; gift to Central Park Conservancy, 140; Partnerships for Parks board, 271n13
Giuliani, Rudolph W. (mayor, 1994–2001), 18, 23, 41, 107, 189, 227, 234; Bryant Park Conservancy and, 142; cuts in Parks staff, 39, 64; Parks Opportunity Program and, 40; Work Experience Program and, 39–40, 64, 192, 195, 242
"giving back," 190, 194–200, 214, 243–44
Goldman Sachs, 241
Gotbaum, Betsy (parks commissioner, 1990–93), 266n12
Gotbaum, Victor, 266n12
governance, 2, 4, 8, 19, 22, 23, 24, 100, 131, 133–34, 142, 171, 184, 186, 194, 216, 231, 232, 239, 242, 248, 256; governance repertoires, 135–36, 156, 169
Gramsci, Antonio, 19, 22, 169, 214
Green Applied Projects for Parks (GAPP), 58–59, 82
grievances, 5, 7, 29, 31, 48, 63, 120, 122, 144, 194, 212. *See also* out-of-title work; union rules
Guthrie, Doug (*Politics and Partnerships*), 133, 147

Hammond, Robert, 244, 275n27
High Line, the, 24, 156, 157, 190, 223
Historic Harlem Parks, 255–56
Hodson, Randy, 102
Human Resources Administration (HRA), 7, 21, 39, 42, 82, 98, 127, 147

ideal types, 170, 271n5
"in-house" titles, 27, 29, 30, 35

290

integral state: civic discourse and, 194, 214, 243; definition,19, 22, 169; and neoliberalism, 169, 190, 193, 216, 220, 239, 242, 251; and public-private partnerships, 171, 184, 187, 188, 190, 193, 224–25, 254, 255–56. *See also* citizenship; civic discourse and mission; Gramsci, Antonio

invisibilization, 194, 198, 209, 231, 248

invisible work, 193, 238

"It's My Park" days, 88, 160, 199, 209

Jessop, Bob, 24, 135, 170, 239, 264n23, 264n24

Job Training Participant (JTP), *11*, 46, 69, 72, 85, 95, 96, 120, 174, *215*, 217, 240, 248, 255, 256, 258; budgetary savings, 226; competition at worksite, 60, 100, 103–5; in conservancies, 147, 150, 157; definition, 7; demographics, 1, 15, 27, 45, 65, 78, 21, 218; "dirty work," 28, 78–79, 98; initiative, 122–23; job mobility, 43–44, 124, 126; justification of, 193–203, 215; mobile crews, 28, 56, 58, 61, 71, 83, 94, 115, 198, 209; operational disadvantages of, 53, 94, 237–39, 241; overtime, 59, 113; prevalence at worksite, 51, 56, 65, 78, 95–96, 106, 124, 147; program change, 41, 95–96, 252–53; resistance, 121–22, 249; seasonal change in number, 58–59, 78; sexual economy and sexual harassment, 15, 45, 113–18, 129, 241, 245, 251–52; supervisory discretion and, 111–14, 126–29, 211, 214; tasks, 51–53, 61–62, 70–71, 74–76, 82–83; union representation, 41; visibility of, 1, 206–9; wage, 28, 41, 218, 252–53; WEP and, 41–43, 45, 60, 65–66, 95–96, 100, 196–98, 206, 241–42, 252–53. *See also* Parks Opportunity Program

Katz, Cindi, 264n23

Koch, Edward I. (mayor, 1978–89), 23, 39, 64, 107, 131, 138, 192

labor market segmentation. *See* primary labor market; secondary labor market; segmentation of labor markets

leaves, 9, 47, 52, 54, 61, 72–74, 78, 83, 96, 124, 202

legitimation, 19, 187, 193; and accumulation, 220; and integral state, 169–70, 214–16; of neoliberalism, 188, 219, 242–44; of partnerships, 132, 133, 147, 149–50, 188; of repertoires, 135–36, 153, 164–66; of worksite authority, 104, 106

Legal Aid Society, 252

Lindsay, John V. (mayor, 1966–73), 6, 136, 137, 269n7

*Long Beach* decision, 35, 266n7. *See also* civil service; civil service examinations

Madison Square Park, 233; concessions and programming, 10, 24, 87, 155–56, 166, 181, 223, 227

Madison Square Park Conservancy, 21, 82, 227; commercialization, 181, 223; contract with the City, 154, 155–57, 164, 256; division of labor in, 51–52, 58, 73, 82, 181, 223, *227*, 256

Manhattan, 1, 10, 18, 21, 24, 26, 44, 53, 55, 67, 71, 77, 81, 88, 93, 106, 115, 116, 138, 147, 155–57, 164, 165, 173, 179, 185, 199–202, 204, 221–23, 232, 233

mayor, 164, 173, 177, 224, 257; strong mayor system, 40, 186, 238. *See also* Beame, Abraham; Bloomberg, Michael R.; Dinkins, David N.; Giuliani, Rudolph W.; Koch, Edward I.; Lindsay, John V.; Wagner, Robert F., Jr.

Millstein, Ira, 271n13

moral discourse, 97, 118–20, 152, 169, 178, 187, 188–91

Morningside Park, 43, 88, 138, 160, 183, 255, 256

Moses, Robert (parks commissioner, 1934–60), 163; labor strife, 5, 7, 246, 262n9, 266n12; park houses, 60; playgrounds, 27, 32; pools, 157; Riverside Park, 157

Muehlebach, Andrea, 191

neocommunitarianism, 24, 135, 239

neocorporatism, 24, 135, 239

neoliberalism, 4, 19, 20, 133, 214, 216, 231, 237–39, 245; definitions, 4, 169–70, 178; and ideal types, 135, 271n5; institutional aspects, 24, 135; integral state and, 214, 216, 220, 239–44, 251; moral discourse of, 189–91; and paternalism,

## INDEX

neoliberalism (*continued*)
265n29; philanthropic, 186–88; roll-out and roll-back, 262n7

neoliberalization, 171, 173, 190, 191, 193, 246; definition, 170; de-neoliberalization, 255; and the integral state, 214–16, 239–41. *See also* Gramsci, Antonio

neostatism, 24, 135, 239

New Public Management (NPM), 188–89, 242–43

New York City Parks Advocates, 85, 89, 179, 182, 183; testimony, 180. *See also* Croft, Geoffrey

New Yorkers for Parks (NY4P), 34, 52, 91, 92, 138, 153, 222, 224; evaluations of parks conditions, 87, 235; position on conservancies and equity, 179, 180, 183, 185, 225, 227, 232, 234, 244; relationship to conservancies, 179, 271n13

Open Space Alliance for North Brooklyn (OSA), 62, 157, 241

organizing drive, 12, 13, 111, 118, 125, 152

out-of-title work, 29, 31, 35, 120, 144, 152, 193, 210–14

ownership, sense of, 48, 128, 160, 195, 198–200

painting, 27, 80–82, 83, 87, 152, 176; community service and, 54, 58; volunteers and, 52–54, 62, 65, 81–82, 163

Parks Administrator, 11, 17, 51, 54, 62, 73, 77, 83, 131–32, 154, 156, 165, 180, 190, 233, 234, 244, 255; creation of, 6, 107–8, 136–39, 144; dual employment, 146, 157–58, 168, 171–72, 180, 184–85

Parks Council, 138, 179

Parks Department. *See* Department of Parks and Recreation

Parks Enforcement Patrol (PEP), 11, 79, 128, 182, 238; allocation of, 32–34, 183, 220, 232, 237, 250, 256; duties, 33; and homeless people, 34, 121, 123; new hires, 235

Parks Inspection Program (PIP), 33, 85, 86, 87, 126, 127, 173, 174, 179, 189, 212–13

Parks Manager (APRM), 11, 17, 50, 59, 61, 68, 72, 126, 106, 110, 112, 113, 117, 120–21, 128, 161, 189, 198, 209, 210–13; promotion to, 27, 35

Parks Opportunity Program (POP), 12, 18, 27–28, 30, 240; changes in the program, 40–41, 129; definition, 7; orientation and sexual harassment, 115, 117; origins of, 40, 206; programs administered by, 59, 75, 89, 253. *See also* Job Training Participant; seasonal work

Parks Supervisor (PS1 and PS2), 11, 41, 43, 45, 50, 61, 71, 78, 79–80, 84, 87, 89, 91, 92, 93, 102, 107, 119, 137, 144, 150, 151, 198, 201, 205, 209, 251, 253, 255, 260; broadbanding and, 30; challenges of, 33, 42, 45, 67–68, 75–77, 80, 85–86, 91, 106, 126–29, 196, 210–13, 253; and community service sentencees, 57; discretionary power of, 35, 59, 111–13, 120–22, 126–30; in-house title, 30; promotion to, 27, 31, 35, 59, 65, 128; and sexual economy, 114–17, 129–30, 251; and volunteers, 51, 53–54, 56, 82, 88, 160–61, 203. *See also* Principal Park Supervisor

Partnerships for Parks, 21, 46; civic engagement and, 176–77, 200; cultivation of "Friends of" groups, 52, 55, 65, 159–61, 164–65, 176–77, 199, 254; origins, 159; sense of ownership, 200, 203; shared public-private cost, 172; tree pruning, 55, 90; volunteers, 14, 55, 65, 82, 88, 90–99, 199, 202, 209. *See also* "It's My Park" days

passive revolution, 169

paternalism, 108–10

Paul's Park, 203

Peck, Jamie, 170, 239

philanthropic repertoire, 136, 146, 148, 150–57, 162, 166, 169, 171, 186

philanthropy, 16, 132, 134, 138, 139, 141, 149, 168, 171, 189, 228, 244; accountability of, 191; labor and, 152, 171, 185; motivations for, 141, 147–48, 159, 162, 183–84, 190, 223, 234, 243; neoliberal philanthropy, 186–87, 243. *See also* philanthropic repertoire

pools, 32, 59, 62, 96, 157, 249

Prener, Christopher, 193

primary labor market, 36–38, 43, 45, 60. *See also* segmentation of labor markets

Principal Park Supervisor (PPS), 11, 27, 30, 212, 268n6

promotion, 43–44, 107, 110, 122–24, 247; broadbanding, 29–31; and civil service, 27, 30, 34–35, 65, 128–29, 144, 211, 268n6; competition for, 31, 102–3, 246; labor-market segments and, 36–38, 43, 45; provisional promotions, 35, 59; non-civil service, 47–50, 111. *See also* broadbanding; civil service examinations; competition; out-of-title work; segmentation of labor markets; step-ups

Prospect Park, 9–10, 89, 138, 251; distressed conditions (1970s–80s), 131, 137, 140; Hurricane Irene, 93; programming, 144; real estate and, 145, 228, 257. *See also* Carmen's Garden; Prospect Park Alliance; Vale of Cashmere

Prospect Park Alliance, 21, 132, 138, 140, 159, 175, 190, 244; civic repertoire and, 136, 144, 148–49, 157, 161, 190; community committee, 146, 180, 270n11; concessions, 154, 156; conservancy reform and, 183, 255; division of labor, 10, 50–51, 95, 146–47, 150, 154; entry into study through, 8–10, 89; inequality and, 149, 257; labor relations, 151; origins, 5–6, 24, 107–8, 136–37, 139, 144–46, 240; public and private employment, 59, 154, 172; volunteering, 9–10, 46–47, 51, 69, 74, 82, 132, 202–3, 241. *See also* Prospect Park; Thomas, Tupper

Pruners, 30, 90, 92, 235, 238, 257. *See also* citizen pruners; Climbers

public-private partnership, 3, 4, 8, 11, 14, 21, 24, 62, 131–66, 167, 168, 179, 185, 186; accountability of, 171–72, 174, 176, 180, 182, 184; development of, 6, 185–86; fissuring of the workplace and, 60; innovativeness, 177; integral state and, 19, 188; legitimacy of, 147–53, 178, 180, 182; noncontractual, 158–61; regimes and, 6, 133–35; repertoires and, 135–36, 186; revenues, 153–56. *See also* conservancies; Partnerships for Parks

Queens, 14, 32, 43, 52, 56, 90, 91, 92, 93, 105, 111, 113, 122, 123, 124, 159, 162, 192, 200, 202

race, 13, 25, 134, 141, 219, 265n29, 268n6, 269n7

real estate, 6, 19, 24–25, 141, 149, 150, 221–23, 242, 257; maintenance links to, 21, 158, 223, 244, 245, 247–48; role in more complex circuits of value extraction, 224–30

reciprocity, 194–97, 205, 214, 244. *See also* "giving back"

regimes, 6, 22, 133–36, 169, 191, 239–41, 246, 264n25

repertoires, 135–36, 147, 153, 161–62, 169, 170. *See also* civic repertoire; corporate repertoire; philanthropic repertoire

Riverside Park, 138; Conservancy, 157–58; and Riverside South development, 158, 223, 244; and volunteers, 199

Rockefeller Brothers Fund, 141, 149

Rogers, Elizabeth Barlow (Betsy), 5, 163, 190, 241; founding of the Central Park Conservancy, 138–40, 143–44; reflections on union workers, 143–44, 150–51; view on philanthropy, 147–48

roll-back, roll-out policy (Peck and Tickell), 4, 170, 171, 239, 241

Rosenzweig, Roy (*The Park and the People*), 18

Savas, Emmanuel S., 138, 185, 190

Schram, Sanford S. (*Disciplining the Poor*), 265n29

seasonal work, 25, 41, 58–59, 79–80, 84, 96, 98, 157, 232; in conservancies, 48–49, 58, 72, 84, 95; in the Parks Opportunity Program, 28, 40, 41, 114, 206, 253; secondary labor market, 43–44, 46

secondary labor market, 36–38, 43, 45, 60, 228. *See also* seasonal work; segmentation of labor markets

segmentation of labor markets, 36–39, 44–46, 80, 94, 100, 193, 215, 228, 247, 252, 267n18; and broadbanding, 28, 35; in conservancies, 46–52, 101; defined, 20, 28; and the "fissured" workplace, 60–63; race and gender and, 70; seasonal, 58. *See also* dirty work; primary labor market; secondary labor market

segregation, 208, 209, 214, 215

sexual economy, 21, 100, 114, 117, 129, 130, 250

INDEX

sexual harassment, 15, 45, 115, 125, 208, 219, 241, 245, 249; contested accounts of, 116–17; official evasion of, 117, 250, 251–52; workplace power and, 21, 100, 114, 129, 247, 251–52
"shops," the, 85, 95, 192, 213
Simmel, Georg, 187–89
slavery, 45, 196, 215, 239
snow, 47, 52, 67, 69, 72, 76–77, 89, 96, 106, 249
Soros, George, 138, 143
Soss, Joe (*Disciplining the Poor*), 265n29
Squadron, Daniel (state senator), 183, 186, 225, 234, 254
Staten Island, 70, 88, 90, 159, 176
step-ups, 58–59, 65, 249. *See also* promotion
Stern, Henry (parks commissioner, 1983–90, 1994–2000), 39, 107, 108, 268n6; budgets, 174–75; and civil service, 23, 35; "Class Of" program, 35, 107, 268n6; history in Parks, 107; and partnerships 142, 154, 159, 163, 173; privatization experiment, 192; workfare and, 192, 195. *See also* "Class Of" program; *Wright v. Stern* lawsuit
Sulzberger, Iphigene, 138, 141, 271n13
Summer Youth Employment Program (SYEP), 2, 32, 38, 46, 58, 61–62, 80–81, 89, 157, 211

Theodore, Nik, 170, 262, 275, 278, 283
Thomas, Tupper: advocacy for conservancies, 183; confirmation of sexual harassment, 251; Prospect Park Alliance, 6, 107, 136–37, 139–40, 145–49, 151–52, 190; views on changes under Mayor de Blasio, 254, 257; views on parks staffing, 51, 147, 251
Tickell, Adam, 170, 239
Tilly, Charles: categorical inequality, 209, 273n12; repertoires, 135, 153; *Work Under Capitalism*, 36–37, 56, 62
Tilly, Chris, 36–37, 56, 62
trash. *See* garbage
trees, 10, 56, 60, 61, 72, 76, 87, 89–93, 140

uniforms, 23, 129, 137, 174, 205, 206, 208
union contract, 35, 100, 175, 266n7
union drive (in Central Park Conservancy), 12–14, 49, 101, 111, 118–20, 125–26, 129, 152. *See also* unions: hostility toward; unions: and nonprofits
union rules, 23, 31, 35, 63, 97, 100, 120, 125, 143–44, 152, 212–13, 231. *See also* grievances; out-of-title work
unions, 1, 4, 7, *11*, 28, 30, 41, 45, 46, 63, 64, 136, 181, 193, 220, 226, 228, 236, 246, 268n6; hostility toward, 2, 4, 13, 16, 23, 47–49, 97, 101, 110–11, 129, 143–44, 150–52, 173, 185, 239, 241, 243; and nonprofits, 6, 47–49, 97, 134, 146, 151–52, 178, 248, 256, 263n12; public sector, 2, 5, 7, 23, 262n9, 264n25, 266n7, 266n12, 269n7; and workfare, 40, 252. *See also* District Council 37; union contract; union drive; union rules
Union Square Park, 24, 155, 156, 181, 182, 232
unpaid work, 3, 19, 56, 71, 164, 192, 193–94, 197–99, 209, 210, 214, 219, 220, 226, 228, 245, 246

Vale of Cashmere (Prospect Park), 9, 202
Vallas, Steven, 193
value: moral value, 41, 45, 87, 203, 205, 270–71n15; of work, 19, 25, 41, 96, 189, 193, 226–28, 229, 230, 231, 236–37. *See also* real estate
volunteers, 1, 2, *11*, 21, 23, 34, 60, 67, 69, 133, 162, 198, 217, 259, 273n11; civic discourse and, 168, 177, 189–90, 194–95, 198–200, 202–5, 238, 243; in conservancies, 1, 8–10, 14, 16, 46–47, 50–51, 52, 60, 95, 101, 132, 135, 138–39, 144–46, 148–50, 152–53, 157–58, 164, 168, 171–72, 176, 213; corporate, 52, 54, 81–82, 132, 153, 201, 205, 208–9, 239, 241, 256; entry into research and, 8–10, 14, 16, 73–74; as free labor, 3, 5, 7, 38, 164–65, 193, 201–2, 210, 215, 226, 236; in "Friends of" organizations, 5, 45–46, 52–53, 65, 132, 135, 158, 160–61, 163, 164, 242; interaction with other workers, 1, 9, 16, 50–51, 100–101, 144, 196, 199, 201–2, 209, 214–15, 239; legitimacy and, 147, 149, 242–43; management of, 53–54, 62, 89, 145–46, 150, 152–53, 171–72, 189, 203–4, 209, 210, 238, 241; non-labor resources provided by, 81–82, 201; organization of, 14, 45,

294

53, 55, 60, 88, 95, 132, 145–46, 160–61, 167, 176, 200; prevalence of, 52, 60, 65, 218, 240; rewards of, 55, 148, 191, 199, 208; sense of ownership, 54, 200–205; tasks performed by, 9, 16, 47, 50–54, 62, 69, 72, 74, 78, 81–82, 88, 91–92, 97–98, 194, 198; training, 55, 91, 161; types of, 52, 158, 247; uniform, 1, 208, 217, 247; value of, 53, 65, 69, 148, 174, 176, 189, 195, 198–205, 215–16, 238, 270–71n15; visibility of, 14, 162, 177, 193, 205, 208, 215, 247. *See also* "It's My Park" days; Partnerships for Parks

Wacquant, Loïc, 25
Wagner, Robert F., Jr. (mayor, 1954–1965), 5, 45
Washington Square Park, 168, 176, 184, 185, 190, 232, 233
weeding. *See* weeds
weeds, 1, 9, 16, 27, 47, 51–52, 54, 58, 74–75, 78, 81–82, 84, 87, 89, 97–98, 123, 202, 204, 208, 217
Weil, Mark, 29, 38, 60
White, Veronica, 132, 154, 167
Wolch, Jennifer (*The Shadow State*), 264n24

Work Experience Program (WEP), *11*, 30, 39, 52, 56, 58, 60, 61, 94, 100, 104, 128, 157, 174, 198, 249; as cheap or free labor, 40, 45, 95–96, 192–93, 196, 215, 226, *227*, 239–41; compared to Job Training Program, 40–43, 45, 62, 65–66, 95–96, 196–97, 205–6, 209, 241–42, 252; definition, 39; operational problems of, 41–42, 237–38, 241; politics of, 40, 95, 241–42, 247; reciprocity and, 194–97, 199–202; sexual harassment and, 114, 129, 241; status markers, 205–6, *207*, 209; tasks, 72, 78, 89, 98. *See also* dirty work; slavery; workfare
workfare, 7, 12, 21, 23, 25, 30, 38–39, 46, 63–65, 192–96, 214, 216, 218, 237, 241, 245. *See also* unpaid work; Work Experience Program
*Wright v. Stern* lawsuit, 35, 122, 266, 268
Wurf, Jerry, 266n12

Zone Assistant, 9, 10, 12, 16, 50. *See also* Central Park Conservancy; volunteers
Zone Gardener, 8, *11*, 16, 47, 48, 50, 72, 84, 89, 92, 125, 144, 158, 181